USA Immigration & Orientation

Sixth Edition, Revised

Book 1 - USA Immigration: Getting In
Solving the Immigration Process

Book 2 - USA Orientation: Getting Settled
Adjusting to U.S. Living

Bob & Mary McLaughlin

Wellesworth Publishing
Satellite Beach, Florida

Published by:

Wellesworth Publishing
P.O. Box 372444
Satellite Beach, FL 32937-2444
U.S.A.

McLaughlin, Bob
    USA Immigration & orientation / Bob & Mary McLaughlin
    Includes bibliographical references and index.
    1. United States--Emigration and immigration
    2. Naturalization--United States--Handbooks, manuals, etc.
    I. McLaughlin, Mary   II. Title
JV6543.M44

ISBN 0-9657571-6-1

Library of Congress Control Number: 2003103233
325.73--dc21

Printed in the United States of America
Sixth Edition, Revised

Contents

Foreword

America is not only a nation of immigrants, but a nation that continues to rekindle its basic spirit with new immigrants who look for opportunity in their new country. As the world leader, the United States is a desirable home for many families around the globe seeking freedom, business and educational opportunities, and the security provided by a nation of laws. We cannot accept all of those who desire to enter through our ports, and as a result, a complex body of laws, rules and regulations has evolved in order to admit immigrants who serve the national interest.

Bob and Mary McLaughlin have, through extensive research and recent editing to incorporate the new immigration laws, produced a very comprehensive and useful immigration reference book.

The McLaughlins have presented the material in a well organized and easily understandable manner which can be followed by the non-lawyer. The book outlines immigration law, policy and practice in such a way that the general theory behind immigration law can be understood, while also giving specific information about substantive areas of law.

During my term as Commissioner of the Immigration and Naturalization Service, one of our goals was to simplify immigration procedures so that all persons would be able to avail themselves of immigration benefits without the need of an attorney. With the enactment of reform measures in 1986, 1990 and 1996, however, immigration laws have become more complicated and procedures more complex so that now, the immigration lawyer may be more necessary than before. While a reader with a specific immigration purpose should contact an immigration lawyer for advice, the McLaughlin book is well written and gives the reader a good idea where to start and how to negotiate the twists and turns necessary to achieve the benefits and opportunities available.

The subject of immigration is rapidly rising to the top of the world's agenda. This book represents a real service to many who are interested in this expanding and important field. It will certainly find its way, to the desks of many practitioners who specialize in immigration law. I recommend *USA Immigration & Orientation* to the reader, and commend the McLaughlins for their practical treatment and excellent organization of the immigration laws and procedures.

Gene McNary
Former Commissioner, Immigration and Naturalization Service
Attorney at Law
Saint Louis, Missouri

Preface

USA Immigration & Orientation is packed with over 500 pages of vital information with many important 1999, 2000, 2001 and 2002 procedural changes to help you navigate very complex processes of immigrating and adjusting to U.S. living.

In fact, **USA Immigration & Orientation** is actually two books for the price of one. Both are written by people who have lived the immigration experience first hand and have written the book to share what they have learned with others who are about to follow. This is truly a layman's guide, by and for the layman.

The book provides information the authors wish they had been aware of both during and after the immigration formalities. Without knowing where to turn for answers, one can easily form the impression that the system has no answers or compassion. Yes, it is complex and often prolonged. It is also both thorough and fair. So, don't be discouraged and don't try shortcuts.

This book is our way of thanking the many civil servants whose patience and understanding turned our immigration process into an adventure with a happy ending. Countless hours of intensive interviews with experienced members of the Immigration and Naturalization Service (INS) and the Department of State (DOS) confirmed that the roles of these bodies are both independent and interdependent.

The patience and understanding of the DOS and INS officers have provided us with the basics of Book 1, USA Immigration: Getting In which identifies all the immigration classification options and explains what is necessary to qualify for each. It also puts in perspective the role of the participating government agencies in the processing of applications for each classification.

Equal emphasis was placed on the many agencies in both the private and public sector which play a role in the adjustment to life in the United States. What you will read in Book 2, USA Orientation: Getting Settled, is the result of the explanations of patient and helpful practitioners and participants in many fields.

Book 2, USA Orientation: Getting Settled, deals with the administrative and social aspects of life in the United States. Health care, banking, taxation, buying or renting a home and many other important topics are explored.

Taken together, Book 1 and Book 2 offer a comprehensive reference about the intricacies of getting in and getting settled in the United States. Both are divided into five parts to help you concentrate on your most important needs.

The authors hope that **USA Immigration & Orientation** will save you both time and frustration as you do your own research, identify your priorities, pick your classification, develop a realistic plan and decide whether you need to hire professionals who can help you deal with the specifics of your case, for a fee.

The authors welcome your input for use in future editions.

Acknowledgments

In compiling this reference book, the authors have interviewed expatriates from many countries, officials in government departments across the continent and experts in many other fields.

We would like to thank all who have contributed information and, in particular, the following persons and organizations without whose expertise this book would not be possible.

Barbara Artz	Parent, Brevard County, Florida
Pat Bouchard,	Pruitt Real Estate, Melbourne, Florida
Susan Brandt	Department of State
John Bulger	Immigration and Naturalization Service
Giraldo Carratala	Miami, Florida
Joe Carroll	WKMG-TV
Marisa Carroll	Student, Brevard County, Florida
Mary Ann Carroll	Ribbitt Productions
Edward Christensen	Certified Public Accountant
Dan Dease	Xerographic
Karen Eckert	Immigration and Naturalization Service
Sally Gober	Department of State
Bill Greer	Space Coast Writers Guild
John Hogan	Immigration and Naturalization Service
Stella Jarina	Immigration and Naturalization Service
Krissa Jensen	San Diego, California
Bill Johnson	Board of Education, Brevard County, Florida
Neal Johnson	Melbourne, Florida
James Krampen	Specialty Risk International Insurance
Gary McLaughlin	WWWB-TV, Charlotte, North Carolina
James McLaughlin	Computall Services, San Diego California
Edward Odom	Department of State
Ingo Pakleppa	San Diego, California
Thomas Petersen	Petersen International Insurance Brokers
Dale Rumbarger	Department of State
Joan Smith	Department of State
Jean Sparks	Florida Institute of Technology
Samuel Tiranno	Immigration and Naturalization Service
Rick Wiggins	JPMorgan Chase Finance, Melbourne, Florida
Lemar Wooley	Immigration and Naturalization Service

Disclaimer

USA Immigration & Orientation is sold with the understanding that the publisher and authors are not engaged in rendering individual financial, legal or any other professional advice. If formal assistance is required, the services of a competent professional should be sought.

The authors of **USA Immigration & Orientation** have made every effort to research, refine and verify the information in this book, to make it as complete and accurate as possible and to present it from the layman's perspective.

Since U.S. immigration procedures and many aspects of everyday U.S. living are constantly changing, each situation may be unique and thus open to interpretation. Consequently, the publisher and authors assume no liability or responsibility to any person or entity with respect to any loss or damage caused, or alleged to be caused, directly or indirectly, by reading and acting on the information contained herein.

If you do not wish to be bound by the above, you may return this book with your sales receipt to the publisher for a refund of your purchase price.

Book 1

USA Immigration: Getting In

Solving
the Immigration Process

Book 1

Introduction

Book 1, **USA Immigration: Getting In** is devoted to helping you understand the complexities of immigration and select the process best meeting your aspirations. Book 1 also shows you how several U.S. government agencies work together to assess your situation and determine whether you and your adoptive country are right for each other.

In 2001, the Census Bureau released the results of a survey which showed that the immigrant population exceeds 30 million, or 11.1 percent of the total population.

As an indication of the extent of U.S. immigration, here are a few statistical surprises. The Immigration and Naturalization Service (INS):

In Fiscal Year 2002:   *Ref: INS Statistics, 2002*
- Counted 35 million nonimmigrant admissions
- Estimated 5 million illegal aliens (some estimate 11 million in 2001)
- Naturalized 589,810
- Denied 139,779 Naturalization petitions

In Fiscal Year 2001:   *Ref: INS News Release, August 30, 2002*
- Admitted 1,064,318 new immigrants (Green Card holders)
  - 411,059 were processed by the State Department abroad
  - 653,259 were processed by the INS in the United States

After many meetings with helpful and knowledgeable practitioners from the Department of State (DOS) and Immigration, the authors are pleased to include several of their useful suggestions on this very first page.

Do:
- Follow both the spirit and the letter of the law
- Be wary of anyone who promises to get you a visa
- Be over-prepared for all interviews
- Make copies of every document you submit
- Take as much documentation as possible to support your case including previously submitted evidence

- Carefully read and follow the requirements for each application
- Try to process your application in the off-season (avoid summers if possible)
- Send all mail certified, return receipt requested

Don't:
- Try to beat the system, you won't win
- Accept free advice from friends, neighbors and non-professionals
- Delay the processing of other cases by calling the INS or DOS to ask questions that are answered by documents you have obtained

Book 1, Getting In, is set out in five parts that introduce you to the intent and structure of the immigration process as well as the various options available for both temporary and permanent residence in the United States.

Part I - Immigration Laws

Part I explains how laws in general and immigration laws in particular are made and implemented in the United States. Also included is a detailed explanation of the role of the principal players, the U.S. Departments of Homeland Security, State and Labor.

Part II - Temporary Status

Part II is a major examination of the rationale and criteria for all of the available temporary or nonimmigrant visa classifications.

This part is divided into six chapters devoted to a group of similar classifications each created to meet a specific need. The means to qualify for each classification is described on a step-by-step basis.

Part III - Green Cards

Part III contains four chapters that explain how to qualify for a Green Card:
- Family-Sponsored
- Employment-Based
- Diversity (DV) Lottery
- Refugee/Asylee

Part IV - U.S. Citizenship

Part IV discusses the acquisition, advantages and responsibilities of U.S. citizenship with 100 naturalization interview test questions.

Part V - Research Resources

Part V introduces sources of research information available to those who wish to further explore the particular aspect of the immigration process relevant to them.

Part I

Immigration Laws

The immigration laws of the United States control the admission of aliens and the distribution of benefits to qualified recipients.

A Brief History of Immigration Laws

The cornerstone of immigration and nationality laws has been, and remains, the **Immigration and Nationality Act** (INA or the Act) of June 27, 1952 that took effect on December 24, 1952. The INA, as it will be identified in this book, was a major revision of existing laws such as the earlier acts of 1917, 1924 and 1950.

Since 1952, a series of new laws has served to amend the INA without taking away from its status as the preeminent U.S. immigration and nationality legislation.

Some of the more notable amendments to the INA include:

- Immigration Reform and Control Act of 1986 (IRCA)
- Immigration Act of 1990 (IMMACT90)
- Miscellaneous and Technical Immigration and Naturalization Amendments of 1991 (MTINA)
- Technical Corrections Amendments Act of 1994
- Illegal Immigration Reform and Immigrant Responsibility Act of 1996 (IIRIRA96)
- American Competitiveness and Workforce Improvement Act of 1998
- American Competitiveness in the Twenty-first Century Act of 2000
- Homeland Security Act of 2002

The **Illegal Immigration Reform and Immigrant Responsibility Act of 1996** (IIRIRA96) contained several key provisions, some may not be implemented. Many are reported throughout Book 1 and summarized in Chapter 17. They include:

- Increased penalties for violations, and
- The tightening of procedures for:
  - employment verification
  - border security
  - recording the whereabouts of violators and legal aliens alike
  - education of the children of illegal immigrants

Changes are being phased in gradually, including several on April 1, 1997. Some of the changes relate to deportation and removal.

Also reported in Chapter 17 are the key provisions of the **American Competitiveness and Workforce Improvement Act**, enacted in response to the 1998 H-1B crisis. The Act was designed to:

- Protect U.S. workers
- Temporarily increase the annual quota of H-1B workers until 2001
- Increase H-1B fees
- Tighten recruitment rules for H-1B-dependent employers
- Establish major penalties for employers who abuse the H-1B program
- Designate fees for job training of U.S. workers

Details on another important piece of H-1B-related legislation are also included in Chapter 17. The **American Competitiveness in the Twenty-first Century Act of 2000** includes such components as:

- An increase in the annual H-1B cap for three years
- Change to another H-1B job as soon as the new employer files a petition
- Change of employer if an Adjustment of Status petition is unadjudicated for 180 days
- Reuse of revoked numbers
- Extension beyond six years if an Adjustment of Status has been pending for 365 days or more
- Exemption of educational institutions and research organizations, and J physicians from the cap

Also in Chapter 17 are details of the **Homeland Security Act of 2002** which created the Department of Homeland Security (DHS) and combined 22 governmental agencies including the INS on March 1, 2003.   *Ref: Pub. L. 107-296*

By law, the DHS has one year from the time the Department became effective to bring all 22 agencies into the new organization. President George W. Bush anticipated that most of the components would have moved into the new department by March 1, 2003 and any incidental transfers would be completed by September 30, 2003.

Pending future reorganizations, readers should assume that immigration services and benefits will continue to be made available similar to the way they always have been. While the name of the agency will have changed, the same forms, immigration classifications, criteria and even fees may be expected. This edition of USA Immigration & Orientation has been extensively updated to reflect the new assignment of immigration functions necessitated by the merger of so many departments.

Immigration Enforcement

The Directorate of **Border and Transportation Security (BTS)** is the enforcement side of Homeland Security headed by Asa Hutchinson, the Under Secretary for Border and Transportation Security. BTS has the mission of border management with emphasis on securing the borders.

Border and Transportation Security has responsibility for:
- Enforcing U.S. immigration laws by:
  - deterring illegal immigration
  - pursuing investigations when laws are broken
- Securing U.S. borders and transportation systems which straddle 350 official ports of entry and airports
- Ensuring the integrity of America's borders and the security of our transportation system
- Administering the Student and Exchange Visitor Information System (SEVIS) program to collect information on nonimmigrant foreign students and other exchange visitors

Law enforcement agents from the following agencies are expected to enable the BTS to provide a coordinated defense against unlawful entry into the United States:
- The United States Customs Service
- The enforcement units of the INS including the Border Patrol and investigative agents
- The Animal and Plant Health Inspection Service
- The Federal Law Enforcement Training Center
- The Transportation Security Administration
- The Federal Protective Service

The Directorate of Border and Transportation Security (BTS) of the Department of Homeland Security includes the **Bureau of Customs and Border Protection (BCBP)** and **Bureau of Immigration and Customs Enforcement (BICE).**

The **Bureau of Customs and Border Protection (BCBP)** is headed by Commissioner Robert C. Bonner who reports to the Under Secretary for Border and Transportation Security. The 30,000 employees in the BCBP are responsible for protecting U.S. borders with security both at and between ports of entry. Consequently, they are now expected to facilitate the swift movement of trade and travelers while keeping dangerous people and their weapons out.

The border agencies brought together into this bureau are:
- The INS inspection services - agents and investigators - detention and removal functions
- The Border Patrol
- The United States Customs Service
- The Animal and Plant Health and Inspection Service (APHIS)

The **Bureau of Immigration and Customs Enforcement (BICE)** (originally to be called the Bureau of Border Security) enforces the laws *after* the borders are crossed. It brings together 14,000 employees including 5,500 criminal investigators, 4,000 employees for immigration and deportation services and 1,500 Federal Protection Service personnel. Its head, the Assistant Secretary of the Bureau is the former Acting Commissioner of the INS Michael Garcia who reports to the Under Secretary for Border and Transportation Security.

The bureau combines the enforcement and investigation arms of:
- The Immigration & Naturalization Service
- The United States Customs Service including air and marine enforcement functions
- The Federal Protective Service

Immigration Services

The Bureau of Citizenship and Immigration Services (BCIS) is the service side of Homeland Security which is responsible for administering immigration adjudications and benefits. Its Director, Eduardo Aguirre, who reports to the Deputy Secretary of Homeland Security, is responsible for providing immigration information, benefits and services to more than seven million applicants each year.

The Bureau handles:
- Immigrant and nonimmigrant sponsorship
- Adjustment of status
- Work authorization and permits
- Naturalization and citizenship
- Asylum and refugee
- Services to new residents and citizens

The **Citizenship and Immigration Services Ombudsman** is a new function which is mandated to:
- Assist individuals and employers in resolving problems in the Bureau of Citizenship and Immigration Services (CIS)
- Identify areas where individuals and employers are having problems and propose changes to mitigate those problems

To help you better understand the immigration process, Part I explores how immigration and other U.S. laws are made, published and regulated.

Chapter 1 - *Making and Publishing Immigration Laws*
- The origin and promulgation of immigration law

Chapter 2 - *The Administration of Immigration Laws*
- The agencies that regulate immigration law

Chapter 1

Making and Publishing Immigration Laws

Immigration is one of many areas of legal specialization with which the United States Congress must deal. To facilitate the reader's understanding of how immigration and other laws are created and enforced, the following brief overview of the process is included.

Public and Private Bills

Congress generates both public and private bills.

Public Bills

Public bills relate to public matters and deal with individuals only by classes.

Private Bills

Private legislation such as immigration and naturalization bills and claims against the government provide relief to individuals and institutions from the unanticipated implications of existing public laws.

There has been a dramatic decrease in private bills in recent years because Congress has given executive agencies increased authority to act on private matters.

How a Bill Becomes Law

Immigration and other private measures are referred to House and Senate subcommittees for processing.

After a private bill is reported out of committee, the floor action is reflected in the Congressional Record. It is signed by the Speaker of the House and the President of the Senate and sent to the President for signature into law or veto.

A bill may become law without the President's signature if he does not veto it within 10 days of being presented to him. However, if the Congress adjourns before that 10-day period ends, a "pocket veto" occurs and the bill does not become law.

In a regular veto, the President returns the bill to its originating chamber with his stated objections. A two-thirds vote in both chambers is needed to override the veto.

Publishing Laws

A **Slip Law** is published as an unbound pamphlet by the Office of the Federal Register. A number is assigned for public and private laws, and this notation runs sequentially through a Congress. Slip laws are competent evidence in all courts, tribunals and public offices.   *Ref: 1 USC 113*

Statutes at Large are a chronological arrangement of slip laws bound as sessional volumes and published at the end of each session. Immigration and other private laws are published in separate sections. These are also legal evidence of the laws contained in them.

The **United States Code (USC)** contains a consolidation of the general and permanent laws of the United States arranged according to subject matter under 50 title headings. The purpose of the USC is to present the laws in a concise and usable form without requiring recourse to the many volumes of the Statutes at Large containing the individual amendments. Title 8 of the United States Code is devoted to immigration matters.

The **Federal Register (FR)** publishes the general and permanent rules of the Executive departments and agencies of the Federal Government.

The **Code of Federal Regulations (CFR)** codifies all current orders, rules and regulations published in the Federal Register under 50 titles representing broad areas subject to Federal regulation.

As in the United States Code, Title 8 is devoted to immigration. It contains all current regulations issued by the Department of Homeland Security and is revised at least once per calendar year, as of January 1.

Title 8 of the Code of Federal Regulations, 8 CFR, is used as the main operating reference manual by Immigration Officers in the field. It is kept up to date by the individual issues of the Federal Register. These two publications must be used together to determine the latest version of any given rule.

Title 22 of the Code of Federal Regulations, 22 CFR.40 et al is known as the State Department's **Foreign Affairs Manual (FAM)**. Volume 9 - Visas, referred to as 9 FAM throughout the book, serves as the basic policies and procedures source of the State Department, its major resource to meet its responsibility for the administration of immigration affairs overseas.

The FAM is updated on a regular basis and Transmittal Letters are issued to reflect the changing administrative guidelines in the Department of State.

Chapter 2

The Administration of Immigration Laws

The Immigration and Nationality Act (INA) regulates the admission of aliens into the United States and designates the Secretary of Homeland Security and the Secretary of State as the principal administrators of its provisions. *Ref: 8 USC 1101*

The INA also provides that an alien who seeks admission or status in certain immigrant or nonimmigrant classifications shall be excluded unless certification from the Secretary of Labor is received.

Each of the U.S. Government departments charged with administering the immigration and naturalization of aliens has a specific well-defined role to play.

The first immigration office was created as far back as 1864. However, the first Federal immigration agency was not established until March 3, 1891 when President Benjamin Harrison signed the Immigration Act of 1891 into law.

The Naturalization Act of 1906 created the Bureau of Immigration and Naturalization with responsibility for administering and enforcing immigration laws, for supervising the naturalization of aliens and for keeping naturalization records. While the immigration and naturalization functions were separated in 1913, they were reunited to stay in 1933 with the creation of the Immigration and Naturalization Service within the Labor Department. In 1940, the INS moved to the Justice Department. Finally, in 2003, jurisdiction moved to the Department of Homeland Security when the Homeland Security Act became law.

Department of Homeland Security

Under the leadership of Secretary John Ridge and Deputy Secretary Gordon England, the Homeland Security Act of 2002 re-assigned 170,000 federal employees from 22 agencies within a single department. Immigration is a major responsibility.

Under 8 CFR 2.1, all authorities and functions of the Department of Homeland Security, to administer and enforce the immigration laws are vested in the Secretary of Homeland Security who may further delegate at his discretion. This replaces the authority of the Attorney General and Commissioner of the INS. *Ref: 68 FR 10921*

The mission of the new department is the safety of the United States homeland while continuing the tradition of welcoming immigrants. Each year 500 million people enter the United States, 330 million of them are not U.S. citizens.

The newly created Department of Homeland Security (DHS) includes the United States Customs Service, the Immigration and Naturalization Service, the Border Patrol, the Animal and Plant Health Inspection Service, the Transportation Security Administration (TSA) which protects the nation's transportation systems and the Federal Protective Service which provides security for federal facilities.

With these diverse components, the DHS is responsible for securing U.S. borders and managing the immigration process. In the past these two important missions were bundled together within one agency, the Immigration & Naturalization Service. However, under DHS, immigration services and border enforcement functions were assigned to separate DHS agencies and the INS was abolished on March 1, 2003.

Under DHS, the newly created **Bureau of Citizenship and Immigration Services (BCIS)** focuses exclusively on providing services such as processing applications for U.S. citizenship and administering the visa, work authorization and permitting programs for new residents and citizens.

The Bureau of Citizenship and Immigration Services was created to meet the following responsibilities:
- Providing immigration benefits to those individuals who are entitled to stay in the U.S. on a temporary or permanent basis including:
  - granting citizenship to those eligible to naturalize
  - authorizing individuals to reside in the U.S. on a permanent basis
  - providing aliens with the eligibility to work in the United States
- Establishing national immigration services policies and procedures
- Advising the Deputy Director on the oversight and performance of all functions transferred

Border security and the enforcement of immigration laws are now handled by the Directorate of **Border and Transportation Security** which absorbed INS Border Patrol and investigative officers along with the U.S. Customs Service. Their mission includes managing the entry and removal of illegal immigrants, securing the borders against illicit drugs, unlawful commerce and the entry and residence of criminal aliens, terrorists and the instruments of terrorism.

The Directorate of Border and Transportation Security (BTS) includes the **Bureau of Customs and Border Protection (BCBP)** and **Bureau of Immigration and Customs Enforcement (BICE).**

The **Bureau of Customs and Border Protection (BCBP)** mission is to:
- Manage illegal immigration, and
- Secure land, sea and air borders against:
  - illegal drugs
  - unlawful commerce

- Stop the entry of terrorists and instruments of terror

The **Bureau of Immigration and Customs Enforcement (BICE)** mission is to:

- Enforce the full range of U.S. immigration and customs laws
- Locate and remove illegal aliens
- Prevent illegal entry
- The protection of specified federal buildings
- Information sharing with the FBI and the U.S. Attorney's office

Department of State (DOS)

The State Department advises the President on the formulation of foreign policy. As Chief Executive, the President has overall responsibility for the foreign policy of the United States.

The Secretary of State is the ranking member of the cabinet and fourth in line of presidential succession.   *Ref: DOS Fact Sheet, May 26, 1995*

The Department of State's Bureau of Consular Affairs, under the direction of one of 19 Assistant Secretaries, is responsible for:

- The administration and enforcement of the immigration and nationality laws that concern the State Department and its Foreign Service
- The protection and welfare of American interests abroad
- The protection and welfare of American citizens traveling or living abroad
- The issuance of passports to U.S. citizens
- The issuance of visas and related services to foreign nationals who wish to visit or reside in the U. S.subject to the final authority of the Department of Homeland Security

The consular offices of the Department of State throughout the world are generally the initial contact for aliens who wish to come to the United States. DOS determines the type of visas for which aliens may be eligible and issues those visas.

DOS uses the Foreign Affairs Manual (FAM) as its working procedures and interpretation reference manual in the administration of the immigration laws for which it is responsible. 9 FAM deals with immigration matters. *Ref: 22 CFR.40 et al.*

Department of Labor (DOL)

The Department of Labor is a vital component of the immigration process.

Since immigration law serves as a protection to U.S. workers, the DOL must determine whether an adequate pool of U.S. workers is available to meet the needs of U.S. commerce. Where a shortage of available qualified U.S. workers exists, the DOL must ensure that alien workers seeking admission are fully qualified and appropriately compensated.

Immigration law requires the DOL to be involved in the processing of cases involving certain temporary and permanent classifications. Depending on the classification, the process is called Labor Certification or Labor Condition Application. See www.doleta.gov/regions to locate an office.   *Ref: INA 212(a)(5)(A)*

To locate a Department of Labor Employment and Training Administration office, see www.doleta.gov/regions.

Other Agencies

Several other federal government agencies such as the BCBP, Selective Service, and the Internal Revenue play a major role after the formal immigration proceedings have been completed. Book 2 explains their functions in detail.

The Immigration Process - Step-By-Step

Parts II and III describe the role of these federal bodies in the processing of petitions and applications for both nonimmigrant or temporary status in Part II and immigrant or permanent status in Part III.

To help you understand the normal sequence of events, information is presented throughout Book 1 in the following chronological format.

Step 1 - Clearing the Department of Labor (DOL) in the U.S.

Some aliens require pre-clearance from the U.S. **Department of Labor (DOL)** if they wish to work in certain designated temporary or permanent immigration classifications. This usually involves verification of the aliens's credentials, willingness to pay the going rate for the type of work involved, and sometimes, the employer's inability to find qualified U.S. workers.

Step 2 - Clearing Immigration - Initial Petition

Usually, a prospective employer or a family member will file an Initial Petition with the Bureau of Citizenship and Immigration Services (BCIS) in the United States. However, in some cases, an alien may file a personal application and refugee candidates may file outside the United States. An approved petition accords the alien a particular status under immigration laws.

To boost efficiency and provide more timely service, a state-of-the-art National Records Center was opened in Lee's Summit, Missouri in 1999 to centralize more than 25 million alien records.

Step 3 - Clearing the Department of State (DOS) Abroad

An alien may apply for a visa from the **Department of State (DOS)** at a U.S. Embassy or Consulate serving his or her home outside the United States. However, the consul who handles the application is not bound by an approved BCIS petition.

Only citizens of Canada and Visa Waiver countries do not require State Department visas.

When approved, a visa signifies that an alien has been pre-screened abroad and found to be eligible to apply for admission in a specific classification.

Step 4 - Clearing Immigration at a U.S. Port of Entry

When an alien arrives with a visa at a U.S. port of entry, jurisdiction switches from the State Department. At that point, a Bureau of Customs and Border Protection (BCBP) Inspector must be satisfied that the alien has the right type of visa and intends to engage in activities that are both permitted and consistent with the limitations of the visa.

If satisfied, the inspector will grant entry into the United States in a particular "status" setting out:

- One of the applicable temporary or permanent classifications
- A maximum duration of stay

To avoid confusion, both the "visa" issued abroad by the DOS and the "status" approved by the Immigration Inspector within the United States bear the same name. For example, an E visa issued abroad has the same effect and the same name as E status acquired on entry into the United States.

Step 5 - Extension or Change/Adjustment of Status

Depending on the classification, aliens living in the U.S. may be able to obtain a BCIS change or adjustment of status or extension, or a State Department visa extension without leaving the United States, if they are *In Status* when applying.

Status may be violated and deportation may result if an alien does any of the following:

- Remains beyond the expiration date of the status granted by the BCIS
- Engages in employment without authorization
- Engages in an activity inconsistent with the status under which he or she was admitted

Part II

Temporary Status

Most temporary classifications or categories are identified by a single letter identifier. Every letter from A to V is used plus extras such as NATO and TN (NAFTA). All are described in Part II.

Each classification has been created to meet a unique combination of needs and goals of aliens, employers and government alike. Employment is permitted in some, not all, classifications. So, choose your classification carefully.

When considering your classification, it is important to understand that U.S. immigration law is based on the premise that every alien shall be presumed to be an immigrant until he or she establishes entitlement to a nonimmigrant visa to the satisfaction of the consular officer or immigration inspector. H-1, L and V visas do not require that commitment.   *Ref: INA 214(b)*

Applicants for entry usually must prove they have a permanent residence and other strong ties abroad that would compel them to leave the United States when their temporary stay ends.   *Ref: DOS Publication 9772, June, 1990*

The State Department considers that the longer an applicant has been out of status, the greater the presumption of immigration. *Ref: DOS Policy March 20, 1996*

Try to find out as much as possible before starting an immigration application procedure. USA Immigration & Orientation identifies many sources of information including the internet. It may also be possible to call or meet an officer at certain times in a BCIS or consular office.

When phoning the BCIS or the State Department, have your file number or document identification number available along with a pencil and paper to take full notes of any instructions received. The status of applications filed at Regional Service Centers is available at: https://egov.immigration.gov/graphics/cris/jsps/index.jsp.

How Nonimmigrant Classifications are Grouped in Part II

It is very important to choose the classification that is best for you.

To make your choice easier, Part II has been grouped into six chapters. Each chapter assembles all the current nonimmigrant or temporary immigration classifications that address a similar need.

First, review the following list of chapters and the nonimmigrant classifications which they include to help you decide which best meets your needs and qualifications. Then, turn to the classifications you feel may be the most suitable.

Chapter 3 - Visitor Classifications

- VWP   Visa Waiver Program
- B-1/B-2   Temporary Visitor for Business or Pleasure
- *   Alternative Inspection Programs
- C-1/D   Alien in Transit / Crew member, Sea or Air
- *   Advance Parole
- TWOV   Transit Without Visa

Chapter 4- Educational Classifications

- F   Academic Student
- J   Exchange Visitor
- M   Vocational or Non-Academic Student

Chapter 5- Business Professionals

- E   Treaty Trader or Investor
- H   Professional, Temporary Worker or Trainee
- L   Intra-Company Transferee
- TN   Treaty NAFTA Professional

Chapter 6 - Extraordinary/Internationally-Recognized Persons

- O   Alien of Extraordinary Ability in the Sciences, Arts, Education, Business, or Athletics
- P   Internationally-Recognized Athlete or Entertainer

Chapter 7 - Special Purpose Classifications

- I   Foreign Information Media Representative
- K   Marriage to U.S. Citizen
- Q-1/Q-2   International Cultural Exchange Program Participant/ Irish Peace Process Cultural and Training Program Participant
- R   Alien in Religious Occupation
- S   Alien Witness and Informant
- T   Victim of Trafficking
- U   Humanitarian/ Material Witness
- V   Spouse and Children of Permanent Resident

Chapter 8 - Foreign Government and Organization Representative

- A   Senior Government Official
- C-2/C-3   Alien in Transit to United Nations and Foreign Government Official
- G   Government Representative to International Organization
- N   International Organization Family Member
- NATO   Representative of Member State

Admission Process

As noted in Part I, the process is usually carried out in several steps. What follows is a general overview of how the process evolves for a candidate for nonimmigrant status. For detailed information, you should refer to the section devoted to the specific nonimmigrant classification of interest to you.

Unless you are seeking H-1B, L or V status, be prepared to prove you are not an intending immigrant and that you are entitled to a nonimmigrant visa. If you are unable to prove nonimmigrant intent, it may be necessary to post a bond with the Secretary of Homeland Security.   *Ref: 9 FAM 41.11*

Step 1 - Pre-clearance

Some classifications require pre-clearance before a petition may be filed.

An employer must apply for DOL approval before proceeding with petitions for H-1B, H-2 and some D visas. In those cases, an employer must apply for Labor Condition Application (LCA) for H-1B candidates, Labor Certification for H-2 candidates or file an attestation to allow foreign vessel crew members to do longshore work in Alaskan ports. In all cases, the DOL must be convinced there is a need to admit an alien to carry out a temporary job, that there are no U.S. qualified citizens or residents available, that the going rate will be paid and the U.S. job market will not be adversely affected.

Aliens wishing to study in the United States also require a form of pre-clearance. There are three classifications from which to choose. Prior acceptance is required from an accredited institution in each case.

Step 2 - Clearing the Bureau of Citizenship and Immigration Services (BCIS) - Initial Petition

If DOL clearance is not required, this is usually the first step. However, Canadian applicants for TN - NAFTA status may skip this step and file directly at a U.S. port of entry.   *Ref: Pub. L. 107-296*

The employer or sponsor must usually file a petition and specified supporting documentation with the appropriate BCIS regional Service Center. Forms are available at (800) 870-3676 or www.immigration.gov/graphics/formsfee/forms

Documentation and supporting evidence includes:

- *BCIS forms*
  - nonimmigrant status
- *Fees*
  - appropriate for classification being petitioned for
- *Passports and photographs*
  - passport valid for at least six months beyond intended stay
  - color photographs 40 mm high by 35 mm wide in 3/4 profile showing right ear, no head covering (religious exceptions), light background
- *Current and prior immigration status*
  - such as I-94
- *DOL approvals*
  - such as Labor Certification or Labor Condition Application
- *Professional credentials*
  - such as degrees and/or professional status
- *Employer's supporting documentation*
  - supporting letter confirming salary, function and source of funds
- *Proof of financial support or solvency*
  - I-134, Affidavit of support from family sponsor
  - own funding
- *Civil documents, including dependents*
  - birth
  - marriage
  - divorce
  - death of spouse
- *Police clearance*
  - verification of local police records that may include fingerprinting
- *Medical clearance*
  - if history of medical ineligibility
  - consular medical examination
- *Evidence that U.S. stay is temporary (intent to depart)*
  - binding family ties
  - return tickets
  - no intention to abandon residence abroad

Premium Processing Service

To meet urgent employment-based immigration needs of American business, a Premium Processing Service was introduced in mid-2001. Form I-907 with a fee of $1,000 may be filed for both new and pending E, H, L, O, P, Q-1, R and TN cases along with I-129 petitions and all other I-129 processing fees. Only the petitioner, attorney or representative may seek premium processing. The beneficiary may not.

The BCIS guarantees adjudication within 15 calendar days of delivery to the proper Service Center premium processing address. This may be an approval, request for evidence, intent to deny or notice of investigation for fraud or misrepresentation. A new 15-day period begins upon submission of additional evidence. The $1,000 fee will be refunded if cases go beyond 15 days without a notice of action being mailed. The premium processing fee must be submitted by check or money order separate from other fees.

If filed at the same time as the principal alien, the BCIS offers premium processing to I-539 applications for dependents at no extra cost.

Petitioners who have been designated as non-profit by the IRS may continue to request discretionary expedited service.

Questions about premium processing may be submitted by email to the appropriate regional Service Center. Also, a special telephone number and email address have been established at each Service Center for premium processing customers exclusively. The Office of Business Liaison Customer Assistance Office may be contacted at (800) 357-2099 or by fax at (202) 305-2523.

General Processing Tips

The BCIS will now accept copies of certain documents such as diplomas and certificates if you submit a signed Form ER 750 which certifies that:

- Copies of original documents are exact and unaltered, and
- You will submit original documents, if required

For specific details about the photographs which are required by the BCIS, check www.immigration.gov/graphics/lawsregs/handbook/m-378.pdf.

On approval, the BCIS will issue a Form I-797, Notice of Approval to the petitioner and notify the appropriate consulate if the case is to be processed abroad.

Aliens who are ineligible for entry as a nonimmigrant because of a drug conviction, criminal record, or other reason must file Form I-192, Application for Advance Permission to Enter as a Nonimmigrant with the $195 filing fee, 90 to 120 days in advance of their planned entry. A typical example is a long distance trucker with a drug conviction who must make trips into the United States as part of his or her job. It is important to remember that the United States does not recognize a pardon from a foreign country.   *Ref: INA 212(d)(3)*

Step 3 - Clearing The Department Of State (DOS) Abroad

Virtually all nonimmigrant visa classifications may be processed at U.S. Embassies or Consulates abroad.

Every alien seeking a nonimmigrant visa is required to apply in person before a consular officer except:

- Child under 14 years of age
- A, C-2, C-3, G or NATO

- Applicant for diplomatic or official visa
- B, C-1, H-1 or I
- J-1 who is a leader in a field of specialized knowledge or skill
- D ship or aircraft crew member with a qualifying employer's letter
- Any nonimmigrant category where the consular officer determines that a waiver of personal appearance is warranted   *Ref: 9 FAM 41.102*

The State Department may allow aliens to select any consulate in their home country to process their visa application.

The usual application form required by the DOS is Form DS-156, Nonimmigrant Visa Application which may be waived if the interview has been waived. Many State Department forms are available online at www.travel.state.gov/visaforms.html.

Documentation and supporting evidence includes:

- *DOS form*
  - DS-156, Nonimmigrant Visa Application
- *Fees*
  - $100 for non-refundable Machine-Readable Visa (MRV)
  - visa filing fee may be waived by the Secretary of State for a nonimmigrant alien engaged in charitable activities in the U.S.
  - visa reciprocity fee equating to fees charged in similar circumstances in alien's home country (A, G, C-2/3, NATO exempt)
    (see www.travel.state.gov/reciprocity/index.htm for reciprocity fees)
- *Passports and photographs*
  - passport valid for at least six months beyond intended stay (A, C-3, NATO exempt)
  - every applicant must furnish photograph(s) in the quantity required 50 mm (2") square in reasonable likeness showing full face without head covering (check religious exceptions) against a light background signed on reverse   *Ref: 22 CFR 41.105 (a) (3)*
- *Current and prior immigration status*
  - such as I-94
- *Prior BCIS, DOL, USIA, academic approvals*
  - such as BCIS I-797, DOL Labor Certification or Labor Condition Application, I-20, IAP-66
- *Professional credentials*
  - such as degrees and/or professional status
- *Employer's supporting documentation*
  - letter confirming:
    - salary and source of funding
    - function
    - period of employment
- *Additional evidence*
  - purpose of trip
  - document outlining plans in U.S.

- *Proof of financial support or solvency*
  - arrangements to cover expenses in U.S. such as:
    - I-134, Affidavit of Support from family sponsor
    - own funding
- *Civil documents, including dependents*
  - birth
  - marriage
  - divorce
  - death of spouse
- *Police clearance*
  - police certificate if the consular officer has reason to believe that a police or criminal record may exist (A-1/2, C-3, G-1 to G-4, NATO-1 to NATO-4 and NATO-6 exempt)
- *Medical clearance:*
  - if history of medical ineligibility
  - if applying for K visa
  - if entering for medical treatment   *Ref: 9 FAM 41.108*
- *Evidence that U.S. stay is temporary (intent to depart)*
  - binding family ties
  - return tickets
  - no intention to abandon residence abroad

Unless the requirement is waived, each applicant for a nonimmigrant visa must be interviewed by a consular officer abroad. Based on the documentation presented, the consular officer shall determine the proper nonimmigrant classification and the alien's eligibility to receive a visa. K interviews may not be waived.   *Ref: 9 FAM 41.102*

Information on obtaining or renewing nonimmigrant visas may be obtained by calling (202) 663-1225. You may speak with a Visa Information Officer between 8:30 am and 5:00 pm, Eastern Time, Monday to Friday. You may also take advantage of the Auto-fax system by calling (202) 647-3000.

The 2001 USA Patriot Act requires that all visa applicants are submitted to a name-check to determine whether they have a criminal history or record. If there is a potential name match, the applicant will be required to have fingerprints taken and pay an $85 fee which will be forwarded to the FBI. If a record is found in their NCIC database, the FBI will forward it to the State Department for use by an authorized Consular Officer.   *Ref: 67 FR 8477*

As part of the nonimmigrant visa application process, consular officers at U.S. Embassies and Consulates abroad will identify individuals who must follow the special registration requirements when they apply for admission to the United States.

When arriving for interviews at consular or BCIS offices, do not be afraid to ask for directions if you find the signs are confusing or not helpful. Be prepared to leave briefcases with security. As waits may be long, take a good book such as this to read.

Grounds for Denial

Aliens are ineligible to obtain visas if the consular officer believes that any of the following impediments apply:

Examples	Grounds
• Physical or mental disorder posing a threat	• Health-related
• Criminal activity, convictions, prostitution	• Criminal and related
• Terrorist activity, adverse effect on foreign policy, past memberships	• Security and related
• Likely to become a public charge	• Public charge
• Lack of determination by Secretary of Labor	• Labor certification
• Previously deported, stowaways	• Illegal entrants and immigration violators
• Smugglers	• Missing required documents
• Draft dodgers	• Permanently ineligible for citizenship
• Polygamists, international child abductors	• Miscellaneous

In 2001, the State Department added two additional grounds of ineligibility:
- A crewman intending to land to join a vessel involved in a strike or lockout
- Study at a public elementary or publicly-funded adult education program or a public secondary school unless the stay is less than one year and the student has fully reimbursed the institution.   *Ref: 66 FR 10363*

State Department officials discourage dealing with U.S. Embassies and Consulates in third countries such as Mexico and Canada as they do not have the time or resources to verify information with authorities in your home country. It is better to deal with a U.S. Embassy or Consulate while living or visiting at home.

At a cost of $100, the U.S. Embassy or Consulate will place a Machine-Readable Visa (MRV), also called a foil or sticker, in the applicant's passport. It contains:
- Passport number
- Date of birth
- Nationality
- Entry: M (multiple) or 01 (single), 02 (double) or other numerical limit
- Dates of issue and expiration

Step 4 - Clearing the BCBP at a U.S. Port of Entry

BCBP Immigration Inspectors at a U.S. port of entry have the right and responsibility to ensure that all medical reports and other required documents are in order for entry under the chosen nonimmigrant classification. They do, after all, have the final responsibility for making a determination on your eligibility for entry in your desired classification regardless of whether you have a DOS visa in your hand.

While Immigration Inspectors are not expected to second guess the work of other agencies with whom you have dealt, they must be satisfied that you have supplied all the necessary paperwork along the way. To expedite processing, you are encouraged to bring copies or originals of all documents you have filed in previous steps.

With the exception of entries in E and K status, Canadians are not required to have obtained Department of State visas (MRVs).

In special cases, an alien may apply for and obtain a waiver of the visa and passport requirement under INA 212(d)(4)(A) without the prior concurrence of the Department of State if, either prior to the alien's embarkation abroad or upon arrival at a port of entry, the responsible District Director of the Bureau of Customs and Border Protection (BCBP) in charge of the port of entry concludes:

- The alien is unable to present the required documents because of an unforeseen emergency, and
- The alien's claim of emergency circumstances is legitimate, and
- Approval of the waiver would be appropriate under all the attendant facts and circumstances

Ref: FR Vol. 64, No. 103, May 28, 1999; 8 USC 1104 41.2(j);22 CFR 41 and 42

Applicants are cautioned to be truthful and avoid raising suspicions as Immigration Inspectors who suspect fraud may order "Expedited Removal" that bars an alien from entering the U.S. for five years. In some BCBP districts, the Immigration Inspector at the port of entry must obtain permission from the district duty officer before initiating this process.

Documentation and supporting evidence includes:

- *BCIS form*
  - I-94, Arrival/Departure Record
- *Fees*
  - $6 for I-94
  - $3 for commercial air and sea passengers (except Great Lakes)
- *Passports and photographs*
  - passport valid for at least six months beyond intended stay
  - color photographs 40 mm high by 35 mm wide in 3/4 profile showing right ear, no head covering (religious exceptions), light background
- *Current and prior immigration status*
  - such as I-94, Arrival/Departure Record

- *Prior DOL and DOS approvals*
  - DOL Labor Condition Application or Labor Certification
  - DOS Machine-Readable Visa (MRV) in passport
- *Professional credentials*
  - such as university diploma
- *Employer's supporting documentation*
  - supporting letter confirming salary, function and source of funds
- *Proof of financial support or solvency*
  - I-134, Affidavit of Support from family sponsor
  - own funding
- *Civil documents, including dependents*
  - birth, marriage or divorce
  - death of spouse
- *Police clearance*
- *Medical clearance*
  - if history of medical ineligibility
  - Consular medical examination
- *Evidence that U.S. stay is temporary (intent to depart)*
  - binding family ties
  - return tickets
  - no intention to abandon residence abroad

Entry Formalities

Your I-94 or passport may be stamped for single-entry or multiple-entry depending on how a U.S. citizen is treated in similar circumstances in your home country and may differ from the terms of the visa issued by the State Department.

Citizens of Iran have only single-entry visas that are canceled on entry. However, nationals of other countries with single-entry visas may be able to visit Canada or Mexico for fewer than 30 days without surrendering their I-94.

When meeting a BCBP Immigration Inspector:

- Tell the *whole* story of what you are trying to accomplish
- Have a passport, birth certificate, I-94 in your hands
- Have all other required documents immediately available
- A Driver's License is not acceptable proof of immigration status

An alien who makes an application for a visa or for admission into the United States is required to possess a passport that:

- Authorizes the alien to return to the home country, and
- Is valid for a minimum of six months beyond the date of the expiration of the initial period of the applicant's admission or contemplated stay in the United States, or
- Is issued by a country that the U.S. accepts as having agreed that their passports will be valid for reentry up to six months after expiring

Ref: FR Volume 63, Number 196, October 9, 1998

Grounds of Inadmissibility

There are a number of Grounds of Inadmissibility including:

- Being present in the U.S. without having been admitted or paroled
- Being in the U.S. unlawfully for more than 180 days after April 1, 1997
- Inciting terrorist activity to cause death or serious bodily harm
- Lacking a legally binding family-sponsored immigrant's affidavit of support
- Nurses failing to have a certificate from the Commission on Graduates of Foreign Nursing Schools or approved equivalent
- Intending immigrants without the required vaccinations
- Failing to attend a proceeding to determine inadmissibility
- Falsely claiming to be U.S. citizens
- Violating the new student visa terms
- Accompanying other aliens inadmissible for medical reasons
- Voting in a U.S. election
- Renouncing U.S. citizenship to avoid taxation

Ref: INS Fact Sheet, March 26, 1997

If you must enter despite your inadmissibility as a nonimmigrant, a Form I-192, Application for Advance Permission to Enter as a Nonimmigrant with the $195 filing fee plus an additional $50 for fingerprints must be filed with the District Director and approved before you may enter. Processing may take four months. Form I-601 should only be used for immigrant visa cases. Be prepared to offer such proof as:

- Fingerprint evidence
- A list of convictions and dispositions
- A letter from your employer with reasons why you must enter the U.S.
- A letter of clearance from your physician if narcotics are on your record
- Letters of reference

Counting from April 1, 1997, aliens seeking to enter the U.S. after being out of status (unlawfully present) in the U.S. from six months to a year are barred from admission for three years while those out of status for one year or more are barred for ten years.

Ref: IIRIRA96.301

Address changes must be reported to the BCIS within ten days. Either a letter or Form AR-11 may be used. Form AR-11 may be ordered online or by telephone and may be handed in to the local BCIS office or mailed to P.O. Box 7134, London, KY 40742-7134.

Special Registration Entry-Exit Strategy

In light of recent events and the security concerns which they raised, Congress has mandated that a comprehensive entry-exit program must be implemented by 2005 to further ensure the country's security while protecting the rights of inviduals coming in to the country.

In late 2002, a Special Registration strategy was initiated to register certain designated aliens applying for admission as well as those already in the United States.

National Security Entry-Exit Registration System (NSEERS)

The National Security Entry-Exit Registration System (NSEERS) was introduced in 2002 to meet several important national security objectives including using the national database to check for wanted criminals, known terrorists, visitors who have overstayed their visa as well as confirmation of entries and exits. It is also intended to more closely monitor where foreign visitors are living and what they are doing.

Phase One of Special Registration - Individuals Registered at a Port of Entry

The first phase of Special Registration of selected individuals to be fingerprinted, photographed and interviewed under oath at U.S. ports of entry continues.

As part of the nonimmigrant visa application process, consular officers at U.S. Embassies and Consulates abroad identify individuals who must follow the special registration requirements in the United States.

Who must always be registered at a port of entry ?

- Citizens or nationals 14 and over from Iran, Iraq, Libya, Sudan and Syria are registered at each entry regardless of any dual nationality
- Males 16 to 45 from Pakistan, Saudi Arabia and Yemen
- Nonimmigrants who have been designated by the State Department
- Any other nonimmigrants identified by immigration officers for Special Registration at airports, seaports and land ports   *Ref: 8 CFR 264.1(f)(2)*

Immigration officers at ports of entry may identify nonimmigrants for registration each time they apply for admission to the United States for a temporary period of time if they meet a combination of intelligence-based criteria and are identified as presenting elevated national security concerns. Those identified are sent to a special area for registration.

Registration takes the form of an interview under oath with an immigration inspector. The enrollment process includes the taking of specific biometric information, fingerprints and photograph. Itineraries and addresses are recorded.

Effective October 1, 2002, registrants became subject to the following requirements:

- If you remain in the United States for 30 days or longer, you must report in person to a Special Registration immigration district or sub-office between the 30th and 40th day after entering the U.S. to show that you are following your travel plans or statement of intentions made when entering. No appointment is necessary. A waiver may be obtained from a District Director.
- If you remain more than one year, you must report in person to a Special Registration office within ten days of the anniversary of the date you were

last admitted to the United States to show that you are still following your travel plans or statement of intentions made when you entered
- If you change your address, employer or school after remaining in the United States more than 30 days, you must notify the BCIS in writing within ten days of the change
- When you leave the United States, you must appear in person before an immigration inspecting officer at a designated port of departure to have your departure documented and you must leave that port on the same day
- Anyone failing to report their departure might not be permitted to return to the United States unless a consular or immigration officer is satisfied with the reasons for failing to report the departure

Phase Two of Special Registration - Call-In Registration

In the Second Phase of Special Registration, selected nationals and citizens of designated countries who previously had been admitted to the U.S. were called in to register at an immigration office or sub-office.   *Ref: INA 263(a) and 265(b)*

The four Call-In groups are:
- Group 4 - Bangladesh, Egypt, Indonesia, Jordan, Kuwait
- Group 3 - Pakistan, Saudi Arabia
- Group 2 - Afganistan, Algeria, Bahrain, Eritrea, Lebanon, Morocco, North Korea, Oman, Qatar, Somalia, Tunisia, United Arab Emirates, Yemen
- Group 1 - Iran, Iraq, Libya, Sudan, Syria

The call-in required the registration of males 16 and over who are citizens or nationals of these countries and:
- Were last admitted to the U.S. before September 30, 2002, and
- Were still in the United States after a late 2002 or early 2003 residence deadline which varied by country
- Met the early 2003 registration deadline applicable to their group

Registrants are given an I-94 Arrival/Departure Record annotated with a Fingerprint Identification Number (FIN) to show that they have registered.

Registrants were also subject to the following:
- Reporting to a designated Special Registration office for an interview, fingerprinting and photograph by the early 2003 deadline for their group
- Reporting for an annual interview at a Special Registration office within ten days of their anniversary date if they remain in the U.S.
- Submitting a Form AR-11 to the BCIS within ten days of changing their address, employment or educational institution
- Reporting to an immigration officer at a port of entry on the day they depart the country

Exempted were U.S. citizens, legal permanent residents, refugees, asylees, asylum applicants, nonimmigrants in A or G status and those paroled in to the United States.

The group of nonimmigrants subject to registration was estimated at 7,200 by the INS. Most of those required to register were students, extended business travelers or individuals visiting family members for extended periods.

Step 5 - Application for Employment

The rules for accepting employment vary from classification to classification. However, as a general principle, employment must be temporary and, in certain cases, it should not displace a U.S. citizen or legal permanent resident and the alien should be paid the prevailing rate for the specific type of work in the area.

To avoid misunderstandings, read the employment parameters of your chosen classification and discuss your conclusions with the DOL and/or the BCIS.

The IIRIRA96 and subsequent H-1B legislation have changed some of the H-1B employment practices to protect the U.S. worker while enabling employers to fill urgently needed job vacancies with skilled foreign workers.

By way of example, the 1996 legislation, among other things:
- Increased the fines for hiring illegal aliens
- Established three pilot programs of employment eligibility confirmation
- Established a toll-free telephone or electronic media to provide confirmation on an alien's identity and authorization to be employed

The 1998 Act:
- Increased the annual quota of temporary professionals for three years
- Required H-1B-dependent employers to attempt to employ qualified U.S. workers before employing foreign workers
- Introduced an additional $500 filing fee (now $1,000). A training program for low income students and stiffer penalties for infractions

The 2000 laws:
- Further increased the annual quota of skilled foreign professionals
- Gave aliens more flexibility in changes of employer
- Increased the supplementary filing fee to $1,000

Normally, a Form I-765, Application for Employment Authorization is submitted to the BCIS regional Service Center having jurisdiction over your location. In 1997, the INS began issuing Form I-766, Employment Authorization Document (EAD) cards meant to be more tamper proof. Form I-688A and I-688B EADs are being phased out.

Step 6 - Application for Renewal or Change of Status

Application to the BCIS within the United States

Aliens living in the United States as legal nonimmigrants may be able to renew their temporary status or change to another classification without leaving the United States. Usually, this is done by filing with the BCIS. Frequently, either Form I-539, Application to Extend/Change Nonimmigrant Status or Form I-129, Petition for a Nonimmigrant Worker is used, depending on the classification and whether the petition is on behalf of the principal alien or a dependent.

Application for renewal or change of status may be filed and the alien remain in the United States during the grace period which follows a period of admission. However, the alien may not work until approval is received.

To avoid unnecessary problems, be sure to:
- Use forms that are not out of date
- Fill out the forms correctly and completely
- Enclose the correct filing fee and documents
- Sign all papers requiring a signature
- Answer all questions, if not applicable, answer N/A
- Make a checklist and mark off each item to be remembered
- Not conceal information or submit false information or documents
- Keep photocopies of all papers filed
- Send all mail certified, return receipt requested

BCIS Regional Service Centers - Where to File

Generally, an alien filing an application for an extension of status or a change to another temporary or permanent classification, should file the application with the BCIS regional Service Center having jurisdiction over his or her place of residence. However, certain types of transactions must be filed at one specific Service Center. For example, most Reentry Permits are to be filed with the Nebraska Service Center.

The following list is included for reference only. Always check the BCIS address before submitting any paperwork as addresses may vary according to the benefit.

Vermont Service Center
75 Lower Welden Street
Saint Albans, VT 05479-0001

(802) 527-4913

Serving: Connecticut, Delaware, District of Columbia, Maine, Maryland, Massachusetts, New Hampshire, New Jersey, New York, Pennsylvania, Puerto Rico, Rhode Island, Vermont, the Virgin Islands, Virginia, West Virginia.

Texas Service Center

4141 St. Augustine Road   7701 N. Stemmons Freeway
Dallas, TX 75227   Dallas, TX 75247

(214) 381-1423

Serving: Alabama, Arkansas, Florida, Georgia, Kentucky, Louisiana, Mississippi, New Mexico, North Carolina, Oklahoma, South Carolina, Tennessee, Texas.

California Service Center

P.O. Box 30111
24000 Avila Road
Laguna Niguel, CA 92607-0111

(949) 831-8427

Serving: Arizona, California, Guam, Hawaii, Nevada.

Nebraska Service Center

100 Centennial Mall North, Room B-26
Lincoln, NE 68508

(402) 323-7830

Serving: All other states.

Note: With the exception of the initial NAFTA application made by Canadians at a U.S. port of entry, all Mexican and Canadian TN (NAFTA) applications should be filed with the Director of the Nebraska Service Center.

A Nonimmigrant L or Immigrant Alien Worker petition should be mailed to the Vermont Service Center if the beneficiary will be located within the jurisdiction of either the Vermont or Texas Service Centers. Otherwise petitions should be filed with either the California or Nebraska Service Centers, as defined above.

Visa Revalidation by the Department of State (DOS)

After the BCIS has extended your stay, your visa may need to be renewed before attempting to reenter the U.S. from a business or pleasure trip of more than 30 days outside the contiguous U.S. and Canada. Depending on how U.S. citizens are treated in your home country, your original visa may have been restricted to a limited number of entries and short period of validity. If so, you need to renew your visa. Visas are a State Department document and cannot be issued at a BCBP port of entry. Only E status requires Canadians to hold temporary visas for reentry to the U.S.

Application for visa renewal may be made at a U.S. Embassy or Consulate in your home country or by Third-Country Nationals (TCNs) at a U.S. Consulate in Mexico or Canada by calling (900) 443-3131. For security reasons, the automatic revalidation of nonimmigrant visas is no longer available to aliens from countries identified as supporting terrorism when they attempt to reenter the U.S. with an unexpired I-94,

I-20 or IAP-66 following a visit of not more than 30 days to other North American countries or adjacent islands, except Cuba.   *Ref: 67 FR 10322*

A, G, E, H, I, L, O, P and NATO classifications may be renewed by mail by the DOS in the U.S. Tourist visas and student visas may not.   *Ref: 22 CFR 41.111(b)*

Completed applications may be sent by mail to:

> U.S. Department of State/Visa
> P.O. Box 952099
> St. Louis, MO 63195-2099
> Fax: (202) 663-1608

Completed applications may also be sent by courier to:

> U.S. Department of State/Visa (Box 2099)
> 1005 Convention Plaza
> St. Louis, MO 63101-1200
> Fax: (202) 663-1608

Prior refusals being returned to the State Department for processing will be treated as new applications at the beginning of the reissuance process. The reapplication should include a new DS-156, Nonimmigrant Visa Application and 50 mm (2") square photograph with the complete application packet mailed to:

> Department of State
> CA/VO/P/D
> 2401 E Street, N.W.
> Washington, DC 20522-1016

It is not possible to obtain expedited processing or status reports. If you do not have time to get your visa renewal in the U.S., you should apply in person to the consular office of the country of destination.

Documentation and supporting evidence includes:

- *DOS form*
  - DS-156, Nonimmigrant Visa Application
- *Fees*
  - $100 for non-refundable Machine-Readable Visa (MRV)
  - visa reciprocity equating to fees charged in similar circumstances in alien's home country
- *Passport and photograph*
  - passport valid for at least six months beyond intended stay
  - 50 mm (2") square photograph facing camera directly without head covering (check for religious exceptions) against a light background
- *Current and prior immigration status*
  - original current I-94 (no copies)
  - copy of I-171C (H's or L's) or I-797 Petition Approval Notice

- *Employer's supporting documentation*
  - detailed letter identifying:
    - the employee and his or her position
    - travel itinerary

When a fee is charged for visa reciprocity, include two certified checks or money orders, one for the visa application and one for the reciprocity charge. Personal checks cannot be accepted.

Further recorded information may be obtained by calling (202) 663-1213. It may be possible to speak with an officer between 2 and 4 pm, Monday to Friday.

An alien living in the United States or Canada must pay a fee for a call to a central number to obtain visa information or book a visa appointment interview with a consular officer at any of the U.S. Consulates along the U.S. border with Canada or Mexico.

The system is run by a contractor in Canada and can be reached by calling:
- (900) 443-3131 to book an appointment from the U.S.
- (900) 656-2222 for operator-assisted visa information from the U.S.
- (900) 451-2778 to book an appointment from Canada
- (900) 451-6663 for operator-assisted visa information from Canada
- (900) 451-6330 for recorded visa information from Canada
- (888) 840-0032 to make an appointment (pay for service)
- (888) 611-6676 to cancel an appointment (toll-free)

Operators are available to make appointments from 7 am to 10 pm, Eastern Time, Monday to Friday. Appointments may also be booked on the internet at www.nvars.com at a cost of $CDN 10 charged to a major credit card.

The contractor will send the applicant a Form DS-156, information sheet and instructions about what is needed at their interview and confirmation of the details of the appointment. It should only be necessary to contact a consulate for information not provided by the contractor.

Third Country National (TCN) processing is no longer available at Canadian and Mexican border posts to nationals of the seven counties designated as state sponsors of terrorism. These countries are North Korea, Cuba, Syria, Sudan, Iran, Iraq and Libya. Nationals of these countries must file an additional form DS-157 and appear for an interview.

The Border Posts are:

Tijuana, Mexico
The U.S. Consulate-General is located at Tapachula 96, 22420 Tijuana, Baja California Norte, across from San Diego, California. Telephone: 52 66 81-7400.

Matamoros, Mexico
   The U.S. Consulate is located at Tamaulipas Calle Primera 2002, Matamoros Mexico, across the border from Brownsville, Texas. Telephone: 52 88 12-4402. Central booking appointments are not made for this U.S. Consulate.

Ciudad Juarez, Mexico
   The U.S. Consulate-General is located at Chihuahua, Avenue Lopez Mateos 924N 32000, Ciudad Juarez across the border from El Paso, Texas. No Mexican visa is necessary to go to the consulate. Telephone: 52 16 11-3000.

Vancouver, B.C., Canada
   The U.S. Consulate-General is located at 1095 West Pender Street, 21st Floor, Vancouver, BC V6E 2M6. Telephone: (604) 685-4311.

Calgary, Alberta, Canada
   The U.S. Consulate-General is located at 615 Macleod Trail, S.E., Room 1050, Calgary, AB T2G 4T8. Telephone: (403) 266-8962.

Toronto, Ontario, Canada
   The U.S. Consulate-General is located at 360 University Avenue, Toronto, ON M5G 1S4. Telephone: (416) 595-1700.

Ottawa, Ontario, Canada
   Visas are issued by the Consular section of the U.S. Embassy at 490 Sussex Drive, Ottawa, ON K1N 1G8. Telephone: (613) 238-4470.

Montréal Québec, Canada
   The U.S. Consulate is located at 1155 St-Alexandre St. Montréal, QC, H2Z 1Z2. Telephone: (514) 398-9695, extension 402.

Québec City, Québec, Canada
   The U.S. Consulate-General is located at 2, Place Terrasse Dufferin, Québec, QC G1R 4T9. Telephone: (418) 692-2095 or 692-4640.

Halifax, Nova Scotia, Canada
   The U.S. Consulate-General is located at 2000 Barrington Street, Suite 910, Cogswell Tower, Halifax, NS B3J 3K1. Telephone: (902) 429-2480 or 429-2485.

   Approved out-of-district visas generally will be ready for pickup by specified times on the following business day.

   General information is available from the American Citizen Services Consular Information Telephone Service by calling (800) 529-4410 from the U.S. or Canada.

Chapter 3

Visitor Classifications

F oreign nationals who meet the intent of the law may enter the United States as visitors for varying periods and purposes. Most, but not all visitors are required to obtain visas.

In general, visitors are those aliens who are coming to the United States:
- For a relatively short period, and
- Will not become either temporary or permanent residents

Since this chapter deals with the vacations, business trips and brief stop overs, you need to review the following criteria before deciding what option applies to your situation:
- The purpose of your trip
- The duration of your trip
- Your home country

Vacationers who will leave after a set period are easy to characterize as visitors. They have different options depending on how long they will stay and the country they are from.

People on business trips are more difficult to categorize as they may require more formal visa and status arrangements.

Aliens who are passing through the country constitute a third group. Their status depends on why they are passing through and what they plan to do while they are in the United States.

Canadians and Mexicans are visa exempt in certain circumstances.

Visitors from several other countries may also come to the United States without a visa if their country is a participant in the U.S. tourist promotion Visa Waiver Program.

VWP

Visa Waiver Program

T he Visa Waiver Program (VWP) permits nationals from designated countries who participate in the VWP to apply for admission to the United States for 90 days or less as nonimmigrant visitors for business or pleasure, without first obtaining a B-1/B-2 nonimmigrant visa from a U.S. consular office.   *Ref: INA 217*

The Secretary of Homeland Security, in consultation with the Secretary of State, is authorized to operate a program which waives the necessity of obtaining a visa by an alien who meets the following requirements:

- Seeking entry as a visitor for pleasure or business
- Entering for 90 days or less
- National of a Visa Waiver Program country
- Is not inadmissible   *Ref: H.R. 3767; 9 FAM 31.2(l)*

All other entries may require the issuance of a visa.

The Visa Waiver Pilot Program became permanent on October 30, 2000 when President Clinton signed legislation which requires:

- The identity of waiver applicants to be checked for inadmissibility against an automated electronic data base
- A visa application to be made in a consular office abroad when grounds of inadmissibility are identified
- Information on each applicant to be retained for ten years

As of January 1, 2003, travellers from Visa Waiver Program countries arriving and departing from U.S. air and sea ports will not be admitted unless they arrive on carriers or vessels that electronically transmit detailed entry and exit passenger control data to the BCBP via the Interagency Border Inspection System (IBIS) database. The stated purpose of the process is to safeguard U.S. law enforcement and reduce the ability of inadmissible aliens to enter the U.S.   *Ref: Pub. L. 106-396; 67 FR 63246*

Aliens entering under the terms of the Visa Waiver Permanent Program are called Visa Exempt. Since they are limited to 90 days, it may be preferable to enter with a visa if there is a possibility of requesting an extension or change to another status.

Regular sub-categories are:

- WB - Visa Waiver, Business
- WT - Visa Waiver, Tourist

To qualify, a country must:

- Have a nonimmigrant visa refusal rate of less than 2 percent of its nationals over the previous two fiscal year period
- Have a nonimmigrant visa refusal rate of less than 2.5 percent of its nationals in either fiscal year
- Have a machine-readable passport program (operating by October 1, 2003)
- Extend a reciprocal privilege to U.S. citizens

In 2002, entry was available to the following countries:

Andorra	Ireland	San Marino
Australia	Italy	Singapore **
Austria	Japan	Slovenia
Belgium	Liechtenstein	Spain
Brunei	Luxembourg	Sweden
Denmark	Monaco	Switzerland
Finland	Netherlands	United Kingdom*
France	New Zealand	Uruguay **
Germany	Norway	
Iceland	Portugal**	

*   United Kingdom includes only British citizens who have the unrestricted right of permanent abode in England, Scotland, Wales, Northern Ireland, the Channel Islands, and the Isle of Man.

**   Terminated April 15, 2003.   *Ref: 64 FR 42006*

Under the Guam Visa Waiver Program, citizens of qualifying countries may visit Guam for up to 15 days without a nonimmigrant visitor visa.   *Ref: Pub. L. 99-396*

Admission

Single Step - Clearing the BCBP at a U.S. Port of Entry

A passport is necessary and, unless you are entering overland from Canada or Mexico, you may need to produce a round trip ticket when you enter.

An I-94W, Arrival/Departure Record must be filled out and stamped by a BCBP Immigration Inspector at a U.S. port of entry. It may be stamped Multiple Entry.

Other Visa Waiver aliens arriving at ports of entry must also obtain an I-94W.

Documentation and supporting evidence includes:

- *BCIS form*
  - completed and signed I-94W, Arrival/Departure Record

- *Fee*
  - $6
- *Passport*
  - passport valid for at least six months beyond intended stay
- *Proof of financial support or solvency*
  - proof of financial solvency
- *Special conditions*
  - be seeking entry into the U.S. for business or pleasure
  - waive the right to a hearing of exclusion or deportation
  - not be a threat to U.S. welfare, health, safety or security
  - not have failed to comply with the conditions of any previous visa waiver admission
  - not ineligible under INA
  - not change status, work or study
- *Evidence that U.S. stay is temporary (intent to depart)*
  - if entering by air or sea:
    - have a round-trip transportation ticket issued on a carrier that has a signed an agreement with the U.S. government to participate in the waiver program
    - arrive in the United States aboard such a carrier
      Ref: 8 CFR 217, 60 FR 15855, April 1, 1995

Effective March 17, 2003, citizens of most countries except Canada and the Visa Waiver countries require State Department visas.

Canadian citizens do not require B-2 tourist visas and passports to enter for up to six month periods. However, the Canadian Government and U.S. border officers recommend that all Canadians carry passports for all U.S. visits.

Mexican nationals with a border crossing identification card do not need a visa and passport when applying for admission as a temporary visitor for business or pleasure.   *Ref: DOS TL: Visa-94, 9-30-94*

The voluntary departure period may be extended for nonimmigrant aliens admitted under the visa waiver program who require U.S. medical treatment. The annual limit of waivers is 300. Statements must be submitted to BCIS headquarters from a district office:

- From the physician and health care facility respecting medical diagnosis and non-public payment of health services
- From the alien with evidence of the ability to pay without public assistance
  Ref: H.R. 2961

Aliens entering in WB status may accept honoraria with a written invitation.

B

Temporary Visitor for Business or Pleasure

The B classification is reserved for those who have a home in a foreign country where they will return after a short stay in the U.S. and their stay is for:

- Business - to attend meetings, buy goods, negotiate contracts, act as representative of a foreign employer
- Pleasure - to tour, visit friends or family, sightsee   *Ref: ER 806 3-8-94*

Sub-categories are:

- B-1 - Temporary Visitor for Business
- B-2 - Temporary Visitor for Pleasure
        Ref: INA 101(a)(15)(B); 9 FAM 41.12, 41.31

Visitors may be admitted for professional or commercial endeavors but not employment. Although compensation must be earned and paid from abroad, B-1 and B-2 scholars who in engage in academic activities may receive honoraria in exchange for services that benefit an academic institution provided that the student has not received honoraria from more than five institutions during the previous six months.
Ref: INS Memorandum, November 30, 1999

Canadians and Mexicans have special status. They are covered under four nonimmigrant classifications of the North American Free Trade Agreement (NAFTA) including B, Temporary Visitor for Business or Pleasure.

Canadian Snowbirds

A maximum admission period of six months is generally the norm for Canadian retirees planning to winter in the U.S. Those who wish to stay longer may apply for an extension once they are in the U.S.

Canadian Visitors to the U.S.

To enter the U.S., a Canadian citizen must establish both identity and citizenship. A birth or citizenship certificate or passport proves citizenship and a driver's license, health card or other government photo identification may establish identity. The requirements of U.S. authorities for identification upon entering the country have become more strict and less predictable. The Canadian Department of Foreign Affairs and International Trade recommends that all Canadians carry a Canadian passport for all visits to the U.S. A Canadian citizen arriving in the U.S. from outside the Western Hemisphere is required to present a passport. See: www.immigration.gov/graphics/lawenfor/bmgmt/inspect/docrequirements.htm.

B-1 Visitor for Business

Aliens with B status are not permitted to accept employment during their stay in the U.S. However, certain supervisory, training and sales activities may be permitted.

In separate BCIS and DOS notices published on September 19, 2001, it is confirmed that an alien may enter as a B-1 non immigrant:

- To perform activities incident to international trade and commerce
- To train or supervise others in building or construction work but not perform such work themselves
- To install, service or repair commercial or industrial equipment or machinery purchased from a company outside the United States, if he or she possesses specialized knowledge
- If compensation is not from sources within the United States

Because installation and service of equipment is permitted under B-1 and building and construction is not, the BCIS and DOS are considering a more formal definition of building and construction work.   *Ref: 66 FR 48223*

In a June 21, 2001 Memorandum, DOS provided for closer scrutiny of Visa Waiver Country business visitors.

B-2 Visitor for Pleasure

A B-2 is usually the appropriate classification when a tourist visa becomes necessary. It is used when an alien enters for activities of a recreational character including tourism, amusement, visits with friends or relatives, rest, medical treatment and activities of a fraternal, social or service nature.   *Ref: 9 FAM 41.31(2)*

When inviting a friend or relative to visit the United States, the BCIS suggests sending a personal letter of invitation and a completed I-134, Affidavit of Support to the person abroad. These and other personal documents that show ties to their home country should be taken to the nearest U.S. Consulate.   *Ref: ER-722*

Intending student status is permitted for aliens who enter the U.S. in B-2 status to visit schools that may be of interest. In these cases, if your B-2 is issued with the annotation "Intending Student" and, after being accepted by an accredited school, you may apply for a Change of Status to one of the student classifications without leaving the United States. BCIS approval must be received before enrolling.

Medical treatment for U.S. visitors is permitted. Be prepared to produce a letter from a U.S. doctor who will undertake treatment and from a specialist in your home country confirming that treatment is not available there. Also, be prepared to prove that you have the necessary funds to pay for your treatment and living expenses.

Medical externships are permitted on B-2 visas. You may observe but may not be paid or provide any direct patient care.

Seeking employment is permitted although you may be under more scrutiny if there is any feeling that you may not leave the U.S. by the end of your period of admittance. Factors considered on whether you will be admitted include your:

- Financial support
- Intent to depart
- Commitment to remain within the terms of your admittance

Proof that may be required includes your:

- Residential lease or home ownership in your home country
- Bank statements
- Utility bills
- Employer's letter

Honoraria may be accepted as a gratutitous payment for an activity for which no fee is legally required. If arranged before arrival, entry is in B-1 status and requires an invitation letter from the institution which describes the event, date and location of the activity. Honoraia are also permitted if participation is arranged after arrival in B-2 status. Incidental expenses such as travel and supplies may be covered. Such activities are limited to nine days at each of five organizations over a six-month period. This was originally proposed by the INS on May 30, 2002.   *Ref: 67 FR 37727*

Admission Process

Step 1 - Clearing the Department of State (DOS) Abroad

If you are not Canadian, Mexican or from a Visa Waiver country, you should generally apply for your visitor visa at the U.S. Embassy or Consulate having jurisdiction over your place of permanent residence. Although you are permitted to apply at any consular office abroad, it may be more difficult to qualify for the visa outside your country of permanent residence.

Ref: DOS Publication, November, 1995

Visitors for Business or Pleasure usually obtain a visa from a U.S. Consulate in their home country. The visa may be valid for applications to the BCBP for visits over periods of up to ten years by aliens who are:

- Nationals of countries that offer a reciprocal treatment of U.S. citizens
- In possession of a valid passport
- Bona fide visitors and will continue to enter the United States only for such purpose for an indefinite period of time   *Ref: 9 FAM 41.112*

Documentation and supporting evidence includes:

- *DOS form*
  - DS-156, Nonimmigrant Visa Application
- *Fees*
  - $100 for non-refundable Machine-Readable Visa (MRV)
  - visa reciprocity fee equating to fees charged in similar circumstances in alien's home country
- *Passport and photograph*
  - passport valid for at least six months beyond intended stay
  - 50 mm (2") square photograph facing camera directly without head covering (check for religious exceptions) against a light background
- *Employer's supporting documentation*
  - letter confirming function, amount and source of salary
- *Special conditions*
  - classifiable as a visitor under U.S. law
  - purpose of the trip
- *Proof of financial support or solvency*
  - letters confirming your financial support, if applicable
  - letters of invitation from hosting relatives or friends
  - confirmation of participation in planned tours
- *Additional evidence*
  - classifiable as a visitor under U.S. law
  - purpose of the trip
- *Evidence that U.S. stay is temporary (intent to depart)*
  - binding family ties
  - employment abroad
  - copy of return tickets
  - no intention to abandon residence abroad

The Form DS-156 and any additional evidence furnished by the alien shall be retained in the consular files. A Machine-Readable Visa (MRV) valid to apply to the BCBP for entries for up to ten years is placed in the applicant's passport or on Form OF 232, Nonimmigrant Visa Stamp in some circumstances.   *Ref: 9 FAM 41.113*

Members of observer missions to the United Nations who apply for B-1 visas receive a waiver of visa application and issuance fees.   *Ref: 65 FR 52306*

Step 2 - Clearing the BCBP at a U.S. Port of Entry

Application for entry should be made at a U.S. port of entry no later than the expiration date on the visa.

The bearer of the visa is subject to inspection by a BCBP Immigration Inspector who has the authority to determine how long a visitor may stay or deny admission. To lessen this risk, a visitor should carry any evidence originally presented when the visa was issued by the consulate abroad, unless entry is based on the 90-day Visa Waiver Program.

A Visitor for Pleasure is now automatically admitted for six months. However, a an immigration inspector has the discretion to admit for up to 12 months. It is usually wise to pay $6 for an I-94 as proof of the approved entry period.

The BCBP now permits the entry, in B-2 status, of long-term cohabiting partners of principal aliens. Such accompanying partners must:

- Not plan on being employed
- Have a pre-determined departure date
- Have a residence outside the U.S. to return to
- Apply for extensions normally beyond six months

It is important to tell the truth about your reason for coming to avoid the risk of expedited removal which comes with an automatic five-year ban on future entry. It is acceptable to be looking for work but very important to prove that you do not intend to work, that you have a permanent residence abroad and you intend to depart the U.S. by the expiration date of your visitor status. For more information on inspection, see www.immigration.gov/graphics/howdoi/legadmit.htm.

It is not acceptable to say that you are on vacation when your real intent is to get married. That is seen as fraudulent and carries serious consequences. On the other hand, if you suddenly have an unanticipated change of plans such as getting married, you may be able to change status without leaving the United States. However, it must be unanticipated and you should be able to prove it.

Option 1 - *Mexicans and Canadians*

Mexican nationals are now issued an I-94, Arrival/Departure Record instead of an I-444, Mexican Border Visitors Permit for visits up to six months. An unexpired passport, State Department Laser Visa or "Mica" must still be presented.

Under the terms of NAFTA, both Mexican and Canadian citizens and permanent residents may apply directly at a U.S. port of entry without obtaining employment authorization and without numerical restriction provided that:

- They comply with other immigration measures applicable to temporary entry
- Their entry does not affect adversely:
  - the settlement of any labor dispute at the place of employment
  - the employment of any person involved in the labor dispute

Documentation and supporting evidence includes:

- *Proof of Citizenship*
  - passport or other proof of citizenship
- *Employer's supporting evidence (B-1)*
  - how the business person will be engaged

- description of the purpose of entry
- the proposed business activity is international in scope
- the business person is not seeking to enter the local market, including:
  - the primary source of remuneration for the proposed business activity is outside the territory of the United States
  - the business person's principal place of business and the actual place of accrual of profits, at least predominantly, remain outside the United States (proof is normally an oral declaration or, if required, a letter of attestation from the employer)

Ref: NAFTA Annex 1603

Option 2 - Non-NAFTA

The expiration date on the visa is the last day you may apply at a U.S. port of entry for permission to enter the United States.

The decision on whether to admit you is up to a BCBP Immigration Inspector who may refuse admission if something is discovered contrary to your declared intention.

Grounds for Exclusion include:

- Discovery of documents indicating the applicant is planning to get married and live in the United States
- Past criminal convictions
- Past immigration violations
- Certain diseases

Documentation and supporting evidence includes:

- *BCIS form*
  - I-94, Arrival/Departure Record
- *Fee*
  - $6
- *Passport*
  - passport valid for at least six months beyond intended stay
- *Prior DOS approval*
  - DOS Machine-Readable Visa (MRV) in passport
- *Professional credentials*
  - qualifications need not be proven
- *Evidence to support request*
  - employer's letter explaining role in project, source of salary (B-1), or
  - letter of invitation (B-2)
- *Proof of financial support or solvency*
  - I-134, Affidavit of Support from family or friend sponsor
  - own funding
- *Evidence that U.S. stay is temporary (intent to depart)*
  - binding family ties
  - employment abroad

- copy of return tickets
- no intention to abandon residence abroad

If your admission is approved, your I-94, Arrival/Departure Record may be validated for six months. The charge for issuing the B is approximately the same as is charged to U.S. citizens in your home country.   An I-797 is not issued.

An alien may request a written statement of the factual and legal reasons for denial and a copy may be sent to the alien's attorney for review.

Step 3 - *Revalidation/Extension or Change of Status by the BCIS within the United States*

You should file with the BCIS regional Service Center having jurisdiction over your place of residence at least 45 days before your stay expires for either:

- An extension of B status
- Change of status from another classification to B
  Ref: INS Instructions - Form I-539; DOS Publication 10311, November, 1995

It may be possible to obtain a change of status without leaving the country, depending on the circumstances. Once your extension application is filed, you may remain in status until a decision is made.

Documentation and supporting evidence includes:

- *BCIS form*
  - I-539, Application to Extend/Change Nonimmigrant Status
  - supplement for dependents
- *Fee*
  - $140
- *Current and prior immigration status*
  - original I-94, Nonimmigrant Arrival/Departure Record
- *Evidence to support request*
  - employer's detailed written explanation of why an extension is required
  - other supporting documentation to extend Visitor for Pleasure
- *Proof of financial support or solvency*
  - proof of financial support
- *Evidence that U.S. stay is temporary (intent to depart)*
  - binding family ties
  - copy of return tickets
  - firm ties to home country that you have no intention of abandoning

Pending Green Card or Labor Certification applications are not considered to be valid reasons for an extension. Otherwise, you are normally permitted to remain while an extension is being processed. While there are no formal rules on how often an alien may enter on a B visa, it is important to maintain your permanent residence abroad.

Alternative Inspection Programs
Land, Air and Water Expedited Entry

Expedited entry programs are available to make the entry of low risk U.S. and foreign travelers faster and easier without sacrificing border security.

Mexicans   *Ref: 64 FR 45162*

Mexican Combination B-1/B-2/Visa and Border Crossing Card

Mexican nationals may use either a Border Crossing Card (BCC) or a valid passport with a U.S. visa to enter the U.S. as a visitor. If they are eligible to receive a B-1 or B-2 visa, they may apply for a Form DSP-150 combined B-1/B-2/BCC card. It is credit card style and contains the applicant's digitized image and a machine-readable biometric identifier. As of October 1, 2002, the old style I-586 card is no longer valid.

Application is made at the U.S. Embassy in Mexico City or at one of the nine U.S. Consulates throughout Mexico. Applicants must:

- Be a citizen of Mexico - residing in Mexico
- Be seeking to enter the U.S. as a temporary visitor for business or pleasure for periods of stay not exceeding six months
- Be eligible to receive a B-1/B-2 visa, or
- Have received a waiver of a ground of ineligibility for at least ten years

Documentation and supporting evidence includes:

- *Form*
  - DS-156, Nonimmigrant Visa Application
- *Fee*
  - $100 ($13 for a child under 15 valid only until 15th birthday)
- *Evidence of Mexican citizenship and residence*
  - Mexican passport, or
  - Certificate of Mexican Nationality (CMN) and either:
    - an additional piece of photo identification, or
    - a valid or expired U.S. visa, BCC or B-1/B-2/BCC (not voided)
- *Photograph and fingerprints taken at the time of the application*
  - digitized photographic image
  - digitized impression of applicant's index fingers

Further information is available from the U.S. Embassy in Mexico City at 01-900-849-4949 or at: www.usembassy-mexico.gov.

Canadians

Border Crossing Card

The Canadian Border Crossing Card (BCC) I-185 has been terminated.

Ref: 67 FR 71443

Canadians visitors may generally travel to the U.S. without a visa. Canadians may also enter with a Form I-194, Waiver of Grounds of Inadmissibilty which is valid for up to five years. The I-194 serves as a notice of approval of advance permission to enter as a nonimmigrant.

Canadian Border Boat Landing Program (Seasonal Permit)

The I-68 program is available to U.S. citizens, Green Card holders, Canadian nationals and certain landed immigrants of Canada to enter the United States without further inspection by means of a water pleasure craft for visits of a maximum of 72 hours within 25 miles of the border shoreline.   *Ref: 8 CFR Part 235.1(e)*

Each applicant must appear in person before an Immigration Officer for inspection once a year at a port of entry within the jurisdiction of the intended place of landing. If approved, a Form I-68, Canadian Border Boat Landing Permit bearing the applicant's photograph and fingerprint is issued. Application for renewal cannot be made by mail.

U.S. and Canadian citizens, Green Card holders and Commonwealth residents of Canada as well as nationals of Visa Waiver Program countries without I-68s must appear for inspection at a port of entry or use a free Outlying Area Reporting Station (OARS) videophone at a marina, gas dock or state park to communicate with an Immigration Inspector. Entry may also be permitted with evidence of enrollment in any other BCBP Alternative Inspections Program such as INSPASS.

The BCBP reserves the right to conduct inspections. Inspection upon returning to Canada is required.

Documentation and supporting evidence includes:
- *BCIS form*
  - I-68, Canadian Border Boat Landing Permit
- *Fees*
  - $16 or $32 for husband, wife and minor children
- *Supporting attestations*
  - Evidence of citizenship status
  - Copy of previous I-68, if issued

Canadian Permanent Commuters

Canadians holding Green Cards who work in the U.S. may live in Canada if they obtain Canadian Permanent Commuter status.

Automated Inspection Services (AIP) Programs

U.S. citizens, Green Card holders and citizens of Canada and Landed Canadian Immigrants who are citizens of British Commonwealth countries are eligible to apply for all Automated Inspection Services programs. Additional qualified groups, as noted in the specific program, may participate.

Participants are subject to periodic compliance checks.

AIP programs are also known as Port Passenger Service System (PORTPASS) and are available in certain identified ports of entry to provide access to the U.S. for a group of low-risk border crossers. Alien participants are personally inspected, identified and screened by an Immigration Inspector prior to approval and may enter the U.S. through a Dedicated Commuter Lane (DCL) or and Automated Permit Port (APP). Each successful use of PORTPASS constitutes a completed inspection and application for entry. U.S. citizens who qualify are subject to all rules, procedures and conditions.
Ref: 8 CFR 235.7

The criteria for designation of a port of entry for PORTPASS access is:
- Identifiable group of low-risk border crossers
- Institution of PORTPASS will not significantly inhibit normal traffic flow
- The port of entry has a sufficient number of BCBP personnel to perform primary and secondary DCL inspection functions

Application Process

Each participant in each program must submit a separate Form I-823, Application - Alternative Inspection Services in person or by mail to the principal port of entry having jurisdiction over the port for which the applicant intends to request entry.

Original documentary evidence must be provided to meet the following terms prior to issuance, and at any time thereafter:
- U.S. Citizenship or lawful permanent residency or eligible nonimmigrant
- Proof of employment or residence
- Current driver's license, vehicle registration and insurance

An interview may be scheduled prior to acceptance. Approval is valid for one year unless revoked.

Cards may only be used for the purpose for which they were authorized. Card holders are not exempt from normal examination when entering for any other purpose.

All applicants who have been denied permission to participate in the DCL or APP programs or have had their participation revoked, must wait 90 days before reapplying.

Automated Permit Port Program (APP)

An APP has limited hours of operation and is located at a remote location on a land border. This program is limited to the northern border of the United States.

Ref: 8 CFR 235.7

Entry to the United States during hours when a port of entry is not staffed may only be made through a port designated by the BCBP to provide access to the U.S. by an identified low-risk border crosser through the use of automation.

In addition to the qualified nationals noted above, certain nonimmigrants may participate. Application may be made in person or by mail at the port of entry having jurisdiction over the APP for which access is requested.

Documentation and supporting evidence includes:

- *BCIS forms*
  - I-823, Application - Alternative Inspection Services
  - I-823, Automated Permit Port Applications Supplement
- *Fees*
  - none
- *Supporting attestations*
  - full vehicle inspections
  - agreement to checks of criminal information databases
  - use of DCL limited to authorized vehicle
  - agreement to all fees including fingerprint fee
  - all devices to identify and inspect remain the property of U.S. government
  - proof that registrant has permission to register vehicle

SENTRI Dedicated Commuter Lane Program (DCL)

A Dedicated Commuter Lane (DCL) is a special lane at a port separated from the normal flow of traffic at a land border port of entry. It allows an accelerated inspection of low-risk travelers. This program is limited to the northern border of the United States and the California-Mexico border. The period of enrollment for SENTRI and INPASS was extended to two years on February 28, 2003.   *Ref: 68 FR 10143*

SENTRI is the world's first automated Dedicated Commuter Lane advanced Automatic Vehicle Identification (AVI) technology to meet stringent law enforcement needs at the border while providing more efficient means of traffic management, with reduced traffic congestion. With SENTRI DCL, the BCBP may inspect and clear certain low risk pre-enrolled border crossers at selected ports of entry in less than three minutes. The system was introduced in Otay Mesa (San Diego), California in 1995 and subsequently in El Paso, Texas, Buffalo, New York and Detroit, Michigan.

In addition to the qualified nationals noted above, the Dedicated Commuter Lane Program is also available to certain citizens of Mexico and certain nonimmigrants.

As an example of how one expedited entry program works, when a participating SENTRI traveler crosses the border, a transmitter located on the participant's vehicle causes the system to automatically validate the vehicle and its occupants against data in the enrollment system computer. This data includes digitized photographs of the vehicle's pre-authorized occupants. Upon reaching the booth, the driver swipes his or her electronically-coded PortPass card through a magnetic stripe card reader. If both the inspector and the electronic equipment approve, the traffic light turns green, the gate raises, the tire shredders retract and the driver can drive into the United States.

Documentation and supporting evidence includes:

- *BCIS forms*
    - I-823, Application - Alternative Inspection Services
    - I-823B, Dedicated Computer Lane Participants Supplement
- *Fees*
    - $25 for initial application
    - $50 for fingerprinting
    - $80 for final processing ($160 for husband, wife and minor children)
    - $42 for each additional vehicle
- *Supporting attestations*
    - full vehicle inspections
    - agreement to checks of criminal information databases
    - use of DCL limited to authorized vehicle
    - all devices to identify and inspect remain U.S. government property
    - proof that registrant has permission to register vehicle

Applications may be submitted in person or by mail to the port of entry sponsoring the DCL. Replacement fees are $25 for a card and $42 for a transponder.

You may call (877) 265-1335 for more information about the SENTRI program.

BCBP Passenger Accelerated Service System (INSPASS) - Land and Airport

INSPASS is an automated immigration inspection system that eliminates the in-person inspection interview for frequent business travelers and reduces processing time. INSPASS does not relieve the traveler of the responsibility for carrying valid travel documents such as a passport or visa, if required. The INSPASS kiosk is similar to a bank ATM. All persons using automated inspection kiosks are subject to automated random or discretionary compliance reviews to ensure U.S. laws are respected and for quality control.

INSPASS has been installed at a number of airports including Detroit, JFK in New York, Pearson International in Toronto as well as Newark, Miami, Los Angeles, San Francisco, Washington-Dulles and Vancouver where 20,000 inspections are carried out each month. INSPASS is being phased in at other airports and land border ports.

Air travelers insert their enrollment card and align their hand to the hand geometry biometric reader at an INSPASS kiosk. If the identity is validated, an I-94 is printed and the gate opens. If the check is not successful, the traveler is referred to a nearby Immigration Inspector.

Enrollment is on Form I-823 and may be submitted by mail or fax. However, persons under 14 may not enroll in either INSPASS program. It is necessary to be interviewed at an INSPASS enrollment office where a card is issued. The processing officer will enter your data, collect a digital photograph, fingerprints, hand geometry or other biometrics. You will be issued a PortPASS card.

Each airport serves as an enrollment center. INSPASS applicants may apply at a BCBP port of entry in person or by mail. Details may be found online at: www.immigration.gov/graphics/lawenfor/bmgmt/inspect/faqs.htm

Documentation and supporting evidence includes:

- *BCIS forms*
  - I-823, Application - Alternative Inspection Services
  - I-823, INSPASS Airport Participants Supplement
- *Fee*
  - none
- *Additional supporting evidence*
  - Visa Waiver Program participants complete form concerning record of diseases, arrests, convictions, espionage, sabotage, withholding children from U.S. citizen custodial parent

NEXUS Dedicated Lane Program - Expedited Entry to U.S. and Canada

The NEXUS Alternative Inspection Program was established to allow pre-screened low-risk travelers to be processed by Canadian and U.S. Customs and Immigration officials with little or no delay. The NEXUS program uses dedicated lanes and is expected to be expanded to all high-volume crossings in 2003. Application is made on Form I-823N available at www.ccra-adrc.gc.ca. It requires a security check, interview and fingerprinting. The application costs $US 50 and it is good for five years. Further information is available at (866) 639-8726.

Checkpoint Pre-enrolled Access Lane (PAL)

The INS established a PAL program to allow U.S. citizens and residents to use a specifically designated lane to pass through the Border Patrol's checkpoint on Interstate Highway I-5 at San Clemente, California. Form I-866 must be filed. Further information is at www.immigration .gov/graphics/lawenfor/bmgmt/pal.htm.

C–1/D

Alien in Transit/
Crew Member, Sea or Air

These two visa categories may be issued separately as a C-1 or D or, alternatively, as a joint C-1/D classification.

In general terms, the D portion facilitates the entry to the United States and controls the activities of crew members of cruise ships, cargo ships and aircraft while the C-1 permits transit within the country of these and other foreign visitors.

The individual classifications are:

- C-1 - Alien in Transit
- D   - Crew member, Sea or Air   *Ref: INA 101(a)(15)(C)*

Specifically, the C-1 classification is used by visitors with confirmed onward reservations who stop in the U.S. to:

- Change planes or ship
- Pass through the United States with permission to enter a third country and will leave the U.S. in a few days
- Make a short shore visit from a cruise or cargo ship

D status is for bona fide crew members of foreign ships or aircraft. This includes aliens:

- Who come to a U.S. land or water port to take on or offload cargo or passengers
- Whose work is required for the normal operation of the ship or aircraft

Admission Process

Immigration and Consular Officers issue the joint C-1/D Classification to accommodate crew members who spend short periods in the U.S. between assignments and may have to leave from a different location than the one in which they arrived.

Each time cargo ship crew members enter a U.S. port, they are placed in C-1/D status and issued a new I-95, Crewman's Landing Permit, that is good for a maximum of 29 days. Cruise ships have their entire ship inspected and new crew lists made every 90 days and the BCBP is advised of changes to the crew list as they occur. Crew members have no rights other than entry unless prior permission is obtained for longshore work.

Step 1 - Clearing the Department of Labor (DOL)

This step applies only to alien crew members who intend to perform longshore activities in U.S. ports. Others may skip Step 1.

The loading and unloading of vessels in U.S. ports has traditionally been performed by U.S. longshore workers. Until the passage of IMMACT90, INS had allowed alien crew members to do this kind of work because longshore work was considered to be within their scope of permitted employment. The IMMACT90 limited this practice to provide greater protection to U.S. longshore workers.

The use of alien crew members for longshore activities is governed by prevailing practice in a given U.S. port. In certain circumstances, employers are required to submit attestations to the DOL and then apply for permission to use alien crew members to perform specified longshore activities.

Before undertaking longshore work, it is advisable to determine whether longshore work is permitted under prevailing practice or the Department of Labor's Employment and Training Administration (ETA) requires an attestation. Further information should be obtained from the regional ETA office having jurisdiction over the state in which the port is located. See Appendix G for telephone numbers.

DOL Form ETA 9033, Attestation by Employer using Alien Crew members for Longshore Activities in U.S. Ports still exists but is currently not being used. If it were to be used, it would apply only to ports in the lower 48 states where the overriding principle is that U.S. workers must not be displaced and alien crew members may only perform a particular activity of longshore work if that work were permitted by the prevailing practices in the port during the preceding 12-month period.

Ref: 60 FR.12, 1995

The process has been modified for Alaskan ports. The Coast Guard Authorization Act of 1993 amended the INA and established a new Alaska exception to the general prohibition on the performance of longshore work by alien crew members in U.S. ports.

While the Alaska exception is intended to provide a preference for hiring U.S. longshoremen over the employer's alien crew members, the prohibition does not apply where an employer has filed, with the Department of Labor, a successful attestation with accompanying documentation for the performance of specified longshore work at a particular location in the State of Alaska. The attestation process, as administered by ETA, became effective October 7, 1996.   *Ref: 20 CFR, part 655, Subpart F and G*

The information collection requirements of the Form ETA 9033-A under the Alaska exception were published in the Federal Register on January 19, 1995 (60 FR 3950). The ETA estimates that employers will be submitting 350 attestations per year under the Alaska exception.

Alaska is served by the ETA's Region 6 (six) office in Seattle, Washington. Information on submitting an attestation may be obtained by calling (415) 975-4617.

Documentation and supporting evidence includes:

- *DOL form*
  - Form ETA 9033-A, Attestation by Employers Using Alien Crew members for Longshore Activities at Locations in the State of Alaska
- *Employer's supporting attestation*
  - the employer will:
    - make a bona fide request for help and employ qualified and available U.S. longshore workers from contract stevedoring companies and private dock operators before using alien crewmen to perform the activity specified in the attestation
    - provide notice of filing the attestation to such stevedoring companies and private dock operators, and to labor organizations recognized as exclusive bargaining representatives of U.S. longshore workers
    - not use alien crew members to perform longshore activities to influence the election of a bargaining representative for workers in the State of Alaska

Exceptions are permitted in:

- The use of an automated self-unloading conveyor belt or vacuum-actuated system unless the Administrator has determined that it is not the prevailing practice in a specific location
- The loading or unloading of hazardous cargo

Step 2 - Clearing the Department of State (DOS) Abroad

Usually the foreign vessel personnel will make arrangements for C-1/ D visa issuance. Application may be made at a U.S. Embassy or Consulate abroad.

The requirement of a personal appearance before a consular officer may be waived in the case of an aircraft crewman seeking a C-1 or D visa classification if the application is supported by a letter from the employing carrier certifying that the crewman is employed as an aircraft crewman, and the consular officer is satisfied that an appearance is not necessary.

Step 3 - Clearing the BCBP at a U.S. Port of Entry

Visitors in Transit

Only certain designated U.S. ports of entry process applications for C-1 Visitor in Transit status. Before arriving in the United States you are required to fill out an I-94, Arrival/Departure Record if you:

- Are a non-U.S. Citizen or Permanent Resident, and
- Are in transit to a country outside the United States, and
- Do not hold a valid U.S. visa
- Hold a common carrier ticket or other evidence of outbound travel arrangements

The bottom portion of the I-94 (Departure Record) must be kept with your passport until you leave the United States.   *Ref: INA 238(d)*

Crew members

Application for crew members to enter the United States in C-1/D status is made on Form I-418, Passenger - Crew List. An I-95, Crewman's Landing Permit - Land or Sea is issued. Aircrews may use International Civil Aviation Organization (ICAO) or Customs Form 7507, General Declaration in lieu of Form I-418.   *Ref: 9 FAM 41.42*

Cargo crews receive an I-95 each time they come into port while the entire crew of cruise ships are inspected every three months and the cruise line reports interim crew changes.

Crew members performing longshore work

Before longshore work may be performed, the BCIS must be satisfied that the Department of Labor concurs.

The maximum period of admittance is 29 days. It is not renewable*Ref: INA 248*

Step 4 - Change of Status

An alien may not change to or from another classification.   *Ref: INA 248*

Parole

P arole is an extraordinary measure, used sparingly, which authorizes an apparently inadmissible alien to enter the U.S. without a visa for a specific period due to a compelling emergency. Parole is a delegated discretionary power.

Parole does not confer immigration benefits or constitute formal admission into the United States. Parolees must depart at the end of their parole authorization or adjust to immigrant status. Aliens may apply to the BCIS to extend their parole status but requests are granted on a case-by-case basis for a specific period of time

Because of the terms of their immigration status, many non-citizens living in the United States may not travel abroad and return to the U.S. without Advance Parole authorization.   *Ref: 9 FAM 42.1 N4.4*

Types of parole include:

- Advance Parole
- Humanitarian Parole
- Significant Public Benefit Parole
- Deferred Inspection
- Port of Entry Parole
- Overseas Parole   *Ref: INA 212(d)(5)*

Advance Parole

Advance Parole may apply to aliens living outside the U.S. who need to enter before receiving final approval of their immigration application. It may also apply to those living in the U.S. whose immigration application is under review and who need to leave the U.S. briefly and reenter without abandoning their pending application.

Advance Parole does not guarantee admission as the final decision is made by the Immigration Inspector at the port of entry.

Advance Parole is needed by aliens who have:

- To travel abroad for emergent business or personal reasons
- A pending Adjustment of Status application
- Been granted benefits under the Family Unity Program
- Been granted Temporary Protected Status (TPS)
- An asylum application pending
- Refugee or Asylee status and need to apply for an immigrant visa in Canada

Advance Parole is not available to aliens who are:
- In the U.S. illegally (they risk a three or ten year ban when attempting to reenter)
- The beneficiary of a private bill
- Under removal proceedings
- Admitted as a nonimmigrant
- Admitted as a Refugee or granted Asylum (require Refugee Travel Document to reenter the United States after a trip abroad)
- Subject to the J-1 Exchange Visitors Home Residency Requirement

Inside the United States

Most aliens who have pending applications for immigration benefits such as Adjustment of Status or Change of Status, need to seek Advance Parole by filing Form I-131, for a Reentry Permit to avoid the termination of their application when attempting to reenter the United States after a trip abroad. Aliens in H-1, L-1, V or K-3/4 status and their dependents who are applying for Adjustment of Status do not require Advance Parole when returning to the United States.

Documentation and supporting evidence includes:

- *BCIS form*
  - I-131, Application for Travel Document
- *Fee*
  - $110 for I-131
- *Photographs*
  - 2 color photographs 40 mm high by 35 mm wide in 3/4 profile showing right ear, no head covering (religious exceptions), light background
- *Proof of financial support or solvency*
  - statement of how medical, housing, transportation and other subsistence expense needs will be met
- *Supporting documentation*
  - evidence to demonstrate why Advance Parole is necessary
  - any documents issued by the BCIS showing present status
  - copy of filing receipt of Adjustment of Status, Asylum or Refugee status, as applicable
  - Consular appointment notice if traveling to Canada, as applicable

Parole requests should identify potential sources of financial support.

The application should be sent to the BCIS District Office or Sub-Office with jurisdiction over your place of residence or to the Service Center where your case is pending. I-512 Parole Authorization may be issued to a principal alien by the District Director .

Applications for a Form I-571, Refugee Travel Document which is valid for one year should be sent to the Nebraska Service Center.

The principal alien must return within four months of the date of the parole authorization. However, an alien required to remain abroad in connection with his or her qualifying profession or occupation must return within one year from the date of issuance of parole authorization, including multiple applications.

An alien under exclusion, deportation or removal proceedings loses any protection from a pending Green Card petition by departing the U.S. However, departure before a decision on an application for a Reentry Permit or refugee travel document will not affect the application.

Applicants who are the beneficiary of a private bill or are under deportation proceedings must file at:

> Bureau of Citizenship and Immigration Services
> Office of International Affairs
> Parole and Humanitarian Assistance Branch
> 425 I Street, N.W.
> Attn: International Affairs
> Washington, DC 20536

Since filing procedures vary widely throughout the BCIS system, applicants should contact their local BCIS office to confirm filing requirements.

Aliens in detention who are subject to final orders of removal may submit a written request for release on the ground that there is no significant likelihood that the INS will be able to remove them in the reasonably foreseeable future in accordance with the judgment of the Supreme Court in Zadvydas v. Davis. Any detained alien who believes that he or she may be eligible for release under the Zadvydas decision should submit a written request for release along with supporting documentation to:

> Post-Order Detention Unit
> 801 I Street, N.W. Unit 900
> Washington, DC 20536   *Ref: 66 FR 44646*

Outside the United States

When applying for Advance Parole to enter the United States from abroad, you must submit:

Documentation and supporting evidence includes:

- *BCIS forms*
  - I-131, Application for Travel Document
  - I-134, Affidavit of Support , or
  - I-864, Affidavit of Support (Green Card applicants)
- *Fee*
  - $110 for I-131

- *Photographs*
  - 2 color photographs 40 mm high by 35 mm wide in 3/4 profile showing right ear, no head covering (religious exceptions), light background
- *Proof of financial support or solvency*
  - statement of how medical, housing, transportation and other subsistence expense needs will be met
- *Supporting documentation*
  - details of why a U.S. visa cannot be obtained
  - details of efforts to obtain a waiver of inadmissibility
  - copy of any decision or details on pending immigrant petition
  - complete description of emergent reasons for, and requested duration of, parole
  - evidence of how medical, housing, transportation and other subsistence expenses will be met

The BCIS will inform the Consular post if a medical examination must be performed by a post panel physician.

A Reentry permit shall be valid for two years and a refugee travel document shall be valid for one year. Neither may be extended. An alien who presents a valid unexpired refugee travel document, or whose application for a refugee travel document, has been approved, shall be examined as to his or her admissibility under the Act.

In special cases, application for Advance Parole may be made to enter the United States for multiple entries for one year, to leave and return as often as necessary.

Applications should be submitted to:

Bureau of Customs and Immigration Services
Office of International Affairs and Parole
425 I Street N.W., Room 1203
Washington, DC 20536

It should be noted that an applicant outside the U.S. who wishes to enter to apply for Adjustment of Status may request parole authorization with the Texas Service Center. The director of the Texas Service Center may issue an Authorization for Parole Form I-512 to allow the alien to be paroled into the U.S. The alien shall have 60 days from the date of the parole to file the application for Adjustment of Status.

Ref: Pub. L. 105-100, Section202

Humanitarian Parole

The Secretary of Homeland Security may parole an otherwise inadmissible alien into the United States, temporarily, on a case-by-case basis, for urgent or compelling humanitarian reasons. Humanitarian Parole is an extraordinary measure which is used sparingly.

Humanitarian Parole should be a last option for persons who:
- Have urgent humanitarian reasons such as medical emergencies
- Are otherwise ineligible for a visa
- Cannot benefit from a waiver   *Ref: 9 FAM 42.1 N4.2*

Humanitarian Parole may be requested by interested parties in the U.S. or abroad on behalf of persons who are outside the United States. Requests may be submitted by anyone on Form I-131, Application for Travel Document with the $110 fee. The BCIS says that Humanitarian Parole applications are generally adjudicated within 60 to 90 days and may be granted for up to one year. Ineligibility is considered against the need to travel.

Humanitarian Parole is sometimes available for:
- Adopted children
- Disabled or immigrant visa beneficiaries who have aged out(turned 21)

Applications should be sent to:

> Office of International Affairs
> Parole and Humanitarian Assistance Branch
> ULLICO Building, 3rd floor
> 425 I Street N.W.,
> Washington, DC 20536.

A Consular Officer who believes that exceptional circumstances or grave humanitarian concerns warrant the use of Humanitarian Parole, should cable or fax this office.

A medical examination is only conducted by the Consular post physician when the BCIS advises that it is required.

Documentation and supporting evidence includes:
- *BCIS and DOS forms*
  - I-131, Application for Travel Document
  - I-134, Affidavit of Support
  - DS-2053, Medical Examination for Immigrant or Refugee Applicant (if examination required by BCIS)
- *Fees*
  - $110 for I-131
  - DS-2053 fee, as applicable
- *Supporting documents*
  - justification for parole request
  - certification that CLASS name check has been made for the principal alien and dependents with results (printout not included with transportation letter)
  - information on officers and/or agencies concurring in the request

- information on the individual or agency bearing financial responsibility
- expected travel itinerary
- certification by appropriate State Department official

When the individual has applied directly to the BCIS, the Consular officer must verify that the necessary financial funds are available.

After receiving BCIS approval, the Consular post issues a transportation letter to be carried with a copy of the State Department's VISAS Ninety-one cable attached to be presented to the BCBP at the U.S. port of entry.

Significant Public Benefit Parole

An alien may be paroled into the United States, on a case-by-case basis for significant public benefit. The terms are often more restrictive than those in Humanitarian Parole authorizations.

Significant Public Benefit Parole may be granted in cases of clear U.S. Government interest where a need to admit an individual to the United States as quickly as possible exists. This option is not used in lieu of normal refugee processing except for compelling reasons of public interest. An individual must be in imminent danger and unable to travel to a third country for refugee processing.

Ref: 9 FAM 42.1 N4.3

The more common form of SPBP cases are requested through the Department of Justice by law enforcement agencies (LEAs) or intelligence agencies that require the presence of an alien in connection with legal cases or investigations. The SPBP option may be available to certain child abductors to attend custody hearings in Hague cases.

Consular posts must submit their requests to the State Department's relevant country desk with a copy to Immigration. The country desk will coordinate with other interested government agencies. The Deputy Secretary of State for Visa Services sends the recommendation to the Office of International Affairs (IAO), Parole and Humanitarian Assistance Branch (PHAB) for a decision.

Upon approval, the PHAB will inform the port of entry and District Director that SPBP has been authorized. Transportation letters are issued by consulates with a copy of the State Department's VISAS Ninety-one cable attached to be presented at the U.S. port of entry.

Documentation and supporting evidence includes:

- *BCIS and DOS forms*
  - I-131, Application for Travel Document
  - I-134, Affidavit of Support
  - DS-2053, Medical Examination for Immigrant or Refugee Applicant (if examination required by BCIS)

- *Fees*
  - $110 for I-131
  - DS-2053 fee, as applicable
- *Supporting documents*
  - justification for parole request
  - certification that CLASS name check has been made for the principal alien and dependents with results
  - information on officers and/or agencies concurring in the request
  - information on the individual or agency bearing financial responsibility
  - expected travel itinerary
  - certification by appropriate State Department official

Deferred Inspection

Deferred inspection may be conferred by an Immigration Inspector at the port of entry. The alien may be paroled in if a preliminary examination and review of their documentation leaves questions about their admissibility which can best be answered at their destination point.

Port of Entry Parole

Port of Entry Parole may be authorized at the port when the alien arrives. This option applies to a wide variety of situations and is used at the discretion of the supervisory Immigration Inspector, usually to allow short periods of entry. Examples include allowing in aliens, who could not be issued the necessary documentation within the required time period, or who were otherwise inadmissible, to attend a funeral or permit the entry of emergency workers such as fire fighters to assist with an emergency.

Overseas Parole

Overseas Parole is authorized at a District or suboffice while the alien is still overseas. It is designed to constitute long-term admission to the United States. In recent years, most of the aliens the INS processed through Overseas Parole have arrived under special legislation or international migration agreements.

TWOV
Transit WithOut Visa

T ransit WithOut Visa or TWOV status (pronounced by Immigration Officers as trove or twove) is reserved for travelers, or air or ship crews, who are transit aliens traveling without a nonimmigrant visa and are stopping in the United States solely for the purpose of changing to planes or ships headed to a remote foreign destination. Confirmed immediate onward reservations or crew assignments are required.

INA authorizes the State Department and the BCIS to waive the passport and nonimmigrant visa regulations for aliens from participating countries who are proceeding in immediate and continuous transit through the United States en route to a specified foreign country and are using a carrier that has entered into a Form I-426, Immediate and Continuous Transit Agreement (TWOV) contract with the INS.

A country's participation is based on such factors as their abuse of the TWOV privilege, nonimmigrant refusal rate, the stability of their country, whether their citizens are linked to terrorist, narcotics, or international criminal activity, the existence of a restricting Presidential proclamation and security concerns. The list changes periodically.   *Ref: 8 CFR 212*

Application Process

Application for Transit WithOut Visa (TWOV) can only be made at certain designated U.S. land and sea ports of entry.

Before arriving in the United States each family member must complete their own Form I-94T, Arrival/Departure Record - Transit WithOut Visa if they:

- Are a non-U.S. Citizen or Permanent Resident, and
- Are in transit to a country outside the United States, and
- Do not hold a valid U.S. visa, and
- Do not need to be admitted to the United States

Aliens in this status are not admitted, and may not leave the secure landing station area. However, they may be left in the care of an airline or ship representative for eight hours or until their departure, whichever is earlier. The bottom portion of the I-94T must be kept with the alien's passport until leaving the U.S. The carrier turns in the completed I-94T Departure Record to the BCBP.

Chapter 4

Educational Classifications

$\mathbf{T}$hree classifications are available to foreign students who wish to further their education in the United States. For the most part, they pursue post-secondary education. In 2002, 582,996 international students were enrolled in U.S. colleges and universities.   *Ref: Open Doors 2002, Institute of International Education*

The appropriate classification is determined, in part, by who pays and how formal is the training. Regardless of the classification, there are strict rules which are meant to ensure that the student's educational expectations are met with a minimum of financial and administrative distractions.

F is the most flexible student status as it enables students with financial support to take full advantage of the U.S. educational process while providing some access to career-oriented employment opportunities. The description of this classification may be found on the following pages.

J, the most complex and varied student classification, permits an alien with limited resources to participate in an exchange visitor program approved by the U.S. Department of State. The student or exchange visitor may take advantage of financial support from the home country or the United States. J status is frequently offered with the proviso that the new skills are practiced at home for a minimum of two years after graduation. Details are furnished in the J section, Step 8.

M, the least formal student status, has been established to permit vocational training, non-academic schooling or training in a language other than English. Details about this visa may be found in the M section.

Introduction of SEVIS

In May, 2002, as part of the ongoing effort to enhance homeland security, a new system was introduced to significantly improve the ability to track foreign students while they are in the U.S.   *Ref: Pub. L. 107-56*

Mandated by the USA Patriot Act, the INS introduced the new foreign student monitoring system called Student and Exchange Visitor Information System (SEVIS) to automate the paper-driven process of reporting and record keeping about F academic students, J exchange visitors and M vocational students.

SEVIS is an internet-based system which permits the timely electronic flow of information between the educational institution or Exchange Visitor Program's Principal Designated School Official (PDSO) or one of up to nine Designated School Officials (DSOs) and the BCIS and State Department concerning past, present and incoming students and exchange visitors and their dependents throughout their U.S. stay.   *Ref: 67 FR 76256 and 76307*

A DSO must sign and complete a Form I-20 or DS-2019 for each prospective continuing student or exchange visitor and their dependents. The PDSO or DSO must be a U.S. citizen or legal permanent resident and named by the person in charge of the school or school system.

SEVIS is designed to collect information on the student's:

- Enrollment at school
- Start date of the next term or session
- Failure to enroll within 30 days of the registration deadline
- Dropping below full course of study without authorization
- Other failure to maintain status
- Graduation before authorized program end date
- Change of legal name or address or that of dependents
- Disciplinary action by the school as a result of a criminal conviction

Schools and exchange visitor programs are required to use SEVIS to issue documentation and report pertinent information to the BCIS and State Department. SEVIS is also expected to improve accountability and to implement reasonable and clear standards governing the maintenance, extension and reinstatement of student status. It is expected to be self-funded through fees paid by students and exchange visitors. Fees for SEVIS I-20s and DS-2019s are being considered and applicants should check to determine whether they have been introduced.

Schools and exchange visitor programs were given until February 15, 2003 to join SEVIS and begin issuing SEVIS documents although they could continue to use previously issued non-SEVIS forms until August 1, 2003. To register and obtain a temporary user ID and password see www.immigration.gov/sevis. The SEVIS help desk may be reached at (800) 892-4829.   *Ref: 67 FR 76307*

Until SEVIS could be made fully functional, the Border Security Act required the State Department to establish a temporary electronic system known as Interim Student and Exchange Authentication System (ISEAS) to monitor the visa adjudication process, visa issuance and to facilitate the collection and transmission of information pertaining to foreign student and exchange visitor visa applicants.

Accreditation of educational institutions

SEVIS requires the accreditation of each educational institution that receives foreign students. The BCIS is required to review all schools within two years to ensure they are bona fide and financially viable and reviewed every two years thereafter.

All schools previously approved to accept students on visas had to obtain SEVIS approval by February 15, 2003 to continue to be authorized. Schools which participated in a preliminary enrollment have until May 14, 2004 to complete the review process.

Other schools, including M status flight schools (Pub. L. 107-71) that were not eligible for preliminary enrollment, were given until November 15, 2002 to apply for certification under the Interim Certification Rule which included a full review with on-site visit. Schools that delayed their application, risked missing the implementation deadline and the ability to submit data electronically and enroll new students.

Private elementary and private secondary schools were permitted to apply for SEVIS if they were previously approved by the BCIS for three years and are a member organization in the Council for the American Private Education (CAPE) or the American Association of Christian schools (AACS). Post-secondary, language and vocational schools could also apply if they were accredited by an accrediting agency recognized by the U.S. Department of Education.

Application for F and M schools to participate in SEVIS is made electonically by Form I-17 and $580 paid through pay.gov. State Department approval of new J Exchange Visitor program participants is obtained by filing Form DS-3036.

How SEVIS Operates

August 1, 2003 is the date after which the records of all current and continuing students must be entered in SEVIS and all non-SEVIS I-20s and DS-2019s will no longer be valid. Data on all F, J and M nonimmigrants must be in the SEVIS system by that date. After August 1, 2003, only SEVIS I-20s and DS-2019s will be valid.

To ensure the integrity of the system, U.S. Consulates abroad will enter data into SEVIS and advise the school or exchange visitor administrator that a visa has been issued. The BCBP will also advise the school or exchange visitor program when the alien has been admitted at a port of entry. The BCIS must be notified if the student fails to register within 30 days of the registration deadline.

Students and exchange visitors must advise their DSOs of any change of address or legal name within ten days and this information must be entered into SEVIS.

A student who transfers to another school or finishes post-completion optional practical training, has five months to begin studies at the new school. Only the school which is responsible for the student or exchange visitor may access the SEVIS records.

Post-approval requirements

Once a school is approved for SEVIS, it must be used for reporting and information exchange and retention purposes. It is also to be used to generate any new I-20 or DS-2019 forms electronically for both new students and exchange visitors and those extending their program of study. A student or dependent must present a SEVIS I-20 or DS-2019 issued in his or her own name by a BCIS-approved school or State Department approved Exchange Visitor Program.

F

Academic Student

F status is reserved for those who will be studying an academic course at a school authorized to allow foreign students to attend. They must have a home in a foreign country to which they will return when they complete their studies.

Students may be admitted for study at the elementary level through the post-graduate and doctoral level. However, there are severe restrictions on pre-university study as explained in Step 4 - Maintenance of Status.

The F classification can include a spouse and unmarried children under 21 years of age.   *Ref: INA S ER 806 3-8-94*

Sub-categories are:
- F-1 Student (academic or language training program)
- F-2 Spouse and minor children of alien classified F-1
- F-3 Border Commuter Student - Canada or Mexico   *Ref: 67 FR 54941*
  Ref: 9 FAM 41.12; INA 101(a)(15)(F)

To be eligible, a student must:
- Be enrolled in a BCIS-accredited institution
- Be proficient in English or engaged in English language courses leading to English proficiency
- Demonstrate sufficient financial resources to complete studies without having to work
- Show that there is no intent to abandon residency in the home country
- Be studying on a full-time basis if at the undergraduate level (normally at least 12 academic hours per semester)

Students may be permitted to pursue part-time study if their foreign student advisor recommends this for academic reasons, illness or the need to improve English skills. English as a Second Language (ESL) places students at their appropriate levels; reading, writing, and speaking are practiced.

F-3 border commuter students may engage in full or part-time studies at an approved F school. In 2002, the rules were amended to permit Mexican and Canadian nationals residing near the U.S. border to regularly commute to study at a U.S. educational institution within 75 miles of the border.

Ref: 67 FR 54941; Pub. L. 107-274

At the graduate level, the definition of full-time is left up to the school as work on a thesis or dissertation may constitute full-time work even if no credit hours are taken.

Financial aid may not be available to international students. However, they may qualify for academic or athletic scholarships. Because of visa regulations, academic pressures and a competitive employment market, international students should not count on financing their education by part-time employment.

Admission Process

Step 1 - Acceptance by a BCIS-Accredited Educational Institution

Application for a school to participate in SEVIS is made electonically by Form I-17 and paid through pay.gov. The filing fee is $230 plus $350 for the on-site review for a total charge of $580.

A student must be accepted by a SEVIS-approved institution before being processed for a visa by a U.S. Embassy or Consulate abroad.

Documentation and supporting evidence includes:
- Application for admission
- School transcripts
- Diplomas, official reports (translated into English)
- Standardized test scores - SAT or ACT
- Evidence of English proficiency, such as TOEFL
- Recent photograph

Additional supporting documentation that may be required includes:
- Application fee/tuition deposit
- Housing application and deposit
- Personal recommendations
- Health information

Upon acceptance of a student, the school:
- Issues letter of acceptance
- Issues SEVIS I-20, Certificates of Eligibility
- Electronically transmits evidence of acceptance to DOS
- Enters certain information into SEVIS electronic system database

Under SEVIS rules, each principal alien and dependent is issued their own SEVIS Form I-20 and unique identification number which allows them to enter 30 days before their studies begin. Non-SEVIS I-20s are void effective August 1, 2003 and will no longer be acceptable. All students must also be protected by health insurance and may also need to submit proof of required immunization.

Step 2 - Clearing the Department of State (DOS) Abroad

Application is made to the visa officer at the U.S. Embassy or Consulate serving the student's home country.   *Ref: 9 FAM 41.61*

Documentation and supporting evidence includes:

- *DOS form*
  - DS-156, Nonimmigrant Visa Application
- *Fees*
  - $100 for non-refundable Machine-Readable Visa (MRV)
  - visa reciprocity equating to fees charged in similar circumstances in an alien's home country
- *Passport and photograph*
  - passport valid for at least six months beyond intended stay
  - 50 mm (2") square photograph facing camera directly without head covering (check for religious exceptions) against a light background
- *Prior approval*
  - SEVIS I-20, Certificate of Eligibility, issued by the university
- *Additional evidence*
  - proof of adequate English language skills
- *Proof of financial support or solvency*
  - evidence of adequate financial resources to cover expenses for full proposed period of study without work, including:
    - school financial aid
    - personal and family funds
    - government assistance
      (anticipated employment earnings not included as resources)
- *Evidence that U.S. stay is temporary (intent to depart U.S.)*
  - job prospects upon returning home
  - details about immediate family members back home
  - student's involvement in community organizations
  - financial ties and assets in the home country
  - why the same quality of education is not available at home

The Consular Officer may not issue a visa until they receive and review the electronic acceptance data submitted by the approved institution. Under SEVIS rules, DOS must notify the school when a visa is issued for a new student or for a renewal.

Although it is not normally required, the consul has the right to request that a student post a Maintenance of Status and Departure Bond with the local BCIS office.

Depending on which country a student is from, it may be necessary to apply for a multiple-entry visa to permit periodic trips back home. Whether a single-entry or multiple-entry visa is issued depends on how U.S. citizens are treated in similar circumstances in the student's home country.

Some U.S. Embassies or Consulates abroad allow a student to apply by mail.

Step 3 - Clearing the BCBP at a U.S. Port of Entry

As in other classifications, the BCBP has the obligation to reexamine all documents including proof of financial solvency submitted to, and visas obtained from, a U.S. Embassy or Consulate abroad. A BCBP Immigration Inspector may refuse entry if not satisfied that the documents presented meet the intent of the law. If admitted, the BCBP must advise the school of the admission.

A potential student may enter as a B-2 visitor to compare schools with the notation "intending student" on the I-94. However, no B nonimmigrant may enroll in school until the intending student has applied for, and the BCIS has approved, a Change of Status to F-1.   *Ref: 67 FR 18062*

Canadians with all necessary documentation from the school may apply directly at a port of entry. All other students apply for admission after the MRV is placed in their passport at the U.S. Embassy or Consulate.

If the SEVIS I-20 or evidence of financial support are not available, the BCBP Inspector may allow temporary entry. If confirmation of admission has been received from the school, Form I-515, Notice to Student or Exchange Visitor must be completed and Form I-515a, 30 Day Admission Notice issued to the student who will have 30 days to submit the missing documentation to the BCBP office.

Documentation and supporting evidence includes:
- *Prior approval*
  - SEVIS I-20, Certificate of Eligibility, issued by the university with DOS endorsement in the passport
- *Additional evidence*
  - copies of evidence presented to DOS including proof of financial solvency and intent to return to home country at completion of studies

Foreign students are normally issued an I-94 Arrival/Departure Record at the port of entry which admits them for Duration of Status (D/S). Under D/S, they may stay in the U.S. for the entire period of enrollment in the academic program plus any period of authorized practical training and a 60-day grace period to leave the country.

Under SEVIS, the BCBP is required to notify the institution when the incoming student is admitted. If the student fails to register, the institution must notify the BCIS within 30 days of passing the registration deadline.

Step 4 - Maintenance of Status

A student must complete the academic program prior to the date of expiration on the I-20 issued by the Designated School Official (DSO). However, a student eligible to return to school may take a summer vacation in the United States between semesters. A student has 60 days to depart after graduation or authorized practical training.

The Illegal Immigration Reform and Immigrant Responsibility Act of 1996 included several provisions that have impacted on foreign students including:

- Exclusion on violation of their F-1 status
- A limit of 12 months at a public elementary or secondary school
- Loss of status by transferring from a private to public high school

A spouse who wishes to begin post-secondary eduction must apply for an F-1. However, the spouse and minor children (under age 21) who are admitted in F-2 status may study on a full-time or part-time basis in an elementary, middle or high school.

A student must inform the DSO of a change of name or address within 10 days and the DSO must advise the BCIS within 21 days.

The DSO may authorize a reduction in course load for up to 12 months and must inform the BCIS within 21 days.

The DSO may consider reinstatement if a student has not been out of status for more than five months. A Form I-539 with $140 fee and the DSO's recommendation must be submitted to the BCIS.

Step 5 - Employment/Training

Congress has decided that since **undergraduate** foreign students need time to adjust to U.S. college life, they may not accept off-campus employment during the first academic year even if employment is required for their degree.

Graduate students, on the other hand, may begin off-campus work immediately if employment is required for their degree. Otherwise, they must complete their first academic year of study before beginning employment.

The role of the Department of Labor in the foreign student employment process has been changed. The filing of DOL Form 9034 and the U.S. employers' worker recruitment process to which it was tied have been eliminated.

The level of involvement of the Bureau of Citizenship and Immigration Services (BCIS) depends on whether the job opportunity is on-campus or off-campus and how closely it relates to the student's course of study or financial situation.

Job opportunities and the process of qualifying for them generally fall within three broad categories:

- **On-campus employment** providing a service to students, or
- **Off-campus employment** directly related to their area of study, or
- **Other off-campus employment**, in cases of substantial unanticipated economic hardship or internship with an international organization

On-campus Employment

F-1 students may accept on-campus employment provided that the school's Designated School Official (DSO) has determined that the student is in good academic standing and is otherwise qualified. The BCIS is not involved in the on-campus employment qualifying process. Employment may not begin earlier than 30 days before classes begin.

To meet on-campus employment rules, jobs must:

- Be 20 hours or less per week when school is in session but may be full-time when school is not in session
- Be filled traditionally by students
- Not displace U.S. residents
- Be on school premises, including on-location commercial firms that provide services for students on campus, such as a school bookstore or cafeteria, or
- Be at an off-campus location which is educationally-affiliated with the school and associated with the school's established curriculum, or
- Be related to contractually-funded research projects at post-graduate level

On-campus jobs may not:

- Be with on-site commercial firms, such as a construction company building a school structure, which do not provide direct student services
- Be continued unless a student:
  - intends to enroll for the next regular academic year, or
  - is authorized for practical training

Off-campus Employment

Off-campus employment encompasses two options.

The first option includes practical training employment opportunities directly related to a student's area of study. The second option includes jobs which may be unrelated to a student's major area of study such as those obtained to meet an unforeseen economic necessity or through an internship with an international organization.

F-1 students may accept off-campus employment provided that the school's DSO has determined that they are in good academic standing and meet several important conditions which vary significantly according to the category of off-campus employment opportunity. If a student fails to maintain status, these employment opportunities are automatically terminated.

In most situations, before accepting off-campus employment, students must:

- Have completed at least one full academic year (nine months)
- Have the approval of their Designated School Official (DSO) (foreign student advisor)

- Be in good academic standing
- Be currently pursuing a full course of study
- Demonstrate that the employment will not interfere with their carrying a full course of study
- Accept an employment limit of 20 hours a week or less when school is in session or full-time during holiday or vacation periods
- Not displace U.S. residents

The process wherein an employer submits a formal DOL labor and wage attestation has been terminated.

Option One - Practical training related to student's major area of study

Practical training is available to F-1 students (except students in English language training programs) who have been lawfully enrolled on a full-time basis in a BCIS-approved college, university, conservatory or seminary for at least nine months. An eligible F-1 student may request employment authorization for practical training in a position directly related to their area of study.

There are two types of practical training available.

Curricular practical training programs

An F-1 student may be authorized by the DSO to participate in a curricular practical training program that is an integral part of an established curriculum.

Curricular practical training is defined to be alternate work/study, internship, cooperative education, or any other type of required internship or practicum which is offered by sponsoring employers through cooperative agreements with the school.

Curricular practical training employment authorization may be possible if any of the following apply:

- The job is an integral or important part of the student's curriculum
- Employment is required for the degree
- Course credit is available for the employment
- It is listed in the school's course handbook and is overseen by a faculty member
- It applies to a full-time student
- It is unavailable back home

Exceptions to the one full academic year pre-requirement are provided for students enrolled in graduate studies requiring immediate participation in curricular practical training.

The student must submit a request for authorization of curricular practical training to the Designated School Official who shall:

- Determine whether the employment is directly related to the student's major area of study

- Update the student's SEVIS record
- Issue a new SEVIS I-20 to the student

A student may begin curricular practical training on receipt of the SEVIS I-20 with the DSO endorsement. Form I-538 is no longer submitted.

A student who does the maximum of one year of curricular practical training while working toward a degree is ineligible for post-completion academic training.

Optional practical training

Like curricular practical training programs, optional practical training programs require that the employment opportunity be directly related to the student's major area of study.

The total periods of authorization for optional practical training shall not exceed a maximum of 12 months. Part-time practical training of 20 hours per week or less shall be deducted from the available practical training at one-half the full-time rate.

Unlike curricular practical training, the rules for optional practical training do not require that the job be an integral part of an established curriculum. The down side is that the application process is longer and more complex.

There is a 60 day grace period following graduation during which time students may remain in the United States and apply for optional practical training. It may take four to six weeks to get approval.

A student may remain in the U.S. up to five months after the end of optional practical training or before starting classes at a new (transfer) school. A student who returns home for five months or more and returns to a new course of studies, gets 12 more months of employment authorization.

A job offer is not required but it is desirable because the clock starts ticking on the practical training time limits as soon as the EAD card is issued.

A student may apply for optional practical training up to 90 days before completing one full academic year but the start date cannot be before completing at least one academic year.

Students who have received one year or more of full-time curricular practical training are ineligible for post-completion practical training.

Temporary employment for practical training may be authorized:

- During the student's annual vacation and at other times when school is not in session if the student is currently enrolled, eligible and intends to register for the next term or semester
- While school is in session, provided that practical training does not exceed 20 hours a week
- After completion of all bachelor's, master's, or doctoral degree course requirements (excluding thesis)

- Within the 14 months following the completion of the course of study

The authorization process is in two parts.

Initial request for authorization to accept practical training must be made to the Designated School Official (DSO) of the school the student is authorized to attend.

In making a recommendation for practical training, the DSO must:
- Update the student's record in SEVIS as being recommended for optional practical training
- Print and sign the SEVIS I-20 employment page and give it to the student

The **second part** of the process requires that the student apply to the BCIS regional Service Center having jurisdiction over location of the school for an Employment Authorization Document (EAD) for optional practical training.

Ref: 8 CFR 274a

Documentation and supporting evidence includes:
- *BCIS form*
  - Form I-765, Application for Employment Authorization
- *Fee*
  - $120
- *Prior DSO recommendation*
  - SEVIS Form I-20 endorsed by the DSO within the past 30 days for full-time or part-time employment with start and end dates

The BCIS shall adjudicate the I-765 and issue an EAD on the basis of the DSO's recommendation unless the student is found otherwise ineligible. Employment may not begin until the I-766 or I-688B Employment Authorization Document is received.

The applicant cannot appeal a denial.   *Ref: 60 FR 21973*

Any employment authorization, whether part of an academic program, is automatically suspended upon certification by the DOL to the BCIS that a strike or other labor dispute is in progress in the occupation at the place of employment.

The spouse and children of an F-1 student may not accept employment.

Option Two - Non-practical training employment

F-1 students may apply for employment that does not take the form of practical training directly related to their major area of study. These employment opportunities fall within the categories of:
- Severe economic hardship
- Internship with an international organization

Initial request for authorization to accept employment must be made to the Designated School Official (DSO) of the school the student is authorized to attend.

Students must submit Form I-765, Application for Employment Authorization to the BCIS Service Center with jurisdiction over his or her place of residence. Students should also submit the SEVIS I-20 with the employment page and DSO's comments and certification.

Severe economic hardship

If other employment opportunities are not available or are otherwise insufficient, an eligible F-1 student may request off-campus employment work authorization unrelated to his or her major area of study based upon severe economic hardship caused by unforeseen circumstances beyond the student's control such as:

- Loss of financial aid or on-campus employment
- Currency fluctuations
- Inordinate tuition and living increases
- Unexpected changes in the financial condition of the student's source of support
- Other substantial and unexpected expenses

In cases of severe economic hardship, the DSO must certify that the student has demonstrated that:

- Employment is necessary due to unforeseen circumstances beyond the student's control, and
- Authorized on or off-campus employment is unavailable or otherwise insufficient to meet the needs that have arisen as a result of the unforeseen circumstances

Internship with an international organization

A bona fide F-1 student who has been offered employment by a recognized international organization within the meaning of the International Organization Immunities Act (59 Stat. 669) may apply for employment authorization.

Written certification from the international organization is required to demonstrate that the proposed employment is within the scope of the organization sponsorship.

Documentation and supporting evidence includes:

- *BCIS form*
  - I-765, Application for Employment Authorization
- *Fee*
  - $120
- *Prior DSO recommendation*
  - SEVIS I-20 endorsed by the DSO within the past 30 days for full-time or part-time employment with start and end dates
- *Supporting documentation - severe economic hardship*
  - affidavits that further detail the unforeseen economic circumstances that cause the request

- evidence of unavailability or insufficiency of on-campus or off-campus employment opportunities in area of study
- *Supporting documentation - internship with an international organization*
  - international organization's letter of certification that the proposed employment is within the scope of its sponsorship

SEVIS has eliminated the use of the I-538 DSO certification form.

If employment is authorized, the adjudicating officer shall issue an endorsed EAD and notification to the student which permits off-campus employment. The employment authorization may be granted in one-year intervals up to the expected date of completion of the student's course of study. No appeal of a denial is permitted.

Off-campus employment authorization may be renewed by the BCIS only if the student is maintaining status and good academic standing. However, it is automatically terminated whenever the student fails to maintain status.   *Ref: Service Law Books*

Because of the economic hardship arising from the devaluation of their home currencies, the INS temporarily eased the employment rules for students from Indonesia, Malaysia, the Philippines, South Korea and Thailand. The 20-hour limit is lifted and the minimum course load is reduced.

Step 6 - Reinstatement/Revalidation/Extension/Change of Status

Application to the BCIS within the United States

An application for reinstatement, revalidation or change of status should be filed with the appropriate BCIS regional Service Center. However, the DSO at a SEVIS school may grant an extension by updating the student's SEVIS record and issuing a new SEVIS Form I-20. The DSO may grant the extension at any time prior to the end date listed on the student's original SEVIS I-20.

An F-1 student with Duration of Status (D/S) is not required to apply for an extension of stay if he or she is making normal progress toward the completion of the educational objective.

The school DSO will access SEVIS and update the student's records electronically for entry/exit data, changes of name or address, program extensions and changes in program of study.

No B nonimmigrant may enroll in school until the student has applied for, and received, BCIS approval for a Change of Status to F-1.   *Ref: 67 FR 18062*

Documentation and supporting evidence includes:

- *BCIS form*
  - I-539, Application to Extend/Change Nonimmigrant Status
- *Fee*
  - $140

- *Passport*
  - passport valid for at least six months beyond intended stay
- *Prior approval*
  - original I-20 issued by the school
- *Current and prior immigration status*
  - original I-94, Arrival/Departure Record, or
  - I-102, Application for Replacement/Initial Nonimmigrant Arrival/Departure Record, if applicable
- *Proof of financial support or solvency*
  - proof of financial support

Change of School or Program

A student in good standing academically and with the proper financial resources may transfer to another school. A new SEVIS I-20 must be obtained from the transfer school and sent to the BCIS with a copy to the old school. The student is required to notify the DSO at the transfer school within 15 days of the program start date

The DSO will advise the BCIS regional Service Center within 30 days. No notification is required when changing majors, but still pursuing the same degree.

Out of Status Prior to Completion of Program

A student who goes out of status should submit evidence to prove that:

- The violation of status was solely due to circumstances beyond his or her control, or
- Failure to receive reinstatement would result in extreme hardship
- The student is pursuing or will pursue a full course of study at the school listed on the SEVIS I-20
- The student has not engaged in unauthorized off-campus employment, or
- Any unauthorized off-campus employment was related to a scholarship, fellowship or assistantship
- A U.S. resident was not displaced
- The student is not in deportation proceedings

A student who has been out of status less than five months may be able to regain status by departing and reentering the United States using a valid F-1 visa and SEVIS I-20 validated by the DSO.

Change To or From F-1

H-4s wishing to change their status to F-1 may:

- File by mail for a status change with the appropriate BCIS regional Service Center, or
- Apply at a U.S. Consulate in Mexico or Canada with an I-20, proof of financial support and other F-1 documents

F-1s wishing to change their status to H-1 will not go out of status if their practical training expires while an H-1 petition is pending. However, they must await receipt of the H-1 before starting work.

Students with an F-1 visa who marry a Green Card holder may remain in the United States as long as they stay in school. However their spouse should file an I-130 Green Card application with the BCIS.

Visa Revalidation by the Department of State (DOS)

A student who is unable to complete the program within the deadline indicated on the I-20 may seek the approval of both the school's DSO or foreign student advisor and the State Department to extend their stay.

A request to extend an F-1 may be processed by the State Department in a student's home country, but not in the United States. However, renewal in Canada or Mexico is permitted. It is advisable to check whether a Canadian visitor's visa is required to enter Canada.

A request should be submitted within 30 days of the expiration of the I-20 and should normally be granted if a student:

- Applies on time
- Has maintained status without violation
- Can demonstrate that the extension is required because of compelling medical or academic reasons

As long as their I-94 is valid, students may reenter the United States regardless of whether their F-1 renewal is approved abroad.

Documentation and supporting evidence includes:

- *Passport*
  - passport valid for at least six months beyond intended stay
- *Prior approval*
  - valid I-20
- *School's evidence to support request*
  - letter from your department explaining why you need the extension
- *Proof of financial support or solvency*
  - proof of financial resources

It is advisable to retain the I-94 for reentry when leaving the United States for State Department processing in case your visa application is denied. It may also be used if the visa is granted.

Change of Status to H-1B After Completion of Studies - Effect of H-1B Cap

Following completion of their studies or program, F-1 nonimmigrant aliens may seek employment in H-1B status. However, since there is an annual cap on the number of H-1Bs issued in any BCIS Fiscal Year, petitions on behalf of F-1 aliens may not be processed for a work start date in the current BCIS Fiscal Year if the H-1B cap has already been reached.

A new rule implemented on June 15, 1999 permits the BCIS to extend the period of duration of status of certain F-1 nonimmigrant aliens who are still in status for such time as is necessary for the BCIS to act on the petition for a change of their status to H-1B with a work start date in the following fiscal year. Such F-1 aliens and their F-2 dependents will not be required to depart the United States to avoid going out of status and may remain in the U.S. to wait for H-1B numbers to again become available at the start of the next fiscal year beginning October 1.   *Ref: 64 FR 32146*

Employment or other activities inconsistent with the terms of their F-1 status is not permitted without BCIS authorization until H-1B visa numbers become available and the BCIS has approved the change of status for a date no earlier than October 1.

H-1B amended petitions, extensions of stay and petitions filed on behalf of an H-1B alien by a new or additional employer are not counted against the cap.

J

Exchange Visitor

J status is reserved for persons from other countries to participate in educational and cultural visitor, work, study or training exchange programs that implement the Fulbright-Hays Act of 1961. Its stated objective is:

- To mutually increase understanding between the people of the United States and the people of other countries by means of educational and cultural exchange

Sub-categories are:

- J-1 - Exchange visitor
- J-2 - Spouse and children of alien classified J-1

Ref: 9 FAM 41.12: INA 101(a)(15)(J)

Background

This act and the INA provide nonimmigrant status for a person having a residence in a foreign country that he or she has no intention of abandoning, who seeks to enter the United States temporarily, and who has been selected to participate in an Exchange Visitor Program.

Each year, some 175,000 foreign nationals enter the United States in the Exchange Visitor Program as part of the public diplomacy efforts of the United States Government designed to promote peaceful relations and mutual understanding with other countries. At the end of their program, the visitors are expected to return home within thirty days to share their experiences and new skills with their fellow citizens.

Program Operation

In October, 1999, the Foreign Affairs Reform and Restructuring Act of 1998 was implemented and as a result the exchange visitor functions of the former program administrator, the United States Information Agency (USIA) were absorbed into the Department of State. Consequently, the functions related to operation of the Exchange Visitor Program were delegated to the Under Secretary of State for Public Diplomacy and Public Affairs. The functions related to the waiver of the foreign residency requirement were delegated to the Assistant Secretary for Consular Affairs in the Waiver Review Division of the Office of Legislation, Regulation and Advisory Assistance in the Visa Office of the Bureau of Consular Affairs. Now, participation is contigent upon accreditation by and full participation in SEVIS. *Ref: Pub. L. 105-277, 107-56*

Program participants include students, medical and on-the-job trainees, teachers, professors, research scholars and international visitors coming for the purpose of travel, observation, consultation, research, training, sharing, or demonstrating specialized knowledge or skills, or participating in organized people-to-people programs.

Although many large companies participate as sponsors, J status is grouped with other educational classifications in this chapter because of its heavy educational concentration. However, as an indication of its diversity, J status may apply to the following classifications:

	22 CFR	Maximum Program
• Education		
• professors and research scholars	(62.20)	three years
• short-term scholars	(62.21)	six months
• college and university students	(62.23)	duration of status or non-degree - 24 months
• teachers	(62.24)	three years
• secondary school students	(62.25)	one year
• Other employment		
• specialists	(62.26)	one year
• alien physicians	(62.27)	seven years
• camp counselors	(62.30)	four months
• au pairs	(62.31)	one year
• Other visitors		
• trainees	(62.22)	18 months
• international visitors	(62.28)	one year
• government visitors	(62.29)	18 months
• summer student travel/work	(62.80)	four months

Each classification may contain a number of sub groups. For example, au pairs now include two distinct programs. The original program provides for a maximum of 45 hours of child care a week plus not less than six semester hours of academic credit. A second program, called EduCare, provides for a maximum of 30 hours of child care and the au pair must pursue a minimum of 12 semester hours of academic credit. Both programs are limited to one year. In each, one and a half days off per week and two weeks paid vacation must be provided.

An estimated 100,000 Exchange Visitors are currently subject to a statutory provision of 8 USC 212(e) which requires that they return to their country of citizenship or last permanent residence for a period of two years when their exchange program is completed and their J-1 or J-2 status expires. Waivers of this requirement are possible but not necessarily easily attainable. Details follow in Step 8.

Health insurance is mandatory. Some scholarships include coverage for the J-1 visa holder. In those cases, coverage must still be purchased for the dependents. If the scholarship does not include health insurance, then the alien must find coverage.

Admission Process

Step 1 - Obtaining Approval of Programs

U.S. educational institutions, U.S. government agencies, foreign or U.S. private organizations wishing to apply for approval as an exchange visitor program must register online at www.immigration.doj.gov/sevis for a temporary ID and password. It is also necessary to submit a Form DS-3036, Exchange Visitor Program Application by mail with the $799 fee and required supporting documentation. The DOS will update SEVIS on receipt of the application.

Currently designated sponsors must also register in SEVIS to continue sponsoring nonimmigrants as exchange visitors. They must have submitted Form DS-3036 to enroll in SEVIS by the February 15, 2003 registration deadline.

Information is available from the SEVIS Help Desk at (800) 892-4829 or by writing:

Department of State
Program Designation
301 4th Street S.W.
Washington, DC 20547

The application must be returned with:

- The applicant's proposed exchange program activity and ability to comply
- Evidence of legal status and financial responsibility of the organization
- Accreditation, if a post-secondary institution
- Evidence of licensure if required by law
- Certification that chief executive and responsible officers are U.S. citizens

Program information is available from the State Department fax-on-demand information line by calling (202) 205-8237 from your fax machine.

Step 2 - Clearing the Approved Sponsoring Agency

In order to participate, a foreign national must be accepted by one of the approximately 1,400 designated sponsoring agencies issuing the Form DS-2019, Certificate of Eligibility for (J-1) Exchange Visitor.

As of February 15, 2003, each exchange visitor program approved by the Department of State for J Exchange Visitors must issue a SEVIS DS-2019 to each J-1 principal alien and to each J-2 spouse and minor child applicant. Until SEVIS was fully operational, schools and program sponsors had to electronically register visa applicants into both SEVIS and ISEAS.

The Accreditation Council for Graduate Medical Education (ACGME) is responsible for the accreditation of U.S. post-MD medical training programs. See www.acgme.org.

International medical graduates must have a valid certificate from the Educational Commission for Foreign Medical Graduates (ECFMG). See www.ecfmg.org.

Each approved program has a Designated School Official (DSO) or responsible officer named to assist applicants with the immigration process.

Step 3 - *Clearing the Department of State (DOS) Abroad*

After being accepted in an approved program and receiving the DS-2019, Certificate of Eligibility, an alien living abroad must apply to the U.S. Embassy or to a Consulate in his or her home country.   *Ref: 9 FAM 41.62*

Documentation and supporting evidence includes:
- *DOS forms*
  - DS-156, Nonimmigrant Visa Application
  - DS-158, Contact Information and Work History for Nonimmigrant Visa Application
- *Fees*
  - $100 for Machine-Readable Visa (MRV) is waived in this classification
  - reciprocity equating to fees charged in similar circumstances in an alien's home country
- *Passport and photograph*
  - passport valid at least six months beyond intended stay
  - 50 mm (2") square photograph facing camera directly without head covering (check for religious exceptions) against a light background
- *Prior approval*
  - DS-2019, Certificates of Eligibility for J-1 Student and J-2 dependents
- *Additional evidence*
  - proof of sufficient scholastic preparation unless the exchange program is designed to accommodate non-English speaking participants
  - proof of adequate knowledge of English
- *Proof of financial support or solvency*
  - sufficient funds to cover all expenses while participating in the exchange program, or
  - funds provided by the sponsoring organization in the form of a scholarship or other stipend
- *Evidence that U.S. stay is temporary*
  - proof of binding ties to the home country and intent to depart the United States after completing the program

If you are taking a spouse and minor children with you, additional documentation is required.

Documentation and supporting evidence includes:

- *Passport and photograph*
  - passports of dependents
  - 50 mm (2") square photograph facing camera directly without head covering (check for religious exceptions) against a light background
- *Civil documents*
  - proof of marriage
  - proof of parenthood of each child

If an alien is found to be an appropriate candidate and all necessary documents are in order, the consulate will place a J visa stamp in the alien's passport.

Although Canadians do not need passports or visas to enter, the Canadian Government recommends that Canadians have passports to enter the U.S.

Step 4 - Clearing the BCBP at a U.S. Port of Entry

An alien must apply for entry with the BCBP at a port of entry.

Documentation and supporting evidence includes:

- *Passport and photograph*
  - a valid passport with its valid J visa stamp
- *Prior DOS and program approval*
  - SEVIS-generated DS-2019, Certificate of Eligibility for Exchange Student (J-1)
  - DOS Machine-Readable Visa (MRV) in passport
- *Proof of financial support or solvency*
  - evidence of financial support

A spouse and minor children may be granted J-2 status.

The BCBP will issue an I-94 Arrival/Departure Record card and transcribe the I-94 number on the SEVIS DS-2019 and return it to the alien. They should be kept with the passport as proof of J-1 status.

The Immigration Inspector makes the determination of whether the Exchange Visitor is subject to the two-year home residency requirement. Key indicators are whether any funding of the exchange visitor's program is from either the home country or the United States. Also, if the exchange visitor's skills are on a shortage list at home, he or she will be subject to the two-year home residency requirement under which a total of two years must be spent in the home country, not just outside the United States. However, it may be possible to eliminate the two-year requirement by working in a third country for a home country employer such as a government agency.

An alien may be admitted 30 days before the program begins and is usually admitted for the period of time necessary to complete the program. Check the maximum program participation period for each classification of Exchange Visitor. There is a 30-day grace period to depart after successfully completing the program.

Canadian citizens and landed immigrants in Canada who are British subjects or citizens of a Commonwealth country or citizens of Ireland do not need to obtain a J visa from a U.S. consular office. Persons from those countries should present proof of citizenship and landed immigrant status, financial support evidence and DS-2019 directly to the Immigration Inspector at a port of entry.

If the DS-2019 or evidence of financial support are not available, the BCBP Inspector may allow temporary entry. If confirmation of admission has been received from the school, Form I-515, Notice to Student or Exchange Visitor must be completed and Form I-515a, 30 Day Admission Notice issued to the exchange visitor who will have 30 days to submit the missing documentation to the BCBP office.

Step 5 - Maintenance of Status

An Exchange Visitor must complete the program for which he or she was admitted prior to the date of expiration of their status. However, a student eligible to return to school may take a summer vacation in the United States between semesters.

Sponsors must notify the State Department program administrators in writing when an Exchange Visitor has withdrawn from or completed a program 30 or more days before the ending date on his or her DS-2019, or if he has been terminated.

An Exchange Visitor must notify the DSO within ten days of a name or address change. The DSO has 21 days to update SEVIS.

J-2 dependent children may enroll for full-time study in an elementary, middle or high school. J-2 spouses may not enroll for post-secondary education without obtaining F-1 or J-1 status. The J-1 principal alien may not accept employment unless prior approval is obtained. See Step 6 which follows.

Step 6 - Employment/Training

There are several avenues available for employment and training.

Option One - Student Employment

Application for employment must be made in writing to your school's J-1 responsible officer or international student advisor who must evaluate your proposed employment in relation to your academic program and your personal situation. If approved, employment may be permitted for up to one year at a time.

J-1 student employment is limited to 20 hours per week except during school breaks and annual vacations.

There are three types of Student Employment.

- **Scholarship, fellowship or assistantship** required employment usually occurs on campus with the school as the employer. However, it is possible to obtain work such as in a government or private research laboratory if your major professor supervises you in work that would count toward your degree.
- **On-campus** jobs unrelated to study are allowed for work in which the school is not the employer and the work is unrelated to the study program.
- **Off-campus** jobs are permitted in cases of serious, urgent, and unforeseen economic circumstances that have arisen since your arrival in the U.S.

Option Two - Academic Training

Academic Training is the name used for certain types of study-related employment. It offers a variety of employment situations to supplement an academic program both during and after completion of the study program.

Academic training is divided into training **before completion of your program of study** and **after completion of your program of study**.

Before completion of your program of study

You may interrupt study to work full-time while you are writing a thesis. The limit is 18 months or the time that you have been a full-time student, whichever is shorter, unless the employment is a degree requirement.

After completion of your program of study

You will be eligible for academic training if you submit a written offer of appropriate employment within 30 days after the end of your program. The limit is 18 months or the time that you were a full-time student, whichever is shorter minus any previous academic training.

After receiving a doctorate, you become eligible for any postdoctural training minus any academic training prior to receipt of the doctorate.

Academic Training allows part-time work when classes are in session and full-time during vacation periods and other times such as when a thesis is being written.

To be eligible for employment:

- Your primary purpose must be study rather than academic training
- You must be in good academic standing at the school on your DS-2019
- The proposed job must be directly related to your major field of study
- You must maintain permission to remain in the United States throughout your training
- You must maintain health insurance for yourself and your dependents throughout your academic training

Employment may be authorized for the length of time necessary to complete the goals and objectives of the training, provided that:

- The amount of time is approved by both the academic dean or advisor and the responsible officer
- The employment does not exceed the period of:
  - the full course of study or 18 months, whichever is shorter, or
  - 36 months in the case of a Ph.D.
- Any Academic Training after completion of the program must be reduced by any prior periods of Academic Training
- Any Academic Training after completion of the program involves paid employment
- A written job offer is presented to the Responsible Officer within 30 days of the completion of the program

If Employment Authorization is not obtained before leaving the country, reentry may be difficult.

J-1 students in non-degree programs are also eligible for Academic Training.

To qualify, it is necessary to:

- Obtain a written offer from your prospective employer including:
  - your job title
  - brief description of the goals and objectives of your job
  - dates and location of employment
  - number of hours per week
  - the name and address of your training supervisor
- Have your academic advisor write a letter recommending your academic training to your J-1 Responsible Officer setting forth:
  - the goals and objectives of the specific training program
  - a detailed description of the training program
  - how the training program relates to the major field of study
  - why it is an integral or critical part of the academic program
  - adviser's approval of the length of time necessary to complete the goals and objectives of the training
- If in agreement, your J-1 responsible officer must write you a letter of approval
- The Responsible Officer must issue a new DS-2019 for a maximum of 18 months of post-doctoral training at a time

A maximum of 36 months of practical training is permitted including all periods before and after completion of your program.

Option Three - All Other Employment Options

As listed in the introduction to this J Exchange Visitor section, there are several options for a person who wishes to enter the United States temporarily to gain job experience. These range from the graduate medical student and professor to the au pair and camp counselor. Each has its own rules and restrictions on employment.

J Status U.S. jobs may be arranged for a fee through placement organizations that have the authority to issue an DS-2019 to allow a student, recent graduate, or young professional to obtain temporary J-1 status. The following internet addresses are offered without recommendation as a service to those who may wish to consider the use of a placement agency.

AIESEC: www.us.aiesec.org/index.asp
Association for International Practical Training: www.aipt.org/index.html
CDS International: www.cdsintl.org/cdsctpinusaprogram.html
Institute of International Education: www.iie.org

Spousal Employment

A spouse may work on a J-2 visa during the J-1's stay after submitting an application and receiving permission from the BCIS regional Service Center. The process takes about four weeks.

A J-1 student should take the most recent Form DS-2019 and a new DS-2019 will be issued for the spouse.

Documentation and supporting evidence includes:

- *BCIS form*
  - I-765, Application for Employment Authorization
- *Fee*
  - $120
- *Photographs*
  - two color photographs 40 mm high by 35 mm wide in 3/4 profile showing right ear, no head covering (religious exceptions), light background
- *Prior program approval*
  - DS-2019
- *Current and prior immigration status*
  - copy of the I-94s of principal alien and dependent
- *Dependent's evidence to support request*
  - letter explaining why employment is desired and that it is not necessary to support J-1 spouse
- *Additional evidence*
  - letter from Foreign Student Advisor confirming that student is enrolled and making satisfactory progress toward graduation
- *Proof of financial support or solvency*
  - source and amount of principal alien's financial support of spouse evidence that job income is not required to support the J-1

Step 7 - Change of Programs

If a student decides to change schools before graduation and before the J-1 expires the action you take depends on whether your I-94 shows a specific expiration date or Duration of Status (D/S).

If your I-94 shows Duration of Status or D/S, there are three parts to the process.

Part One - Preparing the Form
- Fill out and sign the white page of the Form DS-2019

Part Two - Release to Another Program
- Have your present J-1 Responsible Officer complete and sign the lower right-hand corner of all three copies of your DS-2019 form to release you to the second school's sponsorship

Part Three - Notifying the BCIS
- Take Form DS-2019 to the second school's International Office which will:
  - mail the yellow copy to the BCIS
  - return the pink copy to you

If your I-94 shows a specific expiration date, you must mail your application to the BCIS regional Service Center having jurisdiction over your new school.

Documentation and supporting evidence includes:
- *BCIS form*
  - I-539, Application to Extend/Change Nonimmigrant Status
- *Fee*
  - $140
- *Prior approval*
  - both sides of the white page of the DS-2019
- *Current and prior immigration status*
  - copies of prior DS-2019s
  - copies of front and back of I-94 Arrival/Departure Record cards of principal alien and J-2 dependents

Work for the new school cannot begin until documents are received from BCIS.

Step 8 - The Two-year Home Residency Requirement (HRR)

Option 1 - Serving the Two-year HRR

As previously noted, the BCBP makes a determination of who is subject to the two-year HRR when they first obtain J status. This is to ensure that designated Exchange Visitor Program participants share with their countrymen the knowledge, experience and impressions gained during their sojourn in the U.S.

Ref: 9 FAM 41.53; INA 101(a)(15)(H); 8 USC 212(e)

Exchange Visitors are currently subject to the two-year return home requirement (HRR) if they:

- Receive U.S. or foreign government financing for any part of their studies or training in the U.S.
- Are engaged in studies or trained in a field deemed of importance to their home government and such field is on the "skills list" maintained by the program administrator in consultation with foreign governments
- Entered the U.S. to pursue graduate medical education or training

An alien is subject to the two-year HRR unless evidence is produced to demonstrate that all of the following terms have been met:

- A preliminary decision has been made by the immigration officer on the initial DS-2019 stating that the alien is not subject to the HRR (see the bottom left corner of the DS-2019 and the visa stamp in the passport)
- The J-1 participation was not funded in whole or in part, directly or indirectly, for the purpose of exchange, by either the home government or the U.S. government
- The skills on the alien's training program as described on the DS-2019 are not on the home country's list of urgently needed skills (per the U.S. government's Exchange Visitor Skills List)
- The J-1 did not participate in a graduate medical education or training program
- The J-2 is not the dependent of an Exchange Visitor subject to the HRR

If an alien is subject to the two-year HRR:

- Visits to the United States are permitted while serving the HRR but the time in the U.S. should be subtracted from the two-year residence time
- Time spent residing in a third country does not meet the intent of the two-year HRR
- Working for a home country employer such as the government in a third country may not meet the intent of the two-year HRR
- It is not possible to change status to permanent resident or nonimmigrant H-1 or L status until evidence is submitted that the two-year HRR has been waived or served   *Ref: 9 FAM 40.202*

It is advisable to provide documentary proof of having resided and worked in the home country for a full two years to satisfy the HRR.

Option 2 - Waiver of the Two-year HRR

Exchange Visitors who are subject to the two-year Home Residency Requirement may apply for a waiver under one of the five following applicable grounds:

- A no objection statement from the visitor's home country
- A request by an interested United States Government agency

- A request by a state on behalf of an exchange visitor who has pursued graduate medical education or training in the U.S.
- A reasonable fear of persecution if returning to his or her home country
- Exceptional hardship to the visitor's U.S. citizen spouse or child

The State Department's Waiver Review Division makes recommendations to the BCIS on waivers of the two-year HRR.

Applicants may obtain general information through a fax-on-demand system by calling (202) 647-3000. The Public Inquiries Division may be reached at (202) 663-1225.

On March 17, 1997, the USIA amended its skills list of experts lacking in a particular country. J-1s studying in a field covered by the list may not change to any other classification before serving the 2-year HRR or obtaining a waiver. The list is online at http://dosfan.lib.uic.edu/usia/GC/gc_docs/j-exchange/jexp.htm

Ref: 62 FR 2448

Applicants should be aware that waivers are not liberally granted, although the law allows an application every six months. With an overall 1997 success rate of 91 percent, five alternative approaches may be followed to obtain a waiver.

Alternative 1 - NORI - No Obligation to Return

This is a "no-objection" statement and issued by the home government, usually through their consulate. In 1997, 68 percent of the 5,752 waiver applications fell within this alternative. The process should be started six months before the J status expires. The NORI is an important aspect of the waiver process but other supporting documentation may also be needed.

Since the NORI is issued routinely by most European countries, it is of limited value. On the other hand, Indian citizens have found this to be a successful approach.

The NORI process includes:

- Obtaining the NORI application forms from the home country's consulate
- Completing the forms in quadruplicate, having them notarized and returned to the consulate
- The consulate endorsing and returning the forms to the alien to obtain a NORI statement or clearance from three home country agencies such as:
  - local passport office
  - state government
  - federal Department of Education
  - Ministry of Health (physicians)
  - police
  - tax authorities
- Each agency sending a NORI statement to the alien and to the country's consulate in the United States for forwarding to their embassy in the U.S.
- The embassy sending a NORI statement to the program administrator

- The program administrator making a recommendation to the BCIS
- The BCIS issuing the final waiver

One cannot appeal a denial to an application for a waiver based on a "no objection" statement.

Alternative 2 - Interested Government Agency

An Interested Government Agency (IGA) such as NASA, the CIA, Departments of Commerce, Health or Defense wanting to hire a J-1 alien subject to the two-year HRR to do security-related, research or other work must file for a waiver of the two-year HRR. This alternative accounted for 15 percent of all waiver applications in 1997.

Submissions must be accompanied by strong and convincing supporting documentation to demonstrate such evidence as:

- Their research or other work will lead to the development of a product or technology that will give the United States a market or technological edge

The Interested Government Agency (IGA) petition process includes the:

- IGA examining the case and deciding whether to apply to the program administrator for a waiver
- Alien completing and submitting an Exchange Visitor Program Data Sheet
- Program administrator forwarding its recommendation directly to the alien's local BCIS office
- BCIS sending the applicant an I-797C Notice of Action acknowledging receipt of the recommendation and advising that it takes 30-60 days to process the case
- BCIS sending the final letter to the applicant (BCIS usually accepts a waiver recommendation)

An employer may write a supporting letter to make the alien the beneficiary of a petition with an interested U.S. government agency. The Interested Government Agency may then act as sponsor for a waiver. However, letters to the program administrator or Congressional Representatives only serve to delay the process.

A university must demonstrate through extensive documentation that the U.S. would get a significant edge in terms of contributions to the education field generally or to the successful completion of a project which is of great interest to the Department of Education.

This process may take four to six months once all necessary papers are submitted to the Interested Government Agency.

The Department of Housing and Urban Development (HUD) announced that it will not process waiver recommendations for physicians subject to the J-1 two-year HRR.   *Ref: HUD, December 13, 1996*

Alternative 3 - Conrad Amendment - State 30 Program

The Conrad Amendment State 30 Waivers for Foreign Medical Graduates enables each participating state to obtain a waiver of the two-year HRR in order to bring in 30 physicians to areas with a shortage of physicians. The program expired in 2002 but was extended to 2004 and the state quota increased from 20 to 30.   *Ref: Pub. L. 107-273*

Almost 10 percent of 1997 waiver requests were on behalf of Foreign Medical Graduates (FMGs) who entered the U.S. for graduate medical education or training and were subject to the two-year home-country physical presence requirement (HRR).

Currently, the Appalachian Regional Commission acts as an interested government agency on behalf of foreign medical graduates seeking a waiver of their two-year HRR. The Department of Agriculture terminated its waiver program in 2002. If a waiver is approved, doctors provide primary medical care to Americans living in a health professional shortage area without adequate access to medical care and where there are few doctors such as in a rural area or inner city. However, only 30 waivers may be allowed for each state each year, hence the name Conrad 30 Program.

Applications must come from each state's designated Department of Health in the form of a letter to the program administrator stating that it is in the public interest that the alien physician remain in the United States together with a completed data sheet. The physicians must demonstrate a bona fide offer of full-time employment at a health facility designated by the Secretary of Health and Human Services as having a shortage of health care professionals and present a signed contract in which the physician agrees to practice medicine for at least three years. The state body should confirm that it intends to renew the contract after the initial three-year period.

Ref: 22 CFR 514.44 (e)

Required documentation

- A three-year employment contract of at least 40 hours per week of primary medical care in a designated primary care Health Professional Shortage Area ("HPSA") or designated Medically Underserved Area ("MUA") or psychiatric care in a designated Mental Health Professional Shortage Area ("MHPSA").
- Two written statements must be included:
  - the facility is located in a designated HPSA, MHPSA, or MUA and the facility provides medical care to Medicaid or Medicare eligible and indigent uninsured patients
  - the medical graduate does not have a pending interested state or federal request awaiting approval and will not request that another agency pursue a request on his or her behalf

Alternative 4 -Fear of Persecution

Less than one percent of all requests for waivers were based on fear of persecution on account of race, religion or political opinion if the visitor were to return to his or her home country.

A BCIS Form I-612 must be filed for a recommendation. If the BCIS makes a preliminary finding of probable persecution, the file is forwarded to the State Department's Bureau of Democracy, Human Rights and Labor for their recommendation. This determination is relied on heavily by the BCIS.

Extreme hardship to a U.S. citizen or permanent resident, spouse or child may constitute grounds for a waiver. Economic hardship or relocation may not be sufficient.

Qualifying residents of the People's Republic of China may take advantage of a blanket waiver.

Alternative 5 - Exceptional Hardship

Six percent of all waiver applications were based on exceptional hardship to a U.S. citizen or legal permanent resident spouse and/or children.

This alternative also requires the filing of BCIS Form I-612. If it determines exceptional hardship, the BCIS forwards the file to the State Department's Waiver Review Division for a recommendation.

If U.S. Government funding was expended on the Exchange Visitor, the opinion of the funding agency is sought. It is then the responsibility of the Waiver Review Division to weigh the relative merits of the program, policy and foreign relations considerations against the exceptional hardship which would befall the U.S. citizen or legal permanent resident and/or children if the two-year HRR were enforced. Decisions are made on a case-by-case basis. Considerations include:

- The amount and source of funding
- General home country conditions
- The absence of any objection
- The spouse and/or child's a chronic medical condition
- The spouse and/or child's safety in the home country
- The existence of a child custody order
- Military service that would prevent the spouse from accompanying
- Applicant's marital status and children

When considering a request for a waiver, be aware that:

- It is not necessary to have a job waiting in the United States in order to apply for a waiver
- An alien who has been granted a waiver of the HRR, becomes subject to the two-year HRR rule all over again by renewing the J-1

- The refund of HRR funds such as college grants does not constitute grounds for a waiver
- Because of the complexity of this process, it may be advisable to consult the International Student office for assistance

Documentation and supporting evidence includes:

- *DOS and BCIS forms*
  - DS-3035, J-1 Visa Waiver Review Application
  - I-612, Application for Waiver of the Foreign Residency Requirement (Use with alternatives 4 and 5 only)
- *Fees*
  - $230 for DS-3035 (Payable to Department of State)
  - $195 for I-612 (Payable to BCIS)
- *Current and prior immigration status*
  - I-94 Arrival/Departure Record if applying in U.S.
- *Additional evidence*
  - documentary evidence relating to exceptional hardship or persecution
- *Civil documents*
  - proof of birth if spouse or child is a U.S. citizen by U.S. birth, or
  - proof of U.S. citizenship of foreign-born spouse or child such as:
    - marriage
    - marriage termination
    - birth certificate
    - statement of dates, ports, means of all U.S. arrivals and departures by spouse and child, or
    - Certificate of Naturalization of spouse or child (if occurred within 90 days of filing Form I-612)

Before requesting other status changes in the Exchange Visitor program, applicants should determine whether proposed additional fees have been implemented.

The State Department operates a service offering status reports on HRR waiver applications by calling (202) 663-1600 or on the internet at http://63.70.23.80. The BCIS information line is (800) 375-5283.

Applications may be sent by Registered Mail, Return Receipt Requested to:

U.S. Department of State
Waiver Review Division
P.O. Box 952137
St. Louis, MO 63195- 2137

Applications may also be sent by courier to:

> U.S. Department of State
> Waiver Review Division
> (Box 952137)
> 1005 Convention Plaza
> St. Louis, MO 63101-1200

Necessary documentation that does not include the processing fee should be sent to:

> U.S. Department of State
> Visa Services
> Waiver Review Division
> 2401 E Street, N.W.
> Washington, DC 20522-0106

Step 9 - Reinstatement/Revalidation/Extension or Change of Status

Application to the Department of State in the United States

When requesting a reinstatement or extension, the State Department must be satisfied that you do not intend to abandon the Exchange Visitor Program.

If your I-94 Arrival/Departure Record shows Duration of Status or D/S instead of a specific expiration date, you may extend your DS-2019 in the United States.

After confirming the necessity for your reinstatement or extension, your J-1 responsible officer will take your DS-2019 and mail the yellow copy to the program administrator and return the pink copy to you.

Application to the BCIS within the United States

Regardless of the instructions on the Form I-539, if your I-94 Arrival/ Departure Record shows a specific DS-2019 expiration date instead of Duration of Status or D/S, you must mail your extension application directly to the BCIS regional Service Center having jurisdiction over your place of residence at least 45 days before your stay expires.

Documentation and supporting evidence includes:

- *BCIS form*
  - I-539, Application to Extend/Change Nonimmigrant Status
- *Fee*
  - $140
- *Current and prior immigration status*
  - original DS-2019 issued by your program sponsor

Retain the copy of the DS-2019 designated for the J-1.

A request for a waiver of the two-year HRR would lead the State Department and sponsor to believe that the alien intends to abandon the exchange program. Hence, any request for an extension of J-1 status might not be successful.

If your application is approved, you will be mailed an approval notice which should be kept with your I-94 and your copy of your DS-2019. These documents together demonstrate your status.

Visa Revalidation by the Department of State (DOS)

Your permission to stay in the United States ends on the date shown on your I-94, Arrival/Departure Record card. However, if your card is marked Duration of Status or D/S you may stay until 30 days after the date on Item 3 of your DS-2019.

To extend your permission to stay in the United States, you must:

- Contact your J-1 Responsible Officer at least three months before the expiration date on your DS-2019
- Be making satisfactory academic progress and have adequate funding, or
- Have completed your program of study and want to participate in an academic program, or
- Be participating in an authorized academic training program and need an extension to finish the program (within the established time limits)

Leaving and Reentering the United States

If you leave and reenter the country using your new DS-2019, this will extend your permission to stay. This is not an option if you are in Canada, Mexico or the Caribbean for periods of fewer than 30 days as the BCBP Inspector may not record your reentry and thus "turn on" your new DS-2019.

If you leave North America you will need a valid J-1 visa stamp in your passport. If yours has expired, you will need to apply for a new one at a U.S. Embassy or Consulate abroad.

Documentation and supporting evidence includes:

- *DOS form*
  - DS-156, Nonimmigrant Visa Application
- *Fees*
  - $100 for non-refundable Machine-Readable Visa (MRV)
  - visa reciprocity equating to fees charged in similar circumstances in an alien's home country
- *Passport and photograph*
  - passport valid for at least six months beyond intended stay
  - 50 mm (2") square photograph facing camera directly without head covering (check for religious exceptions) against a light background
- *Prior approval*
  - DS-2019

- *Additional evidence*
  - dependents' passports
- *Proof of financial support or solvency*
  - proof of funding and support
- *Civil documents*
  - proof of marriage and parenthood

Application to the BCIS for Change of Status to J within the United States

If you and your dependents are filing for a change to J status, you must mail your application to the BCIS regional Service Center having jurisdiction over your location.

Documentation and supporting evidence includes:

- *BCIS form*
  - I-539, Application to Extend/Change Nonimmigrant Status
- *Fee*
  - $140
- *Prior approval*
  - DS-2019, Certificate of Eligibility for (J-1) Exchange Visitor
  - original I-94, Arrival/Departure Record for principal alien and dependents (if none available, file Form I-102, Application for I-94 with $100 fee)

Retain your copy of the DS-2019. The BCIS issues an I-797, Notice of Approval that serves as evidence of the change of status.

Application to the BCIS for Change of Status from J within the United States

A petition for change in status to H-1 or Green Card may be made as soon as a favorable recommendation is received on the request for a waiver of the two-year HRR. It is not necessary to wait for the final waiver from BCIS. This is advisable as the LCA or Labor Certification processes take a long time in many states.

An applicant may apply for H-1B or permanent residency while serving the HRR. If approved, the visa can be issued the day the two years are up. This is particularly advisable for those who can get permanent visas without Labor Certification such as on the basis of family preference. You can apply at a U.S. Embassy or Consulate in your home country.

It is possible to accept a tenure track university position on the basis of completing the first 18 months on a J-1 visa as practical training, then return home for two years before returning to the United States. An applicant must ensure that:

- The employer is willing to keep the position open for two years and sponsor the alien for an H-1 visa and a return to the United States, or
- If a waiver of the HRR has been applied for, and there is a reasonable assurance that it will be issued, the employer can sponsor for an H-1 visa

A J-1 Exchange Visitor subject to the foreign residency requirement who has not received a waiver is not eligible to change status to H-1B, L or V.

A J-1 Exchange Visitor whose status was for the purpose of receiving graduate medical training is ineligible for change of status unless a waiver is obtained under the Conrad 30 Program.

Change of Status to H-1B After Completion of Studies - Effect of H-1B Cap

Following completion of their studies or program, J-1 nonimmigrant aliens may seek employment in H-1B status provided that they are not subject to the HRR. However, since there is an annual cap on the number of H-1Bs issued in any BCIS Fiscal Year, petitions on behalf of J-1 aliens may not be processed for a work start date in the current BCIS Fiscal Year if the H-1B cap has already been reached.

A new rule implemented on June 15, 1999 permits the BCIS to extend the period of duration of status of certain J-1 nonimmigrant aliens who are still in status for such time as is necessary for the BCIS to act on the petition for a change of their status to H-1B with a work start date in the following fiscal year. Employment or any other activity inconsistent with the terms of their J-1 status is not permitted without BCIS authorization until H-1B visa numbers become available and the BCIS has approved the change of status for a date no earlier than October 1.   *Ref: 64 FR 32146*

J-1 aliens and their J-2 dependents will not be required to depart the United States to avoid going out of status and may remain in the U.S. to wait for H-1B numbers to again become available at the start of the next fiscal year, October 1.

Ref: 64 FR 32146

M

Vocational or Non-Academic Student

$\mathbf{M}$status is reserved for "those who will be studying at a vocational or other non-academic school and who have a home in a foreign country to which they will return after they complete their studies. This classification can include a spouse or unmarried children under the age of 21."   *Ref: INS ER 806 3-8-94*

Although the M is for less formal academic studies, it has many of the same prerequisites and limitations that apply to the F. An alien is admitted initially for a maximum of one year with extensions possible if the study extends longer.

An M-1 student may not change status to an H classification if the training received as an M-1 helped him or her qualify for H status. However, transfer to another school during the first six months and change of status to F-1 is permitted.

Sub-categories are:
- M-1 - Vocational Student or Other Recognized Nonacademic Student
- M-2 - Spouse and children of alien classified M-1
- M-3 - Border Commuter Student - Canada or Mexico   *Ref: 67 FR 54941*
  Ref: 9 FAM 41.12; INA 101(a)(15)(M)

Admission Process

Step 1 - Acceptance by an Accredited Institution

The application process is similar to that for the F-1.

A student must be accepted by a SEVIS-approved institution before submitting a visa application to a U.S. Embassy or Consulate abroad. A SEVIS I-20 is issued to the student and each dependent.

Documents required by the institution include:
- Application for admission
- Diplomas, official reports (translated into English)
- School transcripts
- Recent photograph
- Evidence of English proficiency, such as TOEFL

Additional documentation which may be required includes:
- Application fee/Tuition deposit
- Housing application and deposit
- Personal recommendations
- Health information

Upon acceptance, the school issues:
- Letter of acceptance
- SEVIS Form I-20 - Certificate of Eligibility to each principal alien and dependent with their own ID number

All students must be protected by health insurance. If they choose not to take the insurance available through the school, they should find adequate coverage elsewhere. Students may also need to submit proof of required immunization.

In 2002, the rules were amended to permit M-3 Mexican and Canadian nationals residing near the U.S. border to regularly commute to a U.S. educational institution within 75 miles of the border to study on a full or part-time basis.

Ref: Pub. L. 107-274

Step 2 - Clearing the Initial Application

Option 1 - By the BCIS in the United States

A student who is already in the United States with legal immigration status, may make application at the local BCIS office having jurisdiction over the area where the institution is located.

Documentation and supporting evidence includes:
- *BCIS form*
  - I-539, Application to Extend/Change Nonimmigrant Status
- *Fee*
  - $140
- *Passport*
  - passport valid for at least six months beyond intended stay
- *Prior approval*
  - SEVIS Form I-20 - Certificate of Eligibility for Nonimmigrant (M-1) from school
- *Proof of financial support or solvency*
  - the applicant has sufficient funds to pay school-related expenses and to support himself or herself during the program

Option 2 - By the Department of State (DOS) Abroad

Application must be made to a U.S. Embassy or Consulate. The Consular Officer may not issue an M-1 visa until they receive the electronic acceptance data submitted by the approved institution for both the student and dependents. DOS must notify the school when a visa is issued to a new student or for a renewal.

Documentation and supporting evidence includes:
- *DOS form*
  - DS-156, Nonimmigrant Visa Application
- *Fees*
  - $100 for non-refundable Machine-Readable Visa (MRV)
  - visa reciprocity equating to fees charged in similar circumstances in an alien's home country
- *Passport and photograph*
  - passport valid for at least six months beyond intended stay
  - 50 mm (2") square photograph facing camera directly without head covering (check for religious exceptions) against a light background
- *Prior approval*
  - SEVIS I-20, Certificate of Eligibility for Nonimmigrant (M-1) issued by the school
- *Alien's evidence to support request*
  - proof of adequate English language skills
- *Proof of financial support or solvency*
  - evidence of adequate financial resources to cover expenses for the full program including:
    - school financial aid
    - personal and family funds
    - government assistance
- *Evidence that U.S. stay is temporary (intent to depart U.S.)*
  - bona fide evidence that the student intends to return home

Step 3 - Clearing the BCBP at a U.S. Port of Entry

A potential student may enter as a B-2 visitor to compare schools with the notation "intending student" on the I-94. However, no B nonimmirant may enroll in school until the intending student has applied for, and the BCIS has approved, a Change of Status to M-1. An M-1 student and M-2 spouse and minor children may enter 30 days before studies begin.   *Ref: 67 FR 18062*

Documentation and supporting evidence includes:
- *Passport*
  - passport valid for at least six months beyond date of entry (citizens of Canada exempt)
- *Prior approval*
  - SEVIS I-20 from the academic institution
  - DOS visa

- *Additional evidence*
  - copies of all documentation previously submitted to the U.S. consulate abroad
- *Proof of financial support or solvency*
  - evidence of financial support for full term

The Immigration Inspector should:

- Issue and date an I-94 to the student and each family member
- Admit an eligible spouse and minor children in M-2 status
- Send SEVIS Form I-20 to the BCIS for processing
- Notify institution when the student and each family member is admitted
- Advise that unauthorized employment is not permitted

If the student fails to register, the institution must advise the BCIS within 30 days of passing the registration deadline.

If the SEVIS Form I-20 or evidence of financial support are not available, the BCBP Inspector may allow temporary entry. If confirmation of admission has been received from the school, Form I-515, Notice to Student or Exchange Visitor must be completed and Form I-515a, 30 Day Admission Notice issued to the student who will have 30 days to submit the missing documentation to the BCBP office.

Documentation and supporting evidence includes:

- *Passport*
  - passport valid for at least six months beyond date of entry
- *Prior approval*
  - the principal alien's I-20
- *Proof of financial support or solvency*
  - evidence of financial support

Each M-1 or M-2 nonimmigrant must present an original SEVIS I-20 issued in their name by the current school. The student is admitted for a fixed time period, the time necessary to complete the course of studies plus practical training after the completion of studies as well as an additional 30 days to depart the U.S. but not to exceed a total of one year.

Step 4 - Maintenance of Status

A student must complete the vocational or non-academic program prior to the expiration of status. A student who is eligible to return to school may take a summer vacation in the United States and dependents may attend elementary or high school.

The Illegal Immigration Reform and Immigrant Responsibility Act of 1996 included several provisions that impact on foreign students.

The DSO may reduce a course of study for up to five months and must update SEVIS.

The M-2 spouse may not engage in full-time study at a post-secondary institution but M-2 children may engage in full-time study in an elementary, middle or high school. M-2 dependents may not engage in employment.

Step 5 - Employment Authorization by the BCIS

Part-time employment is permitted on campus but off-campus employment is restricted to practical training required for the certificate or degree and the permission of the BCIS must be obtained. Students may apply for paid practical training upon completion of their program.

The maximum time for training is one month for each four months of full-time study to a maximum of six months plus 30 days to depart the country.

Obtaining work authorization is now a two-part process.

Part One - Designated School Official

Certification of the school's Designated School Official (DSO) is required.

The former requirement to submit a paper Form I-538 attached to a paper Form I-20 has been completely eliminated. This is now an electronic function as the DSO enters the certification data in SEVIS.   *Ref: 67 FR 76256*

Part Two - Application to the BCIS

The student applies in person to the BCIS for an Employment Authorization Document (EAD) up to 90 days before the program ends.

Documentation and supporting evidence includes:

- *Form*
  - I-765, Application for Employment Authorization
- *Fee*
  - $120
- *Required approval*
  - SEVIS I-20 endorsed for practical training by DSO

The BCIS issues the student:

- Authorizing I-766
- Endorsed I-20

Employment without authorization makes an alien subject to deportation.

Step 6 - Change of School by the BCIS Within the United States

When transferring from the current school to the transfer school, the student must notify the current school which will update SEVIS to show that the student is transferring out. The student must submit a Form I-539 to the BCIS at this point. The student has 15 days to advise the DSO after receiving BCIS approval.

The transfer school must generate a SEVIS I-20 and the student may begin classes while awaiting BCIS adjudication.

Documentation and supporting evidence includes:

- *BCIS form*
  - I-539, Application to Extend/Change Nonimmigrant Status
- *Fee*
  - $140
- *Prior approval*
  - I-20 from the new school
- *Current and prior immigration status*
  - Student's old I-20
- *Additional evidence*
  - I-94s for student and family

Electronic filing of I-539s is expected in 2005.

Step 7 - Revalidation/Extension/Change of Status

Application to the BCIS within the United States

An M-1 student must not go out of status. An M-1 student is considered to be legally in the United States as long as he or she has met and continues to meet all the requirements for maintaining status. To extend their stay, M-1 students should apply to the BCIS regional Service Center having jurisdiction over their school 15 to 60 days before their stay expires.

The student must apply for an extension on Form I-539 and must include spouse and children on the application. The cumulative time of extensions is limited to three years from the M-1 student's original start date plus 30 days to leave the U.S.

No B visitor may enroll in school before the BCIS has approved a Change of Status.

Documentation and supporting evidence includes:

- *BCIS form*
  - I-539, Application to Extend/Change Nonimmigrant Status
- *Fee*
  - $140

- *Prior approval*
  - new I-20, if applicable
- *Current and prior immigration status*
  - student's old I-20
- *Additional evidence*
  - I-94s of dependents, if any

The student should not send his or her I-94 or passport to the BCIS.

Visa Revalidation by the Department of State Abroad

The State Department does not do M visa renewals in the United States. However, renewals can be done at a U.S. Embassy or Consulate abroad by filing the same documents as required in the initial entry.

Chapter 5

Business Professionals

Several visa options are available to business professionals wishing to work in the United States on a temporary basis. Some classifications permit a stay of several years.

Chapter 5 focuses on four of the less restrictive classifications that permit the entry of business entrepreneurs, transferees and trainees as well as professionals who benefit from the NAFTA agreement. Included are:

- E   Treaty Trader or Investor
- H   Professional, Temporary Worker or Trainee
- L   Intracompany Transferee
- TN   Treaty NAFTA - Professional

In selecting the most appropriate classification you should consider:

- The length and purpose of your proposed stay
- Your future immigration plans
- Your professional credentials and experience
- The availability of U.S. workers with similar qualifications, and
- The willingness of U.S. employers to undertake a potentially complex, expensive and protracted visa application process

Depending on the length of the U.S. stay or other circumstances, Mexican and Canadian applicants may be able to enter the United States on business for short periods without obtaining a formal visa. (See Chapter 1).

Chapters 6, 7 and 8 describe classifications with more restrictive or specialized entry criteria.

E

Treaty Trader or Investor

E status is available only to an alien who is a national of a country that has a treaty of commerce and navigation with the United States. These treaties are sometimes called friendship treaties or bilateral investment treaties.

To qualify, an alien must be coming to carry on substantial trade in goods or services principally between their home country and the United States.

Sub-categories are:

- E-1 Treaty trader, spouse and children
  - the person represents a company that will carry on trade with the United States (the U.S. office must do a substantial amount of its business or trade with the person's country), or
- E-2 Treaty investor, spouse and children
  - the person is directing and developing a business in which they have invested a substantial amount of capital.
  Ref: INS ER 806 3-8-94; INA 101(a)(15)(E)(i),(ii); 9 FAM 41.12

While there are not firm financial guidelines on the amount of investment required, $100,000 is often used as a benchmark.

E status should not be confused with Employment-Based immigrant (Green Card) status that provides for aliens willing to invest between $500,000 and one million dollars in a U.S. enterprise. This is described in Part III of Book 1.

To qualify for Treaty Trader (E-1) status in the United States:

- You must:
  - be a national of your treaty country
  - have the same nationality as your trading firm
  - be employed in a supervisory or executive capacity, or
  - possess highly specialized skills essential to the efficient operation of the firm
- Your trading firm must:
  - have a volume of international trade of goods, services and technology which is sizeable and continuing and more than 50 percent of the trade must be between the United States and your home country

- produce evidence of substantial trade supported by three or more of the following:
  - bills of lading
  - customs receipts
  - letters of credit
  - insurance papers documenting commodities imported
  - carrier inventories
  - trade brochures
  - sales contracts

To qualify for Treaty Investor (E-2) status in the United States:
- You must:
  - be a national of your treaty country
  - be coming to the United States to develop and direct the operation
  - have control of the funds and the investment must be at risk
  - in a partnership, submit copies of partnership agreements with a statement of proportionate ownership
- Your investment must:
  - be a new or pre-existing active U.S. business
  - be substantial enough to ensure the successful operation of the enterprise
  - be a real operating enterprise, not speculative and not idle (uncommitted funds do not count)
  - have a significant impact in the United States and may not be marginal, generating only a living for the investor and family
  - not have loans secured with the assets of the enterprise
  - be supported by:
    - articles of incorporation
    - payments for the rental of business premises or office equipment
    - business licenses
    - stock certificates
    - office inventories
    - insurance appraisals
    - advertising invoices
    - annual reports
    - net worth statements from certified professional accountants
    - business bank accounts for routine operations and escrow

Both categories are available to Canadians and Mexicans under the terms of NAFTA.   *Ref: DOS Publication 10074, August, 1995*

Admission Process

Step 1 - Clearing the Department of State (DOS) Abroad

The consular officer must be satisfied that the alien qualifies under the provisions of INA 101(a)(15)(E).   *Ref: 9 FAM 41.51*

If you are living outside the United States, the employer is not required to file a BCIS petition in order to apply for an original E-1 or E-2.
Ref: INS Instructions - Form I-129

The State Department advises that visa applicants should generally apply at the U.S. Embassy or Consulate having jurisdiction over their place of permanent residence although they may also apply in a third country, if eligible. After a brief suspension in late 2001 for security reasons, the Third Country National (TCN) program was reinstated.

Few of the Canadian and Mexican border posts handle E cases. Although Canadian nationals all require an E visa, the U.S. Consulate in Toronto is the only Consulate in Canada which processes E visa applications for Canadian Citizens and Landed Immigrants of Canada as well.   *Ref: 9 FAM 41.2(m)*

The U.S. Consulate in Ciudad Juarez only accepts cases from residents of Chihuahua and those with a business enterprise in New Mexico or West Texas. The U.S. Consulate in Tijuana will not accept applications for E visas from persons not legally resident in Mexico.

The DOS also advises that none of the participating posts will accept applications from TCN E Visa applicants who are not resident in their consular districts.
Ref: DOS Publication - TCN Present in United States

Documentation and supporting evidence includes:
- *DOS forms*
  - DS-156, Nonimmigrant Visa Application
  - DS-156E, Nonimmigrant Treaty Trader/Investor Application
- *Fees*
  - $100 for non-refundable Machine-Readable Visa (MRV)
  - visa reciprocity equating to fees charged in similar circumstances in alien's home country
- *Passports and photograph*
  - passport valid for at least six months beyond intended stay
  - 50 mm (2") square photograph facing camera directly without head covering (check for religious exceptions) against a light background
- *Current and prior immigration status*
  - I-94, Arrival/Departure Record, as an example

- *Professional credentials*
  - university diploma(s)
  - supporting documentation
- *Evidence to support request*
  - very detailed explanatory letter from the company
  - forms required by the consular officer to ensure that the enterprise meets the requirements of the law
- *Proof of financial support or solvency:*
  - extensive documentation to demonstrate financial solvency such as a letter from the bank
  - employer's supporting letter confirming salary, function and source of funds
- *Medical clearance*
  - if history of medical ineligibility
- *Evidence that U.S. stay is temporary (intent to depart)*
  - binding family ties
  - copy of return tickets
  - no intention to abandon residence abroad

The reciprocity charge for issuing the E-1 or E-2 is approximately the same as the fee charged to U.S. citizens in your home country.

Ref: DOS Publication 10311, November, 1995

Step 2 - Clearing the BCBP at a U.S. Port of Entry

The initial E-1 or E-2 is valid for a maximum of two years from the date of entry. Holders may reside in the United States as long as they continue to maintain their status with the enterprise.

Aliens with E-1 or E-2 status may bring a spouse and unmarried children under 21 years of age. Under Public Law 107-124, a spouse may accept employment.

Option 1 - NAFTA Only

- Under the terms of NAFTA, citizens of Canada and Mexico may apply directly at a U.S. port of entry without obtaining employment authorization and without numerical restriction provided that they:
  - have established all necessary documentation and obtained a visa at a U.S. Embassy or Consulate serving their home country
  - carry on substantial trade in goods or services principally between their home country and the United States
  - establish, develop, administer or provide advice or key technical services to the operation of an investment to which a substantial amount of capital is committed
  - act in a capacity that is supervisory, executive or involves essential skills   *Ref: NAFTA Annex 1603*

Option 2 - Non-NAFTA

The expiration date on the visa issued by the consular officer abroad is the last day you may apply at a U.S. port of entry for permission to enter the United States.

The decision on whether to admit you is up to the BCBP Immigration Inspector. If admission is approved, the officer will validate your I-94, Arrival/Departure Record and note the length of stay permitted.

Documentation and supporting evidence includes:
- *Prior DOS approval*
  - DOS Machine-Readable Visa (MRV) in passport
- *Evidence to support request*
  - employer's letter confirming function, amount and source of salary
  - details of how enterprise qualifies for E status
- *Evidence that U.S. stay is temporary (intent to depart)*
  - binding family ties
  - copy of return tickets
  - no intention to abandon residence abroad

Step 3 - Revalidation/Extension or Change of Status

Application to the BCIS within the United States

The **Principal Alien** must apply between 60 days before or one year after expiration. The alien is permitted to remain while the extension is being processed.

The employer of the principal alien should file with the BCIS regional Service Center in Texas or California depending on the location of the enterprise for either:
- An extension of E status, or
- A change to E status from another classification   *Ref: INS- Form I-129*

The decision to grant or deny a request is made solely by the BCIS which issues an I-797, Notice of Approval of the extension or change of status. Extensions are for periods up to two years with no maximum number.

Documentation and supporting evidence for the principal alien includes:
- *BCIS forms*
  - I-129, Petition for a Nonimmigrant Worker
  - E Classification Supplement page
  - I-126, Report of Status by Treaty Trader or Investor
  - I-907, Request for Premium Processing, if requested
- *Fees*
  - $130 for I-129
  - $1,000 for I-907, if requested
- *Passports and photographs*
  - passport valid for at least six months beyond intended stay and

containing the present visa for the same classification (may be in a previous passport)
  - color photographs 40 mm high by 35 mm wide in 3/4 profile showing right ear, no head covering (religious exceptions), light background
- *Current and prior immigration status*
  - copy of I-94, Arrival/Departure Record
- *Professional credentials*
  - evidence of the applicant's special knowledge, skills, training, education
- *Employer's supporting documentation*
  - letter from the petitioner explaining the reasons for the change of status
- *Proof of financial support or solvency*
  - substantial trade in the case of an E-1 petition
  - substantial investment in the case of an E-2 petition
  - the unavailability of U.S. workers in the case of a non-executive/managerial employee
  - ownership and nationality such as:
    - lists of investors with their nationalities
    - stock certificates
    - certificates of ownership issued by a foreign embassy
  - supporting letter confirming salary, function and source of funds
- *Civil documents to confirm relationship with accompanying dependents*
  - birth
  - marriage
  - divorce
  - death of spouse
- *Medical clearance*
  - if history of medical ineligibility
- *Evidence that U.S. stay is temporary (intent to depart)*
  - binding family ties
  - return tickets
  - no intention to abandon residence abroad

Dependents

Dependents of principal E status aliens should file with the BCIS regional Service Center having jurisdiction over their state to change or extend their status. They may study on a full or part-time basis.

The alien spouse may obtain employment authorization as a result of a bill to provide for work authorization for nonimmigrant spouses of treaty traders and treaty investors which was signed into law on January 16, 2002.   *Ref: Pub. L. 107-124*

Documentation and supporting evidence for E-1 and E-2 dependents includes:

- *BCIS form*
  - I-539, Application to Extend/Change Nonimmigrant Status

- *Fee*
  - $140
- *Passports and photographs*
  - passport valid for at least six months beyond intended stay and containing the present visa for the same classification (may be in a previous passport)
  - color photographs 40 mm high by 35 mm wide in 3/4 profile showing right ear, no head covering (religious exceptions), light background
- *Current and prior immigration status*
  - copy of I-94, Arrival/Departure Record
- *Professional credentials*
  - evidence of the applicant's special knowledge, skills, training, education
- *Employer's supporting documentation*
  - letter from the petitioner explaining the reasons for change of status
- *Principal alien's supporting documentation*
  - the petition filed for the principal alien or evidence that it is pending
  - a copy of the principal alien's I-94, Arrival/Departure Record or approval notice showing status granted
- *Proof of financial support or solvency*
  - supporting documentation from principal alien
- *Civil documents to confirm relationship with principal alien*
  - birth
  - marriage
  - divorce
  - death of spouse
- *Evidence that U.S. stay is temporary (intent to depart)*
  - binding family ties
  - copy of return tickets
  - no intention to abandon residence abroad

Visa Revalidation by the Department of State (DOS)

After the BCIS has extended your stay, your visa may need to be renewed before attempting to reenter the United States after a business trip abroad. Depending on how U.S. citizens are treated in your home country in similar circumstances, your original visa may have been issued with restrictions on the number of entries into the United States and its period of validity, perhaps six months or a year.

Application for visa renewal may be made at a U.S. Embassy or Consulate in your home country. Revalidations may also be made at a U.S. Consulate in Mexico or Canada by calling (900) 443-3131 for an appointment.

It is not possible to obtain expedited processing or status reports. If you do not have time to get your visa renewal in the U.S., you should apply in person to the consular office of the country of destination.

As a service to aliens in a few classifications such as E, the Department of State renews visas by mail in the U.S., if time permits. Full information on revalidations is available from the State Department web site at www.travel.state.gov/revals.html. You may download the required Form DS-156 there.

Documentation and supporting evidence includes:
- *DOS forms*
  - DS-156, Nonimmigrant Visa Application
  - DS-156E, Nonimmigrant Treaty Trader/Investor Application
- *Fees*
  - $100 for non-refundable Machine-Readable Visa (MRV)
  - visa reciprocity equating to fees charged in similar circumstances in alien's home country
- *Passport and photograph*
  - passport valid for at least six months with previous visa
  - 50 mm (2") square photograph facing camera directly without head covering (check for religious exceptions) against a light background
- *Current and prior immigration status*
  - original current I-94 (no copies), or
  - I-797 Petition Approval Notice
- *Employer's supporting documentation*
  - financial statement, income tax and W-2 forms (E-2) 10 or fewer staff
  - detailed and signed letter on letterhead identifying:
    - the employee and his or her position and travel itinerary

When a fee is charged for visa reciprocity, include two certified checks or money orders, one for the visa application and one for the reciprocity charge. Personal checks cannot be accepted.

Applications should be sent in a padded envelope with a stamped padded envelope enclosed for return mailing. If return by courier is requested, an air bill is required. Processing may take six to eight weeks. Call (202) 663-1213 for further information.

Completed applications may be sent by mail to:

U.S. Department of State/Visa
P.O. Box 952099
St. Louis, MO 63195-2099

Completed applications may also be sent by courier to:

U.S. Department of State/Visa (Box 2099)
1005 Convention Plaza
St. Louis, MO 63101-1200

H

Professional, Temporary Worker or Trainee

Hstatus meets a broad spectrum of employment, training and residency needs ranging from the experienced professional to the trainee. It is reserved only for "those who are coming to the United States to work in a temporary job." *Ref: ER 806 3-8-94*

Sub-categories are:
- H-1B Professionals or other skilled workers
  - specialty occupations and fashion models
- H-1C Nurses in Health Professional Shortage Areas
  - registered professional nurses (similar to former H-1A)
- H-2A Temporary services for general labor - Agricultural Services
- H-2B Temporary services for general labor - Non-agricultural Services
  - skills in short supply
  - seasonal services unavailable in the United States
- H-3   Occupational Trainee/Special Education Visitor
  - H-3 Trainee
    - in an established formal occupational training program
    - program not available in the home country
    - skills to be used outside the United States
  - H-3 Special Education Exchange Visitor
    - participant in structured special education exchange visitor program providing practical training and experience in the education of children with physical, mental or emotional disabilities
- H-4   Dependents
  - H-4 Spouse and unmarried children under 21 of principal alien classified H-1, H-2, or H-3   *Ref: 9 FAM 41.12/53; INA 101(a)(15)(H)*

An H-1B nonimmigrant may be admitted for up to three years initially, normally extendable for another three years or longer as noted on the following pages. After the expiration of the full H-1B term including extensions, aliens must remain outside the U.S. for one year before returning for a new period as an H-1B, unless they have a special one-year extension as noted on the following page. However, entry in a status other than H, L, V or permanent resident is possible.

With the exception of aliens in H-1, L and V status, nonimmigrants living in the U.S. risk losing their status when they apply for a Green Card. The doctrine of dual intent provisions of the INA permits aliens with nonimmigrant H-1, L and V status to simultaneously seek permanent resident or immigrant status without jeopardizing their nonimmigrant status. The dual intent doctrine does not apply to aliens with TN - NAFTA status. The L, V and TN processes are discussed later.

The requirement that an H-1 nonimmigrant have a residence in a foreign country that he or she has no intention of abandoning was removed, effective October 1, 1991, by Section 205(e) of IMMACT90.   *Ref: Pub. L. 101-649*

A fully qualified alien may enter with spouse and unmarried children. Although dependents may not accept employment, they may do volunteer work with public service organizations such as the American Red Cross without compensation.

The American Competitiveness and Workforce Improvement Act of 1998
When the annual quota of 65,000 H-1B entries ran out four and a half months before the end of the 1998 fiscal year, Congress passed a short-term H-1B compromise, the American Competitiveness and Workforce Improvement Act of 1998 (ACWIA) that was included in the Omnibus Budget Bill, signed by President Clinton on October 21, 1998. An additional $500 fee and increased annual quotas to a maximum of 115,000 in Fiscal Years 1999 and 2000 were added.

The American Competitiveness in the Twenty-first Century Act of 2000
After the revised annual cap of 115,000 ran out in March, 2000, Congress developed yet another piece of legislation, the American Competitiveness in the Twenty-first Century Act of 2000 to benefit such fields as information technology, health care and education. It was signed into law by President Clinton on October 17, 2000.   *Ref: S.2045; Pub. L. 106-313*

The Act raised the annual cap to 195,000 for Fiscal Years 2001, 2002 and 2003. It exempted:
- Anyone employed or offered employment by an institution of higher education or related nonprofit entity
- An employee of a nonprofit or government research organization
- Physicians who have received J waivers of the two-year HRR and changed status to H-1B
- Persons counted toward the cap during the past six years
- Beneficiaries of multiple applications - only the first is counted

Notes   - persons moving to a non-exempt job become subject to the quota
        - all cases filed before September 1, 2000 are counted against the 2000 cap

Other features of the Act include:
- Extensions in one-year increments beyond the six-year limit:
  - if Labor Certification or an employment-based I-140 petition has been filed over one year

- until the adjudication of the Adjustment of Status application of an H-1B worker who is the beneficiary of an employment-based petition and subject to the per-country limit
- H-1B workers in status may transfer jobs as soon as a new employer files an I-129W petition (authorization ends if the petition is denied)
- H-1B workers may change to another employer in the same or similar occupational classification as the job for which the original petition was filed if the Adjustment of Status has been pending for more than 180 days
- Extension of the authority for Department of Labor attestation and investigative provisions
- Reuse of numbers from revoked visas
- Incorporates the Immigration Services and Infrastructure Improvement Account Act to eliminate backlogs and reduce processing times to 180 days for Green Cards and 30 days for temporary status *Ref: Pub. L. 106-313*
- Separate 2000 legislation increased employer's fee from $500 to $1,000, and exempted the following employers filing before October 1, 2003:
  - a primary or secondary education institution
  - an institution of higher education
  - a nonprofit related or affiliated entity
  - a nonprofit entity which engages in established curriculum-related clinical training of registered students
  - a nonprofit research organization
  - a government research organization   *Ref: H.R. 5362; Pub. L. 106-311*

The additional fee of $1,000 applies to an initial grant of H-1B status, an extension of stay or a change of employer. Fees, which have totalled $212 million as of October 1, 2002, are deposited into an H-1B nonimmigrant petitioner account and used for technical skills training of U.S. workers. Applications for grants under the Workforce Investment Act are made to the Department of Labor. Further details are at www.doleta.gov or (877) US2-JOBS.

H-1B-dependent employers

Although the rules remain basically unchanged for employers with a relatively small share of H-1B nonimmigrants in their workforce, on December 20, 2000 the DOL published the more restrictive ACWIA implementation rules for employers with a higher proportion of their workforce employed as H-1B nonimmigrants.

H-1B-dependent employers are so defined if they have:

- 25 or fewer full-time equivalent employees in the U.S. of whom eight or more are H-1B nonimmigrants, or
- From 26 to 50 full-time equivalent employees in the U.S. of whom 13 or more are H-1B nonimmigrants, or
- At least 51 full-time equivalent employees in the U.S. of whom 15 percent or more are H-1B nonimmigrants   *Ref: ACWIA.412 (b) (3) (A)*

Admission Process

Qualifying for H-1 or H-2 status is a multi-step process requiring the cooperation of the federal Departments of Justice, State and Labor to collectively establish the eligibility of a temporary worker for admission. H-3 and H-4 aliens do not require Department of Labor clearance.

Step 1 - Blanket Application

A blanket application is available for aliens who will apply for their visas at the same consulate or, if they do not need visas, will enter at the same port of entry and may be included in one petition filed by the employer or agent in the following classifications if the dates of employment are the same and they are also:

- H-1B   members of the same entertainment group or athletic team and accompanying aliens, or
- H-2A/B   on the same labor certification performing the same duties, or
- H-3   receiving the same training

Step 2 - Qualifying - Entry Criteria

The necessary qualifications vary according to the sub-category.

H-1B - Aliens in Specialty Occupations and as Fashion Models

The petitioner (employer) must establish that the position is a specialty occupation and that the beneficiary (alien worker) meets H-1B qualifications.

To qualify in an H-1B specialty occupation, the beneficiary must meet one of the following criteria:

- Holds the required U.S. baccalaureate or higher degree from an accredited college or university, or a foreign degree determined to be equivalent
- Holds a degree common to the industry in parallel positions that the employer normally requires for the position
- Holds an unrestricted state license, registration or certification
- Has equivalent education, training and experience plus recognized expertise through progressively responsible positions
- The nature of the duties are so specialized, complex or unique that the knowledge required to perform the duties is usually associated with a baccalaureate or higher degree

The beneficiary may also be required to demonstrate:

- Theoretical, practical application of a body of highly specialized knowledge
- Membership in a professional organization
- The source of awards including the reputation, size, standing and membership requirements of the awarding organization

H-1C - Registered Nurses

The H-1C classification was created in the Nursing Relief for Disadvantaged Areas Act of 1999 (NRDAA) and implemented on April 19, 2000 for four years. It allows the entry of registered nurses to deliver health care to underserved or health professional shortage areas.   *Ref:INA 101(a)(15)(H)(i)(c); Pub. L. 106-95*

The unique features of the H-1C include:

- Admission for up to three years
- The classification will end in four years, unless extended by Congress
- A limit of 500 visas per year
- A limit of 50 visas to states over 9 million (25 visas to other states)
- Eligible hospitals must have at least:
    - 190 acute care beds
    - 35 percent of patients on Medicare
    - 28 percent on Medicaid

H-2A - Temporary Agricultural Service Workers - U.S. Workers are Not Available

This category covers alien workers who are needed to perform agricultural labor or services of a temporary or seasonal nature.

H-2B - Other Temporary Workers - U.S. Workers are Not Available

This is a broad category to cover aliens in non-agricultural occupations such as sports instructors and minor league professional athletes, instrumental musicians, stable attendants, crab meat and fish roe workers, and housekeeping cleaners. Others may be unskilled. H-2B temporary workers must be needed to meet a specific project of not more than one year with a defined end. Portions of the annual allotment of 60,000 H-2B visas may also be used for the planned temporary Q-2 classification.

Step 3 - Clearing the Department of Labor

Step 3 applies only to H-1 and H-2 candidates who must first obtain a job offer and Department of Labor (DOL) approval before a BCIS petition may be filed.

More than one alien may be requested on an application if they are:

- To do the same work on the same terms and conditions
- In the same occupation and area(s) of employment during the same period

Effective January 14, 2002, the DOL has introduced a new electronic LCA filing process. H-1B filings may be done online at www.lca.doleta.gov. The system will automatically determine within minutes if the submitted LCA is certified or denied.

Upon receipt of the certified LCA, the employer must print and sign the Form ETA 9035E and file a copy with the visa petition.

The new three-page Form ETA 9035 may also be used for filing H-1B cases by mail or fax. It is available at www.ows.doleta.gov/foreign/preh1bform.asp and may be either faxed to (800) 397-0478 or mailed to:

ETA-H-1B
P.O. Box 13640
Philadelphia, PA 19101

Documentation and supporting evidence includes:

- *DOL form*
  - Form ETA 9035, Labor Condition Application (three-page form only)
- *Employee's professional credentials*
  - Bachelor's degree in a narrowly defined subject area, or
  - an Associate degree plus three years of equivalent experience for each required year of schooling in a narrowly defined subject area may be sufficient
- *Employer's evidence to support request - Attestation on Form ETA 9035*
  - job data - question 7
    - three-digit occupational group code from Dictionary of Occupational Titles (converting to O*Net OnLine database - see Appendix E)
  - wage statement - question 8 (a)
    - required wage will be paid for the entire period of employment
    - the greater of the actual or prevailing wage will be paid
    - wage sources in order of priority:
      - State Workforce Agency (SWA) determination
      - independent authoritative source
      - another legitimate source of wage information
  - working conditions statement - question 8 (b)
    - hiring of the alien will not adversely affect the working conditions of similarly employed workers in the area
  - no strike or lockout statement - question 8 (c)
    - there is currently no strike or lockout in a labor dispute in the occupational classification at the place of employment
  - labor condition statement - question 8 (d)
    - if there is no bargaining representative, posted notice of filing a total of 10 days
- *Additional evidence - registered professional nurses only*
  - the nurse:
    - has received appropriate nursing education in the United States or Canada or has a full and unrestricted license to practice
    - pending a final ruling on IIRIRA96.343, the BCIS and DOS have agreed to waive the certification requirement *Ref: INS 10/14/98*
    - is fully qualified, eligible and will practice as a registered nurse in the place of intended employment
  - the employer:
    - will comply with any limitations that the laws in the state place on the nurse's services

- *Additional evidence - foreign physicians performing direct patient care*
  - the physician must have:
    - a license or authorization required by the state of employment
    - a full and unrestricted license to practice medicine in a foreign country, or
    - graduated from a medical school in the U.S. or a foreign country
    - completed a medical residency in the U.S. (see exception below)
  - the employer must confirm that:
    - it is a nonprofit educational or research institution or agency and if the physician will teach or conduct research, or
    - the foreign doctor has passed the Federation Licensing Examination (FLEX) or an equivalent accepted by the U.S. Department of Health and Human Services and is:
      - competent in spoken and written English, or
      - a graduate of a medical school accredited by the U.S. Department of Education

If the H-1B nonimmigrant agrees, an employer that is a school or other educational institution may pay an annual salary in disbursements over fewer than 12 months to the H-1B nonimmigrant in accordance with an established salary practice that applies equally to U.S. workers in the same occupational classification.

Canadian physicians

Since the U.S. Department of Education has accredited all U.S. and Canadian medical schools, Canadians are not usually required to have completed a medical residency in the United States. Nevertheless, they must still have passed the FLEX, NBME, or USMLE licensing examinations. The Canadian LMCC is accepted in some states.

Additional rules for H-1B-dependent employers

The American Competitiveness and Workforce Improvement Act of 1998 (ACWIA) basically left the old H-1B process in place for employers with a limited H-1B workforce. However, it established more stringent rules for H-1B-dependent employers who must attest that they:

- Will not displace any similarly employed U.S. worker within 90 days before or after the filing an H-1B petition
- Will not place any H-1B nonimmigrant with any other employer or at another employer's worksite unless the employer has made a bona fide inquiry on whether the other employer has displaced or intends to displace a similarly employed U.S. worker within 90 days of the placement
- Took or will take good faith steps according to industry wide standards to recruit U.S. workers with compensation at least as great as required to be offered to the H-1B nonimmigrant (does not apply to "priority workers")

Ref: ACWIA.212(n)(1)

Some additional teeth are added in the legislation under section 212 (n) (2) (C), in which H-1B-dependent employers face new penalties, after notice and opportunity for a hearing if:

- Labor Secretary finds a failure or a substantial failure to meet a condition, or misrepresentation of fact, the Homeland Security Secretary may:
  - impose a maximum $1,000 penalty, and
  - not approve H-1B petitions for that employer for at least one year
- Secretary finds a wilful failure to meet a condition or wilful misrepresentation of material fact in an application:
  - a civil penalty of up to $5,000 per violation may be imposed, and
  - the Homeland Security Secretary shall not approve that employer's H-1B petitions for at least two years
- Secretary finds a failure to meet a condition or a wilful misrepresentation of material fact resulting in the displacement of a U.S. worker within 90 days of the filing of any visa petition and if the placing employer knew or had reason to know of the displacement:
  - a monetary penalty not exceeding $35,000 may be imposed, and
  - the Homeland Security Secretary shall not approve H-1B petitions for three years
- It is also a violation for an employer to:
  - discriminate against an employee or former employee who cooperates or seeks to cooperate in the investigation of a possible violation
  - require that an H-1B nonimmigrant pay a penalty for ceasing employment prior to a mutually agreed date
  - require that an H-1B nonimmigrant reimburse the employer for any part of the fee for the petition; a maximum $1,000 monetary penalty may be imposed and the amount paid returned to the nonimmigrant
  - place an H-1B nonimmigrant designated as a full or part-time employee in nonproductive status or to fail to pay the nonimmigrant full wages due to a decision by the employer or due to the nonimmigrant's lack of a permit or license (this clause does not apply to non-work-related factors such as the nonimmigrant's voluntary request for an absence or inability to work)
  - fail to offer benefits and eligibility for benefits to an H-1B nonimmigrant on the same basis and criteria as offered to U.S. workers

Arbitration process

In an effort to ensure equitable treatment, the new legislation has established a detailed arbitration process with several key elements including:

- The Secretary of Homeland Security shall establish an arbitration process for complaints concerning an employer's failure or misrepresentation
- Homeland Secretary may request the Federal Mediation and Conciliation Service to appoint an arbitrator to initiate binding arbitration proceedings

- If the arbitrator concludes that there is a failure or misrepresentation, the Homeland Security Secretary may impose administrative remedies up to $5,000 per violation and not approve petitions for up to two years
- An employer on probation may be subject to random investigations for a period of five years after a wilful failure to meet a condition or wilful misrepresentation of material fact
- Such actions may only be set aside in a U.S. Court of Appeals

Mechanisms for enforcement

The DOL does not require proof that the employer has been unable to find qualified U.S. workers unless the employer is H-1B-dependent. Although the job does not have to be advertised outside the company:

- The employer:
  - must post a labor attestation at the work site to indicate the presence of an H employee
  - must pay the greater of the actual or prevailing rate
- Co-workers:
  - should report alleged H status violations to the Department of Labor
- DOL:
  - may initiate independent investigations

H-1C - Registered Nurses (RNs)

U.S. health care providers may file for up to 500 nurses a year in a four-year (2000 - 2004) H-1C program for nurses in health shortage areas. The nurse must have:

- Been educated in the U.S. , or hold
- A full unrestricted license to practice nursing in country where educated
- A full unrestricted license in the state of employment, or
- Passed an appropriate examination approved by the Department of Health and Human Services and offered by the Commission on Graduates of Foreign Nursing Schools (CGFNS)
- Been fully qualified and authorized to work as a registered nurse in the place of intended employment

Documentation and supporting evidence includes:

- *DOL form*
  - ETA 9081, Attestation for H-1C Nonimmigrant Nurses
- *Fee*
  - $250 payable to U.S. Department of Labor   *Ref: Pub. L. 106-95*
- *Attestation by employer*
  - the facility meets the required definition of facility
  - employment will not adversely affect the wages and working conditions of other similarly employed registered nurses
  - the alien will be paid the wage rate of other similarly employed nurses
  - it is taking steps to recruit and retain U.S. nurses

- there is no strike or lockout in progress
- notice of filing has been provided to the union, if any, or to staff
- it will not employ more than 33 percent of its RNs as H-1Cs
- it will not assign the H-1C to other than its worksites *Ref: 65 FR 51138*

Send attestations to:

> Chief, Division of Foreign Labor Certifications
> Office of Workforce Security
> Employment and Training Administration
> U.S. Department of Labor
> 200 Constitution Avenue, N.W., Room C-4318
> Washington, DC 20210

H-2A - Temporary Agricultural Service Workers

An employer who anticipates a shortage of H-2A U.S. workers needed to perform agricultural labor or services of a temporary or seasonal nature must apply for temporary alien agriculture labor certification to the Regional Administrator (RA) in whose region the intended employment is located.   *Ref: INA 101(a)(15)(H)(ii)(a)*

Most H-2A petitions are filed before the petitioner has identified or named the H-2A workers (beneficiaries). In 2000, the total number of employers using H-2As was approximately 4,400.

The H-2A regulations at 20 CFR 655.101 require the simultaneous submission of an H-2A application to the Regional Office of the Department of Labor (DOL) and the State Workforce Agency (SWA) in the area of intended employment. Most states have transferred the H-2A functions to a centralized location within the state to better coordinate the programmatic efforts between the State and the Regional Office of the Department of Labor.   *Ref: 66 FR 19984*

The petition for an H-2A may be filed by the employer or the employer's agent or an association of U.S. agriculture producers as a joint employer on the Labor Certification.

Under the Connelly Amendment, the application must be filed no less than 45 calendar days before the first date of need and the Regional Administrator (RA) must make a determination to grant or deny by 30 calendar days before the date of need. The employer must show that an advertisement and job order have been placed before issuance of the Labor Certification. The job order initiates a search of potential interstate and intrastate sources of U.S. workers.   *Ref: Pub. L. 106-78*

On an annual basis the ETA revises its Adverse Effect Wage Rates (AEWR). The H-2A must be paid the higher of the AEWR, the applicable prevailing hourly wage rate or the legal federal or state minimum wage rate. Housing must be in compliance 20 days before occupancy and predetermined travel and meal allowances paid.   *Ref: 20 CFR 655.102(b)(9)*

By ETA General Administration Letter (GAL) No. 3-01, March 28, 2001, sheep and goat herders and cooks in agricultural labor camps are to be treated by the SWA under H-2A regulations. Also, under ETA GAL 1-01, March 22, 2001, the employer must notify the SWA in writing within 48 hours of becoming aware of the abandonment of employment or termination for cause.

Labor Certification is granted only for enough H-2A workers to fill the employer's job opportunities for which U.S. workers are not available. If a Labor Certification is denied, the RA also denies the petition for lack of Labor Certification. The Regional Administrator (RA) makes a determination to grant or deny by 20 calendar days before the date of the need.   *Ref: 57 FR.181*

Documentation and supporting evidence for H-2A includes:

- *DOL form*
  - ETA 750, Application for Alien Employment
- *Fees*
  - $150 for Labor Certification - ten or fewer jobs, or
  - $250 for Labor Certification - ten to 99 jobs, or
  - $1,000 maximum (employer or joint employer association)
  - payable within 30 calendar days of granting Labor Certification
- *Employer's declaration*   *Ref: 20 CFR 655.90*
  - recruitment of U.S. workers
  - free housing
  - meals and transportation
  - worker's compensation
  - tools and supplies
  - guarantees of employment 3/4 days of contract
  - accurate records
  - not replacing workers on strike or in lockout

Form ETA 750 is filed with the DOL and Form I-129 with the BCIS.

The rule under which the BCIS would have delegated authority for the adjudication of H-2A petitions to the DOL was withdrawn on September 24, 2002. Consequently, the proposed combined DOL Labor Certification and BCIS petition was also withdrawn.   *Ref: 67 FR 59779*

H-2B - Other Temporary Workers - U.S. Workers are Not Available

The employer's need for services must be one of:

- One-time occurrence
- Seasonal need
- Peak load need
- Intermittent need

As a general rule, the employer's need must be one year or less and the Labor Certification application may not exceed 12 months. However, if there are unforeseen circumstances where the employer's need exceeds one year, a new certification is required for each period beyond one year to a three year maximum.

Applications for certification shall be filed with the State Workforce Agency (SWA) serving the area of employment between 60 and 120 days before the Labor Certification is needed. The SWA will prepare a job order and place it into the regular ES system for ten days. Walk-in applicants and those in SWA files will be referred to the employer.

The employer must advertise the job opportunity for three days in the most appropriate general circulation newspaper, professional, trade or ethnic publication to attract U.S. workers before aliens may be considered.

The SWA office will forward the application to the appropriate Regional Administrator, Employment and Training Administration (ETA).

The regional Certifying Officer shall determine whether to grant the temporary Labor Certification based on:

- Availability of U.S. workers for the temporary employment
- Whether the employment of the alien will adversely affect wages and working conditions of similarly employed U.S. workers
- Whether the job opportunity contains restrictions that preclude consideration of U.S. workers   *Ref: 20 CFR 655.3*

The Certifying Officer who makes a temporary Labor Certification determination sends the employer the certified application containing the official temporary Labor Certification stamp and other documents including the Temporary Determination Form. These documents should all be submitted to the BCIS.

In 1995, only 2,398 visas were issued.

Documentation and supporting evidence includes:

- *DOL form*
  - Form ETA 750, Part A, Application for Alien Employment Certification
- *Employer's evidence to support request*
  - documentation of any efforts to recruit U.S. workers
  - statement explaining:
    - why the job opportunity is temporary
    - why the need meets the standard of:
      - a one-time occurrence
      - a seasonal or peakload need
      - an intermittent need
- *Aerospace engineer documentation*
  - SWA job order
  - employer's blind ad in a newspaper or engineering publication
  - offer of reemployment to laid-off engineers
  - identification of alien engineer's work location

- employee's contract
- all certification job orders in interstate and intrastate clearance
- *Construction worker documentation*
  - union representatives contacted to determine availability of U.S. workers when ten or more workers in the same occupation requested within six months
- *Boilermaker documentation*
  - in emergency situations, boilermaker applications must be sent directly to National Office of the U.S. Department of Labor, Washington
  - in nonemergency situations, applications are processed like all H-2s

H-3 - Temporary Trainee, and
H-3 - Special Education Exchange Visitor

Department of Labor attestation is not required.

H-4 - Spouse and Minor Children

Department of Labor attestation is not required but the working spouse must complete the admission process before the spouse and minor children may be admitted.

Step 4 - Clearing the BCIS - Initial Petition

After receiving Department of Labor approval, the employer may file a petition with the BCIS regional Service Center having jurisdiction over the state in which the alien will be working. If approved, the BCIS issues an I-797, Notice of Approval which the DOS requires.

In December, 1999, the four BCIS Service Centers briefly stopped processing H-1Bs so that they could do an audit on the number of cases being processed and bring the Service Centers in line. It was expected that these periodic holds could continue.

Physicians may be admitted in H-1B status if their entry is primarily to teach or conduct research at or for a public nonprofit public educational or research institution or agency in which no patient care will be performed except that which is incidental to the teaching or research. Doctors may also be admitted for direct patient care on a case by case basis on the approval of the appropriate BCIS regional Service Center. In such cases, the physician must have a state license or authorization and a full degree.

A second simultaneous H-1B petition may be filed while the first is still in force. A spouse and minor children are processed with the principal alien as H-4s.

All H-1C petitions must be filed by the facility on Form I-129, Petition for Nonimmigrant Worker. Petitions must be filed at at the BCIS Vermont Service Center with a copy to the ETA National Office at the address listed in Step 3.

Documentation and supporting evidence includes:

- *BCIS forms*
  - I-129, Petition for a Nonimmigrant Worker

- H Classification Supplement page which confirms:
  - that the job is new to the alien
  - the job description, proposed duties and location
  - details about the business
  - details about the alien and his or her qualifications
  - agreement to return transportation if the alien is dismissed early
  - compensation at the average current wage for the job in the area
  - the dates of employment   *Ref: INS ER-721 EFC*
- I-129W, Data Collection and Filing Fee Exemption (Version 12/18/00) (Complete Part B if claiming exemption)   *Ref: ACWIA*
- I-907, Request for Premium Processing Service, if requested
- *Fees*
  - $130 for I-129
  - $1,000 for H-1B supplementary fee (except exempt organization)
  - $1,000 for I-907, if requested
- *Prior DOL approval*
  - copy of Form ETA 9035, Notice of Acceptance from the Department of Labor
- *Employer's evidence to support request*
  - letter describing the job and sponsorship in detail
  - contract describing who controls the alien's work and whether he or she controls the work of others
  - company's annual report
  - agreement to pay the alien's return fare home
  - evidence of nonprofit organization status if claiming fee exemption
- *Employee's professional credentials*
  - work experience, résumé, diplomas, professional memberships and qualifications, as applicable

The employer must be prepared to make available the additional documentation filed with the Department of Labor as noted previously. Also, submit the following additional documentation to the BCIS for **H-1B Registered Professional Nurses** and **practicing physicians**:

- Letter from health care facility to the Department of Labor containing:
  - statement that employment will be as a registered nurse or physician
  - proof of the alien's professional credentials

The petitioner must submit additional documentation for **H-3 Temporary Trainees** including:

- Written description which details:
  - duration of the different phases of training including classroom work
  - the professional instructors who will provide the training
  - the reading and course work required during the training
  - why the training is not available at home
  - the job the alien will occupy at home at the end of the training period

The petitioner must submit additional documentation for **H-3 Special Education Exchange Visitors:**

- Written description of the training program
- Written description of the facility's professional staff
- Written description of the alien's participation in the training program
- Evidence that the alien is nearing completion of a baccalaureate degree or higher, or has extensive prior training and experience in teaching children with physical, mental or emotional disabilities

Upon approval, the BCIS will:

- Issue an I-797C Notice of Action approval to the petitioner with the bottom portion being the I-94 to be cut off and retained by the worker
- Cable the notice of approval to the American consulate if the alien will be processed abroad for a visa
- Grant approval for an initial three-year period

After receiving BCIS approval, the petitioner should forward the approval notice to the alien so that he or she may make a visa application at a U.S. Embassy or Consulate abroad. It should take a few weeks to get the H-1B Visa after the LCA is approved by the Department of Labor. However, you may not begin work until the employer has all necessary approvals.

An employer who believes that a visa was denied as the result of an error in law, may file a request for reconsideration with the regional BCIS office. Filing does not authorize employment.

Step 5 - Clearing the Department of State (DOS) Abroad

Unless visa exempt, in order to finalize visa proceedings, the first time an H visa is issued, it usually means a trip to a U.S. Embassy or Consulate in your home country or in a third country such as Canada or Mexico when the program is operating.

After approval is received from the BCIS by the alien and the consular officer, the alien should make an appointment for State Department processing at a U.S. Embassy or Consulate abroad where you will file documents according to the requirements of the requested classification. If you qualify, you will be issued a visa to be presented at a U.S. port of entry. Canadians do not require visas.

Former J Exchange Visitors who are subject to the two-year Home Residency requirement are ineligible to apply for H visas. *Ref: 9 FAM 41.53*

At the Consulate, be prepared for the consular officer's questions about your residence at home, your job and employer, your financial situation and your future immigration plans. Be truthful and try to focus your answers on the questions asked.

Since it is the consular officer's responsibility to evaluate an applicant's credentials, it is important to take all your evidence to your interview. A credentials evaluation agency's report may be helpful but one senior consular officer called it just another piece of paper.

The visa issued by the State Department is presented at the a U.S. port of entry. A single-entry visa generally allows an alien to make a trip of less than 30 days to Canada and Mexico. However, visas of Iranians are canceled on entry.

Some H-1 visas issued abroad do not permit unlimited entry to the U.S. but application may be made to permit multiple-entry at U.S. Consulates near the Canadian or Mexican borders.

H-1B - Aliens in Specialty Occupations and as Fashion Models

Documentation and supporting evidence includes:

- *DOS form*
  - DS-156, Nonimmigrant Visa Application
- *Fees*
  - $100 for non-refundable Machine-Readable Visa (MRV)
  - visa reciprocity equating to fees charged in similar circumstances in alien's home country
- *Passport and photograph*
  - passport valid for at least six months beyond intended stay
  - 50 mm (2") square photograph facing camera directly without head covering (check for religious exceptions) against a light background
- *Prior BCIS and DOL approvals*
  - certified copy of employer's petition Form ETA 9035, Labor Condition Application (LCA) including copy of DOL certification
  - original I-797, Notice of Approval for each applicant
- *Current and prior immigration status*
  - I-94, Arrival/Departure Record when the United States was last entered, if applicable
  - previous visa, if applicable (may be in a previous passport)
- *Professional credentials*
  - university degree and/or other professional certification (including nurse's nursing diploma)
- *Employer's evidence to support request*
  - letter from employer giving such information as job title, salary, date of joining company
  - letter from your immediate supervisor confirming the need to travel abroad on company business if multiple-entry visa is required
  - copies of all documents filed with the BCIS by employer
  - forms required to ensure that the enterprise meets legal requirements
- *Additional evidence*
  - certified copies of all your documentation if your spouse and children are applying separately
  - proof of CGFNS or other certification (nurses)   *Ref: 67 FR 77158*

- *Proof of financial support or solvency*
  - extensive documentation to demonstrate the alien's financial solvency such as a letter from the bank
- *Evidence that U.S. stay is temporary (intent to depart)*
  - binding family ties
  - copy of return tickets
  - no intention to abandon residence abroad
- *Payment by bank check or money order*

MRV and reciprocity visa fees require separate payment made payable to "Department of State"   *Ref: DOS instructions, January 3, 1995*

H-2A - Temporary Agricultural Service Workers

The process for obtaining a visa is similar to the H-1. However, evidence is required of DOL approval of ETA 750, Part A and professional credentials in keeping with the requirements of the job.

H-2B - Other Temporary Workers - U.S. Workers are Not Available

The process for obtaining a visa is similar to the H-1. However, evidence is required of DOL approval of ETA 750, Part A and professional credentials in keeping with the requirements of the job.

H-3 - Temporary Trainee, and
H-3 - Special Education Exchange Visitor

The process for obtaining a visa is similar to the H-1 without DOL approval and detailed professional qualifications.

Only 50 children per year with physical, mental or emotional handicaps will be permitted H-3 Special Education status. Maximum duration is 18 months.

H-4 - Spouse and Minor Children

Processing is with the principal alien.

Third Country National (TCN) Visa Processing in Canada and Mexico.

The Third Country National processing service allows you to have your visa processed at a Canadian or Mexican consulate. The service was halted briefly in late 2001 for security reasons. An appointment must be made two to three weeks in advance and at your expense by calling a central appointment 900 number or by booking online on the internet at www.nvars.com. 900 service operators are available between 9 am and 10 pm to make appointments.

The key telephone numbers are:
- From the United States:
  - To make an appointment: (900) 443-3131, or
                               (888) 840-0032 (payment required)
  - General visa information: (900) 656-2222

- To speak with a visa officer: (202) 663-1225 (during business hours)
  (202) 663-1213
- From Canada:
  - To make an appointment: (900) 451-2778
  - General visa information: (900) 451-6330
  - To speak with an operator: (900) 451-6663

You may cancel an appointment by calling (888) 611-6676 (have passport handy).

The contractor will send the appropriate forms, detailed instructions about the interview and will confirm the appointment. The contractor may also advise if certain types of applicants may encounter difficulties when they apply for their visas.

U.S. Consulates for obtaining H-1Bs are located in Ciudad Juarez, Tijuana and Matamoros, Mexico and in Halifax, Québec City, Montréal, Ottawa, Toronto, Calgary and Vancouver, Canada.

Step 6 - *Clearing the BCBP at a U.S. Port of Entry*

After being cleared at a Consulate abroad, the last step is to take all papers to a U.S. port of entry and have the passport stamped as a legal nonimmigrant.

A person may enter the U.S. up to ten days prior to their start date to find accommodation and carry out other startup activities in their new location.

Canadians not already in status in the U.S. may apply directly to a U.S. port of entry after receiving Department of Labor Approval and BCIS approval of the initial petition. Canadians may also live in Canada and commute to work in the United States while in H-1B status.

Documentation and supporting evidence includes:
- *Passport*
  - passport valid for at least six months beyond intended period of stay
- *Prior BCIS / DOL / DOS approvals*
  - BCIS I-797, Notice of Approval
  - DOL Labor Condition Application or Labor Certification
  - DOS Machine-Readable Visa (MRV) in passport
- *Current and prior immigration status*
  - such as I-94
- *Professional credentials*
  - copies of documents filed with DOS and DOL
- *Evidence to support request*
  - employer's letter confirming function
- *Proof of financial support or solvency*
  - employer's letter confirming amount and source of salary and period of employment

- *Evidence that U.S. stay is temporary (intent to depart)*
  - all except H-1
  - no intention to abandon residence abroad (H-2, H-3, H-4)

As previously noted, the INA permits an H-1 to have the dual intent of remaining in the United States with a pending Green Card application while maintaining temporary H-1 status. Therefore, it is not necessary to demonstrate that you will at all times maintain a foreign residence during your temporary stay in the United States and consequently, there is no longer a presumption of immigrant intent to overcome for the H-1 visa applicant.   *Ref: INA 214; 8 USC 1184*

However, the rules are quite different for an alien in H-2 or H-3 status.

A spouse or minor child holding an H-4 visa is not permitted to engage in any type of employment in the U.S. To do so is a violation of their immigration status, and could result in deportation and/or denial of future visas, including a Green Card.

Six years is the total cumulative time most aliens are allowed to remain in H status. However, there are exceptions:

- Nurses may remain a total of five years
- Aliens working on a U.S. Department of Defense administered cooperative research and development project may remain a total of ten years
- Temporary workers performing agricultural or other services unavailable in the United States may remain a total of three years
- Special education exchange visitors may remain a total of 18 months
- Trainees in an occupational training program may remain two years
- Certain aliens being processed for Green Cards
- As incorporated in the American Competitiveness in the Twenty-first Century Act of 2000

An employee who resigns or is fired must leave the country unless he or she has legal status in another classification. However, a story published on March 16, 2001, quoted INS spokesperson Eyleen Schmidt as saying that the INS would examine each case to determine how long a laid-off H-1B could remain to seek another job.

Canadian musicians and accompanying crews, who have an engagement within 50 miles of the U.S.-Canadian border may apply directly to a port of entry for admission in H-2 classification for up to 30 days. Application must be made to the appropriate regional Service Center if the engagement is more than 50 miles from the border or longer than 30 days. Certification by the Department of Labor is not required.

An INS interim rule effective July 1, 1999 eliminated the requirement for II-1B nonimmigrants and their dependent family members to obtain Advance Parole prior to traveling outside the U.S. while they have an Adjustment of Status pending.

Ref: 64 FR 29208

Step 7 - Revalidation/Extension or Change of Status

H-1B renewals, amendments, change of employer or additional jobs do not count against the H-1B annual quota.

An alien has 30 days of grace to depart the United States after the expiration of an initial H-1B. An I-129 renewal petition must be filed within ten days of the end of the first H-1B and the beneficiary must be in valid nonimmigrant status both when the petition is filed and on the date on which the requested change becomes effective. The alien is not permitted to work until the new petition is effective. The approval of a permanent Labor Certification, or the filing of a preference petition by an alien in H-2 or H-3 status shall be reason by itself to deny the alien's extension of stay.

Changes of status from F-1 and J-1 for H-1B applicants can be processed as long as the effective date of the H-1B falls within their lawful duration of status. Their status is extended if their H-1B is pending or until October 1 if the annual cap was reached. While their application is pending, they may remain in the U.S. but not work.

When it is not possible to bridge the gap between the end of the first status and the start of the new status for reasons beyond the applicant's control, like in 1998 and 1999 when the H-1B cap was exceeded before the end of the fiscal year, it may be possible to obtain B-2 visitor status. The BCIS says that in such circumstances, the pending H-1B application will not undermine eligibility for visitor status.

H-1 and H-2 candidates must first obtain Department of Labor approval before a BCIS petition may be filed. Original H-2A petitions now have a two-week grace period which eliminates the former need to file with the BCIS for such a short extension. Longer extension applications are made to the DOL.

DOL extensions are not normally permitted if the total work period including past periods and requested extension exceed 12 months or if a short term extension has been granted by the BCIS. Extensions for longer periods not to exceed three years may be granted by the DOL only in extraordinary circumstances.

Department of Labor clearance

Labor clearance applies to aliens in H-1 or H-2 status. If you are applying for H-3 or H-4 status, go directly to Application to the BCIS within the United States.

H-1B - Aliens in Specialty Occupations and as Fashion Models

As in the case of the initial petition, the employer must file for a Labor Condition Application (LCA) renewal with the regional office of the Department of Labor before an H-1B revalidation may be filed. The LCA renewal must be valid for the period of time requested on the BCIS petition to a maximum of three additional years or a total of six years. Nurses are limited to a total of five years.

Documentation and supporting evidence includes:

- *DOL form*
  - Form ETA 9035, Labor Condition Application

- *Employer's attestation to support request*
  - it has offered the prevailing wage for the type of work in the geographical area as proven by:
    - salary data from the state's Department of Labor, or
    - an independent wage analysis by the company, or
    - a relevant industry wage survey
  - employment of the H-1B will not adversely affect the working conditions of workers similarly employed in the area of intended employment
  - there is not a strike, lockout or work stoppage in the occupation in which the H-1B will be employed at the place of employment
  - a copy of the labor attestation will be provided to all H-1Bs affected
  - notice of filing has been provided to the bargaining agent, if any
  - if no bargaining agent, a notice has been posted for 10 consecutive working days in two locations, including the actual work site if other than the main location, to advise other employees that it is filing for a Labor Condition Application for a prospective H-1B employee
- *Employee's professional credentials*
  - Bachelor's degree in a narrowly defined subject area, or
  - an Associate degree plus three years of equivalent experience for each required year of schooling in a narrowly defined subject area may be sufficient

H-2A - Temporary Agricultural Service Workers

H-2B - Other Temporary Workers - U.S. Workers are Not Available

The employer must file Form ETA 750, Part A with the local office of the State Employment Service to request temporary Labor Certification.

The petition for an H-2A may be filed by the employer or the employer's agent or an association of the U.S. agriculture producers named as a joint employer on the Labor certification.

The State Employment Service will instruct the prospective employer on what steps must be taken (such as newspaper or trade magazine ads) to attract U.S. workers before aliens may be considered. If it is satisfied, the DOL will issue certification.

Application to the BCIS within the United States

Aliens in all classifications must apply to the BCIS regional Service Center having jurisdiction over their place of residence. To avoid going out of status, an application must be submitted before the grace period expires after graduation (60 days for F-1s and 30 days for J-1s). Applicants may remain in the United States during this waiting period but may not work until the H-1 is received.

Aliens who are not from a country participating in the Visa Waiver Program may submit an application for renewal between 45 days and four months prior to expiration, to the BCIS regional Service Center having jurisdiction over their place of residence.

Documentation and supporting evidence includes:

- *BCIS forms*
  - I-129, Petition for Nonimmigrant Worker
  - H Classification Supplement page
  - I-129, Petition for Nonimmigrant Worker Filing Fee Exemption (if claiming exempt organization status) (Version 12/18/00)
  - I-907, Request for Premium Processing, if requested
- *Fees*
  - $130 for I-129
  - $1,000 for H-1B supplementary fee (except exempt organizations)
  - $1,000 for I-907, if requested
- *Current and prior immigration status*
  - copy of I-94 Arrival/Departure Record
- *Prior DOL approval*
  - current copy of the Department Of Labor's:
    - certified Labor Condition Application ETA 9035 (H-1), or
    - Labor Certification ETA 750 (H-2A), or
    - blanket DOL team certification letter
    - required supporting documentation
- *Employer's evidence to support request*
  - letter from petitioner explaining the reasons for the extension
  - proof of financial support
  - evidence of nonprofit status if claiming supplementary fee exemption

The BCIS issues an I-797, Notice of Approval which serves as evidence of the extension or change of status.

Dependents

Family members should file Form I-539 for an extension with the BCIS regional Service Center having jurisdiction over their state.

An H-4 spouse may request permission to convert from H-4 to H-1 and obtain permission to work after obtaining a job offer, and an LCA.

Documentation and supporting evidence includes:

- *BCIS form*
  - I-539, Application to Extend/Change Nonimmigrant Status
- *Fee*
  - $140
- *Prior BCIS approval*
  - original Form I-797 (spouse's H-1B working permit)
- *Passports and photographs*
  - passport valid for at least six months beyond intended stay
  - passport photographs
- *Principal alien's evidence of support*
  - letter from H-1 spouse supporting the application

- notarized copy of first five pages of H-1 spouse's passport (including the current visa
- *Employer's evidence of support*
  - letter confirming function, amount and source of salary and period of employment of principal alien
- *Proof of financial support or solvency*
  - bank statement with proof of funds to support H-4 spouse
  - recent paychecks
- *Civil documents*
  - notarized copy of marriage certificate and translation, if not in English
  - wedding photographs and a wedding invitation

Dependents of H aliens may study on a full or part-time basis in the U.S.

Visa Revalidation by the Department of State (DOS)

After the BCIS has extended your stay, your visa may need to be renewed before attempting to reenter the United States after business or personal travel abroad. Depending on how U.S. citizens are treated in your home country in similar circumstances, your original visa may have been issued with restrictions on the number of entries into the United States and its period of validity, perhaps six months or a year.

Application for visa renewal may be made at a U.S. Embassy or Consulate in your home country. Although Canadians do not need visas, others may seek revalidations at a U.S. Consulate in Mexico or Canada by calling (900) 443-3131 for an appointment.

As a service to aliens in a few classifications such as H, the Department of State renews visas by mail in the U.S., if time permits. Full information on revalidations is available from the State Department web site at www.travel.state.gov/revals.html. You may download the required Form DS-156 there.

It is not possible to obtain expedited processing or status reports. If you do not have time to get your visa renewal in the U.S., you should apply in person to the consular office of the country of destination.

Documentation and supporting evidence includes:

- *DOS form*
  - DS-156, Nonimmigrant Visa Application
- *Fees*
  - $100 for non-refundable Machine-Readable Visa (MRV)
  - visa reciprocity equating to fees charged in similar circumstances in alien's home country
- *Passport and photograph*
  - passport valid for at least six months beyond intended stay
  - 50 mm (2") square photograph facing camera directly without head covering (check for religious exceptions) against a light background
- *Current and prior immigration status*
  - original current I-94 (no copies)

- copy of I-171C (H's or L's) or I-797 Petition Approval Notice
- *Employer's supporting documentation*
  - detailed letter identifying:
    - the employee
    - his or her position
    - travel itinerary

When a fee is charged for visa reciprocity, include two certified checks or money orders, one for the visa application and one for the reciprocity charge. Personal checks cannot be accepted.

Applications sent through the U.S. Postal Service should be mailed in a padded envelope with a stamped padded envelope enclosed for return mailing. An airbill is required for return by courier. Processing may take from six to eight weeks.

Completed applications may be sent by mail to:

> U.S. Department of State/Visa
> P.O. Box 952099
> St. Louis, MO 63195-2099

Completed applications may also be sent by courier to:

> U.S. Department of State/Visa (Box 2099)
> 1005 Convention Plaza
> St. Louis, MO 63101-1200

Recorded information may be obtained by calling (202) 663-1213. It is possible to speak with an officer Monday to Friday. The fax number is (202) 663-1608.

Step 8 - Retaining H Status

H-1 Visa Holders must:
- Obtain another H-1 visa to work at a second full or part-time job
- Obtain a new H-1 visa if changing employers (no stamp needed)

H-1 Visa Holders may not:
- Establish a company that sponsors themselves
- Work as a contractor or on a free-lance basis
- Sponsor parents
- Always get their I-94 back when the BCIS approves a petition
- Be placed on absence without pay
- Remain in the United States for more than 30 days after termination of employment if they have no other legal status
- Reenter the U.S. as an H-1B for a year after six years in H-1B status

The Employer should:

- File an explanatory letter when the employee is promoted, provided that the jobs are similar (legal counsel may again be advisable)
- File an explanatory letter with the BCIS when the company changes ownership if there is no change in the employee's status and the successor company undertakes all rights, liabilities, assets and privileges of the previous owner (legal counsel may be advisable)

An INS interim rule, effective July 1, 1999 has eliminated the requirement for H-1B nonimmigrants and their dependent family members to obtain Advance Parole prior to traveling outside the United States while they have an Adjustment of Status pending.

L

Intra-Company Transferee

Lstatus is designed to facilitate the temporary intra-company transfer to the United States of the management, executive and specialized skills of foreign nationals. It also allows a spouse and unmarried children under the age of 21 to accompany the transferee.

The classifications include:

- L-1 Intra-company transferee
  - This status permits the temporary employment of executive, managerial and specialized personnel continuing their employment with an international firm or corporation
    - L-1A - Manager/executive "managing an essential function"
    - L-1B - Aliens with specialized knowledge
- L-2 Spouse and children of L-1 alien
                        Ref: 9 FAM 41.12; INS ER 806 3-8-94

To be eligible, a foreign national must:

- Have been employed abroad by an international company for at least one continuous year within the three years immediately prior to the date of the application for admission
- Be seeking temporary admission to be employed by a parent/branch/ affiliate/subsidiary of that foreign employer
- Be employed in a managerial or executive capacity, or in a position requiring specialized knowledge

                        Ref: INA 101(a)(15)(L)

Although it was originally targeted toward large U.S. multi-national corporations, the L-1 allows the entry of executives or managers of foreign companies with as few as four full-time employees abroad. Visas are valid for up to seven years and allow the alien to work for a newly formed U.S. branch office of the foreign company. Those corporate transferee visas do not require an initial U.S. investment, other than incorporating the U.S. subsidiary, and arranging adequate office space.

While this classification is open to qualified aliens world-wide, it is also specifically identified as available to Canadians and Mexicans under the terms of NAFTA.   *Ref: DOS Publication 10074, August 1995; NAFTA Annex 1603*

The approval of a permanent Labor Certification or the filing of a preference petition shall not be the basis for denying an L petition, a request to extend an L petition or the alien's application for admission, Adjustment of Status or extension of stay. The alien may legitimately come to the United States as a nonimmigrant under the L classification and depart voluntarily at the end of his or her authorized stay, and at the same time, lawfully have the dual intent of seeking permanent U.S. residency.

It may be possible for multi-national business executives or manager and executive Priority Worker Transferees to adjust their status to immigrant after the U.S. company has operated for at least one year and the importance of their role can be demonstrated.

Admission Process

Step 1 - Filing the Blanket Petition

A blanket petition simplifies the process of filing for a number of L-1 workers in the future. It must be filed with the appropriate BCIS regional Service Center by a multinational corporation which has had a U.S. office for one year or more and meets other financial and organizational requirements.

This process is available for L-1A Managers and Executives who will be managing an essential function.

This process is also available for L-1B specialized knowledge professionals who:
- Will be employed in positions requiring the theoretical and practical application of a body of highly specialized knowledge
- Will fully perform the occupation, and
- Require completion of a specific course of education culminating in a baccalaureate degree in a specific occupational specialty

After receiving approval of a blanket petition, the employer may file for individual employees to enter as an L-1A manager/executive or L-1B specialized knowledge professional under the blanket petition.

Step 2 - Initial Petition

Option 1 - Clearing the BCIS in the United States - Non-NAFTA applicants

Existing U.S. Offices

The U.S. subsidiary of the alien's company must file an application on Form I-129 with the appropriate BCIS regional Service Center for a determination of whether the alien is eligible for the L classification and the petitioner is a qualifying organization. This includes proof of the existence of a subsidiary in the country where the alien currently lives.

Documentation and supporting evidence includes:

- *BCIS forms*
  - I-129, Petition for a Nonimmigrant Worker
  - L Classification Supplement page
  - I-907, Request for Premium Processing Service, if requested
- *Fees*
  - $130 for I-129
  - $1,000 for I-907, if requested
- *Employee's evidence to support request*
  - proof of professional job-related credentials, degrees and/or certification
  - six months of continuous employment abroad within the three years preceding petition filing, if blanket petition is filed, one year otherwise
  - the prior year of employment abroad was in a position that was managerial, executive, or involved specialized knowledge
  - prior education, training, and employment qualifies the alien to perform the intended services in the United States
- *Employer's evidence to support request*
  - the employing organization is qualified as defined in 8 CFR 214.2(1)(1)(ii)(G)
  - extensive tax documents to confirm ownership and control
  - extensive job description
  - the alien will be employed in an executive, managerial, or specialized knowledge capacity

If entering as a specialized-knowledge professional:

- A copy of a U.S. degree or foreign equivalent, or
- Evidence establishing that the beneficiary's education and experience is the equivalent of a U.S. degree

If filing under a blanket petition, the application must be accompanied by:

- A copy of the approval notice of the blanket petition
- A letter from the alien's employer detailing:
  - dates of employment
  - job duties
  - qualifications
  - previous three years salary

Form I-129S is filed by employers with an approved blanket waiver to classify employees outside the U.S. as executives, managers or specialized-knowledge professionals.

If the alien worker is living abroad, the petition should be filed with a U.S. consular office if a visa is required. If not required, filing is with the BCIS. Use Form I-129 for the change of status or extension of stay of an employee who is in the U.S.

New U.S. Offices

If a beneficiary is coming to be employed as an executive or manager in a new U.S. office, the petitioner shall submit evidence that:

- Sufficient physical premises exist
- The beneficiary meets the one continuous year in the last three-year requirement
- The beneficiary will be employed in an executive or managerial authority over the new operation
- Within one year the operation will support an executive or managerial position with the following evidence:
  - the scope, structure and goals of the entity
  - the size of the U.S. investment and the ability to remunerate the beneficiary and commence doing business in the United States
  - organizational structure of the foreign entity

If the beneficiary is coming to be employed in a specialized knowledge capacity in a new office in the United States, the petitioner shall submit evidence that:

- Sufficient physical premises exist
- The business entity in the United States is or will be a qualifying organization
- The petitioner has the financial ability to remunerate the beneficiary and to commence doing business in the United States

Option 2 - Clearing the Department of State (DOS) Abroad - Non-NAFTA Applicants

The consular officer must be satisfied that the alien qualifies under INA 101(a)(15)(L).   *Ref: 9 FAM 41.54*

Visa interviews are necessary and must be scheduled by calling the 900 toll appointment number. It may take up to three weeks to get an appointment.

All applicants including minor children must appear for the interview. Although interviews will be in English, outside translators may be used in certain situations.

Depending on the consulate, the visa may be ready for pickup the working day following the interview.

Documentation and supporting evidence includes:

- *DOS form*
  - DS-156, Nonimmigrant Visa Application
- *Fees*
  - $100 non-refundable Machine-Readable Visas (MRV) fee collected at posts which issue MRVs (NAFTA nationals from Canada and Mexico are exempt from this fee)

- visa reciprocity fee equating to fees charged in similar circumstances in alien's home country
- *Passport and photograph*
  - passport valid for at least six months beyond intended stay
  - 50 mm (2") square photograph facing camera directly without head covering (check for religious exceptions) against a light background
- *Current immigration status*
  - evidence of immigration status in the country in which the Consulate is located
- *Prior immigration status*
  - passports, visas, I-20, I-797, I-94, Employment Authorization Document
- *Prior BCIS approvals*
  - the original I-797 Notice of Approval petition and a copy of either:
    - the I-129 that was filed on their behalf with the BCIS, or
    - the approved petition, I-129 on file at the consulate
- *Employee's evidence to support request*
  - evidence of previous employment with the subsidiary company in the home country or abroad
- *Employer's evidence to support request*
  - proof that the employer abroad still exists

Ref: DOS Calgary Appointment Letter

Step 3 - Clearing the BCBP at a U.S. Port of Entry

An alien may be admitted for full-time or part-time work and paid through either the overseas parent or the U.S. subsidiary. It may be useful to check which method of payment is more beneficial for tax purposes.

L-2 visas may be obtained for the spouse and minor children allowing them to enter the U.S. with the principal alien. They may attend school and/or participate in voluntary organizations. Under pending legislation, a spouse may accept employment.

An L-1 petition may be approved initially for managers and executives for up to three years, with the possibility of two-year extensions to a total of seven years. L-2 employees with specialized knowledge may be approved for three years and extended to a total of five years.

In the case of a new enterprise in the United States, the L-1 will be limited to one year initially with extensions depending on whether the new business is successful.

Option 1 - Non-NAFTA

Documentation and supporting evidence includes:

- *Passport*
  - passport valid for at least six months beyond intended stay

- *Prior BCIS and DOS approvals*
  - I-129, Petition for a Nonimmigrant Worker
  - I-797, BCIS Notice of Approval
  - DOS Machine-Readable Visa (MRV) in passport
- *Evidence to support request*
  - copies of employer's evidence to DOS
  - copies of employee's evidence to DOS
- *Evidence that U.S. stay is temporary (intent to depart)*
  - no intention to abandon residence abroad

Option 2 - NAFTA Only

Under the terms of NAFTA, citizens of Canada and Mexico may apply directly at a U.S. port of entry without obtaining employment authorization and without numerical restriction provided that they comply with other immigration measures applicable to temporary entry.   *Ref: NAFTA Annex 1603*

Documentation and supporting evidence includes:

- *BCIS form*
  - I-129, Certificate of Eligibility
- *Fee*
  - $130

The BCBP Immigration Inspector will:

- Issue an I-94, Arrival/Departure Record
- Stamp passport
- Send the application to the appropriate BCIS regional Service Center

The Service Center will:

- Assign a number
- Issue an I-797

The $100 MRV charge per applicant is waived for Canadians and Mexicans in accordance with the NAFTA agreement.

Dependents

The alien spouse may obtain employment authorization as a result of a bill to provide for work authorization for nonimmigrant spouses of intracompany transferees which was signed into law on January 16, 2002.   *Ref: Pub. L. 107-125*

Step 4 - Revalidation/Extension or Change of Status

Application to the BCIS within the United States

Any alien legally in status seeking a change of status to L-1 must apply before their grace period expires to avoid going out of status. They may remain in the United States during this waiting period but may not work until their L-1 is received.

Aliens who are not from a country participating in the Visa Waiver Program may submit an application for L-1A and L-1B renewal between 45 days and four months to the BCIS regional Service Center having jurisdiction over their place of residence.

Applications are to be filed by mail at the BCIS regional Service Center having jurisdiction over their place of residence.

Documentation and supporting evidence for the principal alien includes:

- *BCIS form*
  - I-129, Petition for Nonimmigrant Worker
  - L Classification Supplement page
  - I-907, Request for Premium Processing, if requested
- *Fees*
  - $130 for I-129
  - $1,000 for I-907, if requested
- *Current and prior immigration status*
  - copy of I-94 Arrival/Departure Record
- *Employer's evidence to support request*
  - letter explaining the reasons for the extension
- *Proof of financial support or solvency*
  - financial proof

Dependents of L aliens must file for their extension or change of status with the BCIS regional Service Center having jurisdiction over their state. They may study on a full or part-time basis in the United States.

Documentation and supporting evidence for dependents includes:

- *BCIS form*
  - I-539, Application to Extend/Change Nonimmigrant Status
- *Fee*
  - $140

The BCIS issues an I-797, Notice of Approval which serves as evidence of the extension or change of status.

Visa Revalidation by the Department of State (DOS)

After the BCIS has extended your stay, your visa may need to be renewed before attempting to reenter the United States after travel abroad for business or pleasure. Depending on how U.S. citizens are treated in your home country in similar circumstances, your original visa may have been issued with restrictions on the number of entries into the United States and its period of validity, perhaps six months or a year.

Application for visa renewal may be made at a U.S. Embassy or Consulate in your home country. Revalidations may also be made at a U.S. Consulate in Mexico or Canada by calling (900) 443-3131 for an appointment.

It is not possible to obtain expedited processing or status reports. If you do not have time to get your visa renewal in the U.S., you should apply in person to the consular office of the country of destination.

As a service to aliens in a few classifications such as L, the Department of State renews visas by mail in the U.S., if time permits. Full information on revalidations is available from the State Department web site at www.travel.state.gov/revals.html. You may download the required Form DS-156 there.

Documentation and supporting evidence includes:

- *DOS form*
    - DS-156, Nonimmigrant Visa Application
- *Fees*
    - $100 for non-refundable Machine-Readable Visa (MRV)
    - visa reciprocity equating to fees charged in similar circumstances in alien's home country
- *Passport and photograph*
    - passport valid for at least six months beyond intended stay
    - 50 mm (2") square photograph facing camera directly without head covering (check for religious exceptions) against a light background
- *Current and prior immigration status*
    - original current I-94 (no copies)
    - copy of I-171C (H's or L's) or I-797 Petition Approval Notice
- *Employer's supporting documentation*
    - detailed letter identifying:
        - the employee
        - his or her position
        - travel itinerary

When a fee is charged for visa reciprocity, include two certified checks or money orders, one for the visa application and one for the reciprocity charge. Personal checks cannot be accepted.

Applications sent through the U.S. Postal Service should be mailed in a padded envelope with a stamped padded envelope enclosed for return mailing. If return by courier is requested, an air bill is required. Processing may take six to eight weeks. You may call (202) 663-1213 for more information.

Completed applications may be sent by mail to:

> U.S. Department of State/Visa
> P.O. Box 952099
> St. Louis, MO 63195-2099

Completed applications may also be sent by courier to:

> U.S. Department of State/Visa (Box 2099)
> 1005 Convention Plaza
> St. Louis, MO 63101-1200

Step 5 - Retaining L Status

You may remain in the U.S. after the expiration date of the original visa until the end of your 30 day grace period but may not work until a renewal is received.

The total period of a temporary stay for an executive or manager is seven years and, for specialized knowledge personnel, the maximum stay is five years including all time spent in H status.

After these limits are reached, the alien must reside and be physically present outside the United States for at least one year before being readmitted in H or L status. However, entry in another visa status such as F-1 is permitted.

Dependents of L aliens may study on a full or part-time basis in the U.S.

Loss of Status

An alien whose original visa expires before an application for renewal is filed, becomes out of status and must file for renewal outside the country within 120 days of expiration.

Aliens who lose their L-1 status also lose the right to work and remain in the United States. However, you may remain in the U.S. after the expiration date of the original visa until the end of your grace period but may not work until the renewal is received.

If a petition for a different visa is denied while you still are working with a valid L-1, the denial does not affect any extension petition for the current L-1, if it can still be extended.

If either the U.S. or foreign side of the company ceases to operate, the L-1 visa automatically becomes void and the work permit terminated.

L-1 nonimmigrants and their dependent family members no longer risk loss of status when they travel abroad while they have an Adjustment of Status pending. An INS interim rule effective July 1, 1999 eliminated the requirement to obtain Advance Parole.

TN

Treaty NAFTA Professional

TN status is reserved for business professional citizens of Canada and Mexico to enter the United States temporarily under the terms of the North American Free Trade Agreement (NAFTA) to practice one of the professions listed in the NAFTA Agreement in Appendix 1603.D.1 of Chapter 16.

Legal residents who are not citizens of Canada and Mexico and physicians working in clinical or primary care do not qualify.   *Ref: INS ER 806 3-8-94*

NAFTA classifications include:

- B-1   - Visitor for Business
- E-1/E-2 - Treaty Trader or Investor
- L-1   - Intracompany Transferee
- TN   - Business Professional

TN sub-categories include:

- TN   - Treaty NAFTA - Professional
- TN-1   - Canadian citizen
- TN-2   - Mexican citizen
- TD   - Trade Dependent - Spouse or minor child of NAFTA Professional
                        Ref: INA 214(e)(2); 9 FAM 41.12; NAFTA Annex 1603

A TD spouse and children under 21 may attend school full or part time without a separate student visa. The TD spouse is not permitted to work but may apply for a temporary working visa, study or do volunteer work or, if living in a border community, commute to work in Canada or Mexico.

While TNs are issued a year at a time, they may be renewed indefinitely. The only advantage in converting to H-1 status with its absolute limits is that you may have a Green Card application pending at the same time as you hold temporary status. Dual intent is only permitted in H-1, L and V status, not TN.

A job may be full-time or part-time.

Canada and Mexico permit the entry of U.S. workers on the same basis as Canadian and Mexican workers entering the U.S. under the terms of NAFTA and Canadians do not require Labor Certification.

However, Section D of Annex 1603 of NAFTA permits the United States to establish an annual numerical limit of 5,500 Mexican Trade Professionals for a transition period of up to 10 years.

The $100 Machine-Readable Visa (MRV) fee is waived in this classification.

Admission Process

Step 1 - Qualifying - List of NAFTA Professions

NAFTA Professionals

Profession	Minimum Education Requirements And Alternative Credentials
General	
Accountant	Baccalaureate or Licenciatura Degree; or C.P.A., C.A., C.G.A. or C.M.A.
Architect	Baccalaureate or Licenciatura Degree; or state/provincial license
Computer Systems Analyst	Baccalaureate or Licenciatura Degree; or Post-Secondary Diploma or Post-Secondary Certificate, and three years experience
Disaster Relief Insurance Claims Adjuster (claims adjuster employed by an insurance company located in the territory of a Party, or an independent claims adjuster)	Baccalaureate or Licenciatura Degree, and successful completion of training in the appropriate areas of insurance adjustment pertaining to disaster relief claims; or three years experience in claims adjustment and successful completion of training in the appropriate areas of insurance adjustment pertaining to disaster relief claims
Economist	Baccalaureate or Licenciatura Degree
Engineer	Baccalaureate or Licenciatura Degree; or state/provincial license
Forester	Baccalaureate or Licenciatura Degree; or state/provincial license
Graphic Designer	Baccalaureate or Licenciatura Degree; or Post-Secondary Diploma or Post-Secondary Certificate, and three years experience

Hotel Manager	Baccalaureate or Licenciatura Degree in hotel/restaurant management; or Post-Secondary Diploma or Post-Secondary Certificate in hotel/restaurant management and three years experience in hotel/restaurant management
Industrial Designer	Baccalaureate or Licenciatura Degree; or Post-Secondary Diploma or Post-Secondary Certificate, and three years experience Interior Designer Baccalaureate or Licenciatura Degree; or Post-Secondary Diploma or Post-Secondary Certificate, and three years experience
Land Surveyor	Baccalaureate or Licenciatura Degree; or state/provincial/Federal license
Landscape Architect	Baccalaureate or Licenciatura Degree
Lawyer (including Notary in the Province of Quebec)	LL.B., J.D. , LL.L., B.C.L. or Licenciatura Degree (five years); or membership in a state/provincial bar
Librarian	M.L.S. or B.L.S. (for which another Baccalaureate or Licenciatura Degree was a prerequisite)
Management Consultant	Baccalaureate or Licenciatura Degree; or equivalent professional experience as established by statement or professional credential attesting to five years experience as a management consultant, or five years experience in a field of specialty related to the consulting agreement
Mathematician (including statistician)	Baccalaureate or Licenciatura Degree
Range Manager/ Range Conservationalist	Baccalaureate or Licenciatura Degree
Research Assistant (working in a post-secondary educational institution)	Baccalaureate or Licenciatura Degree
Scientific Technician/ Technologist	Possession of (a) theoretical knowledge of any of the following disciplines: agricultural sciences, astronomy, biology, chemistry, engineering, forestry, geology, geophysics, meteorology or physics; and (b) the ability to solve practical problems in any of those disciplines, or the ability to apply principles of any of those disciplines to basic or applied research
Social Worker	Baccalaureate or Licenciatura Degree
Sylviculturist (including Forestry Specialist)	Baccalaureate or Licenciatura Degree

Technical Publications Writer	Baccalaureate or Licenciatura Degree; or Post-Secondary Diploma or Post-Secondary Certificate, and three years experience
Urban Planner (including Geographer)	Baccalaureate or Licenciatura Degree
Vocational Counselor	Baccalaureate or Licenciatura Degree

Medical/Allied Professional

Dentist	D.D.S., D.M.D., Doctor en Odontologia or Doctor en Cirugia Dental; or state/provincial license
Dietitian	Baccalaureate or Licenciatura Degree; or state/provincial license
Medical Laboratory Technologist (Canada)/ Medical Technologist (Mexico and the United States)	Baccalaureate or Licenciatura Degree; or Post-Secondary Diploma or Post-Secondary Certificate, and three years experience
Nutritionist	Baccalaureate or Licenciatura Degree
Occupational Therapist	Baccalaureate or Licenciatura Degree; or state/provincial license
Pharmacist	Baccalaureate or Licenciatura Degree; or state/ provincial license
Physician (teaching or research only)	M.D. or Doctor en Medicina; or state/provincial license
Physiotherapist/ Physical Therapist	Baccalaureate or Licenciatura Degree; or state/provincial license
Psychologist	State/provincial license; or Licenciatura Degree
Recreational Therapist	Baccalaureate or Licenciatura Degree
Registered Nurse	State/provincial license; or Licenciatura Degree
Veterinarian	D.V.M., D.M.V. or Doctor en Veterinaria; or state/provincial license

Scientist

Agriculturist (including Agronomist)	Baccalaureate or Licenciatura Degree
Animal Breeder	Baccalaureate or Licenciatura Degree
Animal Scientist	Baccalaureate or Licenciatura Degree
Apiculturist	Baccalaureate or Licenciatura Degree

Astronomer	Baccalaureate or Licenciatura Degree
Biochemist	Baccalaureate or Licenciatura Degree
Biologist	Baccalaureate or Licenciatura Degree
Chemist	Baccalaureate or Licenciatura Degree
Dairy Scientist	Baccalaureate or Licenciatura Degree
Entomologist	Baccalaureate or Licenciatura Degree
Epidemiologist	Baccalaureate or Licenciatura Degree
Geneticist	Baccalaureate or Licenciatura Degree
Geologist	Baccalaureate or Licenciatura Degree
Geochemist	Baccalaureate or Licenciatura Degree
Geophysicist (including Oceanographer in Mexico and the United States)	Baccalaureate or Licenciatura Degree
Horticulturist	Baccalaureate or Licenciatura Degree
Meteorologist	Baccalaureate or Licenciatura Degree
Pharmacologist	Baccalaureate or Licenciatura Degree
Physicist (including Oceanographer in Canada)	Baccalaureate or Licenciatura Degree
Plant Breeder	Baccalaureate or Licenciatura Degree
Poultry Scientist	Baccalaureate or Licenciatura Degree
Soil Scientist	Baccalaureate or Licenciatura Degree
Zoologist	Baccalaureate or Licenciatura Degree

Teacher

College	Baccalaureate or Licenciatura Degree
Seminary	Baccalaureate or Licenciatura Degree
University	Baccalaureate or Licenciatura Degree

Ref: NAFTA Appendix 1603.D.1

Actuary and Plant Pathologist are being considered for inclusion. Also, as noted above, not all NAFTA professions require at least a bachelor's degree. Some require as little as two years of post-secondary education and work experience.

Step 2 - Clearing The Department of Labor - Mexicans Only

NAFTA includes a provision that permits a country to require a business person seeking temporary entry to obtain a visa or its equivalent prior to entry. This provision applies to Mexican nationals.   *Ref: NAFTA Annex 1603*

The employer must submit evidence that a Form ETA 9035 has been filed with the Department of Labor for all NAFTA Appendix 1603.D.1 professionals.

Step 3 - *Clearing the BCIS Before Entry - Mexicans Only*

After clearing the Department of Labor, Mexican citizens applying for their initial TN classification must file an application with the Director of the Northern Service Center between 45 days and four months before the proposed employment will begin.

Documentation and supporting evidence includes:

- *BCIS forms*
    - I-129, Petition for a Nonimmigrant Worker
    - I-907, Request for Premium Processing Service, if requested
- *Fees*
    - $130 for I-129
    - $1,000 for I-907, if requested
- *Passport or proof of citizenship*
    - proof of Mexican citizenship
- *Employer's evidence to support request*
    - list of job duties
    - evidence that job applicant meets the educational/ experience requirements
- *Employee's evidence to support request*
    - evidence to satisfy all licensure requirements
    - certification of labor condition application or labor attestation
- *Additional evidence*
    - confirmation that the job is on the NAFTA list
- *Evidence that U.S. stay is temporary*
    - evidence to confirm a foreign residence with no intent to abandon

Under NAFTA Appendix 1603.D.4, the U.S. shall approve as many as 5,500 initial petitions of business persons of Mexico. BCIS issues an I-797, Notice of Approval.

Step 4 - *Clearing the Department of State Abroad - Mexicans Only*

The consular officer need an approved BCIS petition according classification as a NAFTA Professional and be satisfied that the alien is so classifiable and that the proposed stay is temporary and will depart.   *Ref: 9 FAM 41.59*

Step 5 - *Clearing the BCBP at a U.S. Port of Entry*

Canadians are not required to file Form I-129. They may make their initial application at a U.S. port of entry.

The TN is applied for at a Class A port of entry or at a U.S. airport handling foreign traffic or at a foreign airport which handles preflight and preclearance formalities. Immigration lawyers sometimes are retained to assist their TN clients on entry.

The Free Trade Officer has the right to ask such questions or take action to verify the applicant's records. As in other NAFTA classifications and in the spirit of the Department of Labor clearance proceedings, employment authorization may be refused to an alien whose entry might adversely affect:

- Settlement of any labor dispute that is in progress at the employment site
- Employment of any person who is involved in the dispute

If TN status is refused, it is the responsibility of the BCIS to inform the alien and his or her government of the reasons for refusal.

Documentation and supporting evidence includes:

- *BCIS forms*
  - no TN application form
  - I-94 - principal alien and dependents
- *Fees*
  - $50 for entry (principal alien only)
  - $6 for I-94 for principal alien and each dependent
- *Passport*
  - passport valid for at least six months beyond intended stay, or
  - proof of citizenship
- *Prior BCIS and DOS approvals*
  - I-797, Notice of Approval
  - DOS Machine-Readable Visa (MRV) in passport, if required
  - I-94, if previously held
- *Professional credentials*
  - Professional diploma and license, as applicable
  - credentials evaluation
- *Employee's evidence to support request*
  - proof that the applicant meets the education and experience requirements of the job category
  - (transcript may be required)
- *Employer's evidence to support request*
  - signed employment contract with prospective employer including:
    - job description which demonstrates that the job falls within a NAFTA classification
    - salary
    - temporary status
    - time frame - one-year limit
- *Proof of financial support or solvency*
  - financial proof

A dependent spouse who is not a Mexican or Canadian citizen enters as a TD but follows the process as though entering as an H-4. This requires:

- A nonimmigrant visa
- Evidence of the TN's application approval
- I-94, Arrival/Departure Record with validity date

Step 6 - Revalidation/Extension or Change of Status

Application to the BCIS within the United States

Canadian and Mexican citizens may file to renew their TN status by mail with the Director of the BCIS Nebraska Service Center between 45 days and four months before the extension of stay is required. TNs may also be renewed at the border.

Documentation and supporting evidence for principal alien includes:

- *BCIS forms*
  - I-129, Petition for a Nonimmigrant Worker
  - I-907, Request for Premium Processing, if requested
- *Fees*
  - $130 for I-129
  - $1,000 for I-907, if requested

A **dependent** spouse and minor children who are physically present in the United States and requesting an extension of stay or a change of nonimmigrant classification to TD should file Form I-539 with Director of Northern Service Center.

Documentation and supporting evidence for dependents requesting an extension or change to TD status includes:

- *BCIS form*
  - I-539, Application to Extend/Change Nonimmigrant Status
- *Fee*
  - $140 for each dependent
- *Current and prior immigration status*
  - I-129 of the TN Professional

If an alien is not applying for an extension of stay as a TD at the same time that the TN professional is applying, or is applying for a change of nonimigrant status to TD after the TN nonimmigrant obtains status, the alien must present a copy of the TN's Form I-94, Nonimmigrant Arrival/Departure Record, to establish that the TN is maintaining valid nonimmigrant status.

The BCIS issues an I-797, Notice of Approval which serves as evidence of change of status.

When duties are amended, the alien may apply for another TN at the border or list the new duties in an extension application by mail.

Chapter 6

Extraordinary/Internationally-Recognized Persons

There are two classifications which closely parallel permanent resident criteria.

O and P classifications are reserved for persons who are nationally or internationally recognized in their field.

O status is available to "extraordinary" applicants. To qualify they must have:
- Extraordinary ability in the fields of sciences, arts, education, business or athletics, or
- Extraordinary achievement in the motion picture or television industry

P status is available to "outstanding" applicants. To qualify, they must be:
- Internationally-recognized athletes and entertainers
- Seen as "outstanding" for a "sustained and substantial period of time"

O

Aliens of Extraordinary Ability
in the Sciences, Arts, Education, Business, Athletics

T his new classification was created in the Immigration and Nationality Act of 1990 and moved from H-1B to enable an employer to petition to classify an alien as a nonimmigrant worker who may enter the United States temporarily to perform services or labor as an O-1.

This classification is reserved for "those who have extraordinary ability in the sciences, arts, education, business and athletics as demonstrated by sustained national or international acclaim, whose entry the Secretary of Homeland Security believes will substantially benefit the United States.

This classification can also include those accompanying and assisting the alien as well as a spouse and unmarried children under the age of 21."

Ref: 9 FAM 41.12; INS ER 806 3-8-94

Sub-categories are:
- O-1 - Aliens with extraordinary ability in sciences, arts, education, business or athletics
- O-2 - Accompanying alien to assist alien in athletic or artistic performance
- O-3 - Spouse or child of O-1 or O-2   *Ref: INA 101(a)(15)(O)(i),(ii),(iii)*

Applicants in the fields of sciences, arts, education, business or athletics must be able to prove their "extraordinary ability" by:
- Meeting very high standards
- Having a level of expertise attained by a person who is one of a small percentage and who has risen to the top of their field
- Having extensive documentation of sustained national or international acclaim

Applicants in motion pictures and television must be able to prove a demonstrated record of "extraordinary achievement" by demonstrating distinction.

Accompanying aliens may be admitted in O-2 status to assist in the artistic or athletic performance of the O-1 alien. However, if their entry is to support a motion picture or television alien, they must:

- Have the necessary skills and experience with the alien, and
- Have a longstanding or pre-existing relationship with the alien
- Be performing a role that is essential to the successful completion of the production, if it is taking place both inside and outside the United States

As in most other categories, the INA requires that aliens admitted in O status maintain a foreign residence to which they intend to return.

Admission Process

Step 1 - Establishing Eligibility

Aliens in the Sciences, Arts, Education, Business or Athletics

Aliens with extraordinary ability in the sciences, arts, education, business, or athletics require:

- A consultation from a labor organization or peer group representing their area of occupational specialization containing:
- A description of their ability and achievements in the field
- A description of the duties to be performed
- A determination of whether the position requires the services of an O-1, alien of extraordinary ability

The standards for determining "Extraordinary Ability" are very detailed and include receipt of a major international award. Three of the following pieces of documented evidence are required:

- National or international prizes or awards
- Involvement in the field of outstanding achievement
- Major publication of material about the alien and his or her work
- Panel or judge of work of others in alien's specialty field
- Contribution of scholarly work or contributions in specialty field
- Authorship of professionally published scholarly articles
- Employment in organizations with distinctive reputations

Ref: Code of Federal Regulations

Aliens in the Motion Picture or Television Industries

Aliens of extraordinary achievement in the motion picture or television industries require:

- A consultation report from an appropriate union representing their occupational peers, and

- A consultation report from a management organization in their area of expertise containing:
  - a description of their ability and achievements
  - a description of the duties to be performed
- A determination of whether the position requires an O-1 alien of "extraordinary achievement or extraordinary ability in the arts" such as:
  - recipient or nominee for prestigious international awards such as an Emmy, Grammy or Directors Guild award
    OR
  - three of the following pieces of documented evidence:
    - performance as a lead in productions with a distinguished reputation
    - nationally or internationally published recognition
    - performance as a lead or in a starring role for organizations with a distinguished reputation
    - published record of major box office success, standing in the field, research, product development and occupational achievements
    - significant recognition for achievements from acknowledged leaders in the field
    - record of commanding a high salary in relation to others in the field, or
    - other comparable evidence

Step 2 - Clearing the BCIS in the United States - Initial Petition

A U.S. employer or foreign employer may file with the appropriate BCIS regional Service Center in the United States.

Documentation and supporting evidence includes:

- *BCIS forms*
  - I-129, Petition for a Nonimmigrant Worker
  - O and P Classifications Supplement page
  - I-907, Request for Premium Processing Service, if requested
- *Fees*
  - $130 for I-129
  - $1,000 for I-907, if requested
- *Prior BCIS approvals*
  - written consultation with a peer group
- *Employee's evidence to support request*
  - the alien has received a major, internationally recognized award, such as a Nobel Prize or copies of evidence of at least three of the following:
    - receipt of nationally or internationally recognized prizes or awards for excellence in the field of endeavor

- membership in associations in the field which require outstanding achievements as judged by recognized international experts
- published material in professional or major trade publications or newspapers about the alien and his work in the field
- participation on a panel or individually as a judge of the work of others in the field or an allied field
- original scientific or scholarly research contributions of major significance in the field
- authorship of scholarly articles in the field in professional journals or other major media, or
- evidence the alien commands a high salary or other high remuneration for services

- *Employer's evidence to support request*
  - copy of the contract with the alien or the terms of an oral agreement
  - copies of evidence of the services to be performed:
    - are a specific scientific or educational project, conference, convention, lecture, or exhibit sponsored by scientific or educational organizations or establishments, or
    - consist of a specific business project that requires an extraordinary executive, manager, or highly technical person due to the complexity of the project

The law requires that the BCIS consult with union and management groups in the motion picture and television industries prior to deciding on whether to issue a visa. The union or peer group response to the BCIS must be provided within 15 days. Only after it is received may the applicant file the formal visa application.

The petition may not be filed more than four months before the employment is to begin and should be filed at least 45 days before the employment will begin.

The BCIS reserves the right to request that the applicant provide more information or appear for an interview.

The BCIS issues an I-797, Notice of Approval which must be submitted to the DOS.

Step 3 - Clearing the Department of State (DOS) Abroad

After receiving notice of approval from the BCIS, applicants should normally apply at the U.S. Embassy or Consulate having jurisdiction over their place of permanent residence. Although visa applicants may apply at any U.S. consular office abroad, it may be more difficult to qualify for the visa outside the country of permanent residence.

Documentation and supporting evidence includes:
- *DOS form*
  - DS-156, Nonimmigrant Visa Application
- *Fees*
  - $100 for non-refundable Machine-Readable Visa (MRV)
  - visa reciprocity equating to fees charged in similar circumstances in alien's home country
- *Passport and photograph*
  - passport valid for at least six months beyond intended stay
  - 50 mm (2") square photograph facing camera directly without head covering (check for religious exceptions) against a light background
- *Prior BCIS approval*
  - I-797, Notice of Approval
- *Evidence that U.S. stay is temporary (intent to depart)*
  - no intention to abandon residence abroad

Issue of a visa does not guarantee entry to the United States. That decision rests with the BCBP Immigration Inspector at a port of entry.

Step 4 - Clearing the BCBP at a U.S. Port of Entry

Form I-129 may be submitted by mail or at some U.S. ports of entry when entering the country. As a mail application to a BCIS regional Service Center may take as much as two months, you should select an entry point which admits O applicants.

Documentation and supporting evidence includes:
- *BCIS form*
  - I-129, Petition for a Nonimmigrant Worker
- *Fee*
  - $130 (when applying at the border)
- *Prior DOS approval*
  - DOS Machine-Readable Visa (MRV) in passport

O-2 applicants must:
- Have a long-time professional relationship with the O-1 alien
- Skills which cannot be readily replaced, and
- Demonstrate that they have a foreign residence which they have no intention of abandoning

There is a three-year limit on the initial entry.

Step 5 - Revalidation/Extension or Change of Status

Application to the BCIS within the United States

A petition requesting an extension of stay or change to O status may be filed with the BCIS regional Service Center having jurisdiction over your location.

Documentation and supporting evidence by the principal alien includes:

- *BCIS forms*
  - I-129, Application to Extend/Change Nonimmigrant Status
  - O and P Classifications Supplement page
  - I-907, Request for Premium Processing, if requested
- *Fees*
  - $130 for I-129
  - $1,000 for I-907, if requested
- *Passport*
  - passport valid for at least six months beyond intended stay
- *Current and prior immigration status*
  - copy of I-94, Nonimmigrant Arrival/Departure Record
- *Employer's evidence to support request*
  - letter from the petitioner explaining the reasons for the extension

Where there has been a change in the circumstances of employment, you must also submit the evidence required for a new petition.

Dependents should file Form I-539 to apply for a change of status or extension of stay with the appropriate BCIS regional Service Center.

Documentation and supporting evidence for principal alien includes:

- *BCIS form*
  - I-539, Application to Extend/Change Nonimmigrant Status
  - O and P Classifications Supplement page
- *Fee*
  - $140

The BCIS issues an I-797, Notice of Approval which serves as evidence of an extension or change of status.

Visa Revalidation by the Department of State (DOS)

After BCIS has extended your stay, your visa may need to be renewed before attempting to reenter the United States after travel abroad for business or pleasure. Depending on how U.S. citizens are treated in your home country in similar circumstances, your original visa may have been issued with restrictions on the number of entries into the United States and its period of validity, perhaps six months or a year.

Application for visa renewal may be made at a U.S. Embassy or Consulate in your home country. Revalidations may also be made at a U.S. Consulate in Mexico or Canada by calling (900) 443-3131 for an appointment.

As it is not possible to obtain expedited processing or status reports, you should apply in person to the consular office of the country of destination if you do not have time to get your visa renewal in the U.S.

If time permits, and as a service to aliens in a few classifications such as O, the Department of State renews visas by mail in the U.S. Full information on revalidations is available from the State Department web site at www.travel.state.gov/revals.html. You may download the required Form DS-156 there.

Documentation and supporting evidence includes:

- *DOS form*
  - DS-156, Nonimmigrant Visa Application
- *Fees*
  - $100 for non-refundable Machine-Readable Visa (MRV)
  - visa reciprocity equating to fees charged in similar circumstances in alien's home country
- *Passport and photograph*
  - passport valid for at least six months beyond intended stay
  - 50 mm (2") square photograph facing camera directly without head covering (check for religious exceptions) against a light background
- *Current and prior immigration status*
  - original current I-94 (no copies)
  - copy of I-171C (H's or L's) or I-797 Petition Approval Notice
- *Employer's supporting documentation*
  - detailed letter identifying:
    - the employee and position
    - travel itinerary

When a fee is charged for visa reciprocity, include two certified checks or money orders for the visa application and the reciprocity charge. No personal checks.

Applications sent through the U.S. Postal Service should be mailed in a padded envelope with a stamped padded envelope enclosed for return mailing. If return by courier is requested, an air bill is required. Processing may take from six to eight weeks. Further recorded information may be obtained by calling (202) 663-1213.

Completed applications may be sent by mail to:

> U.S. Department of State/Visa
> P.O. Box 952099
> St. Louis, MO 63195-2099

Completed applications may also be sent by courier to:

> U.S. Department of State/Visa (Box 2099)
> 1005 Convention Plaza
> St. Louis, MO 63101-1200

P

Internationally-Recognized Athlete and Entertainer

This classification was created in the Immigration and Nationality Act of 1990 and moved from H-1B.

This classification is for the use of athletes and entertainers who have achieved international recognition. It allows for the temporary admission of entertainment groups, individual or team athletes and accompanying individuals to permit performance in a specific event.

This is reserved for "those recognized at the international level, entering under a reciprocal exchange program or entering in a culturally unique program. This classification can also include a spouse and unmarried children under the age of 21.
Ref: INS ER 806 3-8-94

Sub-categories are:
- P-1- Internationally recognized athlete or member of internationally recognized entertainment group
- P-2 - Artist or entertainer in a reciprocal exchange program
- P-3 - Artist or entertainer in a culturally unique program
- P-4 - Spouse or child of P-1, P-2 or P-3
Ref: INA 101(a)(15)(P)(I),(ii),(iii),(iv)

The P-1 classification is divided into three separate categories:
- Internationally-recognized individual athletes
- Internationally-recognized athletic teams
- Internationally-recognized entertainment groups

An annual ceiling of 25,000 visas is proposed for P-1 and P-3 visas.

Admission Process

Step 1 - Establishing Eligibility

Individual athletes must demonstrate "international recognition" by coming to the United States with an international reputation to participate in an event which also has a distinguished reputation.

A whole team to be admitted must show evidence that it has achieved international recognition in its sport.

A P-1 petition for an athlete requires:

- A tendered contract with a team in a U.S. league or in an individual sport based on international recognition in that sport, and
- Two of the following pieces of documented evidence:
  - previous participation in a major U.S. sports league
  - previous participation in international competition with a national team
  - previous participation in a U.S. intercollegiate competition
  - statement from league or governing body official detailing how the alien or his or her team is internationally recognized
  - statement from media or sports expert detailing how the alien or his or her team is internationally recognized
  - international ranking of the team or individual
  - significant honor or award in the sport

A P-1 petition for a group of entertainers requires:

- Evidence of performing together for at least one year
- A listing of all members and their date of joining the group
- Evidence of international standing such as nomination for awards or prizes, or by three of the following pieces of documented evidence of:
  - past and future performances in events with a distinguished reputation
  - international recognition and acclaim for outstanding achievement
  - past and future performances for organizations with a distinguished reputation
  - major critically acclaimed successes
  - significant recognition from organizations, critics, experts or government agencies
  - high salaries or remuneration

A P-1 classification may be accorded to an entertainment group who perform as a group but not to an individual to perform apart from his or her group. Except for circus members, 75 percent of the members must have been an integral part of the group for at least a year.

Exceptions may be made in cases where there was limited access to news media or special geographical considerations existed.

A P-2 classification may be accorded to individuals and groups of artists and entertainers participating in a temporary reciprocal exchange program between foreign and U.S.-based organizations.

A P-3 classification may be accorded to artists and entertainers who perform under a program that is culturally unique.

Step 2 - Clearing the BCIS in the United States - Initial Petition

Form I-129 is for an employer to petition for aliens to come to the United States temporarily to perform services or labor as a P-1, P-2.

For P-3 nonimmigrant workers, a petition is always required for both an initial visa or entry for new or concurrent employment, and any extension or change of status.

Documentation and supporting evidence includes:
- *BCIS forms*
  - I-129, Petition for a Nonimmigrant Worker
  - I-907, Request for Premium Processing Service, if requested
- *Fees*
  - $130 for I-129
  - $1,000 for I-907, if requested

A U.S. employer may file to classify an alien in a P-2 classification if:
- They are members of the same group (accompanying aliens must be filed for on a separate petition)
- They will accompany the same P-2 alien or group for the same period of time, in the same occupation, and in the same location(s)

P-2 alien coming temporarily to perform as an artist or entertainer, individually or as part of a group, under a reciprocal exchange program between an organization in the U.S. and an organization in another country

The petition must be filed by the sponsoring organization or employer in the United States with:
- Written consultation with an appropriate labor organization
- A copy of the formal reciprocal exchange agreement between the U.S. organization(s) sponsoring the aliens, and the organization(s) in a foreign country which will receive the U.S. artists or entertainers
- A statement from the sponsoring organization describing the reciprocal exchange, including the name of the receiving organization abroad, length of their stay, activities in which they will be engaged and the terms and conditions of their employment
- Copies of evidence the aliens and the U.S. artists or entertainers are experienced artists with comparable skills and that the terms and conditions of employment are similar

P-2 support personnel

Accompanying support personnel are highly skilled aliens coming temporarily as an essential and integral part of the competition or performance of a P-2, or because they perform support services that cannot be readily performed by a U.S. worker and which are essential to the successful performance or services by the P-2. The aliens must each also have significant prior work experience with the P-2 alien.

The petition must be filed in conjunction with the employment of a P-2 alien with:

- Written consultation with a labor organization in the skill in which the alien will be involved
- A statement describing the alien's prior and current essentiality, critical skills and experience with the P-2
- Statements or affidavits from persons with first hand knowledge that the alien has had substantial experience performing the critical skills and essential support services for the P-2
- A copy of any written contract with the alien or a summary of the terms of the oral agreement under which the alien will be employed

Step 3 - Clearing the Department of State (DOS) Abroad

After receiving notice of approval of their petition from the BCIS, applicants should normally apply at the American Embassy or Consulate having jurisdiction over their place of permanent residence. Although visa applicants may apply at any U.S. consular office abroad, it may be more difficult to qualify for the visa outside the country of permanent residence.   *Ref: 9 FAM 41.56*

Documentation and supporting evidence includes:

- *DOS form*
  - DS-156, Nonimmigrant Visa Application
- *Fees*
  - $100 for non-refundable Machine-Readable Visa (MRV)
  - visa reciprocity equating to fees charged in similar circumstances in alien's home country
- *Passport and photograph*
  - passport valid for at least six months beyond intended stay
  - 50 mm (2") square photograph facing camera directly without head covering (check for religious exceptions) against a light background
- *Prior BCIS approval*
  - I-797, Notice of Approval
- *Evidence to support request*
  - purpose of trip
- *Evidence that U.S. stay is temporary (intent to depart)*
  - no intention to abandon residence abroad

Issue of a visa does not guarantee entry to the United States. That decision rests with the BCBP Immigration Inspector at a port of entry.

Step 4 - Clearing the BCBP at a U.S. Port of Entry

Form I-129 may be submitted by mail or at some U.S. ports of entry when entering the country. As a mail application to a BCIS regional Service Center may take as much as two months, you should select an entry point which admits applicants.

Documentation and supporting evidence includes:

- *BCIS forms*
  - I-129, Petition for a Nonimmigrant Worker (when applying at border)
  - O and P Classifications Supplement page
- *Fee*
  - $130
- *Passport*
  - passport valid for at least six months beyond intended stay
- *Prior DOS approval*
  - DOS Machine-Readable Visa (MRV) in passport
- *Current and prior immigration status*
  - copy of I-94, Nonimmigrant Arrival/Departure Record
- *Additional evidence*
  - peer group
  - labor organization
- *Employer's evidence to support request*
- *Evidence that U.S. stay is temporary (intent to depart)*
  - no intention to abandon residence abroad

Maximum Duration of Stay:
- Individual P-1 athletes: up to 10 years based on the trend of signing long-term contracts
- Teams: one year
- P-2 and P-3: the time involved in the event or events to one-year maximum
- P-4: same length of time as the principal alien

Step 5 - Revalidation/Extension or Change of Status

Application to the BCIS within the United States

A petition requesting an extension of stay or change to P status may be filed by mail with the BCIS regional Service Center having jurisdiction over your place of residence.   *Ref: INS recorded information service*

Documentation and supporting evidence by the principal alien includes:

- *BCIS forms*
  - I-129, Application to Extend/Change Nonimmigrant Status
  - O and P Classifications Supplement page
  - I-907, Request for Premium Processing, if requested
- *Fees*
  - $130 for I-129
  - $1,000 for I-907, if requested
- *Passport*
  - passport valid for at least six months beyond intended stay

- *Current and prior immigration status*
  - copy of I-94, Nonimmigrant Arrival/Departure Record
- *Employer's evidence to support request*
  - letter from the petitioner explaining the reasons for the extension

Where there has been a change in the circumstances of employment, the evidence required for a new petition must be submitted.

Dependents should file Form I-539 to apply for a change of status or extension of stay with the appropriate BCIS regional Service Center.

Documentation and supporting evidence by dependents includes:

- *BCIS form*
  - I-539, Application to Extend/Change Nonimmigrant Status
- *Fee*
  - $140

The BCIS issues an I-797, Notice of Approval which serves as evidence of the extension or change of status.

Visa Revalidation by the Department of State (DOS)

After BCIS has extended your stay, your visa may need to be renewed before attempting to reenter the United States after travel abroad for business or pleasure. Depending on how U.S. citizens are treated in your home country in similar circumstances, your original visa may have been issued with restrictions on the number of entries into the United States and its period of validity, perhaps six months or a year.

Application for visa renewal may be made at a U.S. Embassy or Consulate in your home country. Revalidations may also be made at a U.S. Consulate in Mexico or Canada by calling (900) 443-3131 for an appointment.

As it is not possible to obtain expedited processing or status reports, you should apply in person to the consular office of the country of destination if you do not have time to get your visa renewal in the U.S.

As a service to aliens in a few classifications such as P, the Department of State renews visas by mail in the U.S., if time permits. Full information on revalidations is available from the State Department web site at www.travel.state.gov/revals.html. You may download the required Form DS-156 there.

Documentation and supporting evidence includes:

- *DOS form*
  - DS-156, Nonimmigrant Visa Application
- *Fees*
  - $100 for non-refundable Machine-Readable Visa (MRV)
  - visa reciprocity equating to fees charged in similar circumstances in alien's home country

- *Passport and photograph*
  - passport valid for at least six months beyond intended stay
  - 50 mm (2") square photograph facing camera directly without head covering (check for religious exceptions) against a light background
- *Current and prior immigration status*
  - original current I-94 (no copies)
  - copy of I-797 Approval Notice
- *Employer's supporting documentation*
  - detailed letter identifying:
    - the employee
    - his or her position
    - travel itinerary

When a fee is charged for visa reciprocity, include two certified checks or money orders, one for the visa application and one for the reciprocity charge. Personal checks cannot be accepted.

Applications sent through the U.S. Postal Service should be mailed in a padded envelope with a stamped padded envelope enclosed for return mailing. If return by courier is requested, an air bill is required. Processing may take from six to eight weeks. Further recorded information may be obtained by calling (202) 663-1213.

Completed applications may be sent by mail to:

U.S. Department of State/Visa
P.O. Box 952099
St. Louis, MO 63195-2099

Completed applications may also be sent by courier to:

U.S. Department of State/Visa (Box 2099)
1005 Convention Plaza
St. Louis, MO 63101-1200

Chapter 7

Special Purpose Classifications

Several classifications are available for the use of aliens with specialized qualifications and visa needs.

The available categories include:

- I - Foreign Information Media Representative
- K - Fiancé(e) or Spouse of U.S. Citizen
- Q - International and Irish Peace Process Cultural Exchange Programs
- R - Religious Worker
- S - Alien Witness and Informant
- T - Victim of Trafficking
- U - Humanitarian/Material Witness
- V - Spouse and Children of Permanent Resident

I

Foreign Information Media Representative

Istatus is accorded, upon a basis of reciprocity, to an alien who is a bona fide representative of foreign press, radio, film, or other foreign information media, who seeks to enter the United States solely to engage in such vocation, and the spouse and children of such a representative if accompanying or following to join.

Classification is:

- I - Representative of Foreign Information Media, Spouse and Minor Child
Ref: INA 101(a)(15)(I)

Dependents of I aliens may study on a full or part-time basis in the U.S.

Admission Process

Step 1 - Clearing the Department of State (DOS) Abroad

Application should be made to the U.S. Embassy or Consulate in your home country. Canadians are visa exempt.

Documentation and supporting evidence includes:

- *DOS form*
  - DS-156, Nonimmigrant Visa Application
- *Fees*
  - $100 for non-refundable Machine-Readable Visa (MRV)
  - visa reciprocity equating to fees charged in similar circumstances in alien's home country
- *Passport and photograph*
  - passport valid for at least six months beyond intended stay
  - 50 mm (2") square photograph facing camera directly without head covering (check for religious exceptions) against a light background
- *Employer's evidence to support request*
  - comprehensive letter on company letterhead which:
    - is signed by the company's responsible officer
    - describes your job and your business in detail

- justifies the need for the visa
- identifies you
- names your dependents, if any

Any changes to the visa page necessitate the issuance of a different visa. Very few visas are issued in this classification. A separate check must be submitted if there is a visa reciprocity fee.

Step 2 - Clearing the BCBP at a U.S. Port of Entry

The admission of an alien of the class defined in INA 101(a)(15)(I) constitutes an agreement by the alien not to change the information medium or his or her employer until he or she obtains permission to do so from the District Director having jurisdiction over his or her residence. An alien classified as an information media nonimmigrant may be authorized admission for the duration of employment.   *Ref: 8 CFR 214(i)*

Documentation and supporting evidence includes:

- *Prior DOS approval*
  - DOS Machine-Readable Visa (MRV)

The Machine-Readable Visa issued by the State Department abroad is subject to electronic verification by the BCBP at U.S. ports of entry where an I-94 is issued.

I visa holders are admitted to the U.S. for the duration of their assignment.

Step 3 - Revalidation/Extension

Visa Revalidation by the Department of State (DOS)

Full information on revalidations is available from the State Department web site at www.travel.state.gov/revals.html and you may download the required Form DS-156. For information call (202) 663-3111.

Completed applications may be sent by mail to:

> U.S. Department of State/Visa
> P.O. Box 952099
> St. Louis, MO 63195-2099
> Fax: (202) 663-1608

Completed applications may also be sent by courier to:

> U.S. Department of State/Visa (Box 2099)
> 1005 Convention Plaza
> St. Louis, MO 63101-1200
> Fax: (202) 663-1608

Applications may be dropped in a mail slot at 526 N.W. 23rd Street in Washington or delivered in person between 11 am and 12 noon, Monday through Friday. A self-addressed, stamped or pre-paid envelope is required for the return of passports.

Application may also be made at a U.S. Consulate along the Canadian or Mexican border. Appointments must be made in advance by calling the State Department's 900 service at (900) 443-3131 from the United States. Proof of immigration status in those countries may be required.

Documentation and supporting evidence includes:

- *DOS form*
  - DS-156, Nonimmigrant Visa Application
- *Fees*
  - $100 for non-refundable Machine-Readable Visa (MRV)
  - visa reciprocity equating to fees charged in similar circumstances in alien's home country
- *Passport and photograph*
  - passport valid for at least six months and containing the present visa for the same classification (may be in a previous passport)
  - 50 mm (2") square photograph facing camera directly without head covering (check for religious exceptions) against a light background
- *Current and prior immigration status*
  - original I-94 issued by the BCBP when last entered the U.S., or, if expired, valid I-797, Notice of Approval for each applicant
- *Prior BCIS approvals*
  - a valid employment petition I-797 showing:
    - applicant's current employer and
    - BCIS-approved extension of temporary stay
- *Employer's evidence to support request*
  - comprehensive letter on company letterhead which:
    - is addressed to the Visa Office, Department of State
    - is signed by the company's responsible officer
    - describes the job and business in detail
    - justifies the need for the visa
    - identifies you and names your dependents, if any
- *Additional evidence*
  - certified copies of all the principal alien's documentation if spouse and children are applying separately
  - proof of your relationship to accompanying dependents
- *Proof of financial support or solvency*
  - arrangements to cover U.S. expenses
- *Evidence that U.S. stay is temporary (intent to depart)*
  - proof of intention to depart after completion of assignment
  - no intention to abandon residence abroad

K

Fiancé(e) or Spouse of U.S. Citizen

This section describes the original K-1 and the new K-3 nonimmigrant status.

K-1 status continues to enable a U.S. citizen to sponsor a foreign national fiancé(e) and his or her children to enter the U.S., obtain work authorization, marry within 90 days and apply for a conditional Green Card.

K-3 status was introduced when the Legal Immigration Family Equity (LIFE) Act became law on December 21, 2000. This nonimmmigrant classification only expedites the entry of alien spouses of U.S. citizens and the alien spouse's children as K-3 or K-4 nonimmigrants. As beneficiaries of pending or approved visa petitions, they may be admitted and remain in the U.S. until they adjust status.   *Ref: Pub. L. 106-553*

Sub-categories are:
- K-1 - Fiancé(e) of United States Citizen
- K-2 - Child(ren) of Fiancé(e) of United States Citizen living abroad
- K-3 - Spouse of a U.S. citizen with a pending immediate relative petition
- K-4 - Child(ren) of K-3 spouse

See also:
- V Visa - Alien Spouse and Children of Permanent Resident -this chapter
- Immediate Relative of U.S. Citizen- Part III
- Second Preference, Spouse and Children of Permanent Resident - Part III

Admission Process

Step 1 - Clearing the BCIS in the U.S. - Initial Petition

Option 1 - Before Marriage in the U.S. - Fiancé(e) living abroad

A U.S. citizen who plans to marry an alien living abroad and bring the alien to live in the United States should file a Form I-129F for a K-1 with the BCIS regional Service Center having jurisdiction over his or her place of residence before the alien's entry. Notice of BCIS approval is sent to a U.S. Embassy or Consulate serving the alien's home country within about 30 to 90 days. The BCIS approval is valid for four months and may be revalidated by a consular officer.

The U.S. citizen fiancé(e) sends Form I-134, Affidavit of Support to the alien fiancé(e) for presentation at the consulate.

Documentation and supporting evidence includes:

- *BCIS forms*
  - I-129F, Petition for Alien Fiancé(e) (Rev. 3/29/01)
  - G-325A, Biographic Information for the petitioner and fiancé(e)
  - I-134, Affidavit of Support
- *Fee*
  - $110 for I-129F
- *Proof of birth of U.S. citizen*
  - U.S. birth certificate, or
  - Certificate of Naturalization or Citizenship, or
  - Form FS-240 Report of Birth Abroad of a U.S. Citizen, or
  - unexpired U.S. passport
- *Photographs*
  - color photograph 40 mm high by 35 mm wide in 3/4 profile showing right ear, no head covering (religious exceptions), light background
- *Evidence to support request*
  - proof of consent if required because of age
- *Civil documents*
  - copy of divorce or death certificate from previous marriage(s)
  - proof of name changes

If documents are unavailable, it may be possible to substitute:

- Church, school or census record
- Affidavits

The petition is subject to denial if the alien applicant:

- Has a communicable disease or a dangerous physical or mental disorder
- Is a drug addict
- Has committed serious criminal acts
- Has entered the United States illegally
- Is ineligible for citizenship

Option 2 - After Marriage - Alien Spouse living abroad

If your alien spouse is living abroad, a two-step process now enables faster entry. To begin the process of obtaining permanent residency for the alien spouse, the U.S. citizen spouse files an I-130, Petition for Alien Relative at the BCIS regional Service Center having jurisdiction over his or her place of residence in the United States.

To expedite the process, while waiting for the finalization of the I-130 petition, temporary (nonimmigrant) entry may be sought in the form of a K-3 for the spouse and a K-4 for the spouse's children through the filing of a Form I-129F, Petition for Alien Fiancé(e). The form is subject to change.

A K-3 nonimmigrant visa is available only to an alien living abroad who:

- Is already married to a U.S. citizen
- Has had the following filed by a U.S. citizen spouse:
  - Form I-130, Petition for Alien Relative
  - Form I-129F, Petition to Classify Nonimmigrant as Fiancé(e)
- Is seeking to enter the U.S. to await the availability of an immigrant visa

The U.S. citizen petitioner is not required to file a Form I-130 immigrant visa petition on behalf of the K-3 alien's children seeking K-4 nonimmigrant status since K-4s are dependent on the K-3 for their status. Nevertheless, the petitioner may wish to file Form I-130 for the children since they would lose their K-4 status when their K-3 parent becomes a Legal Permanent Resident. Nonimmigrants may not change from another nonimmigrant status to K in the U.S. as that is not the intent of the K-3.

Documentation and supporting evidence includes:

- *BCIS forms*
  - I-130, Petition for Alien Relative
  - I-129F, Petition to Classify Nonimmigrant as Fiancé(e) (Form subject to change)
  - G-325A, Biographic Information for the petitioner and spouse
- *Fees*
  - $96 for I-130
  - $110 for I-129F
- *Passport*
  - passport valid for at least six months beyond intended entry
- *Civil documents*
  - marriage certificate
  - proof of termination of previous marriage(s)
- *Photograph*
  - color photograph of husband, wife and child(ren) 40 mm high by 35 mm wide 3/4 profile no head covering (religious exceptions) light background

If there is more than one beneficiary, only one I-129F need be filed.

Applications for K-3/K-4 status should be sent to:

Bureau of Citizenship and Immigration Services
P.O. Box 7218
Chicago, IL 60680-7218

Once the current Form I-129F is approved, the BCIS will notify the American consulate abroad as specified on the petition. If the marriage took place abroad, the BCIS will notify a consulate in the country where the marriage took place.

Aliens applying for K-3/K-4 status are not exempt from the three-year or ten-year bars as a result of extended illegal presence in the United States.

K-3 or K-4 status terminates 30 days after:
- Their authorized period of admission expires
- Their Form I-130 is denied
- Their application for an immigrant visa is denied
- Their application for Adjustment of Status is denied

Step 2 - Clearing the Department of State (DOS) Abroad

Option 1 - Before Marriage - After BCIS Approval - By State Department (DOS)

Under FAM 9 41.2(k), a visa is required of an alien who is classified under INA 101(a)(15)(K). After receiving notification of the approval of the initial petition from the BCIS, the U.S. Consulate will send the alien fiancé(e) a packet explaining the documents to be collected and submitted and the process to be followed. Whenever possible, originals, including documents filed with the BCIS, must be submitted.

Documentation and supporting evidence includes:
- *DOS forms*
  - DS-156, Nonimmigrant Visa Application
  - DS-156K, Nonimmigrant Fiancé(e) Visa Application
  - G-325A, Biographic Information from the petitioner and fiancé(e)
- *Fees*
  - $100 for non-refundable Machine-Readable Visa (MRV)
  - visa reciprocity equating to fees charged in similar circumstances in alien's home country
- *Passport and photograph*
  - passport valid for at least six months beyond intended entry
  - 50 mm (2") square photograph facing camera directly without head covering (check for religious exceptions) against a light background
- *Prior BCIS approval*
  - I-129F, Petition for Alien Fiancé(e).
- *Proof of financial support or solvency*
  - I-134, Affidavit of Support received from U.S. citizen
  - letters from the U.S. citizen's employer and bank
- *Civil documents*
  - birth certificate
  - divorce or death certificate from previous marriage(s)
- *Police clearance*
  - certificate from all residences since alien's 16th birthday
- *Medical clearance*
  - results of medical exam, chest x-ray and blood test by a DOS doctor
- *Additional evidence*
  - evidence of valid relationship with the U.S. petitioner
  - both persons are legally willing and able to marry in the U.S.

- both persons have met in person during the past two years unless the Secretary of Homeland Security waives the requirement

The alien fiancé(e) must be interviewed by a consular officer. If approved, a K-1 visa, good for six months, is issued for presentation at a U.S. port of entry. The nonrenewable visa is valid only for 90 days from the date of entry to the United States.

Option 2 - After Marriage - By the State Department (DOS) Abroad

The LIFE Act requires the petitioner to file a Form I-129F, Petition for Alien Fiancé(e) in the United States for the purpose of obtaining nonimmigrant (K-3) status for his or her spouse. The petition must be approved prior to the issuance of the nonimmigrant visa by the consular officer abroad. In general, visa applications must be filed in the country of residence of the alien spouse.

The applicant is classifiable as a K-3 nonimmigrant spouse when all the following requirements are met:

- The consular officer is satisfied the alien has met applicable requirements in order to receive a K-3 or K-4 nonimmigrant visa
- The consular officer has received an I-129F petition approved by the BCIS that was filed in the United States by the U.S. citizen spouse of the alien
- If the marriage took place outside the United States, the alien is applying in the country where the marriage took place or at a consular post designated to accept immigrant visa applications for nationals of that country
- If the marriage took place in the United States, the alien is applying in is or her country of residence

In order to obtain classification under K-4, the alien must establish that he or she is the child of an alien entitled to K-3 classification.

The K-4 child applicant is classifiable if:

- The consular officer is satisfied that the alien is the child of the K-3 alien and is accompanying or following to join the principal alien
- The alien has otherwise met all other applicable requirements in order to receive a nonimmigrant visa

The LIFE Act does not provide for visa issuance for the child of a child of the spouse or petitioner.

When applicants are being processed for their nonimmigrant K-3 visa, they will be asked whether they wish to determine from the National Visa Center if an approved I-130 immigrant visa has been received from the BCIS. If it has, the applicant may request that the approved immigrant visa be forwarded to the consular post at which the immigrant visa application must be filed. Only after the approved I-130 has been received at the post, may the alien file an immigrant visa application.

The State Department is authorizing the issuance of ten-year multiple entry visas to K-3 and K-4 visa recipients. However, a shorter period of validity may be necessary in cases of age-out, approaching 21st birthday of the child, security concerns or ineligibility waiver limitations.

K-3 and K-4 visa applicants will be processed via the modified immigrant visa procedure applicable to fiancé(e)s. In general, this procedure requires a medical examination and law enforcement check of the alien. The alien is exempt from the labor certification and vaccination requirements.

The new nonimmigrant K status will terminate following the denial of the relative visa petition or application or application immigrant status based on such petition. In such cases, the nonimmigrant K status will terminate 30 days following the denial and the alien(s) must leave the United States. These petitions or applications are denied when the applicable administrative appeal has been exhausted or the period to appeal has expired. Marriage fraud also results in termination of K status. Another LIFE amendment provides for a "bona fide" marriage exception to the general rule that an alien may not adjust to permanent status while in exclusion, deportation or removal proceedings.   *Ref: 66 FR 19390*

Documentation and supporting evidence includes:

- *INS and DOS forms*
  - I-693, Medical Examination
  - DS-156, Nonimmigrant Visa Application
- *Fee*
  - $100 for non-refundable Machine-Readable Visa (MRV)
- *Passport and photograph*
  - passport valid for at least six months beyond intended entry
  - 50 mm (2") square photograph facing camera directly without head covering (check for religious exceptions) against a light background
- *Supporting documents*
  - INS approval of Form I-129F, Application for Alien Fiancé(e)
  - marriage certificate
  - proof of termination of previous marriage(s)
- *Proof of financial support*
  - I-864, Affidavit of Support
- *Police clearance*
- *Medical clearance*

For cases for which expedited K-3 entry is not requested, most U.S. Embassies or Consulates abroad will allow the filing of all documents with them:

- If your wedding takes place abroad
- If you are both present there, and
- If the consulate is acting for the BCIS
- Regardless of whether the citizen resides in the consular district

An applicant for an immigrant visa or K nonimmigrant visa who is inadmissible and seeks a waiver of inadmissibility shall file an application on Form I-601, at the consular office considering the visa application. The consular officer shall transmit the Form I-601 to the BCIS for decision.

Financial Support

The U.S. citizen sponsor will be notified later by the Department of State when to submit an I-864 to guarantee financial support.

Sponsors should be aware that a new binding Form I-864, **Affidavit of Support**, has been introduced to ensure that an intending immigrant has adequate means of financial support and is not likely to become a public charge. Effective June 1, 2002, a $65 fee is being charged for I-864 review and assistance at the National Visa Center or through a call center. The financial obligation of the Affidavit of Support remains in place until the sponsored immigrant becomes a U.S. citizen, is credited with 40 qualifying quarters of work, departs the U.S. permanently or dies.

The sponsor's household income must equal or exceed 125 percent of the Federal Poverty Line, adjusted annually, for the sponsor's household size which includes the sponsor and all other persons who are related and living with the sponsor as well as previously sponsored immigrants and the intending immigrant and dependents. The Federal Poverty Line is adjusted each year. See http://aspe.hhs.gov/poverty.

In 2003, a U.S. citizen living alone sponsoring an alien spouse with no dependents was required to prove an individual annual income of at least $15,150 if living in the 48 contiguous states or the District of Columbia, more in Alaska and Hawaii. The figures are updated annually.

Qualified co-sponsors and the sponsored immigrant may also file Form I-864A when their income will be used to determine the sponsor's ability to support a spouse and any accompanying minor unmarried children.   *Ref: INA 213A*

Step 3 - Clearing the BCBP at a U.S. Port of Entry

Option 1 - Before Marriage in the United States

Following K-1 consular approval abroad, the alien fiancé(e) must apply to a BCBP Immigration Inspector for entry at a U.S. port of entry. A work permit good for 90 days may be obtained at that time. Then, a Social Security number should be applied for at the local Social Security Office as soon as possible.

An alien fiancé(e) living abroad and entering as a K-1 may not begin the K process at a port of entry or change to another classification after entry.*Ref: INA 248*

Option 2 - After Marriage Abroad

Aliens appearing at U.S. ports of entry with valid K-3 visas will be inspected, and if admissible, will be admitted into the United States for a period of two years. Similarly, aliens appearing with a valid K-4 visa will be admitted for a period of two years or until the day before their 21st birthday, whichever is shorter. K-3 and K-4 aliens are authorized to remain in the United States for the period of time specified on their I-94. Upon arrival, they may apply for employment authorization.

Documentation and supporting evidence includes:
- *BCIS form*
  - I-765, Application for Employment Authorization
- *Fee*
  - $120
- *Prior approvals*
  - INS and DOS approvals

K-3/K-4 status will terminate 30 days after the denial of one of the following:
- The Form I-130 filed on behalf of the alien by the U.S. citizen petitioner
- An application for an immigrant visa by the petitioner
- The alien's I-485 Adjustment of Status application
- The K-3's divorce from the U.S. citizen becomes final
- The marriage of an alien in K-4 status

If any of these happen, the alien will no longer be authorized to reside and work and must leave the United States within 30 days following the administrative appeal applicable to that application or petition has been exhausted.

K-4 status terminates the day before an alien becomes 21 or is married.

Step 4 - Revalidation/Extension or Change of Status

Following the two-year admission period, and 120 days prior to expiration of his or her authorized stay, a K-3 or K-4 nonimmigrant may file a Form I-539, Application for Extension of Stay with the BCIS for an additional two-year increment only if the alien has filed a Form I-485, Adjustment of Status application.

Employment authorization documents issued to K-3/K-4 aliens may be renewed only on a showing that the applicant has an application or petition awaiting approval, equivalent to the showing required for an extension of stay.

Aliens classified K-3 or K-4 seeking to renew their employment authorization will be required to show that they are still pursuing the immigration process and still meet the necessary nonimmigrant classification by having an I-130 application pending, or if approved, an I-485 Adjustment of Status application is pending approval. This may be filed concurrently with an application for extension of stay.

The alien must continue to be married to the U.S. citizen spouse. No appeal of I-539 denials is permitted.

Extensions of K-4 status must be filed concurrently with the K-3 parent's application. If not the alien must await approval of the original I-130.

The alien's K-3 or K-4 status will be terminated after two years if the alien does not file a request for extension of stay.

Aliens wishing to extend their period of stay as a K-3 or K-4 alien must show:

- A Form I-130 petition filed by the alien's U.S. citizen spouse who filed the I-129F
- An application for an immigrant visa based on a Form I-130
- A Form I-485, Adjustment of Status application based on a Form I-130

Documentation and supporting evidence includes:

- *BCIS forms*
  - I-539, Application to Extend/Change Nonimmigrant Status
  - I-765, Application for Employment Authorization
- *BCIS fees*
  - $140 for I-539
  - $120 for I-765
- *Supporting documentation*
  - I-130 or I-485 approval pending
  - marriage continuing

Applications should be sent to:

Bureau of Citizenship and Immigration Services
P.O. Box 7218
Chicago, IL 60680-7218

If the BCIS intends to deny, the applicant will be sent a notice and given 30 days to submit additional information in rebuttal.

Step 5 - Adjustment of Status by the BCIS in the United States

A U.S. citizen's spouse and children remain eligible to file for permanent residency at any time if the original U.S. citizen petitioner files Form I-130 and the beneficiary files Form I-485, Application for Adjustment to Permanent Status.

While pending, the spouse of the U.S. citizen and his or her child may remain in the United States, without accruing unlawful presence and obtain work authorization by filing Form I-765, Application for Employment Authorization and the fee and permission to travel outside the U.S.

If married less than 24 months, Adjustment of Status is subject to the requirement of conditional residency. In such cases, a petition to remove the conditional status must be filed within 90 days of the two-year anniversary of receiving conditional permanent residence status. Aliens who adjust status more than two years after the original marriage are not subject to the conditional residency requirements.

K-3 and K-4 nonimmigrants do not have to wait for a visa number to become current and may apply for Adjustment of Status on Form I-485 at any time following approval of their I-130 petition as immediate relatives of U.S. citizens. Both may be filed concurrently for the K-4. Aliens entering as K-1/K-2 will be treated the same as K-3/K-4 and will be required to file a Form I-864, Affidavit of Support Contract between Sponsor and Household member at the time of adjustment.

An alien admitted to the United States as a K-3/K-4 alien may not adjust to permanent resident status in any way other than as a spouse or child of the U.S. citizen who originally filed the petition for that alien's K-3/K-4 status.

If you have both been living legally in the United States, as soon as possible after your marriage, you should both go to the local BCIS office to file a petition to adjust status to Permanent Resident or Green Card holder. A minor unmarried child admitted with the alien spouse may also apply based on the parent's adjustment application.

Aliens who entered as a K-1 or K-2 nonimmigrant and who later filed to adjust status will continue to be required to obtain advance parole to avoid abandonment of their adjustment application on departure. This is because K-1/K-2 aliens have only a 90-day period of admission prior to be required to marry the citizen petitioner and file an adjustment application. Aliens in K-1/K-2 will have no status to fall back on following the filing of their adjustment application.

Aliens present in the United States in a K-3/K-4 classification may travel outside the United States and return using their nonimmigrant K-3/K-4 visa, even if they have applied for Adjustment of Status. The definition of a K-3/K-4 nonimmigrant does not require that such alien have a foreign residence that they have no intention of abandoning. Accordingly, the BCIS will not presume that their departure constitutes abandonment of their Adjustment of Status application.

Documentation and supporting evidence includes:

- *BCIS forms*
  - I-130, Petition for Alien Relative
  - I-485, Adjustment of Status
  - I-765, Application for Employment Authorization
  - G-325A, Biographic Information for the petitioner and spouse
- *Fees*
  - $96 for I-130
  - $255 for I-485 ($160 for dependents under 14)
  - $120 for I-765
  - $50 for fingerprinting
- *Passport and photograph*
  - passport valid for at least six months
  - two 3/4 frontal color photographs - 40 mm high by 35 mm wide
- *Current and prior immigration status*
  - copy of I-94
- *Proof of financial support or solvency*
  - I-864, Affidavit of Support

- employment letter
- *Civil documents*
  - marriage certificate
  - proof of termination of previous marriage(s)
  - birth certificate
- *Police clearance*
- *Medical clearance*

Step 6 - Green Card Interview

You should be called in for your Green Card interview within six months.

At the interview, it is normal to expect questions to confirm the details of your relationship with and knowledge of the background of your spouse. It may be useful to produce photographs or letters you have written to each other. The examiner must be sure that you:

- Agree that all information in the application is accurate, or
- Correct your petition to reflect actual facts
- Have lawful immigration status in the United States
- Have any necessary proof of financial support
- Resolve any last minute doubts about whether:
  - your marriage was entered into as a "sham" to help the alien spouse evade U.S. immigration laws
  - you have been living together since getting married, or
  - you have valid reasons for not living together

The Marriage Fraud Act of 1986 provides for fines up to $250,000, five years imprisonment of both parties and deportation of the alien if a fraudulent marriage is used as a means to obtain a Green Card.

At the Green Card interview, the alien spouse should receive conditional approval good for two years and have his or her passport stamped to allow international travel until the actual Green Card arrives by mail. Adjustment should be made the same day.

A medical examination shall not be required of an applicant for Adjustment of Status who entered the United States as a nonimmigrant spouse or fiancé(e) of a U.S. citizen or child of such alien if the applicant was medically examined prior to, and as a condition of, the issuance of the nonimmigrant visa. The medical examination must have occurred not more than one year prior to the application for adjustment of status.

If your case is "closed" (approved), the examiner will place a temporary I-551 Green Card stamp in your passport and you will have conditional Green Card status which must be confirmed in two years.

If your case is "continued" because of something missing or incomplete, you must turn in all required additional documentation to the office where the interview was held. If you do not receive written notification of the decision, follow up with the BCIS.

Except for some persons in the U.S. on December 21, 2000 who had a Green Card application in process by April 30, 2001, *Out of Status* aliens may no longer pay a $1,000 fine with Supplement A to Form I-485 to adjust status in the U.S. under INA 245(i). This rule could change again.

Step 7 - Removal of Conditional Status

90 days before the second anniversary of the date of the granting of the Green Card, it is necessary to apply to have the conditional status removed.

A petition should be filed at the BCIS regional Service Center having jurisdiction over your place of residence.

Documentation and supporting evidence includes:
- *BCIS form*
  - I-751, Petition to Remove the Conditions on Residence
- *Fee*
  - $145
- *Passport and photograph*
  - passport valid for at least six months
  - 3/4 frontal color photograph - 40 mm high by 35 mm wide
- *Current immigration status*
  - I-551, Permanent Resident Card
- *Evidence to support request*
  - copies of documents indicating that your marriage was entered into in good faith and not to avoid U.S. immigration laws
  - sworn or affirmed affidavits by at least two people who have personal knowledge of your continuing marriage and relationship
  - lease or mortgage contracts showing joint tenancy
- *Proof of financial support or solvency*
  - financial records showing joint ownership of assets
- *Civil documents*
  - birth certificate(s) of child(ren) born to the marriage

If you choose to not file, you will lose your Green Card on the second anniversary of the date on which you were granted status. However, if you are out of the U.S. at the time of your second anniversary, you must file within 90 days of your return.

Q-1/Q-2

International Cultural Exchange Program Participant (Q-1) and Irish Peace Process Cultural and Training Program Participant (Q-2/3)

Qstatus has been temporarily divided into two parts to permit participation in two special programs.

Sub-categories are:
- Q-1 - Participant in an International Cultural Exchange Program
- Q-2 - Participation in Irish Peace Process Cultural and Training Program
- Q-3 - Dependent of Irish Peace Process Cultural and Training Participant
  Ref: INA 101(a)(15)(Q)(i), (ii) and (iii); Pub. L. 105-319

Q-1 - Participant in an International Cultural Exchange Program

Q-1 status is for "an exchange visa permitting 15 months admission to participate in designated international cultural exchange programs." It is possible to return for a further term after a one-year absence from the U.S.   *Ref: 9 FAM 41.12*

The Q-1 classification was added to the Immigration and Nationality Act in 1990 to:
- Enhance the knowledge and appreciation of different world cultures by the American people by:
  - taking place in a school, museum, business or other establishment
  - exposing the public to the history and traditions of a foreign culture
  - being part of a structured program
  - providing practical training and employment
  - allowing employers such as Disney to bring foreign nationals to the United States for temporary periods to work in places such as Epcot Center in Florida

The prospective Exchange Visitor must be at least 18 years old and able to effectively communicate about his or her home country. But, it is not necessary that the Exchange Visitor derive any cultural benefit from exposure to the American people.

Q-2 - Participant in Irish Peace Process Cultural and Training Program
The Q-2 classification was added temporarily to the Immigration and Nationality Act by incorporating the Irish Peace Process Cultural and Training Program Act of 1998 or Walsh Visa Program which became law on October 30, 1998. It was created to:
- Promote cross-community and cross-border initiatives to build grassroots support for long-term peaceful coexistence
- Develop job skills and conflict resolution abilities in a diverse, cooperative, peaceful, and prosperous environment   *Ref: H.R. 4293*

Participation is limited to aliens:
- Who are 35 years of age or younger who wish to enter the United States with their spouse and children for a period not to exceed 36 months
- From disadvantaged areas of the six counties of Northern Ireland and the counties of Louth, Monaghan, Cavan, Leitrim, Sligo and Donegal in the Republic of Ireland suffering from sectarian violence and structural unemployment, and who can return to their homes better able to contribute toward economic regeneration and the Irish peace process

On October 4, 2002, President Bush signed a bill which extended the Irish Peace Process Cultural and Training Program to 2006.   *Ref: Pub.L. 107-234*

Admission Process

Step 1 - Clearing the BCIS in the United States - Initial Petition
Either a U.S. employer or a foreign employer may submit a petition which must be filed with the appropriate BCIS regional Service Center. A foreign employer's petition must be signed by a senior member of U.S. management who has worked for the organization for the prior year.

Documentation and supporting evidence includes:
- *BCIS forms*
  - I-129, Petition for a Nonimmigrant Worker
  - Q & R Classifications Supplement page
  - I-907, Request for Premium Processing Service, if requested
- *Fees*
  - $130 for I-129
  - $1,000 for I-907, if requested
- *Evidence to support request*
  - evidence that a cultural exchange program exists and is maintained
  - a qualified employee has been designated and will act as program administrator and BCIS liaison
  - the company has been conducting business in the United States for at least two years

- the company will offer the same wages and working conditions as are provided to similarly employed U.S. workers
- the company employs at least five full-time U.S. workers
- *Proof of financial support or solvency*
  - the ability to remunerate participants
- *Additional evidence*
  - the employment or training takes place in a public setting where the alien's culture may be shared with the American people
  - the American people will derive an obvious cultural benefit
  - the cultural component gives an overview of the alien's home country

The BCIS issues an I-797, Notice of Approval to the employer or agent. It is subject to approval by the DOS.

Q-2/3 admission is limited to not more than 4,000 aliens including spouses and minor children in each of three consecutive program years. Each admission will reduce by one the number of H-2B nonimmigrants allowed in a given year. The BCIS is responsible for employment authorization, monitoring status and reporting to Congress.

Step 2 - *Clearing the Department of State (DOS) Abroad*

After receiving BCIP notice of approval, applicants should normally apply at the American Embassy or Consulate having jurisdiction over their place of permanent residence. Although visa applicants may apply at any U.S. consular office abroad, it may be more difficult to qualify for the visa outside the country of permanent residence.

The State Department is responsible for Q-2 and Q-3 program administration, design, policies, procedures and coordination with U.S., Irish and Northern Ireland government agencies. The designated Program Administrator, Northrop Grumman may be contacted for details of the employer approval process by calling (877) 925-7484 or on the internet at www.WalshVisa.net. Q-2 and Q-3 applicants must apply at either the U.S. Embassy in Dublin or the U.S. Consulate in Belfast.

Documentation and supporting evidence includes:

- *DOS form*
  - DS-156, Nonimmigrant Visa Application
  - prior written certification from the Program Administrator (Q-2/3)
- *Fees*
  - $100 for non-refundable Machine-Readable Visa (MRV)
  - visa reciprocity equating to fees charged in similar circumstances in alien's home country
- *Passport and photograph*
  - passport valid for at least six months beyond intended stay
  - 50 mm (2") square photograph facing camera directly without head covering (check for religious exceptions) against a light background
- *Prior BCIS approval*
  - I-797, Notice of Approval

- *Evidence that U.S. stay is temporary (intent to return)*
  - proof of binding ties to a residence outside the United States which you have no intention of abandoning

Issue of a visa does not guarantee entry to the United States.

Step 3 - Clearing the BCBP at a U.S. Port of Entry

The BCBP Immigration Inspector has the authority to deny admission or determine the period for which the alien is authorized to remain in the United States to a maximum of 15 months for Q-1 and 36 months for Q-2 and Q-3.

An accompanying or following spouse and children may enter in Q-3 status. While there is no such provision for Q-1s, their dependents may request admission in B-2 Visitor status or any other classification for which they qualify.

Documentation and supporting evidence includes:

- *Prior approvals*
  - DOS Machine-Readable Visa (MRV) in passport
  - written certification from the Program Administrator (Q-2/3)

The BCBP Immigration Inspector will validate an I-94 Arrival/Departure Record as proof of status. This will serve as employment authorization.

Step 4 - Revalidation/Extension or Change of Status

Application to the BCIS within the United States

If the alien has been in Q-1 status for 18 months, revalidation is not permitted unless the alien has resided outside the United States for the immediate prior year.

A petition requesting an extension of stay may be filed for a Q employee by mail with the BCIS regional Service Center having jurisdiction over your location.

The stay of Q-2 and Q-3 aliens may not be extended beyond a total of 36 months including the original authorized period of stay.

Documentation and supporting evidence for principal alien includes:

BCIS forms
  - I-129, Application to Extend/Change Nonimmigrant Status
  - I-907, Request for Premium Processing Service, if requested (Q-1)
- *Fees*
  - $130 for I-129
  - $1,000 for I-907, if requested
- *Passport*
  - passport valid for at least six months beyond intended stay
- *Current and prior immigration status*
  - a copy of I-94, Nonimmigrant Arrival/Departure Record

- *Employer's evidence to support request*
  - letter explaining the reasons for the extension

Dependents should file for an extension of stay with the BCIS regional Service Center having jurisdiction over their place of residence.

Documentation and supporting evidence for dependents includes:

- *BCIS form*
  - I-539, Application to Extend/Change Nonimmigrant Status
- *Fee*
  - $140
- *Evidence to support request*
  - copies of current documentation of principal alien

All checks and money orders must be drawn on banks or other financial institutions in the United States and must be payable in U.S. dollars.

Submit evidence if a change in the circumstances of employment occurs. The BCIS issues an I-797 Notice of Approval as evidence of the extension or change of status.

Visa Revalidation by the Department of State (DOS)

After BCIS has extended your stay, your visa may need to be renewed before attempting to reenter the United States after travel abroad for business or pleasure. Depending on how U.S. citizens are treated in your home country, your visa may be issued with restrictions on the number of entries into the U.S. and its period of validity.

Aliens may apply for a change of status or extension of Q status at a U.S. Consulate in Mexico or Canada by calling for an appointment on the State Department 900 telephone appointment service. Q revalidations are not processed in the U.S.

Documentation and supporting evidence includes:

- *DOS form*
  - DS-156, Nonimmigrant Visa Application
- *Fee*
  - $100 for non-refundable Machine-Readable Visa (MRV)
- *Passport and photograph*
  - passport valid for at least six months beyond intended stay
  - 50 mm (2") square photograph facing camera directly without head covering (check for religious exceptions) against a light background
- *Prior BCIS approval*
  - approved I-129 petition
  - an original Form I-797
- *Professional credentials*
- *Evidence that U.S. stay is temporary (intent to depart U.S.)*
  - no intention to abandon residence abroad

R

Alien in a Religious Occupation

R status includes ministers of religion, professional religious workers, and other members of religious denominations having a bona fide nonprofit religious organization in the United States.

R status is for those who have been a member of a religious denomination for the preceding two years and plan to carry on the activities of a religious worker.

Ref: INS ER 806 3-8-94

Sub-categories are:
- R-1 - Alien in a Religious Occupation
- R-2 - Spouse or Child of R-1   *Ref: INA 101(a)(15)(R)(I),(ii)*

Initial admission for the religious worker, spouse and children under 21 is for three years with an extension of stay to a maximum of five years.

Ref: Nebraska Service Center

The spouse and minor children of religious workers are eligible for R-2 classification visas that are valid for study but not employment.

Religious workers classifications fall into three categories:
- Professional capacity
  - occupations for which a baccalaureate degree or foreign equivalent is required
- Religious occupation
  - an activity relating to a traditional religious function such as:
  - liturgical worker
  - religious instructor
  - religious counselor
  - cantor
  - catechists
  - worker in religious hospital or religious health care facility
  - missionary
  - religious translator
  - religious broadcaster

- Religious vocation
  - a calling to religious life evidenced by the demonstration of commitment practiced in the religious denomination, like taking vows
  - nuns
  - monks
  - religious brothers and sisters

To qualify, it is necessary to come solely to work for a specified period of time:

- As a minister of that denomination
- In a professional capacity for that organization
- In a religious vocation or occupation for the organization or its nonprofit affiliate

The term "minister" means a recognized religious individual authorized to conduct religious worship and to perform other religious duties. There must be a reasonable connection between the activities performed and the religious calling of the minister. This does not apply to lay preachers not authorized to perform the duties of a minister.

Affiliation between the religious worker and the religious denomination means not only an organization which is closely associated with the religious denomination but also tax-exempt.

Admission Process

Step 1 - Clearing the Department of State (DOS) Abroad

Since no BCIS petition is required, you may apply at a consulate or a port of entry, if visa exempt.

If not visa exempt, aliens may apply for the R-1 visa at the U.S. Embassy or Consulate having jurisdiction over their place of foreign residence or at any other U.S. consular office abroad.   *Ref: 9 FAM 41.58*

Documentation and supporting evidence includes:

- *DOS form*
  - DS-156, Nonimmigrant Visa Application
- *Fees*
  - $100 for non-refundable Machine-Readable Visa (MRV)
  - visa reciprocity equating to fees charged in similar circumstances in alien's home country
  - visa filing may be waived by Secretary of State for alien engaged in charitable activities

- *Passport and photograph*
  - passport valid for at least six months beyond intended stay
  - 50 mm (2") square photograph facing camera directly without head covering (check for religious exceptions) against a light background
- *Professional credentials*
  - if the applicant is a minister, he or she is authorized to conduct religious worship for that denomination and the duties are described in detail, or
  - if the applicant is a religious professional, he or she has at least a baccalaureate degree or equivalent, and that such a degree is required for entry into the religious profession, or
  - if the applicant is to work in a nonprofessional vocation or occupation, he or she is qualified if the type of work to be done relates to a traditional religious function
- *Employer's evidence to support request*
  - letter from an authorized official of the specific unit of the employing organization certifying:
    - if the applicant's religious membership was maintained, in whole or in part, outside the United States, the foreign and United States religious organizations belong to the same religious denomination
    - immediately prior to the application for the R visa, the alien has been a member of the religious denomination for at least two years
    - the name and location of the specific organizational unit of the religious denomination or affiliate for which the applicant will be providing services
    - if the alien is to work for an organization which is affiliated with a religious denomination, a description of the nature of the relationship between the two organizations
- *Proof of financial support or solvency*
  - letter from an authorized official of the specific unit of the employing organization certifying the arrangements for remuneration, including the amount and source of salary, other types of compensation such as food and housing, and any other benefits of a monetary value, and a statement whether such remuneration shall be in exchange for services rendered
  - evidence of the religious organization's assets and methods of operation
  - the organization's papers of incorporation under applicable state law
  - proof of tax-exempt status or eligibility for tax-exempt status
- *Evidence that U.S. stay is temporary (intent to depart U.S.)*
  - no requirement that applicants for R visas have a residence abroad which they have no intention of abandoning, but
  - must intend to depart the United States at the end of lawful status

Ref: DOS, August 1995

Step 2 - Clearing the BCBP at a U.S. Port of Entry

Aliens may apply directly at a port of entry, if visa exempt.

If a visa is issued, it does not guarantee entry into the United States because the BCBP has the authority to deny admission or determine the period for which the alien is authorized to remain in the United States.

Religious workers may be admitted to the United States for an initial period of three years with extensions to a maximum stay of five years.

Documentation and supporting evidence includes:

- *Passport*
  - passport valid for at least six months beyond date of entry
- *Prior DOS approval*
  - DOS Machine-Readable Visa (MRV) in passport
- *Employer's evidence to support request*
  - letter from the authorizing official of the organization which will employ the alien, confirming:
    - that the foreign and United States religious organizations belong to the same religious denomination
    - that immediately prior to the application for the nonimmigrant visa or application for admission, the alien had the required two years of membership in the religious denomination
    - how the alien's religious work qualifies
    - details of the proposed employment
- *Proof of financial support or solvency*
  - particulars of the remuneration for services to be rendered by the alien with the amount and source of any salary including:
    - housing
    - food
    - clothing
    - any other benefits to which monetary value may be affixed
    - a copy of the tax-exempt certificate showing the religious organization which will employ the alien is:
      - a bona fide nonprofit, religious organization in the United States exempt from taxation in accordance with section 501(c)(3) of the Internal Revenue Code of 1986

The BCBP Immigration Inspector will validate an I-94 Arrival/Departure Record to denote the length of stay permitted.

Applicants should be prepared to return directly to their home country if the BCBP refuses entry to the United States.

Step 3 - Renewal/Extension or Change of Status

Application to the BCIS within the United States

Those who wish to stay beyond the time permitted on their I-94 must file with the appropriate BCIS regional Service Center. The decision on whether to grant the request is made solely by the BCIS.

Documentation and supporting evidence includes:

- *BCIS forms*
  - I-129, Petition for Nonimmigrant Worker
  - Q & R Classifications Supplement page
  - I-907, Request for Premium Processing, if requested
- *Fees*
  - $130 for I-129
  - $1,000 for I-907, if requested
- *Passport*
  - passport valid for at least six months beyond intended stay
- *Current and prior immigration status*
  - I-94, Arrival/Departure Record
- *Professional credentials*
  - proof of membership in the religious organization
- *Employee's evidence to support request*
  - evidence of qualifications for employment
  - employment letter indicating the nature, duration and remuneration of employment
- *Additional evidence*
  - proof of the organization's tax-exempt status
- *Proof of financial support or solvency*
  - several recent pay stubs
  - financial proof that you will not become a public charge
- *Evidence that U.S. stay is temporary (intent to depart U.S.)*
  - proof of intent to depart the U.S. upon completion of assignment

Dependents should file for an extension of stay with the BCIS regional Service Center having jurisdiction over their place of residence.

Documentation and supporting evidence for dependents includes:

- *BCIS form*
  - I-539, Application to Extend/Change Nonimmigrant Status
- *Fee*
  - $140
- *Evidence to support request*
  - copies of current documentation of principal alien

Visa Revalidation by the Department of State (DOS)

After BCIS has extended your stay, your visa may need to be renewed before attempting to reenter the United States after travel abroad. Depending on how U.S. citizens are treated in your home country in similar circumstances, your original visa may have been issued with restrictions on the number of entries into the United States and its period of validity, perhaps six months or a year.

Aliens in the United States may apply for an extension of their R status or for a change of status to R at a U.S. Consulate in Mexico or Canada.

An appointment must be made via the State Department's 900 service.

Depending on the consulate involved, the visa will be issued the same day or the following business day.

Documentation and supporting evidence includes:

- *Form*
  - DS-156, Nonimmigrant Visa Application
- *Fee*
  - $100 for non-refundable Machine-Readable Visa (MRV)
- *Passport and photograph*
  - passport valid for at least six months beyond intended stay
  - 50 mm (2") square photograph facing camera directly without head covering (check for religious exceptions) against a light background
- *Prior BCIS approval*
  - copy of I-129 petition
  - original I-797
- *Employee's evidence to support request*
  - evidence of qualifications for employment
  - proof of membership in the religious organization
- *Employer's evidence to support request*
  - proof of the organization's tax-exempt status
  - employment letter indicating the nature, duration and remuneration of employment
- *Proof of financial support or solvency*
  - several recent pay stubs
- *Evidence that U.S. stay is temporary (intent to depart U.S.)*
  - proof of intent to depart upon completion of assignment

S

Alien Witness and Informant

The Violent Crime Control and Law Enforcement Act of 1994 created an S nonimmigrant visa classification which added section 101(a)(15)(S) to the INA. It was further amended by the Illegal Immigration and Immigrant Responsibility Act of 1996. The S classification became permanent when President Bush signed a Senate Bill on October 1, 2001.   *Ref: 67 FR 67108; Pub. L. 105-277, 107-45*

Sub-categories are:
- S-5 - Alien Witness or Informant in a Criminal Matter
- S-6 - Alien Witness or Informant in a Counterterrorism Matter
- S-7 - Qualified family members   *Ref: 9 FAM 41.83; 8 CFR 214.2(t)*

S-5 status provides for the admission of an alien as a nonimmigrant S on application by an interested Federal or state law enforcement authority ("LEA") if the the alien:
- Possesses critical reliable information concerning a criminal organization or enterprise
- Is willing to provide that information to federal and/or state LEA, and
- Is essential to the success of an authorized criminal investigation or prosecution   *Ref: INA 101(a)(15)(S)(i); IIRIRA96.621*

200 visas per fiscal year are available in this classification.

S-6 status provides for the admission of an alien as a nonimmigrant S on application by an interested Federal law enforcement authority ("LEA") if the Secretary of State and the Secretary of Homeland Security jointly consider the alien:
- Possesses critical reliable information about a terrorist organization, enterprise or operation
- Is willing to provide or has provided such information to a federal LEA   *Ref: INA 101(a)(15)(s)(ii); IIRIRA96.621*

50 visas per fiscal year are available in this classification.

S-7 derivative status is available to accompanying or following to join spouse, married and unmarried sons and daughters, and parents of S-5 or S-6 aliens if the Secretary of State and the Secretary of Homeland Security jointly consider it appropriate.

Admission Process

Step 1 - Clearing the BCIS in the U.S. Initial Petition

An S-5 application is filed by an interested Federal or state law enforcement authority (LEA) in the case of an alien witness or informant in a criminal matter.

An S-6 application is filed by an interested Federal law enforcement authority (LEA) in the case of an alien witness or informant in a counterterrorism matter.

A derivative S-7 must be identified by the LEA on a Form I-854 application.

Certifications must be made at the seat-of-government level in Federal cases or at the highest LEA level in state cases.

The completed application is filed with:

> Assistant Attorney General
> Criminal Division
> Department of Justice

Where necessary, an advisory panel of representatives of other government agencies such as the FBI will review the application and prioritize to determine which cases to forward to the Secretary of Homeland Security. Only properly certified applications falling within the numerical limitation are forwarded for approval.

Authority to waive grounds of excludability are delegated to the Secretary. On approval, the Secretary shall notify the Assistant Attorney General, Criminal Division, Secretary of State and appropriate BCIS officers.

Documentation and supporting evidence includes:

- *BCIS form*
  - I-854, Inter-Agency Alien Witness and Informant Record
- *Supporting documentation*
  - signed statement by alien and any beneficiary 18 or older certifying the understanding that he or she is restricted to the terms of the nonimmigrant S classification as the exclusive means to remain permanently in the United States
  - no promises have been made or will be made that the alien may remain in the United States in any other status
  - the LEA shall provide evidence establishing:
    - the nature of the alien's cooperation and need for his or her presence in the United States
    - all possible grounds of excludability
    - all factors and considerations warranting a favorable exercise of discretionary waiver authority on the alien's behalf
    - evidence may take the form of affidavits, memoranda or similar documentation

Step 2 - Clearing the Department of State (DOS) Abroad

The consular officer will process the visa application pursuant to guidance and instruction provided by the Department of State Visa Office. A visa may be authorized for the period necessary pursuant to the certification, but for a period not to exceed the three-year statutory limit.   *Ref: 9 FAM 41.83; Pub. L. 107-45*

Step 3 - Clearing the BCBP at a U.S. Port of Entry

The responsible LEA will coordinate the admission of the alien in S nonimmigrant classification with the Secretary of Homeland Security as to the date, time, place, and manner of arrival.

Admission shall be for a period not exceeding three years.

An S alien may apply for employment authorization by filing Form I-765, Application for Employment Authorization with fee.

Documentation and supporting evidence includes:

- *Passport*
    - passport valid for at least six months beyond intended stay
- *Prior DOS approval*
    - DOS Machine-Readable Visa (MRV) in passport
- *Additional evidence*
    - copies of such documentation as required by the Secretary of Homeland Security and Secretary of State
- *Evidence that U.S. stay is temporary*
    - evidence of intent to depart U.S.

Step 4 - Change of Status

Change of Status from S to another nonimmigrant classification is not permitted. However, aliens in other nonimmigrant classifications may change to that of an Alien Witness or Informant by filing Form I-539, Application to Extend/Change Nonimmigrant Status with filing fee and Form I-854.

Step 5 - Adjustment of Status

Principal aliens and their dependents may be permitted to adjust to permanent status if the principal alien's information substantially contributed to the successful disposition of a criminal investigation or resulted in the prevention of terrorism or the apprehension of a terrorist. Application is filed on Form I-854 with Adjustment of Status on Form I-485.   *Ref: 8 CFR 245.11*

T

Victim of Trafficking

On October 28, 2000, the Trafficking Victims Protection Act of 2000 was signed into law by President Clinton as a component of the Victims of Trafficking and Violence Protection Act of 2000 (VTVPA). It included the creation of this new nonimmigrant T classification as a benefit to a qualifying alien on account of such trafficking.   *Ref: 66 FR 38513; 67 FR 4784; INA 101(a)(15(T); Pub. L. 106-386*

Sub-categories are:
- T-1 - Victim of a severe form of trafficking in persons
- T-2 - Spouse of T-1
- T-3 - Child of T-1
- T-4 - Parent of T-1   *Ref: 66 FR 53711; 67 FR 4784*

The DHS, in cooperation with other law enforcement agencies may arrange for the continued presence and safe haven of aliens who have been the victims of trafficking in persons and are potemtial witnesses to that trafficking so that they will be available to assist with the investigation and prosecution of the traffickers.
Ref: Section 107 (c)

An alien may remain in the United States if the Secretary of Homeland Security determines that the alien:
- Is the victim of a severe form of trafficking of persons, and
- Is physically present in the U.S., American Samoa, the Commonwealth of the North Mariana Islands, or a U.S. port of entry because of such trafficking
- Has complied with any reasonable request for assistance in the investigation or prosecution of acts of trafficking, unless under age 15
- Would be likely to suffer extreme hardship involving unusual and severe harm upon removal from the United States

Admission Process

Step 1 - Support from a Federal Law Enfortcement Agency (LEA)

Any Federal Law Enforcement Agency (LEA) may request an alien's continued presence in the U.S. in order to investigate and prosecute traffickers if the alien is a victim of a severe form of trafficking in persons and a potential witness to such trafficking. The agency may request that an alien be allowed to remain temporarily in the United States.

The submission of a Supplement B serves as primary evidence that the alien is a victim of a severe form of trafficking in persons. Only Federal Law Enforcement Agencies (LEAs) investigating or prosecuting acts of trafficking in persons may fill out the LEA endorsement.

A state law enforcement agency which believes it has encountered a victim who might be eligible for T-1 status should contact the local office of an LEA such as the FBI or U.S. Attorney's office or the Civil Rights Division's Criminal Section. The LEA endorsement must contain a description of the victimization upon which the application is based. Whether to complete an endorsemnt is at the discretion of the LEA. In lieu of an endorsement, the applicant may contact the Department of Justice, Civil Rights Division complaint hotline at (888) 428-7581 to file a complaint and be referred to an LEA.

Step 2 - Clearing the BCIS

Individual applicants may apply without sponsorship from a Federal Law Enforcement Agency (LEA), although it is strongly recommended. Their application is filed with the Vermont Service Center. If an LEA endorsement is not included, the BCIS will make an independent assessment .

Documentation and supporting evidence includes:
- *BCIS forms*
  - I-914, Application for T Nonimmigrant Status
  - Supplement A, Application for Immediate Family Member of T-1, if applicable
  - Supplement B, Declaration of a Law Enforcement Officer for Victim of Trafficking in Persons, if LEA endorsement obtained
- *Fees*
  - $200 for principal applicant
  - $50 for each derivative family member
  - $400 maximum per family
  - $50 fingerprinting fee for all applicants between 14 and 79
- *Supporting documentation*
  - three 3/4 frontal color photographs 40 mm high by 35 mm wide
  - all evidence to support eligibility
  - LEA evidence, if provided, shall establish:
    - that the alien is a victim of trafficking in persons, and
    - the nature of the alien's cooperation and need for his or her presence in the United States

All Nonimmigrant T applicants must be fingerprinted for the purpose of conducting a criminal background check. The BCIS may require an applicant to appear for an interview.

The Secretary of Homeland Security may, in order to avoid extreme hardship, permit the spouse, children and parents of an alien under 21, or the spouse and children of an alien over 21 to accompany or follow to join.

When appropriate, the DHS will use the following means to prevent removal of applicants who have filed bona fide applications:

- Parole
- Stay of removal
- Deferred action
- Nonimmigrant T visa

The BCIS has the discretion to decide to authorize the continued presence of alien victims of trafficking who are not legally present in the United States if they are potential witnesses to trafficking in persons.

Physical presence includes:

- Those present who are being held in some sort of severe form of trafficking in persons
- Were recently liberated from a severe form of trafficking in persons
- Were subject to severe forms of trafficking in persons in the past and remain in the U.S. for reasons directly relating to the original trafficking in persons
- Aliens having escaped from the traffickers before law enforcement became involved must show they did not have a clear chance to leave the U.S.

Victims granted T-1 status will be issued employment authorization without filing the I-765 application. T-2, T-3 and T-4 derivative applicants must file an I-765 for work authorization.

It is the alien's burden of proof to demonstrate a particular means such as force and a particular end such as involuntary servitude.

No person shall be eligible for admission to the United States if there is substantial reason to believe that the person has committed a severe form of trafficking of persons. Removal is also contemplated for conduct after admission or undisclosed before admission.

The number of aliens who may be issued non-renewable visas for three years may not exceed 5,000 in any fiscal year whether or not they were granted continued presence. If the quota is exhausted, approved applicants may be placed on the waiting list and remain in the United States until the next Fiscal Year.

The numerical limitations shall only apply to principal aliens and not to spouses, children, or the alien parents of children who are the principal applicant. The Secretary of Homeland Security shall provide these aliens with employment authorization and may waive a ground of inadmissibility if it is in the public or national interest.

Applicants may apply for T-2, T-3 and T-4 derivative family members at the time of the original application or by filing a separate Form I-914 with attachments and full fee at a later date. Derivative status applicants must include fees, and photographs.

Aliens who are victims of severe forms of trafficking in persons who have been granted contined presence or who have a bona fide application for T Nonimmigrant status are eligible to receive certain kinds of public assistance to the same extent as refugees.

Step 3 - Adjustment of Status

The Secretary of Homeland Security may adjust status of an alien under this section to that of an alien lawfully admitted for permanent residence if the alien:

- Is admissible
- Has been physically present in the U.S. for at least three years since admission in this classification
- Is of good moral character
- Has complied with any reasonable request for assistance in the investigation or prosecution of trafficking acts, or
- Would suffer extreme hardship involving unusual and severe harm upon removal from the United States

Application is to be made during the 90-day period preceding the expiration of the three-year T status. In cases of denial, the applicant can appeal to the Administrative Appeals Office.

U

Humanitarian/Material Witness

On October 28, 2000, the Battered Immigrant Women Protection Act of 2000 was signed into law by President Clinton as a component of the Victims of Trafficking and Violence Protection Act of 2000. It included the creation of this nonimmigrant U classification which facilitates the reporting of crimes by aliens who are victims of physical or mental abuse but are not in lawful immigration status.

In keeping with U.S. humanitarian interests, the U category allows law enforcement officials to regularize the status of those cooperating individuals during investigations or prosecutions of such criminal activity. Accordingly, protection may be offered to victims while law enforcement agencies may detect, investigate, and prosecute cases of domestic violence, sexual assault, trafficking of aliens and other crimes described in the INA.   *Ref: 66 FR 38153; INA 101(a)(15(U); Pub. L. 106-386*

Sub-categories are:
- U-1 - Victim of criminal activity
- U-2 - Spouse of U-1
- U-3 - Child of U-1
- U-4 - Parent of U-1   *Ref: 66 FR 53711*

Admission Process

Step 1 - Clearing the BCIS

To qualify under the U category, the alien must file a petition with the Secretary of Homeland Security and establish that:
- The alien has suffered substantial physical or mental abuse as a result of having been the victim of any one of a list of 26 criminal activities
- As certified by a law enforcement or immigration official, the alien (or if the alien is a child under 16, the child's parent, guardian or friend):
  - posseses information about the criminal activity involved
  - is helpful or likely to be helpful to a Federal, state or local law enforcement official, prosecutor or judge or local authorities in the investigation and prosecution of the criminal activity
- The criminal activity violated U.S. laws and occurred in the United States

While an alien is accorded U status, removal is prevented.

If the Secretary of Homeland Security determines that extreme hardship exists and a law enforcement official certifies that an investigation or prosecution would be harmed without that person's assistance, the spouse, child or parents of the principal alien may accompany or follow to join the principal alien.

The number of aliens who may be issued visas or otherwise provided status shall not exceed 10,000 in any fiscal year. The numerical limitations shall only apply to principal aliens and not to spouses, children, or the alien parents of such children. The Secretary of Homeland Security shall provide these aliens with employment authorization and may waive a ground of inadmissibility if it is in the public or national interest.

Step 2 - Adjustment of Status

The Secretary of Homeland Security may adjust status of an alien under this section to that of an alien lawfully admitted for permanent residence if:

- The alien has been physically present in the U.S. for at least three years since admission in this classification
- The alien's continued presence in the U.S. is justified on humanitarian grounds, to ensure family unity, or is otherwise in the public interest
- A grant is necessary to avoid extreme hardship of a spouse, child or parent of an alien child who did not receive a nonimmigrant visa

V

Spouse and Minor Children of Legal Permanent Resident

On December 21, 2000, the Legal Immigration Family Equity (LIFE) Act was signed into law by President Clinton. It included the creation of this new nonimmigrant V classification to enable backlogged spouses and unmarried minor children of Green Card holders to enter the U.S. until a permanent residency visa becomes available.
Ref: INA 101(a)(15)(V); LIFE Act, Section 1102; Pub. L. 106-553

Sub-categories are:
- V-1 - Spouse of a Legal Permanent Resident
- V-2 - Child of a Legal Permanent Resident
- V-3 - Derivative Child of a V-1 or V-2

Entry Criteria

Alien spouses and unmarried children must establish that they are beneficiaries of a Form I-130, Petition for Alien Relative filed on their behalf by December 21, 2000, and either:
- The I-130 petition has been pending for three years or more, or
- The I-130 petition has been approved and three or more years have elapsed since the filing of the petition and, either:
  - a world wide or per-country numerical limitation immigrant visa number is not available, or
  - an immigrant visa number is available but the application is pending

Eligible aliens may enter, work and continue to reside in the United States while they wait for their family-based Second Preference F2A visa petition to be approved. A child of a petitioned-for spouse or child beneficiary is eligible if accompanying or following to join such an alien.

Their authorized stay is terminated if:
- Their authorized period of admission expires
- Their Form I-130 is denied
- Their application for an immigrant visa is denied
- Their application for Adjustment of Status is denied

An alien is no longer eligible for F2A preference category if the qualifying marriage is terminated, the child reaches the age of 21 or the I-130 petition is withdrawn. The alien is no longer considered to be in valid V Classification 30 days after. However, the spouse and child of an abusive lawful permanent resident may be eligible to file a self-petition.

The period of authorized admission shall terminate 30 days after:

- The permanent residency petition is denied, or
- The subsequent immigrant visa petition is denied, or
- The application for Adjustment of Status is denied

Admission Process

Step 1 - Processing

Processing is possible in the United States or abroad, depending on where the spouse and unmarried minor children are living and their immigration status.

Option 1 - Processing by the BCIS in the United States

If already present in the United States, eligible aliens may obtain V nonimmigrant status while remaining in the U.S.

Documentation and supporting evidence includes:

- *BCIS forms*
  - I-539, Application to Extend/Change Nonimmigrant Status
  - I-539, Supplement A, Filing Instructions for V Nonimmigrant Status
  - I-693, Medical Examination of Aliens Seeking Adjustment of Status
  - I-765, Application for Employment Authorization, if needed
- *Fees*
  - $140 for I-539
  - $120 for I-765
  - $50 for fingerprinting
- *Proof of filing of immigrant petition*
  - I-797, Notice of Action, or
  - Notice of Approval or receipt from the local district office, or
  - correspondence with the BCIS
- *Financial proof*
  - I-134, Affidavit of Support, may be required

Applications are to be submitted to:

Bureau of Citizenship and Immigration Services
P.O. Box 7216
Chicago, IL 60680-7216

The maximum period of admission in V status is two years but may be extended if the alien continues to remain eligible.

The Secretary of Homeland Security shall authorize an alien admitted as a V to engage in employment in the United States and shall provide the alien with an Employment Authorization Document (EAD) to match the period of authorized stay as a V. V-2 and V-3 status terminates upon marriage or on the day before the 21st birthday, at the same time as eligibility for an F2A Adjustment of Status is terminated.

An alien who was granted V nonimmigrant status in the United States by the BCIS will need to obtain a V visa from a consular office abroad in order to be inspected and admitted to the United States as a V nonimmigrant after traveling abroad.

There are special exemptions for an alien in immigration proceedings or the subject of a Final Order of Removal, Deportation or Exclusion.

Option 2 - *Processing by the Department of State (DOS) Abroad*

Eligible spouses and unmarried children under 21 outside the United States may apply for a V nonimmigrant visa at a U.S. consular office abroad and for admission to the U.S. in V nonimmigrant status if they are beneficiaries of an I-130 petition for F2A immigrant visa preference. The alien must personally appear before a consular officer and verify by oath or affirmation the statements contained on Form DS- 230 and all supporting documents.

By March 15, 2001, the Department of State had begun notifying all persons with F2A priority dates which were at least three years old, of the availability of V visas.

Documentation and supporting evidence includes:
- *DOS forms*
  - DS-156 Nonimmigrant Visa Application
  - DS-3052, Nonimmigrant V Visa Application Form
- *Fee*
  - $100 for Machine-Readable Visa (MRV)
- *Passport and photograph*
  - passport valid for at least six months
  - 50 mm (2") square photograph facing camera directly without head covering (check for religious exceptions) against a light background
- *Supporting evidence*
  - medical examination
  - police criminal record statement and name checked by the FBI

Unless they obtain DOS approval to the contrary, applicants must apply at the consular post designated as the processing post in the underlying immigrant visa petition. The State Department has instructed its consular officers to issue visas to qualified applicants for the usual maximum validity period of ten years.

Ref: 22 CFR 41.86

Step 2 - Clearing the BCBP at a U.S. Port of Entry

An alien who obtained a V nonimmigrant visa from a consular office abroad may be inspected and admitted to the United States in V nonimmigrant status as long as the alien posseses a valid unexpired V visa and remains eligible for V nonimmigrant status.

Step 3 - Extension of Stay

If the period of admission is about to expire, a two-year extension may be sought.

Documentation and supporting evidence includes:

- *BCIS forms*
  - I-539, Application to Extend/Change Nonimmigrant Status
  - I-539, Supplement A, Filing Instructions for V Nonimmigrant Status
  - I-765, Application for Employment Authorization, if needed
- *Fees*
  - $140 for I-539
  - $120 for I-765

Applications are to be submitted to:

> Bureau of Citizenship and Immigration Services
> P.O. Box 7216
> Chicago, IL 60680-7216

Extensions are not permitted if the principal alien has been naturalized; in such cases, the I-130 petition will be automatically upgraded to an immediate relative and the spouse and child may apply for Form I-485, Adjustment of Status and Form I-765 for work authorization. A new Form I-130 must be filed for a V-3 Derivative child.

Step 4 - Adjustment of Status

The Secretary of Homeland Security may adjust the status of an alien physically present in the United States if the alien:

- Applies for Adjustment of Status
- Satisfies the requirements
- Is eligible to be admitted to the United States
- Pays an application fee not to exceed $200
- Pays a sum equal to $1,000, if so required, and if eligible

Aliens admitted in V status, like H-1Bs and Ls, are not subject to the constraints of dual intent. They are eligible to apply for Advance Parole. However, if a Form I-485, Adjustment of Status is pending, it is not necessary to obtain Advance Parole prior to traveling abroad per Section 1102(d) of the LIFE Act.

Ref: 66 FR 19392 and 46704; Pub. L. 106-553

Chapter 8

Foreign Government and Organization Representative

Several classifications are used by officials, families and staff of foreign governments and international organizations including:

- A - Senior Government Official
  - ambassador, diplomat or consular officer
  - family and staff
- C-2 - Alien in Transit to United Nations and C-3 Foreign Government Official
  - official
  - family and staff
  - personal employee in transit
- G - Government Representative to International Organization
  - principal or other government representative
  - representative of nonrecognized or nonmember government
  - international organization representative or employee
  - family and staff
- N - International Organization Family Member
  - unmarried son or daughter of a current or former international organization officer or employee
  - surviving spouse of a deceased international organization officer
  - retired international organization officer or employee
  - immigrant spouse of a retired international organization officer or employee
- NATO Representative of Member State
  - principal permanent representative
  - senior NATO executives
  - other NATO officials, representatives, experts and official clerical staff
  - accompanying civilians
  - family and staff

A

Senior Government Official

Astatus is a very formal classification for the use of representatives of foreign governments. It is reserved for "ambassadors, public ministers, diplomats or consular officers assigned to represent a country to the United States". Family, servants or attendants, and their immediate families are also included.   *Ref: INA 101(a)(15)(A)*

Sub-categories are:

- A-1 - Ambassador, Public Minister, Career Diplomat or Consular Officer, or Immediate Family
- A-2 - Other Foreign Government Official or Employee, or Immediate Family (on the basis of reciprocity)
- A-3 - Attendant, Servant, or Personal Employee of A-1 and A-2 Classes or Immediate Family (on basis of reciprocity) *Ref: 9 FAM 41.12, 41.21, 41.22*

The Department of State (DOS) and the BCIS have the joint responsibility for the adjudication of applications relating to A nonimmigrants.

Admission Process

Step 1 - Clearing the Department of State (DOS) Abroad

The sponsoring agency usually handles the processing of these visas.

Applications for entry in this classification may be made at a U.S. Embassy or Consulate abroad. Canadians do not have to go to the U.S. Embassy or Consulate.

Documentation and supporting evidence includes:

- *DOS and BCIS forms*
  - DS-1648, Application for A, G or NATO Visa
  - DS-156 Nonimmigrant Visa Application, or
  - I-566, Inter-Agency Record of Individual Requesting Change/ Adjustment or Dependent Employment Authorization
- *Fee*
  - $100 Machine-Readable Visa (MRV) fee is waived in this classification
- *Passport and photograph*
  - passport valid for at least six months beyond intended stay
  - 50 mm (2") square photograph facing camera directly without head covering (check for religious exceptions) against a light background

- *Third Country immigration status*
  - evidence of current immigration status in third country
- *Current and prior immigration status*
  - (expired) documents relating to previous U.S. visits:
    - passports with visas
    - Forms I-20, I-797, I-94, Employment Authorization Documents
- *Employer's evidence to support request*
  - original letter from the employing embassy/mission/international organization describing nature of your work and length of stay in U.S.
- *Civil documents*
  - proof of relationship of dependents applying for derivative visa status
  - birth and marriage certificates
  - adoption papers

Step 2 - *Clearing the BCBP at a U.S. Port of Entry*

Entry is granted by the BCBP based on the approval of the DOS.

Documentation and supporting evidence includes:

- *Prior DOS approval*
  - DOS Machine-Readable Visa (MRV) in passport

Step 3 - *Extension/Change of Status in the United States*

An extension or change from another nonimmigrant status to A-1 or A-2 is a two-part process. Except for A-3 applicants, first file with the State Department through your diplomatic mission or international organization, then with the BCIS.

Part One - *DOS:*

Documentation and supporting evidence includes:

- *BCIS and DOS forms*
  - I-566, Inter-Agency Record of Individual Requesting Change/ Adjustment or Dependent Employment Authorization
  - DS-1648, Application for A, G or NATO Visa
  - DS-394, Notification of Foreign Government Employment Status, or
  - DS-1497, Notification of Appointment of Foreign Diplomatic Officer
- *Current and prior immigration status*
  - I-94, Arrival/Departure Record

Part Two - *BCIS:*

After you receive your I-566 with a favorable endorsement from the DOS, submit your application to the BCIS office having jurisdiction over your place of residence. File for A-3 status directly with the appropriate BCIS regional Service Center.

If you are a permanent resident who wishes to be employed in an A occupation while retaining your permanent resident status, contact the BCIS office having jurisdiction over your place of residence for procedures under INA 247(b).

Documentation and supporting evidence includes:

- *BCIS forms*
  - I-539 Application to Extend/Change Nonimmigrant Status
  - I-407, Abandonment by Alien of Status as Lawful Permanent Resident
- *Fee*
  - $140 for I-539
- *Prior DOS approval*
  - original I-566 certified by the State Department with favorable DOS endorsement recommending that the request be granted
- *Current and prior immigration status*
  - I-94 Arrival/Departure Record (nonimmigrant)
  - I-551 (Green Card) (immigrant)
- *Additional evidence - A-3 applicants only:*
  - copy of employer's I-94 or approval notice showing G status
  - original letter from employer describing your duties and stating that he/she intends to personally employ you
  - original I-566, certified by the DOS indicating your employer's continuing accredited diplomatic status

The BCIS issues an I-797, Notice of Approval, as evidence of change of status.

Visa Revalidation by the Department of State

After BCIS has extended your stay, your visa may need to be renewed before attempting to reenter the U.S. after travel abroad. The number of entries may be restricted depending on how U.S. citizens are treated in your home country.

As a service to aliens in a few classifications such as A, the Department of State processes A visa renewals in the United States. Forms may be requested by writing:

Department of State
Visa Office
Room L703
2401 E Street N.W.
Washington, DC 20522-0106

Documentation and supporting evidence includes:

- *DOS form*
  - DS-156, Nonimmigrant Visa Application
- *Fee*
  - Machine-Readable Visa (MRV) fee is waived
- *Passport and photograph*
  - passport valid for at least six months beyond intended stay
  - 50 mm (2") square photograph facing camera directly without head covering (check for religious exceptions) against a light background

- *Current and prior immigration status*
  - original current I-94 (no copies)
- *Employer's supporting documentation*
  - detailed letter identifying the employee, position and travel itinerary

Step 4 - Application for Dependent Employment Authorization

Part One - DOS:

In all cases, the alien's diplomatic mission or international organization submits an application to the State Department, Office of Protocol which processes it and forwards it directly to the BCIS Nebraska Service Center.

Documentation and supporting evidence includes:

- *BCIS form*
  - I-566 Inter-Agency Record of Individual Requesting Change/ Adjustment or Dependent Employment Authorization
- *Passport*
  - passport valid for at least six months beyond intended stay
- *Additional evidence*
  - diplomatic note requesting employment authorization
  - employer's offer of employment (when required under the terms of de facto arrangements, name of dependent by name, position description, salary offered, duties, and verification that the dependent qualifies)
  - completed I-765 signed by the applicant
  - no filing fee or fingerprints required
  - two color photographs with the name and mission on the back of each
  - clear photocopy of applicant's photograph from passport, MRV, DOS identification, or other U.S. or sending state identity document
  - copy of I-94 Arrival/Departure Record - front and back

If requesting an extension or reapplying for an EAD, provide photocopies of dependent's previous IRS tax returns. The Nebraska Service Center will direct concerns regarding the sufficiency of an application to the embassy or international organization in the address block of the I-765.   *Ref: 8 CFR 214.2(a) (6) and 214.2(g) (6)*

Part Two -BCIS:

File employment authorization application with the Nebraska Service Center.

Step 5 - Change to Other Status by the DOS and BCIS in the U.S.

To change from A status to either another nonimmigrant or immigrant status, you must first file Form I-566, Inter-Agency Record of Individual Requesting Change/ Adjustment or Dependent Employment Authorization with the State Department.

After clearing the DOS, check the application process for the classification of your choice as detailed elsewhere in this book.

C-2/C-3

Alien in Transit to United Nations (C-2) and Foreign Government Official (C-3)

T he following sub-categories are for foreign government representatives and aliens coming to the United Nations, their families and staff.

- C-2 - Alien in Transit to United Nations Headquarters District under 11.(3), (4), or (5) of Headquarters Agreement with the United Nations
- C-3 - Foreign Government Official, Immediate Family, Attendant, Servant, or Personal Employee in Transit
          Ref: INA 101(a)(15)(C)(ii),(iii); 9 FAM 41.12, 41.23

Admission Process

Step 1 - Clearing the Department of State (DOS) Abroad

Applications for entry in this classification may be made at a U.S. Embassy or Consulate abroad. While the Form DS-156 is used, some consular officials do not require its use.

Aliens in transit to the United Nations who are issued a C-2 visa are subject to travel restrictions imposed by the Secretary of Homeland Security. *Ref: 9 FAM 41.71*

The processing of these visas and related matters is usually handled directly by the sponsoring agency.

The $100 Machine-Readable Visa (MRV) fee is waived in this classification.

Step 2 - Clearing the BCBP at a U.S. Port of Entry

Entry is granted by the BCBP based on the approval of the State Department.

Documentation and supporting evidence includes:
- *Prior DOS approval*
  - DOS Machine-Readable Visa (MRV) in passport

G

Government Representative to International Organization

Gstatus is reserved for "those who are accredited by their government to represent it to an international organization such as the United Nations, World Bank or Red Cross. This classification can include staff, a spouse, unmarried children under the age of 21 and servants and attendants.   *Ref: INS ER 806 3-8-94*

Sub-categories are:

- G-1 - Principal Resident Representative of Recognized Foreign Member Government to International Organization, Staff or Immediate Family

- G-2 - Other Representative of Recognized Foreign Member Government to International Organization, or Immediate Family

- G-3 - Representative of Nonrecognized or Nonmember Foreign Government to International Organization, or Immediate Family

- G-4 - International Organization Officer or Employee, or Immediate Family

- G-5-Attendant, servant, or personal employee of G-1 through G-1 or immediate family   *Ref: INA 101(a)(15)(G);9 FAM 41.12, 41.21, 41.24*

The Department of State (DOS) and the Immigration and Naturalization Service (INS) have the joint responsibility for the adjudication of applications.

Admission Process

Step 1 - Clearing the Department of State (DOS) Abroad

The sponsoring agency usually handles the processing of these visas and related matters.

Applications for entry in this classification may be made at a U.S. Embassy or Consulate abroad.

Documentation and supporting evidence includes:
- *DOS forms*
  - DS-1648, Application for A, G or NATO Visa
  - DS-156 Nonimmigrant Visa Application, or
  - I-566, Inter-Agency Record of Individual Requesting Change/Adjustment or Dependent Employment Authorization
- *Fee*
  - Machine-Readable Visa (MRV) fee is waived in this classification
- *Passport and photograph*
  - passport valid for six months beyond intended stay
  - 50 mm (2") square photograph facing camera directly without head covering (check for religious exceptions) against a light background
- *Third Country immigration status*
  - evidence of current immigration status in third country if eligible to apply as a Third-Country National (TCN)
- *Current and prior immigration status*
  - (expired) documents relating to previous U.S. visits:
    - passports with visas
    - Forms I-20, I-797, I-94 cards, Employment Authorization Documents
- *Employer's evidence to support request*
  - original letter from the employing international organization describing:
    - nature of your work
    - length of your intended stay in the United States
- *Additional evidence*
  - "Howe Letter" from U.N. or similar G-4 visa request letter from other qualifying organizations such as the World Bank
  - employment contract (G-5 applicants) describing:
    - nature of your work
    - length of your intended stay in the United States
- *Civil documents*
  - proof of relationship of dependents applying for derivative visa status
  - marriage certificate
  - birth certificate(s)
  - adoption papers

A "Howe Letter" is named after the former Chief (latterly Bonner) of the Transportation Division of the United Nations who issues letters of request for G-4 visas. Letters are to be sent to the consular section prior to your scheduled appointment.

Step 2 - Clearing the BCBP at a U.S. Port of Entry

Entry is granted by the BCBP based on the approval of the State Department.

The Machine-Readable Visa is subject to electronic verification by the BCBP at U.S. ports of entry.

Documentation and supporting evidence includes:
- *Prior DOS approval*
  - DOS Machine-Readable Visa (MRV) in passport

Step 3 - Extension/Change of Status in the United States

An extension or change from another nonimmigrant status to G is a two-part process. Except for G-5 applicants, it is necessary to first file with the State Department through your international organization. Then, your application is to be filed with the BCIS.

Part One - DOS:

Documentation and supporting evidence includes:
- *DOS forms*
  - I-566, Inter-Agency Record of Individual Requesting Change/Adjustment or Dependent Employment Authorization
  - if applying to be the principal alien:
    - DS-1648, Application for A, G or NATO Visa
    - DS-394, Notification of Foreign Government Related Employment Status, or
    - DS-1497, Notification of Appointment of Foreign Diplomatic Officer
- *Current and prior immigration status*
  - I-94, Arrival/Departure Record

Part Two - BCIS:

After you receive your I-566 with a favorable endorsement from the DOS, submit your application to the BCIS office having jurisdiction over your place of residence.

If filing for G-5 status, file directly with the appropriate BCIS Service Center.

If you are a permanent resident who wishes to be employed in a G occupation while retaining your permanent resident status, contact the BCIS office having jurisdiction over your place of residence for procedures under INA 247(b).

Documentation and supporting evidence includes:
- *BCIS forms*
  - I-539 Application to Extend/Change Nonimmigrant Status
  - I-407, Abandonment by Alien of Status as Lawful Permanent Resident, (Green Card holders only)

- original I-566 certified by the State Department with favorable DOS endorsement recommending that the request be granted
- *Fee*
  - $140 for I-539
- *Current and prior immigration status*
  - I-94 Arrival/Departure Record (nonimmigrant)
  - I-551 Green Card (immigrant)
  - Prior DOS approval
- *Employer's evidence to support request - G-5 only*
  - copy of employer's I-94 or approval notice demonstrating G status
  - original letter from employer describing your duties and stating that he/she intends to personally cmploy you

The BCIS issues an I-797, Notice of Approval, which serves as evidence of the change of status.

Visa Revalidation by the Department of State

After BCIS has extended your stay, your visa may need to be renewed before attempting to reenter the United States after travel abroad. Depending on how U.S. citizens are treated in your home country in similar circumstances, your original visa may have been issued with restrictions on the number of entries into the United States and its period of validity.

As a service to aliens in a few classifications such as A, the Department of State processes A visa renewals in the United States. Forms may be requested by writing:

Department of State
Visa Office
Room L703
2401 E Street N.W.
Washington, DC 20522-0106

Documentation and supporting evidence includes:

- *DOS form*
  - DS-156, Nonimmigrant Visa Application
- *Fee*
  - Machine-Readable Visa (MRV) fee is waived
- *Passport and photograph*
  - passport valid for at least six months beyond intended stay
  - 50 mm (2") square photograph facing camera directly without head covering (check for religious exceptions) against a light background
- *Current and prior immigration status*
  - original current I-94 (no copies)
- *Employer's supporting documentation*
  - detailed letter identifying:

- the employee
- his or her position
- travel itinerary

Your completed application should be mailed to:

Department of State
Visa Office
Room L703
2401 E Street N.W.
Washington, DC 20522-0106

Step 4 - Application for Dependent Employment Authorization

The process for obtaining employment authorization as a G dependent was modified in 1998.

In all cases, the employment authorization application process must start with the alien's international organization submitting an application to the State Department, Office of Protocol, or the United States Mission to the United Nations (USUN) for foreign UN dependents.

The DOS or USUN will process the application and forward it to directly to the BCIS Nebraska Service Center.

Part One - DOS or USUN:

Part one involves the initial submission to the State Department or USUN.

Documentation and supporting evidence includes:

- *DOS form*
  - I-566 Inter-Agency Record of Individual Requesting Change/ Adjustment or Dependent Employment Authorization
- *Passport*
  - passport valid for at least six months beyond intended stay
- *Additional evidence*
  - diplomatic note requesting employment authorization
  - employer's offer of employment (when required under the terms of de facto arrangements (statement must identify the dependent by name, describe the position and salary offered, detail the duties, and verify that the dependent possesses the necessary qualifications)
  - completed I-765 signed by the applicant
  - no filing fee or fingerprints required
  - two color photographs with the name of the applicant and mission on the back of each

- clear photocopy of applicant's photograph from passport, MRV, DOS identification document or other acceptable identity document issued by the sending state or U.S. government
- copy of I-94 Arrival/Departure Record - front and back

If requesting an extension or reapplying for an EAD, photocopies of IRS tax returns for previous years that the dependent worked must be provided. The Nebraska Service Center will direct concerns regarding the sufficiency of an application to the embassy or international organization in the address block of the I-765.

Ref: 8 CFR 214.2(a) (6) and 214.2(g) (6)

Part Two - BCIS:

Applications related to employment authorization should be filed with the Nebraska Service Center.

Step 5 - Change to Other Status by the DOS and BCIS in the United States

To change from G status to either another nonimmigrant or immigrant status, you must first file Form I-566, Inter-Agency Record of Individual Requesting Change/Adjustment or Dependent Employment Authorization with the State Department.

After clearing the DOS, check the application process for the classification of your choice as detailed elsewhere in this book.

N

International Organization Family Member

N status is reserved for "the parent, child or sibling of an alien granted SK-3 special immigrant status under INA Section 101(a)(27)(I) and generally relates to officers or employees of international organizations." It may be available to retired officers and employees previously accorded G-4 status

Ref: INS ER 806 3-8-94

Sub-categories are:

- N-8 - parent of an alien accorded the status of special immigrant under INA 101(a)(27)(I)(I) if and while the alien is a child
- N-9 - child of parent or alien accorded the status of special immigrant under INA 101(a)(27)(I)(ii),(iii),(iv)

Ref: INA 101(a)(15)(N)(I),(ii); 9 FAM 41.82

The classification includes:

- An unmarried son or daughter of a current or former international organization officer or employee
- A surviving spouse of a deceased international organization officer
- A retired international organization officer or employee
- An immigrant spouse of a retired international organization officer or employee   *Ref: INA 101(a)(27)(I)((I),(ii),(iii),(iv)*

Admission Process

Step 1 - Clearing the Department of State (DOS) Abroad

The sponsoring agency usually handles the processing of these visas and related matters.

Applications for entry in this classification may be made at a U.S. Embassy or Consulate serving your home country.

Documentation and supporting evidence includes:
- *DOS Form*
  - DS-156, Nonimmigrant Visa Application
- *Fees*
  - $100 for non-refundable Machine-Readable Visa (MRV)
  - visa reciprocity equating to fees charged in similar circumstances in alien's home country
- *Passport and photograph*
  - passport valid for at least six months beyond intended stay
  - 50 mm (2") square photograph facing camera directly without head covering (check for religious exceptions) against a light background
- *Employer's evidence to support request*
  - comprehensive letter from the principal alien's employer on company letterhead that:
    - is signed by the company's responsible officer
    - describes your job and your business in detail
    - justifies the need for the visa
    - identifies you
    - names your dependents

Upon receipt of satisfactory documentation, the consulate abroad will issue a Machine-Readable Visa. If a visa reciprocity fee is charged, you must submit a separate check.

Step 2 - Clearing the BCBP at a U.S. Port of Entry

Very few visas are issued in this classification.

The Machine-Readable Visa issued by the State Department abroad is subject to electronic verification by the BCBP at U.S. ports of entry.

Documentation and supporting evidence includes:
- *Prior DOS approval*
  - DOS Machine-Readable Visa (MRV) in passport

N visa holders are admitted to the United States for the duration of their assignment.

An I-94, Arrival/Departure Record is issued by the BCBP at a port of entry.

NATO
Representative of Member State

$\mathbf{N}$ATO status is reserved for representatives and staff of member states to NATO.

Sub categories are:

- **NATO-1** - Principal Permanent Representative of Member State to NATO (including any Subsidiary Bodies) Resident in United States and Resident Official Staff Members, Secretary General, Assistant Secretary General, and Executive Secretary of NATO, and other Permanent NATO Officials of Similar Rank, or members of Immediate Family
  Ref: Article 12, 5 UST 1094 and Article 20, 5 UST 1098

- **NATO-2** - Other Representatives of Member State to NATO (including any Subsidiary Bodies) including its Advisors and Technical Experts of Delegations, Members of Immediate Family, Dependents of Member of a Force Entering in Accordance with the Status-of-Forces Agreement or in Accordance with Provisions of the Protocol on status of International Military Headquarters and Members of Such a Force if Issued Visas
  Ref: Article 13, 5 UST 1094 and Article 1, 4 UST 1794

- **NATO-3** - Official Clerical Staff Accompanying Representative of Member State to NATO (including any Subsidiary Bodies) or Members of Immediate Family
  Ref: Article 14, 5 UST 1096

- **NATO-4** - Official of NATO (Other than Classifiable as NATO-1 or Members of Immediate Family
  Ref: Article 18, 5 UST 1098

- **NATO-5** - Expert, Other than NATO Officials Classifiable as NATO-4, employed in Missions on Behalf of NATO, and their dependents
  Ref: Article 21, 5 UST 1100

- **NATO-6** - Member of a Civilian Component Accompanying a Force Entering in Accordance with Provisions of the NATO Status-of-Forces Agreement, Member of a Civilian Component Attached to or Employed by an Allied Headquarters Under the Protocol on Status of International Military Headquarters Set Up Pursuant to the North Atlantic Treaty and their Dependents   *Ref: Article 1, 4 UST 1794; Article 3, 5 UST 877*

- **NATO-7** - Attendant, Servant, or Personal Employee of NATO-1 through NATO-6 Classes or Members of Immediate Family
  Ref: Article 12-20 5 UST 1094-1098; 9 FAM 41.21, 41.25

Admission Process

Step 1 - Clearing the Department of State (DOS) Abroad

Visas in this classification are arranged by the home government directly with their official diplomatic contacts. Submit Form DS-1648, Application for A, G or NATO Visa. The $100 Machine-Readable Visa (MRV) fee is waived.   *Ref: 5 UST 1094-1098*

Step 2 - Clearing the BCBP at a U.S. Port of Entry

Entry is granted by the BCBP based on the approval of the DOS.

Documentation and supporting evidence includes:

- *Prior DOS approval*
  - DOS Machine-Readable Visa (MRV) in passport

Step 3- Extension/Change of Status

Visa Revalidation by the Department of State

Your visa may need to be renewed before attempting to reenter the United States after travel abroad. Depending on how U.S. citizens are treated in your home country in similar circumstances, your original visa may have been issued with restrictions on the number of entries into the United States and its period of validity.

As a service to aliens in the NATO classification, the Department of State processes NATO visa renewals in the United States. Forms may be requested by writing:

> Department of State
> Visa Office
> Room L703
> 2401 E Street N.W.
> Washington, DC 20522-0106

Documentation and supporting evidence includes:

- *DOS forms*
  - DS-156, Nonimmigrant Visa Application
  - DS-1648, Application for A, G or NATO Visa
- *Fee*
  - Machine-Readable Visa (MRV) fee is waived
- *Passport and photograph*
  - passport valid for at least six months beyond intended stay
  - 50 mm (2") square photograph facing camera directly without head covering (check for religious exceptions) against a light background

- *Current and prior immigration status*
  - original current I-94 (no copies)
- *Employer's supporting documentation*
  - detailed letter identifying:
    - the employee
    - his or her position
    - travel itinerary

Your completed application should be mailed to:

> Department of State
> Visa Office
> Room L703
> 2401 E Street N.W.
> Washington, DC 20522-0106

Step 4 - Application for Dependent Employment Authorization

The process for obtaining employment authorization as a NATO dependent was modified in 1998.

In all cases, the employment authorization application process must start with the alien's diplomatic mission submitting an application to NATO's Supreme Allied Commander, Atlantic (SACLANT).

Part One - SACLANT

Part one involves the initial submission to SACLANT.

Documentation and supporting evidence includes:

- *BCIS forms*
  - I-566 Inter-Agency Record of Individual Requesting Change/Adjustment or Dependent Employment Authorization
  - I-765 signed by the applicant
- *Passport*
  - passport valid for at least six months beyond intended stay
- *Additional evidence*
  - diplomatic note requesting employment authorization
  - employer's offer of employment (when required under the terms of de facto arrangements (statement must identify the dependent by name, describe the position and salary offered, detail the duties, and verify that the dependent possesses the necessary qualifications)
  - no filing fee or fingerprints required
  - two color photographs with the name of the applicant and mission on the back of each

- clear photocopy of applicant's photograph from passport, MRV, DOS identification document or other acceptable identity document issued by the sending state or U.S. government
- copy of I-94 Arrival/Departure Record - front and back

If requesting an extension or reapplying for an EAD, photocopies of IRS tax returns for previous years that the dependent worked must be provided. The Nebraska Service Center will direct concerns regarding the sufficiency of an application to the embassy or international organization in the address block of the I-765.

Ref: 8 CFR 214.2(a) (6) and 214.2(g) (6)

Part Two - BCIS

Applications related to employment authorization for the dependents of NATO nonimmigrants should be filed with the BCIS Nebraska Service Center.

Part III

Green Cards

Green Card holders are also known as legal permanent residents, immigrants and landed immigrants. The real name of the Green Card is Permanent Resident Card (formerly Alien Registration Receipt Card) or Form I-551. To reduce document fraud and help employers and government agencies identify valid cards, the BCIS has started production of a new plastic state-of-the-art tamper-resistant Green Card like a credit card at its Service Centers and a production facility in Corbin, Kentucky. The high-tech security features on the front of the card include digital photograph and fingerprint images and a hologram depicting the Statue of Liberty. The laser-etched optical memory strip on the reverse side cannot be altered and must be read by a special BCIS card reader. It contains the cardholder's photograph, signature, date of birth, fingerprint, name and registration number.

Although a Green Card must be renewed every ten years, it offers its holder the privilege of living and working in the United States in what is supposed to be an unrelinquished permanent U.S. residence. While a Green Card makes available many of the benefits enjoyed by U.S. citizens, it also comes with important responsibilities such as good conduct.

An alien who is ineligible for citizenship shall be ineligible for a Green Card. However, those who receive a Green Card may apply for U.S. citizenship after five years in most cases or in three years if married to a U.S. citizen.   *Ref: 9 FAM 40.81*

A nonimmigrant A or G is not eligible to obtain an immigrant visa until executing a written waiver of all rights, privileges, exemptions and immunities which accrue from their immigration status.   *Ref: 9 FAM 40.203*

Entry Criteria

The process of obtaining a Green Card may seem long and frustrating, yet it is actually both thorough and fair. Your chance of success depends on:

- Your qualifications or family relationship
- The parameters of your chosen classification
- The supply of available qualified U.S. workers in your function
- Whether there are other special conditions that influence entry

How Part III is Divided

Part III provides a detailed introduction to the Green Card. Its four chapters offer a step-by-step explanation of each of the main options for obtaining a Green Card.

Chapter 9-Family-Sponsored Preferences
* Four preference options

Chapter 10-Employment-Based Preferences
* Five preference options

Chapter 11-Diversity (DV) Lottery
* Annual worldwide lottery for citizens of underserved countries

Chapter 12-Refugees/Asylees
* Aliens with a well-founded fear of persecution

Overview

The number of permanent visas issued each year is controlled by Congress and their distribution depends on a number of variables.

Unlimited Immigrants obtain permanent residence without numerical limitation and are not counted against the annual quotas. These include:
* Immediate relatives of a U.S. citizen 21 or over
  (spouse, minor children and parents)
* Returning residents - previous U.S. lawful residents returning after more than a year abroad
* Immigrant applying for reacquisition of U.S. citizenship
* Refugees and asylees
* Foreigners in Amnesty Legalization Program (see LIFE - Green Cards)
* Foreigners granted suspension of deportation or registry
* Children born to a permanent resident during a temporary visit abroad
* An unspecified number of visas for qualified aliens

Limited immigrants are subject to certain transitional laws. In Fiscal Year 2002, the available immigrant numbers were:
* Family-Sponsored: no fewer than 226,000 nor more than 480,000 immigrant visas per year
* Employment-Based - at least 140,000   *Ref: INA 201*
* Diversity (Green Card) Lottery - 50,000 immigrant visa numbers annually

In 2001, the **per-country limit** for preference immigrants from independent countries was set at 7 percent or 25,620 and 2 percent or 7,320 for dependent areas. Mexico led all countries of birth in 1997 with 146,865.

INA 203(d) provides that spouses and children of preference immigrants are entitled to the same status and the same order of consideration if accompanying or following to join the principal.

Immigration in Fiscal Year 2001:

- 1,064,318 persons
- 443,964 immediate relatives of U.S. citizens
- 232,143 family preferences
- 179,195 employment preferences
- 108,506 refugees and asylees converting to legal permanent resident
- 42,015 Diversity Program   *Ref: INS News Release, August 30, 2002*

In 1997, the top countries of birth were, in order, Mexico, the Philippines, China, Vietnam and India. California was the leading intended state of residence, followed by New York, Florida, Texas and New Jersey.

The three largest occupational groups were:

- Professional, specialty and technical
- Service occupations
- Executive, administrative and managerial

Admission Process

The following chapters detail the different requirements and processes associated with obtaining a Green Card.

All roads to a Green Card require that the would-be immigrant meet certain criteria and have a reason for coming which is consistent with the spirit and the letter of the Immigration and Nationality Act.

As previously noted, permanent residency is granted generally as a result of:

- A family member filing a petition, or
- A (future) employer filing a petition, or
- Being selected in an annual immigration lottery drawing, or
- Having been granted asylum or refugee status

Often, applicants are living and working or studying in the United States on the basis of a nonimmigrant visa when they are processed for their Green Card. For them, an adjustment of status to immigrant at a U.S. BCIS office is necessary. Others, living outside the United States, will deal with a U.S. Embassy or Consulate abroad.

Step 1 - Labor Certification

Second (EB2) and Third Preference (EB3) Employment-Based classifications require an employer to file for Labor Certification, In those cases, the Department of Labor must be convinced that there is a need to admit an alien to carry out a job for which there are no qualified U.S. citizens or residents available. It should be noted that a Second Preference waiver is possible.

In Fiscal Year 1995, the occupations which received the most Labor Certification approvals were foreign food specialty cook, software engineer, programmer analyst, college or university faculty member, systems analyst and cook.

Step 2 - Clearing the BCIS in the United States - Initial Petition

Many J-1 Exchange Visitors must either obtain a waiver or serve the two-year Home Residency Requirement before they may file for an Adjustment of Status. Also, inadmissible aliens should file Form I-601, Application for Waiver of Grounds of Excludability with $195 to the appropriate Service Center or U.S. Consulate.

A spouse and child not otherwise entitled to an immigrant status and the immediate issuance of a visa are entitled to the same status and the same order of consideration if accompanying or following to join their spouse or parent. An applicant's family or (future) employer may file a petition with the BCIS in the United States on behalf of an alien living in the U.S. or abroad.

All photographs required by the BCIS must meet their stringent standards. See www.immigration.gov/graphics/lawsregs/handbook/m-378.pdf for details.

The date on which a Green Card petition is filed is known as the Priority Date. This is when the properly completed and signed petition is accepted for filing in the first step of the process. Priority Dates have the most impact on Family-Sponsored applicants and EB3 Other Workers.   *Ref: 8 CFR 204.5 (d)*

All immigrant visa applicants are processed in the order of their Priority Date within their classification. Depending on the classification and qualifications involved, the process could take anywhere from a few weeks to several years. This is especially true for natives of India and China who hold more than half of the H-1Bs. Adjustment is thus slower for them and for the many applicants from Mexico and the Philippines.

No fingerprinting fee is submitted if processing will be at a U.S. Consulate abroad. However, the BCIS now requires that a $50 fingerprinting fee be submitted with the petition instead of the fingerprint card, Form FD-258 for all in-U.S. Adjustment of Status cases. The applicant will be advised when and where to have fingerprints taken.

After approval, an I-797, Notice of Approval is sent to the petitioner.

The State Department's National Visa Center at Portsmouth, New Hampshire is notified and holds all approved immigrant visa petitions until the alien's priority date is about to become current and the alien is advised.

Family-Sponsored Petitions - Chapter 9

BCIS Form I-130, Petition for Alien Relative is filed by the U.S. resident family member at the local BCIS office along with an $96 filing fee and documentation.

There are four preference categories:

- First (F1), Second (F2), Third (F3) and Fourth (F4) Preference

Which preference is appropriate is determined by:

- The citizenship of the petitioner
- The relationship, age and civil status of the beneficiary

Employment-Based Petitions - Chapter 10

One of three BCIS forms is filed at the BCIS regional Service Center having jurisdiction over the location concerned.

BCIS Form I-140, Immigrant Petition for Alien Worker is generally filed by the employer along with a $135 filing fee for the following preference categories:

- First (EB1), Second (EB2) and Third (EB3) Preference

BCIS Form I-360, Application for Amerasian, Widow(er) or Special Immigrant is filed along with an $130 filing fee for the following preference category:

- Fourth (EB4) Preference

BCIS Form I-526, Immigrant Petition by Alien Entrepreneur is filed along with a $400 filing fee for the following preference category:

- Fifth (EB5) Preference

Which preference is appropriate is determined by:

- The nature of the employment
- The professional qualifications of the beneficiary
- The special status of the beneficiary
- The status of a multi-national enterprise

Diversity (DV) Lottery - Chapter 11

The annual worldwide lottery is carried out by the State Department for citizens of underserved countries. No BCIS or DOS form is involved in the initial application.

Refugees/Asylees - Chapter 12

BCIS Form I-589, Application for Asylum and Withholding of Deportation may be filed for asylee status by an alien with a well-founded fear of persecution at a U.S. port of entry or at a local BCIS office in the U.S. Form I-590, Registration for Classification as Refugee may be filed by an alien who holds a similar well-founded fear of persecution at a BCIS office or U.S. Consulate or Embassy abroad.

Step 3 - Processing

All family-sponsored applications and those employment-based applications from employers with family ties to the alien require an I-864 Affidavit of Support. BCIS information is at www.immigration.gov/graphics/formsfee/forms/index.htm and State Department is available at www.travel.state.gov/i864gen.html.

As noted in Step 2, all BCIS-approved immigrant visas are retained by the State Department's National Visa Center until they are within a year of being current and a visa number becoming available. At that time they are forwarded to the appropriate U.S. Embassy or Consulate abroad for adjudication by a consular officer and the applicant or attorney is sent a Packet 3 which may also be downloaded from the internet at www.travel.state.gov/nvc.html. If the applicant is adjusting status in the U.S., the appropriate BCIS office is notified. To ensure notification, it is very important that the National Visa Center be advised of any change of address. Their address is:

National Visa Center
32 Rochester Avenue
Portsmouth, New Hampshire, 03801-2909.

Changes of address may also be faxed to (603) 334-0759. A 24-hour automated visa system is operated to provide status of case information by calling (603) 334-0700.

Regardless of whether you take Step 3 by applying for a BCIS Adjustment of Status in the U.S. or for an immigrant visa at a U.S. Embassy or Consulate abroad, you cannot be processed until a visa number is immediately available and your Priority Date, the date of filing your approved petition is earlier than the State Department visa cut-off date for your classification or 'current' as it is called. *Ref: INA 245*

To check on whether your Priority Date has become current, you may call the State Department's 24-hour recorded message service which provides Priority Dates (cut-off dates) for the following month. This service is updated in the middle of each month and may be reached by calling (202) 663-1541. Priority Dates are also available via the internet at: www.travel.state.gov/visa_bulletin.html. Waiting list records of individual visa applicants entitled to an immigrant classification and their priority dates are maintained at posts which will issue the visa. *Ref: 9 FAM 42.52*

Option 1 - Adjustment of Status by the BCIS in the United States

Aliens living in the United States, normally go through the formality of adjusting status to permanent resident via the BCIS in the U.S. although consular processing is also available. Family-sponsored and Diversity Lottery petitions are filed at local BCIS offices, others at Service Centers. Once a bar has kicked in, it is too late for a waiver.

After the initial petition is approved and you are advised that a visa number is immediately available, the next step is to file an application for permanent resident status on Form I-485 (dated February 7, 2000) with the director having jurisdiction over the applicant's place of residence. A separate application shall be filed by each applicant. File Form I-485 with $255 filing fee and concurrently with the I-130 and its $130 filing fee and Form I-765 and its $120 filing fee along with $50 for fingerprinting.

An alien who has been the beneficiary of approved Labor Certifications and I-140s from two different companies may use the earlier priority when filing an I-485, Adjustment of Status if the first employer has not withdrawn the earlier petition.
Ref: 8 CFR 204.5 (e)

If the application for Adjustment of Status is approved, the director shall record the lawful admission of the applicant as of the date of approval. The applicant shall be notified of the decision and, if the application is denied, of the reasons. BCIS advises that the historical denial rate is seven percent. No appeal of the denial may be made but the alien may renew his or her application.

An applicant for Adjustment of Status must have a medical examination by a designated civil surgeon unless medically examined in connection with entry in K Fiancé(e) status. Also, interviews cannot be waived for family-sponsored applicants.

Applicants who have overstayed their temporary status and are still physically present in the United States, are *Out of Status*. They may no longer pay a $1,000 fine with Supplement A to Form I-485 and must be processed in their country unless they prove they were in the U.S. on December 21, 2000 and had a Green Card application in process by April 30, 2001. Out of Status aliens may be able to petition for adjustment in the United States if they have anchor relatives and extreme hardship is involved.

With an application receipt number, the status of an Adjustment of Status case may be checked by calling the BCIS National Customer Service Center at (800) 375-5283 or on the internet at https://immigration.gov/graphics/cris/jsps/index.jsp. Service is available in English and Spanish.

Advance Parole
If you live in the United States, you are placed under a travel embargo:
- After your Priority Date has become current, and
- You have filed an I-485 for Adjustment of Status, and
- Before your final Green Card processing

At this time, the departure of an applicant who is not under exclusion, deportation, or removal proceedings shall be deemed an abandonment of his or her application constituting grounds for termination, unless the applicant was previously granted Advance Parole by the BCIS for such absence and inspected upon returning.

If you must leave and reenter the country prior to your final Green Card processing for emergent, business, personal or humanitarian reasons, you should obtain a Form I-512 by filing an I-131 with the $110 filing fee and an additional $50 for fingerprinting at the appropriate BCIS office or Application Support Center (ASC).

Form I-512 may be issued to:

- A member of the professions or a person having exceptional ability in the sciences or arts who had been granted voluntary departure
- A person who holds valid refugee or asylee status
- An alien who seeks to depart temporarily for any emergent bona fide business, personal or humanitarian reason
- A lawful permanent resident who, because of emergent reasons, must embark before action can be completed on his reentry application

As a word of warning, aliens subject to deportation waive their rights to a deportation hearing and risk being placed in exclusion if they obtain Advance Parole and leave the country before their deportation case is resolved.

Parole authorization on Form I-512 may be issued to a principal alien by the District Director having jurisdiction over the place where the principal alien resides in the United States, and sent to the alien. The multi-page Advance Parole Form I-512 is stamped and issued before departing. Departure before a decision is made on an application for a refugee travel document does not affect the application.

An I-512 may be issued valid for multiple applications for parole into the United States, usually for an alien who frequently leaves the U.S. on business trips.

The remarks block of the I-512 sets forth the time which the alien may be paroled and the conditions for re-parole. If it is marked for multiple applications, generally to a principal alien who, for business purposes, frequently departs the United States, it will be stamped at the port of entry with the arrival date and returned to the alien for future use.

Return of the principal alien shall be required within four months of the date of issuance of the parole authorization, except that the return of an alien who will be abroad in connection with his qualifying profession or occupation shall be required within the time needed for such purpose, not to exceed one year from the date of issuance of parole authorization.

On returning, all copies of the form are stamped with a parole stamp and retained by the traveler except one copy which is sent to the traveler's A file.

An otherwise eligible applicant who is outside the United States and wishes to come to the United States to apply for benefits under section 202 of Pub. L. 105-100 may request parole authorization by filing for Travel Document (I-131) with the Texas Service Center and a photocopy of the I-485 that will be filed on entering the United States. If the Director of the Texas Service Center is satisfied that the alien will be eligible for adjustment of status and will file the application, he may issue an Authorization for Parole Form I-512 to allow the alien to be paroled into the U.S. for a period of 60 days. The alien shall have 60 days from the date of the parole to file the application for Adjustment of Status.

Interviews

The BCIS is moving toward the processing of most Employment-Based adjustment of status cases on an "interview waiver" basis.

When an interview is held, its purpose is to ensure that:

- You agree that all information in the application is correct, or
- You correct your petition to reflect actual facts
- The examiner can resolve any last minute questions or doubts such as:
  - proof of receipt of the salary offered
  - evidence of financial support or lawful employment authorization
  - you have lawful immigration status in the United States

If you are unable to satisfy the examiner that you are legally *In Status* you must meet the following conditions in order to remain and adjust status in the United States:

- A relative or employer must have filed a petition making you eligible for an immigrant visa
- An immigrant visa must be immediately available
- If Out of Status, be in the U.S. on December 21, 2000 with a Green Card application pending by April 30, 2001 and pay a $1,000 fine

If your case is "closed", the examiner will place a temporary Green Card stamp in your passport. However, if your case is "continued", you will be required to submit all missing and necessary documentation to the office where the interview was held within 12 weeks or the case is automatically denied. Written notification of the decision is sent by mail. An alien residing in the U.S. may not be required to produce a passport.

Option 2 - By the Department of State (DOS) Abroad

Aliens who are documentarily qualified, that is who report that they have obtained all the documents specified by the consular officer to meet the requirements of INA 222(b) may apply formally for an immigrant visa.   *Ref: 9 FAM 40.1(g)*

The permanent resident application of aliens (beneficiaries) living outside the United States, normally is processed by a consular officer at a U.S. Embassy or Consulate in their home country or in a third country such as Canada or Mexico.

You may speak with a Visa Information Officer Monday through Friday by calling (202) 663-1225 between 8:30 am and 5:00 pm, Eastern Time, or (202) 663-1213 between 2:00 pm and 4:00 pm Eastern Time.

Effective June 1, 2002, I-864 Affidavit of Support forms sent from the National Visa Center (NVC) and posts abroad are subject to a $65 processing fee to cover the cost of providing NVC or call center assistance to sponsors, co-sponsors and joint sponsors. The fee is charged for each I-864 filed by a sponsor/petitioner but no extra fee is charged for an I-864a filed by a co-sponsor or essentially duplicative I-864 forms such as for parents or other members of one family. If more than one I-864 is needed, one fee will be assessed for each separate affidavit.   *Ref: Pub. L. 106-113*

An alien will normally be sent a "Packet III" which advises which documents will need to be presented. Later, the alien will be sent a "Packet IV" from the National Visa Center to confirm the visa interview appointment and advise that a medical and fingerprinting are necessary. Forms are at: www.travel.state.gov/visaforms.html.

The 2001 USA Patriot Act requires that all visa applicants are submitted to a name-check to determine whether they have a criminal history or record. If there is a potential name match, the applicant will be required to have fingerprints taken and pay an $85 fee which will be forwarded to the FBI. If a record is found in their NCIC database, the FBI will forward it to the State Department for use by an authorized Consular Officer. Applicants from countries listed in FAM where police clearance is not available do not submit police records. But, applicants must provide police records from other countries where they have lived if those records can be obtained.

Panel physicians who conduct medical examinations are required to verify that new vaccination requirements have been met or that it is inappropriate for the applicant to receive vaccinations for one or more of: mumps, measles, rubella, polio, tetanus and diphtheria toxoids, pertussis, influenza, influenzae type b (Hib), hepatitis B, varicella, and pneumococcal.

Instead of adjusting status with the BCIS, aliens with pending I-485s in the U.S. may direct their files for consular processing by filing Form I-824 with a $140 filing fee.

Most consular interviews are brief, routine and in two separate interviews on the same day. The first interview is performed by a document checker who makes certain that an alien has all necessary documents and the information on the forms is correct.

The second interview with a U.S. Foreign Service Officer or consular officer generally occurs shortly afterward. The applicant is placed under oath and swears that all information submitted is correct. The Officer may ask additional questions and must be satisfied that the alien has met the requirements of the requested status. Have available evidence of the disposition of any case before a judge or jury including original or certified copies of law enforcement agency or court record of arrests, charges, indictments, convictions, fines, imprisonment, release, pardons etc.

Advance payment of the $335 immigrant visa processing fee is now required in certain foreign posts before you receive an appointment to appear before a consular officer. The first ten posts represented approximately 40 percent of all immigrant visa applications. Initially, the National Visa center scheduled interviews for Montréal, Canada, Freetown, Sierra Leone and Tirana, Albania. The designated consulates scheduled the others.

Documentation and supporting evidence includes:
- *Fees*
  - $335 for visa processing
  - $65 for Affidavit of Support review

- *Police clearance*
  - copy of police certificate(s)
  - certified copy of prison records
- *Additional evidence*
  - certified copy of military records
  - other documents the consul considers necessary
- *Civil documents*
  - documents establishing relationship of spouse and children to alien
  - records of birth
- *Medical clearance*
  - examination by approved physician
  - seriology and x-ray tests   *Ref: 9 FAM 42.66*

Passports are not required of:

- Certain relatives of U.S. citizens or legal permanent residents
- Returning residents
- Stateless persons
- Nationals of communist countries
- Alien members of U.S. Armed Forces

Visas are not required of:

- Alien members of U.S. Armed Forces
- Aliens entering from Guam, Puerto Rico or the U.S. Virgin Islands
- Child born after the issue of parent(s)' visa
- American Indians born in Canada   *Ref: 9 FAM 42.1*

Successful applicants must return later to pick up their immigrant visa and a sealed envelope of all relevant documents to be carried to the U.S. port of entry.

Step 4 - Clearing the BCBP at a U. S. Port of Entry

An alien living and processed in the United States skips this step.

Applicants must bring their visa and documents issued by the U.S. Embassy or Consulate abroad to a port of entry within six months. A BCBP Immigration Inspector has the right and responsibility to re-check all documentation and decide whether to grant permanent residency and admit the applicant.   *Ref: IIRIRA96.631*

Applicants will be required to complete Form I-89 which provides a copy of their signature and fingerprint. Documentation includes Green Card information, medical and other records. Fingerprints for police clearance are not taken at a port of entry. The applicant must also have a valid passport and agree to keep it valid.

Under INA 289, American Indians born in Canada who possess at least 50 percent American Indian blood may apply for a Green Card and enter by completing Form I-181 at a port of entry. Required documentation for indian, métis and inuit candidates includes a long form birth certificate, a letter from the band council establishing blood quantity and a government status card. Spouses with less than 50 percent American Indian blood do not qualify. A preliminary visit or call to the port of entry is advised.

Step 5 - *Obtaining and Retaining Your Green Card*

Until recently, all Green Cards have come from Arlington, Texas, Now, the distribution is shifted to the BCIS regional Service Centers, the Cards may take up to a year to arrive and are good for ten years. If there is a delay, an inquiry may be filed on Form G-731, available from the BCIS or you may call the responsible BCIS Service Center to inquire about the status of your card.

To avoid the risk of losing your Green Card, you should:

- "Continuously manifest an intention to reside permanently in the U.S."
- Maintain your U.S. principal residence
- Report any change of address to the BCIS within 10 days
- Maintain U.S. bank accounts
- Register with the BCIS within 10 days of turning 14
- Register with Selective Service within 30 days of turning 18 (males only)
- File a U.S. resident tax return on worldwide income and pay all taxes owed

You should not:

- Be involved in illegal activities such as drug use
- Have criminal convictions
- Falsify documents
- Be a security risk or public charge   *Ref: INA 241(a)*
- Leave your Green Card job too soon after starting

Your Green Card allows you to apply for:

- Any U.S. job not requiring U.S. citizenship
- Sponsorship of a spouse and unmarried children under 21 for Green Card
- Naturalization after five years (three years for spouses of U.S. citizens)
- Social Security retirement or disability benefits
- In-state university tuition after a qualifying period
- Scholarships and student loans
- Government-sponsored financial aid for education
- Some welfare, Medicaid and unemployment and some Supplemental Security Income (SSI) benefits

Obtaining a Replacement Green Card

I-551 Green Cards issued since 1989 are only valid for ten years and must be replaced on expiration. Also, I-151 Green Cards issued before 1979 expired on March 20, 1996 and must be replaced.

Without an unexpired Green Card you may experience difficulties when trying to enter a foreign country or reenter the United States.

If your Green Card has expired or will expire within the next six months, you should apply in person at your local BCIS Application Support Center (ASC). For the list of BCIS ASCs see www.immigration.gov/graphics/fieldoffices/ascs/asc.htm.

To replace an expired lost, stolen or erroneous one, you must apply at a local BCIS District or Sub-Office.

Pending arrival of the replacement card, the BCIS will attach a temporary revalidation sticker to your old Green Card to extend its validity.

Renewal applicants who received their Green Cards before their 14th birthday and are now over 14, must be fingerprinted.

Documentation and supporting evidence includes:

- *BCIS forms*
  - I-90, Application to Replace Permanent Resident Card
  - I-751, Petition to Remove the Conditions on Residence (Conditional Residents)
- *Fees*
  - $130 for I-90
    (a waiver to appear is available to infirm or non-ambulatory applicants)
  - $145 for I-751
  - $50 for fingerprinting (applicants who have turned 14)
- *Photographs*
  - two color photographs 40 mm high by 35 mm wide in 3/4 profile showing right ear, no head covering (religious exceptions), light background
- *Prior approval*
  - original I-551 or I-151 Permanent Resident Card
  - photocopy of front and back of the old Green Card
- *Supporting Documentation*
  - Government-issued identification

If you plan to travel, you may need to file an I-131 for a Reentry Permit because of delays in producing replacement cards.

Absences from the United States

Each time you leave the country:

- Carry your Green Card with you to show the BCBP on entering the U.S.
- Keep good records of the dates and reasons for all foreign trips for a future naturalization application and interview
- Reenter legally at a port of entry

If you try to enter the U.S. with your Green Card and are suspected of not actually living in the U.S., the BCBP may place you in exclusion proceedings, a first step in the cancellation of your Green Card. The guidance of competent counsel is advised.

IIRIRA96.110 mandated the Attorney General to implement an automated entry and exit control system to record the exit of every alien and match it to the record of the alien's arrival in the United States. This process has been implemented for students and certain aliens from primarily middle eastern countries. More visas are required at ports of entry than in the past.

A Green Card holder shall not be considered as seeking admission unless he/she:
- Has abandoned or relinquished that status
- Has been absent more than 180 days (see up to 180 days following)
- Has engaged in illegal activity after leaving the United States
- Has departed the United States under legal process
- Has committed an offence identified as criminal and related grounds
- Is attempting to enter at a time or place other than as designated by immigration officers or has not been admitted after inspection

Ref: AERIER

The rules vary depending on the length of time you are out of the United States. However, don't expect to be able to visit the United States once a year and retain your Green Card status. The BCBP advises not to adopt living patterns such as two months in the U.S. and four months outside which indicate that the U.S. is not your permanent and primary residence. Also expect closer scrutiny if you do not have the economic standards to match your traveling patterns.

Up to 180 Days
Green Card holders shall not be considered as seeking admission unless they have been absent for a continuous period in excess of 180 days.   *Ref: AERIER*

As a Green Card holder, you may be away from the United States for up to six months but should be able to demonstrate that you have not abandoned your U.S. residence. Up to 180 days, the burden of proof is on the BCBP to prove that you have abandoned your U.S. residency.

To avoid difficulties, some of the top immigration attorneys recommend keeping trips abroad to a maximum of four months.

The Green Card travel limit does not apply to the spouse or children of a member of the U.S. armed forces or a civilian employee of the U.S. government stationed abroad.

Ref: DOS Pub. 20520, June, 1995

Between Six Months and Two Years
After an absence of six months or more, the burden of proof is on you to prove that you have not abandoned your U.S. residency.

If you are planning to be away from the United States for between six months and two years, and have not been outside the U.S. for more than four of the last five years, it is best to apply to the BCIS for a Reentry Permit on Form I-131 with $110 filing fee at least 30 days before leaving the United States. The permit is good for two years. While it is not renewable, it may be used for multiple reentries. It is also possible to obtain an additional reentry permit after returning to the United States upon presentation of proof of your intent to maintain your permanent U.S. residency. Even though the Reentry Permit demonstrates your intention of not abandoning your permanent resident status, it does not absolutely ensure retention of your Green Card. As noted earlier, Form I-131 is also used for Advance Parole.   *Ref: 8 USC 1203(c)*

There is a special provision for aliens who are employees of the U.S. government and international organizations who, for business reasons, are required to remain outside the United States for over a year. They may be able to have their time outside the country counted toward the naturalization U.S. residency requirement.

Aliens working abroad should submit Form N-470, Application to Preserve Residence for Naturalization Purposes with its $95 fee if:

- They have been a legal permanent resident for at least a year
- They intend to apply for U.S. citizenship

Over Two Years

Should you be unable to return to the United States within six months as a Green Card holder or within two years with a Reentry Permit, you may submit a Form DS-117, Application to Determine Returning Resident Status with a fee of $360 for a special Immigrant Returning Resident (SB-1) visa at your nearest U.S. Embassy or Consulate abroad at least three months in advance. Be prepared to offer convincing evidence why your extended absence is necessary. The SB-1 is issued at the discretion of the consular officer based on proof that:

- You were a lawful permanent resident when you departed the U.S.
- You intended to return to the U.S. when you departed and maintain this intent
- You are returning from a temporary visit abroad
- If your stay was protracted, it was caused by reasons beyond your control for which you were not responsible (e.g. medical incapacitation, employment with a U.S. company, accompanying a U.S. citizen spouse, etc.)
- You are eligible for the immigrant visa in all other respects

If an SB-1 visa cannot be obtained, it may be necessary to apply for a nonimmigrant visa.   *Ref: INA 101(a)(27)(A); DOS Pub. 20520, June, 1995*

The Secretary of Homeland Security may exercise authority under INA 212(c) to grant relief from certain grounds of ineligibility for certain returning aliens.
Ref: 9 FAM 42.22

Being away for two years means that you are treated as a non-resident for tax purposes which also impacts on your naturalization waiting period.

Permanent Commuter

A resident alien who holds an I-151 Green Card may live in a residence outside the United States such as in Canada and commute to work in the U.S. Similarly, a commuter I-151 may be held by a Green Card holder who lives outside the U.S. and commutes to work in the U.S. In both situations, it is necessary to carry formal documentation that must be renewed every six months with the BCIS.

Other Options for Green Cards

Legal Immigration and Family Equity (LIFE) Act - Legalization and Family Unity

Under the Legal Immigration and Family Equity (LIFE) Act of 2000, an alien may be eligible to adjust to legal permanent resident status if he or she:

- Filed a written claim with the Attorney General before October 1, 2000 for membership in one of the following class action lawsuits:
  - Catholic Social Services (CSS) v. Meese
  - League of United Latin American Citizens (LULAC) v. INS
  - Zambrano v. INS
- Entered the U.S. before January 1, 1982 and resided continuously in the U.S. in an unlawful status through May 4, 1988
  (includes aliens entering as nonimmigrants in A, G, F, J or asylee status who remained in unlawful status)
- Was continuously present in the U.S. November 6, 1986 to May 4, 1988
- Is not inadmissible for permanent residence under any provisions of the Act
- Establishes basic English, history and government citizenship skills
- Files an application for Adjustment of Status under LIFE Legalization
- Has a high school diploma or GED or attends an accredited U.S. institution of learning

Each alien who meets these conditions must file a separate I-485 between June 1, 2001 and June 4, 2003. However, requirements may be waived if the applicant is over 65 or developmentally disabled. File with:

> Bureau of Citizenship and Immigration Services
> P.O. Box 7219
> Chicago, IL 60607-7219

Except for a person under 14 or over 79 or when impractical because of health, all aliens filing for Adjustment of Status under LIFE Legalization must be interviewed and fingerprinted. Applicants will be interviewed by an Immigration Officer as determined by the Director of the Missouri Service Center.

An alien may be granted employment authorization in increments not exceeding one year and may return to the U.S. after brief, casual and innocent trips abroad of no more than 30 days or 90 days aggregate.

If the application is granted, any pending proceedings or removal shall be terminated as of the date of approval. However, upon denial, the stay of a final order of exclusion, deportation or removal shall be deemed lifted.

Documentation and supporting evidence includes:
- *BCIS forms*
  - I-485, Application to Register Permanent Residence or Adjust Status
  - I-485, Supplement D, Life Legalization Supplement
  - G-325A, Biographic Information Sheet
  - I-693, Report of Medical Examination
  - I-765, Application for Employment Authorization, if requested
  - I-131, Application for Travel Document (Advance Parole)
- *Fees*
  - $255 for I-485
  - $120 for I-765
  - $110 for I-131
  - $50 for fingerprinting
- *Supporting documentation*
  - two color photographs 40 mm high by 35 mm wide in 3/4 profile
  - evidence of filing CSS, LULAC or Zambrano class action lawsuits
  - evidence of continuous residence in unlawful status

A **spouse and unmarried children under 21** may benefit under the **Family Unity provisions of the LIFE Act Amendments**. Each applicant must establish:
- Entry into the United States before December 1, 1988
- U.S. residence on December 1, 1988
- A qualifying relationship currently exists with the LIFE Legalization alien

A separate form, fee and documentation is filed by each person claiming eligibility. If approved, an authorized period of stay is granted by the Homeland Security Secretary under the Family Unity benefits of the LIFE Act Amendments.

Documentation and supporting evidence includes:
- *BCIS forms*
  - I-817, Application for Family Unity Benefits
  - I-765, Application for Employment Authorization, (one-year validity)
  - I-131, Application for Travel Document (Advance Parole)
- *Fees*
  - $140 for I-817
  - $120 for I-765
  - $110 for I-131
  - $50 for fingerprinting
- *Supporting evidence*
  - 4 color photographs 40 mm high by 35 mm wide in 3/4 profile
  - U.S. residence on December 1, 1988
  - entry into the U.S. prior to December 1, 1988
  - spouse or parent's membership in the CSS, LULAC or Zambrano
  - spouse or parent's filed I-485, if filing after June 1, 2002

Adjustment of Status of Certain Aliens from Vietnam, Cambodia and Laos

Up to 5,000 aliens from Vietnam, Cambodia and Laos may apply for Adjustment of Status. To be eligible, they must have been paroled into the U.S. on or before October 1, 1997 under the Orderly Departure Program, or from a refugee camp in East Asia or from a displaced persons camp in Thailand.

Applicants must be physically present in the U.S. and apply between January 27, 2003 and January 25, 2006 to the Nebraska Sevice Center in Lincoln, Nebraska. Applicants who have obtained Advance Parole may travel abroad. *Ref: Pub. L. 106-429*

Chapter 9
Family-Sponsored Preferences

Green Cards are available, in limited numbers, to qualified relatives of U.S. citizens or permanent residents based on a quota system established by Congress.

Family-sponsored immigration has two basic categories: unlimited and limited.

Unlimited family-sponsored Green Cards are available to immediate relatives of U.S. citizens and returning residents.

There are four Family-Sponsored Preference categories. Each has its own criteria and waiting period. The determination of which preference category is appropriate depends entirely on the relationship of the U.S. petitioner to the beneficiary and the immigration status of the beneficiary. Waiting periods are as of March, 2003.

Preference Categories	Annual Numbers Available	Additional Numbers	Eligibility and Waiting Period
Unlimited Family-Sponsored			
Immediate Relatives of U.S. Citizens	Unlimited	No limit	Spouse, widow(er), unmarried children under 21 of U.S. citizen, parent of U.S. citizen 21 or older Priority Date - Current
Returning Residents	Unlimited	No limit	Lawful Permanent Residents returning after temporary visit abroad of more than one year Priority Date - Current
Limited Family-Based			
First (F1):	23,400	Unused Fourth Preference numbers	Unmarried Sons and Daughters of U.S. Citizens Waiting Period - 3 3/4 years

Second (F2):	114,200	Unused First Preference numbers	Spouses and Children, and Unmarried Sons and Daughters of Permanent Residents
(F2A):	77% of Second Preference limitation	75% exempt from per country limit	Spouses and Children, of Permanent Residents Waiting period - 5 years (Mexico - 7)
(F2B):	23% of Second Preference limitation		Unmarried Sons and Daughters, 21 years of age or older, of Permanent Residents Waiting Period - 8½ years
Third (F3):	23,400	Unused First and Second Preference numbers	Married Sons and Daughters of U.S. Citizens Waiting Period - 6 years
Fourth (F4):	65,000	Unused first three Preference numbers	Brothers and Sisters of Adult U.S. Citizens Waiting period - 12 years (Philippines - 21½ years)

Ref: INA 203

Relatives of U.S. citizens are not counted in quotas.

Section 201 of the Immigration and Nationality Act (INA) sets an annual family-sponsored preference limit of 226,000.

Entry Criteria

Sponsorship by U.S. Citizens

A U.S. citizen may sponsor:
- Sons and daughters
- Spouse
- Brothers and sisters
- Parents

Sponsorship by Permanent Residents

A Green Card holder may only sponsor:
- Spouse and unmarried children
- Second or subsequent spouse if:
  - five years have elapsed since obtaining a Green Card through a previous spouse, or

- it can be proven that the prior marriage was not entered into to evade any immigration law, or
- the prior marriage was terminated by the death of the former spouse
- If they do not depend on public benefits

On August 6, 2002, the Child Status Protection Act addressed the problem of young I-130 dependent applicants **aging out** (i.e. turning 21 and losing their immigration benefits before their Green Card petition is approved), often because of processing delays. The age on the date of filing the I-130 governs a dependent's classification rather than their age on adjudication. The new rules are:

- Immediate relatives under 21 of a U.S. citizen are no longer moved to the backlogged 1st Preference when they turn 21
- 2A applicants who do not marry no longer are moved to the slower 2B if they are under 21 as of the date their petition is filed
- 2A applicants whose parent is naturalized before their petition is processed, are processed as 1st Preference based on their age on the date of their parent's naturalization
- When a marriage termination causes a 3rd Preference applicant to be converted to either a 2A or 1st Preference, the age determination of the dependent is made based on the date of the termination of the marriage
- A 2B applicant automatically becomes a 1st Preference on the naturalization of the parent (unless requesting to remain as a 2B applicant due to an earlier processing date) *Ref: Pub. L. 107-208*

All nonimmigrant classifications except H-1, L and V require that the alien intend to leave the United States at the expiration of their status.

Alien spouses and children who are victims of cruelty, battery or bigamy may apply for Green Cards under the Battered Immigrant Women Protection Act of 2000.

Admission Process

Step 1 - Clearing the BCIS in the United States - Initial Petition

A citizen or permanent resident of the United States, 21 years of age or older, may file Form I-130, Petition for Alien Relative, to establish the relationship and eligibility of certain alien relatives who wish to immigrate to the United States. An alien who is ineligible to become a citizen is also ineligible for a Green Card. *Ref: INA 212(a)(8)(A)*

Documentation and supporting evidence includes:

- *BCIS form*
  - I-130, Petition for Alien Relative
- *Fee*
  - $130

- *Passport and photographs*
  - passport valid for at least six months
  - color photo 40 mm high by 35 mm wide of each dependent - 3/4 profile
- *Current immigration status of petitioner*
  - I-551, Permanent Resident Card, or
  - Certificate of Naturalization (Form N-550)
- *Civil documents*
  - birth certificate of petitioner, or
  - FS-240, Report of Birth Abroad of a United States Citizen or birth certificate for each alien relative
  - marriage certificate
  - documents ending marriages
  - possible substitutes include church, school or census records or affidavits
- *Additional evidence*
  - G-325A, Biographical Information for each alien relative (not necessary to repeat information on I-130)

As previously noted, it may also be possible to file an I-485 and I-765 with an I-130 at the local BCIS office. The alien would be interviewed locally and could begin work immediately if approval would make a visa number immediately available. Otherwise filing is at the appropriate BCIS regional Service Center.

American citizens residing in Canada who wish to apply for Green Cards for their family members must submit their I-130 petitions to the Nebraska Service Center.

Step 2 - Processing

Option 1 - Adjustment of Status by the BCIS in the United States

After an initial petition is approved by the BCIS and an immigrant visa is immediately available, it may be possible for a legal nonimmigrant beneficiary residing in the U.S. to adjust status to permanent resident without leaving the country if you:

- Are filing an application with a complete relative, special immigrant juvenile or special immigrant military petition which, if approved, would make an immigrant visa number immediately available
- Were granted asylum or refugee status and are eligible for adjustment
- Are eligible based on Cuban citizenship or nationality
- Have continuously resided in the U.S. since 1972
- Have maintained legal status
- Are the widow(er) of a deceased U.S. service member and had been married for at least two years

A beneficiary should file with the local BCIS office having jurisdiction over his or her place of residence. If you move, your file stays with this office.

Aliens living in the U.S. who have not maintained lawful status may pay a $1,000 fine with Supplement A to Form I-485 for U.S. processing only if they were in the U.S. on December 21, 2000 and had a Green Card application in process by April 30, 2001.

Adjustment to permanent resident is not permitted where prohibited by the terms of the status under which you entered the U.S. as a nonimmigrant.

Documentation and supporting evidence includes:

- *BCIS forms*
  - I-485, Application to Register Permanent Residence or Adjust Status
  - I-765, Application for Employment Authorization (if required)
  - G-325A, Biographic Information Sheet
- *Fees*
  - $255 for I-485 if the applicant is 14 years of age or over
  - $160 for I-485 if the applicant is under 14 years of age
  - $120 for I-765
- *Passport and photographs*
  - passport valid for six months beyond intended approval date
  - two identical color photographs taken within last 30 days:
    - at least 40 mm high by 35 mm wide
    - unmounted, printed on thin paper
    - glossy, unretouched
    - 3/4 frontal showing right ear and head bare
    - A number or name printed lightly in pencil on back
- *Prior approval*
  - copy of approval notice that a visa number is immediately available
- *Current and prior immigration status*
  - copy of I-94, Arrival/Departure Record, or
  - other evidence of status
- *Additional evidence*
  - supporting documents for special categories, if applicable:
    - copy of K-2 Fiancé(e) approval notice and marriage certificate
    - letter or I-94 showing date of approval of asylum status
    - proof of continuous residence since 1972
    - proof of Cuban citizenship or nationality
    - proof of being spouse or child of another adjustment applicant
    - other proof of eligibility
- *Proof of financial support or solvency*
  - I-864, Affidavit of Support
- *Civil documents*
  - copy of birth certificate
  - marriage certificate
- *Medical clearance*
  - medical examination report on I-693 unless:

> - continuous resident since 1972, or
> - had official nonimmigrant medical examination in past 12 months
- *Police clearance*

After filing an I-765 Application for Employment Authorization, an I-766 (EAD) will be issued to permit the alien to work temporarily while waiting for the Green Card Interview. Some BCIS offices will give permission to work as soon as the I-485 Adjustment of Status is filed. Others will not give permission until the Green Card interview is held several months later. For those working on an H-1B, it is important to seek an extension to avoid going out of status.

Dependents

A spouse and minor children may qualify to adjust status to permanent resident in the United States as long as:

- The relationship with the principal alien existed when the Green Card application was made
- The fiancé(e) entered the U.S. in K status and was married within 90 days
- They are in status in the United States
- They are not subject to the two-year HRR requirement of a J-1 or J-2
- They are processed with the principal alien

While dependents of a U.S. citizen are not subject to the immigrant visa limit and do not have to wait for a visa number, they may still have to wait for a Priority Date.

Option 2 - By the Department of State (DOS) Abroad

Once a visa number is immediately available and your petition is approved by the BCIS in the United States, it will usually be referred to a U.S. Embassy or Consulate in your home country for processing, if you are not living in the United States.

Under urgent circumstances, Consulates may exercise "consular discretion" and assist people by doing work that they have the emergency authority to do. They have been known to expedite the process to enable a minor child approaching his 21st birthday to be processed and cross the border with his family before his birthday.

Police Clearance

A critical step in the process involves having your police record checked to the satisfaction of the U.S. consulate. The 2001 USA Patriot Act requires that all visa applicants are submitted to a name-check to determine whether they have a criminal history or record. If there is a potential name match, the applicant will be required to have fingerprints taken and pay an $85 fee which will be forwarded to the FBI. If a record is found in their NCIC database, the FBI will forward it to the State Department for use by an authorized Consular Officer.   *Ref: 67 FR 8477*

Medical Examination

Also, before the final Green Card interview by a consular official, all applicants must pass a physical examination, tuberculin (TB) skin test (2 years and older) and serologic (blood) test (15 years and older) by physicians designated by the U.S.

government in your home country. All medical work is carried out at your expense. You will be given your results on Form I-693 to be carried in a sealed envelope to your final interview at the U.S. Embassy or Consulate.

Consular Interview

Your interview will be not be scheduled with a consular officer until you have received police and medical clearance.

Documentation and supporting evidence includes:

- *DOS, BCIS and IRS forms*
  - State Department Packets III & IV, including:
    - DS-168
    - DS-230
      - Part I (Biographic Data) and
      - Part II (Sworn Statement)
    - I-864, Affidavit of Support
    - IRS Form 9003, Additional Questions to be Completed by All Applicants for Permanent Residence in the United States
- *Fees*
  - $335 for visa processing
  - $65 for Affidavit of Support review
- *Passport and photographs*
  - passport valid for six months beyond intended date of entry into U.S.
  - two 50 mm (2") square full-face photographs for each person
- *Current and prior immigration status*
  - copy of I-94, if in status in the United States
- *Prior approval*
  - approval notice that a visa number is immediately available
- *Employer's evidence to support request*
  - employment letter, if applicable
- *Civil documents*
  - marriage certificate
  - original of all civil documents required to prove relationship with the Family-Based petitioner
  - certified copy of long form birth certificates for each applicant
  - divorce decree or death certificate of spouse, if applicable
- *Proof of financial support or solvency*
  - evidence of financial support, including, as required:
    - I-864, Affidavit of Support with $65 fee paid
    - evidence of your own assets
    - tax returns
    - bank records
  - proof that the alien will not become a public charge *Ref: 9 FAM 40.41*

- *Police clearance*
    - certificate from all countries where the applicant has resided for six months or more including:
        - all arrests and reason for each
        - disposition of each case
        - court and prison records
        - military record, if applicable
- *Medical clearance*
    - I-693
- *Additional evidence*
    - certified translation of all documents not in English

The National Visa Center has begun mailing out Form I-864 to the petitioner who must forward it to the prospective immigrant. However, if the alien is being processed by Ciudad Juarez, Manila or Santo Domingo, the I-864 has to be returned to the National Visa Center for review.

The scheduling of a Green Card interview does not guarantee the issuance of a visa. Applicants are advised not to give up jobs, dispose of property or make travel arrangements until a visa is actually issued.

Spouses and families cannot work in the U.S. while consular processing is pending abroad. In contrast, spouses may be able to get employment authorization immediately upon application when the principal alien is eligible for final adjustment in the United States.

Step 3 - Clearing the BCBP at a U.S. Port of Entry

All documentation received from the U.S. Embassy or Consulate abroad must be turned over to the BCBP Immigration Inspector at a port of entry.

In line with its responsibility to make a final determination on eligibility for entry, the BCBP may examine any documentation presented by an immigrant in other steps.

While awaiting Green Card processing, the spouse of a Green Card holder who has not been admitted for temporary or permanent residence may be able to obtain permission to visit the U.S. spouse for short visits but should be prepared to provide convincing proof of intent to depart at the end of the approved stay.

If the spouse, sons and daughters of a legal permanent resident are admitted on a conditional basis for two years, the Homeland Security Secretary shall provide for notice to the spouse, son or daughter with the requirements to have the conditional status removed. The legal permanent resident and spouse or alien son or daughter must jointly submit a petition to the Homeland Security Secretary for removal of their conditional status. The Secretary's failure to provide notice shall not affect the enforcement of this section. *Ref:INA 216; 8 USC 1186a*

Chapter 10

Employment-Based Preferences

Green Cards are available, in limited numbers, to qualified alien workers based on a quota system established by Congress. Each of the five Employment-Based Preference categories has its own unique criteria as explored in the following sections.

Available numbers are a percent of the worldwide employment-based level. In Fiscal Year 2001, the limit for employment-based preference immigrants was calculated at 192,074 under INA 201.

Preference Categories	Annual Numbers Available	Additional Numbers	Eligibility and Waiting Period
First (EB1):	28.6%	Unused Fourth and Fifth Preference Numbers	Priority Workers Waiting Period - Current
Second (EB2): *Labor Certification Required*	28.6%	Unused First Preference Numbers	Professionals holding Advanced Degrees or Persons of Exceptional Ability or whose Services are Sought by U.S. Employers Waiting Period - Current
Third (EB3): *Labor Certification Required*	28.6% (10,000 for Other Workers)	Unused First and Second Preference Numbers	Skilled Workers, Professionals and Other Workers Waiting Period - Current (Other Workers - Current)
Fourth (EB4):	7.1%		Certain Special Immigrants or Certain Religious Ministers, Professionals and Other Religious Workers - Waiting Period - Current

Fifth (EB5): 7.1%   Employment Creation (Investors)
              (3,000 in regional centers,   Waiting Period - Current
              and not less than 3,000 in
              targeted rural or high
              unemployment areas)

There may be longer waiting periods for applicants chargeable to India, Mexico and the Philippines.

Entry Criteria

Currently, the number of Employment-Based Preference visas is set at an annual minimum of 140,000. The new Fiscal Year begins in October.   *Ref: INA 201*

The determination of which preference category is appropriate depends on:
- The qualifications of the beneficiary
- The needs of the employer
- The parameters of the job
- The available skills in the local job market's employment pool

Admission Process

Step 1 - Clearing the Job Offer in the United States

In most Employment-Based cases, the prospective U.S. employer must furnish a written job offer stating that the alien will be employed in the United States within the parameters of the chosen Preference category.

Step 2 - Labor Certification

Applicants for First, Fourth and Fifth Preferences skip this step. Second and Third Preference immigrant aliens must meet stringent Department of Labor criteria and they combine this step with Step 3
    Ref: ETA Instructions, Alien Employment Certification, 1980; INA 212(a)(5)

Role of the Department of Labor (DOL)
Any alien who seeks admission or status as an immigrant for the purpose of permanent employment under either Second or Third Preference Employment-Based shall be excluded unless the Secretary of Labor has first certified to the Secretary of State and to the Secretary of Homeland Security that:
- There are not sufficient U.S. workers who are able, willing, qualified and available at the time of application for a visa and admission into the United States and at the place where the alien is to perform the work, and

- The employment of the alien will not adversely affect the wages and working conditions of U.S. workers similarly employed.

Ref: INA 212(a)(5)(A)

Role of the Employer

The DOL requires that employers of nonimmigrant aliens follow a precise program for obtaining Labor Certification.

The employer must:

- Participate in a good faith recruitment
- Not make the job requirements too restrictive or tailored to the alien
- Test the local labor market for qualified and available U.S. workers
- Offer working conditions and wages that are realistic and appropriate for the job
- Review all applicants and be unable to find a qualified U.S. worker willing to take the job
- Demonstrate that the prospective alien employee meets the stated education, training or experience requirements of the job

Ref: 20 CFR 656

There are three ways to clear the Labor Certification process in Second and Third Preference applications. The type of occupation and the circumstances surrounding the application help determine which of the options is applicable.

Option 1 - Labor Certification by the BCIS

The BCIS is mandated to process the Labor Certification applications of:

- Schedule A, Groups I and II, occupations for which there are not sufficient U.S. workers
- Sheepherders (may also be processed for Labor Certification by the State Department abroad)   *Ref: 20 CFR 656*

An alien in the U.S. who is in status and qualified in one of these occupational groups, may apply to a BCIS District Office for Labor Certification. A sheepherder application may also be filed with a U.S. Embassy or Consulate abroad. The application is granted or denied by the BCIS in the United States or the consular office where the application is filed.

Schedule A occupations

Schedule A is a list of occupations for which the Director, United States Employment Service has determined that there *are not* sufficient U.S. workers who are able, willing, qualified and available and that the wages and working conditions of U.S. workers similarly employed will not be adversely affected by the employment of aliens in such occupations.

The Schedule A list is comprised of two groups of precertified occupations (Group I and Group II) which are subject to revision from time to time, based on U.S. labor market conditions.   *Ref: 20 CFR 656.10 and 656.22*

Group I includes Physical Therapists and Professional Nurses.

Group II includes Aliens (except Aliens in the Performing Arts) of exceptional ability in the sciences or arts, including college and university teachers of exceptional ability who have been practicing their science or art during the year prior to application and who intend to practice the same art in the United States.   *Ref: 20 CFR 656.22*

Sheepherders

Sheepherders must have been employed in that capacity for at least 33 of the past 36 months in the United States.   *Ref: 20 CFR 656.21(b)*

Option 2 - **Labor Certification by the Department of Labor**

The DOL processes the Labor Certification applications of:

- Occupations designated for special handling
- Schedule B occupations for which there are sufficient U.S. workers

Occupations designated for special handling

This truncated category includes:

- College or university teacher
- An alien represented to have exceptional ability in the performing arts
                                                    Ref: 20 CFR 656.20

Schedule B occupations

Schedule B is a list of 49 occupations, as of April 1, 2001, for which the Director, United States Employment Service has determined that sufficient U.S. workers *are* able, willing, qualified and available and that the wages and working conditions of U.S. workers similarly employed *will be* adversely affected by the employment of such aliens.   *Ref: 20 CFR 656.11*

An employer may apply to the Department of Labor for Schedule B Labor Certification on behalf of an alien. The application is granted or denied by the Department of Labor.

If the DOL does not approve an application for Labor Certification:

- A further application may not be submitted for six months
- An appeal may be filed

Labor Certification processing times vary widely, depending on where the employing company is located. It could take up to three years in some areas.

If an alien changes location or receives another job offer before the approval of the application to adjust status, a new Labor Certification process must be started.
                                                    Ref: TL:VISA-48, 10-1-91

Option 3 - National Interest Waiver

In Second Preference cases only, it is possible to obtain a National Interest Waiver from the Secretary of Homeland Security and thus avoid the Labor Certification process. If successful, it is not necessary to obtain Labor Certification or have a job waiting.

The complete job description as recorded on Item 13 of Form ETA 750A must be listed on the posting notice. Any person may provide documentary evidence on the application to the Department of Labor and Employment Security or the ETA Regional Certifying Officer.

Step 3 - Clearing the BCIS in the United States - Initial Application

In the case of applications for permanent residency based on Second and Third Preference one of the foregoing three options must be successfully completed before an application for Second or Third Preference permanent residency may be processed.

Petitions for Schedule A occupations, sheepherders and National Interest Waivers, are filed with the BCIS, not the DOL, simultaneously with the petition described in this step. The petition should be filed with the BCIS regional Service Center having jurisdiction over the place where the alien will be employed. Applications for sheepherders may be filed with the BCIS or DOS abroad.

The BCIS forms which are required depend on which of the following preferences is being sought.

First (EB1), Second (EB2), and Third (EB3) Preference
- BCIS Form I-140, Immigrant Petition for Alien Worker
- $135 fee

Fourth (EB4) Preference
- BCIS Form I-360, Application for Amerasian, Widow(er) or Special Immigrant
- $130 fee

Fifth (EB5) Preference
- BCIS Form I-526, Immigrant Petition by Alien Entrepreneur
- $400 fee

In some cases, it may be necessary to provide the BCIS with a credentials evaluation to establish the U.S. equivalent to your foreign degree. A random sampling of evaluators is provided in Appendix D.

In late 2000, budget legislation gave the BCIS authorization to establish an expedited processing of employment-based petitions for which $1,000 would be paid.

Dependents - Derivative Status

The minor child or spouse of an Employment-Based immigrant is entitled to derivative status corresponding to the classification and priority date of the beneficiary of the petition provided that the beneficiary is:

- On a valid visa, if applying in the United States
- Included in the principal alien's petition
- Married before the filing of the I-485, Application to Register Permanent Residence or Adjust Status
- Accompanying or following to join the principal applicant
- Not subject to the two-year HRR requirement of a J-1 or J-2

Ref: TL: VISA-54, 2-28-92

An Employment-Based Green Card applicant who marries after filing a Green Card petition must add the spouse to the petition before the Green Card interview. Otherwise, the spouse will have to wait, currently over four years, for entry as a Family-Sponsored Second Preference applicant.

Spouses who are in the U.S. in legal nonimmigrant status may:

- Not automatically be allowed to remain in the United States
- Not work merely because they are on the waiting list for a Green Card
- Seek a nonimmigrant H-1, L or V visa as permitted under the terms of Dual Intent to permit them to remain and work in the United States while waiting for a Green Card

Step 4 - Processing

Option 1 - Adjustment of Status by the BCIS in the United States

Once an immigrant visa number is immediately available based on the approval of your petition, final processing may be carried out in the U.S. by the BCIS, if you are living in the United States. Therefore, to adjust from a nonimmigrant category to permanent resident status, you should file with the local BCIS office having jurisdiction over your place of residence.

In a change in 2002, an Adjustment of Status Form I-485 with fee may now be filed while a Form I-140 is pending if a visa is immediately available. A copy of a Form I-797, Notice of Action must also be filed to establish the acceptance of the Form I-140. Forms I-765 for Employment Authorization and I-131 for Advance Parole may be filed while the I-485 is pending.   *Ref: 67 FR 49561*

Aliens living in the U.S. who have not maintained lawful status may pay a $1,000 fine with Supplement A to Form I-485 for U.S. processing only if they were in the U.S. on December 21, 2000 and had a Green Card application in process by April 30, 2001.

Documentation and supporting evidence includes:

- *BCIS forms*
  - I-485, Application to Register Permanent Residence or Adjust Status
  - I-765, Application for Employment Authorization (if required)
- *Fees*
  - $255 for I-485 if the applicant is 14 years of age or over
  - $160 for I-485 if the applicant is under 14 years of age
  - $120 for I-765 (if required)
  - $50 for fingerprinting
- *Passport and photographs*
  - passport valid for six months beyond intended date of entry
  - two color photographs 40 mm high by 35 mm wide in 3/4 profile showing right ear, no head covering (religious exceptions), light background
- *Prior approval*
  - copy of notice of approval of immigrant petition making visa number immediately available
- *Current and prior immigration status*
  - copy of I-94, if applicable
- *Proof of financial support or solvency*
  - I-864 Affidavit of Support (submitted if relative/relative's entity filed petition)
  - evidence of your own assets
- *Civil documents*
  - birth Certificate of principal alien and dependents - long form
  - marriage certificate, if applicable
- *Police clearance*
- *Employer's evidence to support request*
  - employment letter

Since the law requires that all temporary residents except those in H-1 and L status intend to leave the United States at the end of the period for which they have been admitted, it is difficult to justify maintaining U.S. residency if a Green Card application is pending.

The BCIS will accept Adjustment of Status applications from aliens who are subject to the 2-year Home Residency Requirement provided that the State Department (formerly USIA) has recommended a waiver. A copy of the recommendation must be attached to the application for Adjustment of Status. *Ref: INS Memorandum 2-17-98*

Option 2 - By the Department of State (DOS) Abroad

Once a visa number is immediately available and your petition is approved by the BCIS in the United States, it will usually be referred to a U.S. Embassy or Consulate in your home country for processing by a consular officer, if you are not living in the United States. *Ref: INA 203(b)*

Beneficiaries with I-140 petitions who have requested Adjustment of Status may file Form I-824, Request for Transfer of Immigrant Visa Petition with the $140 filing fee to have their file transferred overseas for processing. Normally, an alien applying for an immigrant visa applies at the consular office having jurisdiction over his or her last place of residence abroad. However, posts may accept cases under their discretionary authority from applicants not considered resident in their consular district, especially where the applicants are homeless or facing hardship as a result of long delays.   *Ref: State Cable i80792*

Consular officers shall not readjudicate the petition filed with the BCIS, but rather shall review the petition to determine whether:
- The supporting evidence is consistent with the approval
- There was any misrepresentation of a material fact, and
- The alien meets the requirements of the employment offered, if applicable   *Ref: TL:VISA-54, 2-28-92*

An immigrant visa may not be issued to Second and Third Preference applicants until the consular officer is in receipt of Labor Certification by the Secretary of Labor.
                                 Ref: INA 203(b), 212(a)(5)(A); TL:VISA-54; 2-28-92

Regardless of whether they are named in the petition, the child or spouse of an Employment-Based immigrant is entitled to a derivative status corresponding to the classification and priority date of the beneficiary of the petition.
                                            Ref: INA 203(d); TL:VISA-54; 2-28-92

Medical Examination
Before the final Green Card interview by a consular official, all applicants must pass a physical examination, tuberculin (TB) skin test (2 years and older) and serologic (blood) test (15 years and older) by physicians designated by the U.S. government in your home country. All medical work is carried out at the applicant's expense. You will be given your results on Form I-693 to be carried in a sealed envelope to your final interview at the U.S. Embassy or Consulate.

Consular Interview
Your interview will be not be scheduled with a consular officer until you have received police and medical clearance.

If the Employment-Based Green Card interview is not waived, questions may focus on whether your employment status remains exactly the same as at the time the application was submitted and about the accuracy of statements on your application. The interview may be very short. The scheduling of a Green Card interview does not guarantee the issuance of a visa. Applicants are advised to not give up jobs, dispose of property or make travel arrangements until a visa is actually issued.

Documentation and supporting evidence includes:
- *DOS forms*
  - State Department Packet III & IV including:

- DS-230 Parts I and II
- G-325A - Biographic information Sheet
- *Fees*
  - $335 for visa processing
  - $65 for Affidavit of Support review, if I-864 required
- *Passport and photographs*
  - passport valid for at least six months beyond intended date of entry
  - two 50 mm (2") square photographs facing camera directly
- *Prior approval*
  - copy of notice of approval of immigrant petition making visa number immediately available
- *Current and prior immigration status*
  - copy of I-94, if applicable
- *Proof of financial support or solvency*
  - evidence of support
  - I-864, Affidavit of Support (submitted if relative/relative's entity filed petition)
  - notarized offer of employment
  - evidence of your own assets
- *Civil documents*
  - birth Certificate of principal alien and dependents - long form
- *Police clearance*
  - proof of police clearance
- *Medical clearance*
  - I-693, proof of medical clearance

The beneficiary is given a sealed package of documents to carry and give the BCBP Immigration Inspector at a port of entry.

Step 5 - Clearing the BCBP at a U.S. Port of Entry

The issuance of a visa does not guarantee entry into the United States as the BCBP Immigration Inspector reviews all documentation before making a final determination of whether an alien meets the intent of the law.

Step 6 - Retaining Your Green Card

There is no prescribed time during which you must remain with the employer who sponsored you for your Green Card. However, remember that you obtained your Green Card based on your acceptance of a specific "permanent" position. By leaving that position too soon, the BCIS could consider your application to be fraudulent.

It is advisable to seek the opinion of competent counsel before considering an early job change.

Employment-Based First Preference (EB1)

Priority Workers
Aliens with Extraordinary Ability, Outstanding Professors and Researchers, Certain Multinational Executives and Managers

This is the elite of the Employment-Based Preferences. It does not require Labor Certification and, in some circumstances, does not require a job offer. However, in all cases, it requires extensive and conclusive proof that an alien is deserving.

Sub-categories are:

> First Preference (EB1)   Priority workers
>
> A Aliens with Extraordinary Ability (EB11)
> B Outstanding Professors and Researchers (EB12)
> C Certain Multinational Executives and
>   Managers (EB13)
> *Ref: INA 203(b),in part; TL:VISA-55, 3-13-92*

Entry Criteria

A) Aliens of Extraordinary Ability in the Sciences, Arts, Education, Business, and Athletics (EB11)

The alien applicant must:

- Have extraordinary ability in the sciences, arts, education, business or athletics, demonstrated by sustained national or international acclaim
- Be coming to work in the area of extraordinary ability

8 CFR 204.5(h)(2) defines "extraordinary ability" as "a level of expertise indicating that the individual is one of that small percentage who have risen to the top of the field of endeavor".   *Ref: TL:VISA-54, 2-28-92*

B) Outstanding Professors/Researchers (EB12)

The alien applicant must:

- Have at least three years of experience in teaching or research in the academic area
- Be in a tenured or tenure-track position at a university or institution of higher education to teach in the academic area, or
- Be in a comparable position at a university or institution of higher education to teach in the academic area, or
- Be in a comparable position to conduct research for a private employer employing at least three persons in full-time research activities and have achieved documented accomplishments in an academic field
- Have the required written offer of employment
- Have achieved documented accomplishments in the academic field
- Be recognized internationally as outstanding in the specific academic area

C) Certain Multinational Executives and Managers (EB13)

The alien applicant must:

- Have been employed for at least one year in the three years preceding the filing of this petition by a firm or corporation or other legal entity
- Seek to enter the United States to continue to render services to the same employer or to a subsidiary or affiliate in a capacity that is managerial or executive
- Have been employed for one of last three years by a firm or corporation
- Not be coming to open a new office (one-year minimum requirement)

Admission Process

Step 1 - Clearing the Job Offer in the United States

A) Aliens of Extraordinary Ability (EB11)

- Requires evidence of either pre-arranged U.S. employment, or
- Seeks to continue work in the area of extraordinary ability
- May file a petition with the BCIS on their own behalf

Ref: TL: VISA-54, 2-28-92

B) Outstanding Professors and Researchers (EB12)

- The prospective U.S. employer must furnish in writing:
  - a job offer stating that the alien will be:
    - employed in the United States
    - in a teaching or research capacity in the academic area
  - a clear description of the duties to be performed

Ref: TL:VISA-54, 2-28-92

C) Certain Multinational Executives and Managers (EB13)

- The prospective U.S. employer must furnish in writing:
  - a job offer stating that the alien will be:
  - employed in the United States
  - in a managerial or executive capacity
  - a clear description of the duties to be performed

Ref: TL: VISA-54; 2-28-92

Step 2 - Clearing the BCIS in the United States - Initial Petition

While any person, including the beneficiary, may file a First Preference A petition, only a U.S. employer may file a First Preference B or C petition.

A Form I-140, Immigrant Petition for Alien Worker, must be filed with the BCIS regional Service Center having jurisdiction over the place where the alien will be employed as a First Preference alien who qualifies under INA 203(b)(1) under in one of the following three sub-categories:

- A Aliens with Extraordinary Ability
- B Outstanding Professors and Researchers
- C Certain Multinational Executives and Managers

Ref: INA 203(b), in part; TL: VISA-55, 3-13-92

Whether or not named in the petition, the child or spouse is entitled to a derivative status corresponding to the classification and priority date of the beneficiary of the petition.   *Ref: 9 FAM 42.32*

Documentation and supporting evidence includes:

- *BCIS form*
  - I-140, Immigrant Petition for Alien Worker
- *Fee*
  - $135 for I-140
  - $50 for fingerprinting
- *Civil documents*
  - no birth certificate is required
    (as you are not relying on a family connection)
- *Employer's evidence*
  - all necessary supporting documentation as required in First Preference B and C employment letters
- *Proof of financial support or solvency*
  - all necessary proof of financial support
  - I-864, Affidavit of Support (submitted if relative/relative's entity filed petition)
- *Professional criteria*
  - all necessary professional qualifying evidence, as required, on the following pages under A, B or C

The BCIS must approve I-140 petitions of aliens for First Preference *Priority Workers* Employment-Based status in the following sub-categories:

A) Aliens of Extraordinary Ability in the Sciences, Arts, Education, Business, and Athletics (EB11)   *Ref: INA 203(b)(1)(A)*

Any person may file on behalf of an alien applying for First Preference A. No offer of employment or Labor Certification is required.

The alien must:

- Have achievements recognized through extensive documentation
- Include with the petition convincing evidence that he or she is coming to continue work in the area of expertise such as:
  - letter(s) from prospective employer(s)
  - evidence of prearranged commitments, such as contracts, or
  - a statement from the beneficiary detailing plans for continuing work in the United States   *Ref: TL: VISA-54, 2-28-92*

Additional supporting evidence includes:

- One-time achievement such as a major, internationally-recognized award, or prize, or
- at least three of:
  - receipt of lesser nationally or internationally recognized prizes or awards for excellence in the field of endeavor
  - membership in associations in the field which require outstanding achievements as judged by recognized national or international experts
  - published material about the alien in professional or major trade publications or other major media
  - participation on a panel as a judge of the work of others in the field or an allied field
  - original scientific, scholarly, artistic, athletic or business-related contributions of major significance in the field
  - authorship of scholarly books or articles in the field, in professional or major scholarly journals or trade publications with international circulation or other major media
  - display of the alien's work at artistic exhibitions or showcases
  - evidence that the alien has performed in a leading or critical role for organizations or establishments that have a distinguished reputation
  - evidence that the alien has commanded a high salary or other high remuneration for services, or
  - evidence of commercial successes in the commercial arts, as shown by box office receipts, cassette, compact disc, or video sales

If the above standards do not readily apply to the alien's occupation, comparable evidence may be submitted to establish eligibility.

B) Outstanding Professors/Researchers (EB12)   *Ref: INA 203(b)(1)(B)*

A U.S. employer who wishes to employ an outstanding professor or researcher in First Preference B must file this petition.

The alien applicant must:

- Be recognized internationally as outstanding in the specific academic area and have submitted at least two of the following pieces of evidence:
  - major international prizes or awards for outstanding achievement
  - membership in associations in the academic field requiring outstanding achievements of their members
  - published material in professional publications written by others about the alien's work
  - participation as the judge of the work of others in the same or allied academic field
  - evidence of original scientific or scholarly research contributions, or authorship of scholarly books or articles with international circulation in the academic field
  - display of work in exhibitions or showcases
  - leading or critical role for organizations with a distinguished reputation
  - high salary or remuneration in relation to others in the field
                    Ref: 8 CFR 204.5(h)(3); TL: VISA-54; 2-28-92

Initial evidence should be submitted of at least two of the following:

- Receipt of major prizes for outstanding achievement in the academic field
- Membership in associations in the academic field, requiring outstanding achievements of their members
- Published material in professional publications written by others about the alien's work in the academic field
- Participation on a panel, or individually, as the judge of the work of others in the same or an allied academic field
- Original scientific or scholarly research contributions to the academic field
- Authorship of scholarly books or articles, in scholarly journals with international circulation, in the academic field

If the above standards do not readily apply, the petitioner may submit comparable evidence to establish eligibility.

A university or other institution of higher education must provide:

- A letter indicating its intention to employ the beneficiary in a tenured or tenure-track position as a teacher or in a permanent position as a researcher in the academic field, or

A private employer must provide:

- A letter indicating its intention to employ the beneficiary in a permanent research position in the academic field, and

- Evidence it employs at least three full-time researchers and has achieved documented accomplishments in the field

C) Certain Multinational Executives and Managers (EB13)

Ref: INA 203(b)(1)(C)

A U.S. employer who wishes to employ Multinational Executives and Managers First Preference C must file this petition with a statement on behalf of an alien in First Preference C class to demonstrate that:

- If the alien is outside the United States, he or she has been employed outside the United States for at least one year in the past three years in a managerial or executive capacity by a firm or corporation or other legal entity, or by its affiliate or subsidiary, or
- If the alien is already in the United States working for the same employer, or a subsidiary or affiliate of the firm or corporation or other legal entity, by which the alien was employed abroad, he or she was employed by the entity abroad in a managerial or executive capacity for at least one year in the three years preceding his or her entry as a nonimmigrant
- The prospective employer in the United States is the same employer or a subsidiary or affiliate of the firm or corporation or other legal entity by which the alien was employed abroad
- The prospective U.S. employer has been doing business for at least one year, and
- The alien is to be employed in the United States in a managerial or executive capacity and describing the duties to be performed

Executive capacity

If entering in an "executive capacity", an alien must:

- Direct the management of an organization or major component
- Establish the goals and policies of the organization, component or function
- Exercise wide latitude in discretionary decision-making
- Receive only general supervision or direction from higher level executives, the board of directors, or stockholders of the organization

Managerial capacity

If entering in a "managerial capacity" primarily, an alien must:

- Manage the organization, or its department, subdivision, function, or component
- Supervise and control the work of other supervisory, professional, or managerial employees, or
- Manage an essential function within the organization, or its department or subdivision
- Have the authority to hire and fire directly supervised employees or recommend those as well as other personnel actions (such as promotion and leave authorization) or

- Function at a senior level within the organization hierarchy with respect to the function managed if no other employee is directly supervised
- Exercise discretion over the day-to-day operations of the activity or function for which the employee has authority

Supervisory capacity

A first-line supervisor is not considered to be acting in a managerial capacity merely by virtue of supervisory responsibilities unless the employees supervised are professional.   *INA 101(a)(44)(A); TL: VISA-54; 2-28-92*

Multinational

To qualify as "multinational", the qualifying entity, or its affiliate or subsidiary must conduct business in two or more countries, one of which is the United States.

Subsidiary

A qualifying "subsidiary" is a firm, corporation, or other legal entity of which a parent owns:

- Directly or indirectly, 50 percent of a 50-50 joint venture and has equal control and veto power over the entity, or
- Directly or indirectly, less than half of the entity, but in fact controls the entity   *Ref: INA 101(a)(44)(C) and 203(d); 9 FAM 42.31*

Step 3 - Processing

Option 1 - Adjustment of Status by the BCIS in the United States

If you have maintained lawful status in the United States and have been notified that a visa number is immediately eligible, you may apply to adjust status to permanent resident by filing with the local BCIS office having jurisdiction over the place where the alien will be employed.

Aliens living in the U.S. who have not maintained lawful status may pay a $1,000 fine with Supplement A to Form I-485 for U.S. processing only if they were in the U.S. on December 21, 2000 and had a Green Card application in process by April 30, 2001.

Documentation and supporting evidence includes:

- *BCIS forms*
  - I-485, Application to Register Permanent Residence or Adjust Status
  - I-765, Application for Employment Authorization, if requested
- *Fees*
  - $255 for I-485 if the applicant is 14 years of age or over
  - $160 for I-485 if the applicant is under 14 years of age
  - $120 for I-765, if requested
  - $50 for fingerprinting

- *Passport and photographs*
  - passport valid for six months beyond intended date of entry
  - two color photographs at least 40 mm high by 35 mm wide in 3/4 profile
- *Prior approval*
  - copy of approved Notice for immigrant petition making visa number immediately available
- *Current and prior immigration status*
  - copy of I-94, if applicable
- *Proof of financial support or solvency*
  - I-864, Affidavit of Support (submitted if relative/relatives's entity filed petition)
  - evidence of your own assets
- *Civil documents*
  - birth Certificate of principal alien and dependents - long form
  - marriage certificate, if applicable
- *Police clearance*
- *Employer's evidence to support request*
  - employment letter

Option 2 - By the Department of State (DOS) Abroad

An applicant may be processed as an Employment-Based First Preference immigrant at a U.S. Embassy or Consulate abroad after receiving notification that the consular office has received a BCIS Petition approved in accordance with INA 204 and a visa number is immediately available.

The consular officer must be satisfied that the alien is within one of the classes described in INA 203(b)(1).   *Ref: INA 203(b)(1); 9 FAM 42.32*

Documentation and supporting evidence includes:

- *DOS forms*
  - State Department Packet III & IV including:
    - DS-230 Parts I and II
    - G-325A - Biographic information Sheet
- *Fees*
  - $335 for visa processing
  - $65 for Affidavit of Support review (if I-864 required)
- *Passport and photographs*
  - passport valid for at least six months beyond intended date of entry
  - two 50 mm (2") square photographs facing camera directly
- *Prior approval*
  - copy of approved Notice for immigrant petition making visa number immediately available
- *Current and prior immigration status*
  - copy of I-94, if applicable

- *Proof of financial support or solvency*
  - notarized offer of employment
  - evidence of your own assets
  - I-864, Affidavit of Support (submitted if relative/relative's entity filed petition) with $65 review fee paid
- *Civil documents*
  - birth Certificate of principal alien and dependents - long form
- *Police clearance*
  - proof of police clearance
- *Medical clearance*
  - I-693, proof of medical clearance

If the consular officer is satisfied with the evidence presented, an alien will receive a First Preference Employment-Based visa.

Step 4 - Clearing the BCBP at a U.S. Port of Entry

The BCBP has the final authority to review the documents presented for compliance and make a decision on whether to admit the alien.

Employment-Based

Second Preference (EB2)

Professionals Holding Advanced Degrees,
Aliens of Exceptional Ability,
National Interest Waivers

&

Third Preference (EB3)

Skilled Workers,
Professionals, Other Workers

Only some Second (EB2) and all Third (EB3) Employment-Based Preferences require permanent Labor Certification. Since these two Preference categories, the Labor Certification processes, and the agencies which administer them are so interrelated, the two Preference categories are presented together in this section for the sake of clarity.

Second Preference sub-categories are:

Second Preference (EB2):   Professional Holding Advanced Degrees, or

Persons of Exceptional Ability in the Arts, Sciences or Business who will substantially benefit the national economy, cultural or educational interests, or

National Interest Waivers

Third Preference sub-categories are:

Third Preference (EB3):   Skilled Workers with at least two years of specialized training for which qualified workers are not available in the U.S.

Members of Professions with a Baccalaureate Degree

Other Unskilled Workers to perform labor for which qualified workers are not available in the United States
(Only 10,000 visas are available)

Ref: INA 203(b)(3)

Entry Criteria - Second Preference (EB2)

In order to qualify for Second Preference status, you must meet the entry criteria and offer supporting evidence in one of the following three sub-categories:

A) Members of the professions holding advanced degrees or their equivalent

Advanced degree means:

- Any U.S. academic or professional degree, or foreign equivalent degree above that of baccalaureate

The conference committee report (H.R. Rep. No. 101-955) states that a bachelor degree plus five years of progressive experience in the professions should be considered as the equivalent of a master's degree.

B) Aliens of exceptional ability in the sciences, arts, or business who will substantially benefit prospectively the national economy, cultural or educational interests, or welfare of the United States

Exceptional ability means:

- A degree of expertise significantly above that ordinarily encountered
- Something more than what is usual and requires some rare or unusual talent or skill, or extraordinary ability in a calling which requires that talent or skill
- Status in a field wherein contemporaries recognize exceptional individual ability

The possession of a college or university degree, diploma, certificate or similar award or certification shall not by itself be considered sufficient evidence of such exceptional ability.

C) National Interest Waiver

National Interest means:
- Exceptional ability or as a member of the professions holding an advanced degree and,
  - the alien's past record and the prospective national benefit outweigh the national interest of the Labor Certification process
- The alien seeks employment in an area of substantial intrinsic merit
- The proposed benefit will be national in scope
- Exemption from the job offer and labor certification by Secretary of Homeland Security would be in the national interest
- The national interest would be adversely affected if waiver denied

A finding by the Board of Immigration Appeals in 1998 helped to further define the criteria for a National Interest Waiver (NIW) as follows:
- An individual alien cannot establish the importance of a field or the urgency of an issue as a benefit to the national interest simply by working in the field or seeking an undiscovered solution
- A shortage of workers does not constitute grounds for a NIW

The National Interest Waiver expects unique knowledge, abilities or experience that will be of significant benefit to the U.S. and the field.

Many successful cases hold masters or doctoral degrees, require exceptional ability and may require a license and professional membership. They may also reflect a higher degree and salary than most in the field and at least ten years experience and significant contribution to the field.

In an interim INS rule published September 6, 2000, a physician who is willing to practice full-time in an area designated by the Secretary of Health and Human Services (HHS) as having a shortage of health care professionals or in a facility operated by the Department of Veterans Affairs (VA) may petition for a National Interest Waiver. Practice includes only family or general medicine, general internal medicine, pediatrics, obstetrics/gynecology and psychiatry.   *Ref: 65 FR 53889*

The period fixed by the statute, in most cases, is five years within a maximum six-year period. Former J-1s subject to the HRR may count time served as an H-1B toward the five-year requirement. However, time spent as a J-1 does not count. In all cases, the alien must obtain a determination that the work is in the public interest from the HHS, VA, another Federal agency, or a State Department of Health. Physicians may not finalize their Adjustment of Status until they complete their five years of service.

Entry Criteria - Third Preference (EB3)

In order to apply for Third Preference (EB3) status, you must meet the entry criteria and offer supporting evidence in one of the following three sub-categories.

A) Skilled Workers

Skilled Workers are those persons:

- Capable of performing skilled labor, requiring at least two years training or experience
- For whom relevant post-secondary education may be considered as training for the purposes of this provision
- Whose job is not of a temporary or seasonal nature and there are no qualified workers available in the United States *Ref: TL: VISA-54, 2-28-92*

B) Professionals

Professionals are those persons who hold baccalaureate degrees and are members of a profession.

Profession includes but is not limited to:

- Architects
- Engineers
- Lawyers
- Physicians and surgeons
- Teachers in elementary or secondary schools, colleges, academies, or seminaries

An occupation may generally be considered to be a profession if the attainment of a baccalaureate degree is usually the minimum requirement for entry into that occupation. *Ref: INA 101(a)(32)*

C) Other Workers

Other workers are qualified aliens capable, at the time of petitioning, of performing unskilled labor:

- Requiring less than two years training
- Not of a temporary or seasonal nature
- For which there are no qualified workers available in the United States

Due to the annual limit of 10,000 "Other Workers" visas, there is a large backlog. *Ref: TL: VISA-54, 2-28-92*

Admission Process

Step 1 - Clearing the Job Offer in the United States

Except in National Interest Waiver cases, the prospective U.S. employer must furnish a written job offer establishing that the alien will be employed in the U.S. within the chosen Preference sub-category. Labor Certification must also be cleared.

Step 2 - *Labor Certification or National Interest Waiver*

National Interest Waivers, like First Preference EB1s, do not require either Labor Certification or a job offer. Both are faster than classifications which require labor clearance and both allow the applicant to sponsor himself or herself.

Other than National Interest Waiver cases, all U.S. jobs which fall within Second (EB2) or Third (EB3) Employment-Based Preferences must satisfy the Labor Certification requirement before an I-140, Immigrant Petition for Alien Worker may be processed. National Interest Waiver applicants go directly to Step 3.

Labor Certification, or Alien Employment Certification as it is also known, is a finding by the U.S. Department of Labor (DOL) that:

- There are not sufficient U.S. workers who are able, willing, qualified and available at the time of the application
- Employment of the alien will not adversely affect the wages and working conditions of U.S. workers similarly employed   *Ref: 20 CFR 656.1*

Labor Certification clearance may take one of three forms:

- Option 1 - a formal filing with BCIS to meet Department of Labor criteria
- Option 2 - a formal filing with the Department of Labor for:
  - a waiver of its standards to permit the entry of an alien where sufficient qualified U.S. workers are available (Schedule B), or
  - occupations designated for special handling
- Option 3 - a waiver of Labor Certification by the Secretary of Homeland Security in the national interest

Although the supporting documentation varies within these three options, the following is required of all labor certification applications.

Documentation and supporting evidence required:

- *DOL forms*
  - ETA 750A, Application for Alien Employment Certification
  - ETA 750B, Statement of Qualifications of Alien
  - G-28, if represented by an attorney
- *Fee*
  - no DOL filing fee
- *Additional evidence - by employer*
  - full description of the job
  - funds available to pay the alien
  - wage offered and paid equals or exceeds the prevailing wage for the occupation in the geographical area
  - wage is not based on commissions, bonuses or other incentives
  - employer can place the alien on the payroll immediately on entrance into the U.S.

- job opportunity does not involve unlawful discrimination
- job opportunity does not relate to a strike, lockout or labor dispute
- terms are not contrary to Federal, state or local law
- job is open to any qualified U.S. worker
- notice of filing provided to bargaining representative or if none, posted 10 consecutive days in a conspicuous place at the location of employment   *Ref: 20 CFR 656.20*

- *Additional evidence - by alien applicant*
  - offer of employment
  - alien's signed statement of qualification for the occupational group
  - any necessary supporting documentation
- *Additional evidence - physicians and surgeons*
  - passed Part I and II of the National Board of Medical Examiners Examination (NMBMEE), or
  - passed Educational Commission for Foreign Medical Graduates (ECFMG), or
  - practiced in the U.S. in 1978, or
  - graduated from a school of medicine accredited by the Secretary of Education

After the initial petition is approved, applications for permanent residency for the applicants and their families may be filed and permission for work authorization may be received within two months. Approval of residency may take several months longer.

Forms may be downloaded from http://edc.dws.state.ut.us/forms.htm.

Option 1 - Labor Certification by the BCIS

The BCIS handles the Labor Certification petitions of aliens in Schedule A and sheepherders in accordance with Department of Labor standards. Applications are submitted to the BCIS in Step 3 together with Form I-140, Immigrant Petition for Alien Worker. Sheepherders have the option of filing their Labor Certification application with a U.S. Embassy or Consulate abroad before submitting their I-140.

Schedule A occupations

Schedule A is the Department of Labor's list of precertified occupations in short supply which will not adversely affect the employment of U.S. workers.

Schedule A is divided into two groups.

- Group I consists of:
  - Physical Therapists, and
  - Professional Nurses
- Group II consists of:
  - aliens of exceptional ability in the sciences or arts, including college and university teachers of exceptional ability who have been practicing

their science or art during the year prior to application and who intend to practice the same art in the U.S.   *Ref: 20 CFR 656.10*
- *Additional evidence - Schedule A*
  - alien's work experience in the last 12 months and intended U.S. work which will require exceptional ability
  - alien has exceptional ability in the sciences or arts
  - copy and details of at least one advertisement in an appropriate national publication
  - unions unable to refer equally qualified U.S. workers, if applicable
- *Additional evidence - Schedule A - Group I Physical Therapists*
  - certification of professional qualifications and English competency by designated organization
- *Additional evidence - Schedule A - Group I Professional Nurses*
  - certification of professional qualifications and English competency by designated organization (Commission of Graduates of Foreign Nursing Schools (CGFNS)
- *Additional evidence - Schedule A - Group II aliens of exceptional ability in the sciences or arts*
  - documentary evidence testifying to the widespread acclaim and international recognition accorded to the alien by recognized experts in the field
  - documentation showing that the alien's work in that field during the past year did, and the alien's intended work in the U.S. will, require exceptional ability
  - documentation from at least two of the following seven groups within the field for which certification is sought:
    - internationally-recognized prizes or awards for excellence
    - membership in international associations
    - published material in professional publications about the alien
    - participation on a panel or as a judge of the work of others
    - original scientific or scholarly research contributions of major significance
    - authorship of published scientific or scholarly articles
    - display of the alien's work at artistic exhibitions in more than one country

An Immigration Officer shall:
- Determine whether the employer and alien have met the applicable requirements
- Review the application, and
- Determine whether the alien is qualified for and intends to pursue the Schedule A occupation

Although the Immigration Officer may request an advisory opinion from the U.S. Employment Service, the Schedule A determination of the BCIS is conclusive and final.

The Immigration Officer shall forward a copy of the Form ETA 750 to the DOL Director without attachments. At this point, the I-140 may be processed.

Ref: 20 CFR 656.22

Health Care Workers

Section 343 of the Illegal Immigration Reform and Immigrant Responsibility Act of 1996 (IIRIRA96) created a new ground of inadmissibilty. This requires that aliens seeking to be admitted for permanent residence or adjust their status in a category involving a health care occupation must first obtain a certificate issued by a specified independent credentialing organization. Verification ensures that education, training, licensing, experience and English competency are comparable to American health care workers. Applicants from Canada (except Quebec), Australia, New Zealand, Ireland, the United Kingdom and the U.S. are exempt from the English competency requirement. As of February 24, 2003, others must pass the TOEIC or IELTS English language test.

The INS amended the regulations to expand the role of the Commission on Graduates of Foreign Nursing Schools (CGFNS) to the issuance of certificates to aliens seeking admission as, or Adjustment of Status to, permanent resident on the basis of the following occupations: speech language pathologist and audiologist, medical technologist (clinical laboratory scientist), physician assistant, and medical technician (clinical library technician). The CGFNS was already authorized to issue certificates on behalf of occupational therapists, physical therapists and nurses. This latest ruling is said to ensure that foreign health care workers have the same training, education and licensure as similarly employed U.S. workers. *Ref: INA 212(a)(5)(C); 66 FR 3440*

Sheepherders

An employer shall apply for a Labor Certification to employ an alien who has been employed legally as a nonimmigrant sheepherder for at least 33 of the preceding 36 months. *Ref: 20 CFR 656.21(b)*

Petitions for aliens who have been employed as sheepherders for at least 33 of the previous 36 months are filed in Step 3 with either the BCIS in the U.S. or at a U.S. Embassy or Consulate abroad together with an I-140, Petition for Alien Worker.

The determination of the Immigration or Consular Officer shall be conclusive and final. They shall forward a copy of the Form ETA 750 to the DOL Director without attachments. At this point the I-140 may be processed *Ref: 20 CFR 656.21a*

Option 2 - Labor Certification by the Department of Labor

State employment and U.S. Department of Labor offices carry the responsibility for the certification of three groups:

- Occupations designated for special handling

- Schedule B occupations
- Applicants for Reduction in Recruitment (RIR)

Occupations designated for special handling

The DOL has determined that special labor market tests and an abbreviated process are appropriate for occupations which have been designated for special handling. These are:

- College and university teacher
- Alien represented to be of exceptional ability in the performing arts

Ref: 20 CFR 656.20

College or university teacher

An employer shall apply for a Labor Certification to employ an alien as a college or university teacher or an alien represented to be of exceptional ability by filing Form ETA 750, Application for Employment Certification with the local Employment Service office serving the area where the alien proposes to be employed.

The employer must submit clear documentation to show:

- The alien was selected for the job opportunity in a competitive recruitment
- The alien was found to be more qualified than any U.S. worker applicant
- Additional evidence
  - signed statement of details of the recruiting process
  - number of applicants
  - reasons why the alien is more qualified
  - copy of at least one job advertisement in a national professional journal
  - all other recruitment sources utilized
  - attestation of the alien's educational or professional qualifications and academic achievements

Application is made within 18 months after the selection is made.

Alien represented to be of exceptional ability in the performing arts

If the application is for an alien represented to have exceptional ability in the performing arts, the employer shall the following evidence:

- The alien's work experience during the past 12 months
- The alien's intended work in the U.S. will require exceptional ability
- Additional evidence
  - documents attesting to the alien's widespread acclaim and international recognition
  - receipt of internationally recognized prizes or awards for excellence
  - published material by or about the alien
  - documentary evidence of earnings commensurate with the claimed level of ability
  - playbills and starbills
  - documents attesting to the outstanding reputations of establishments in which the alien has performed or will perform

- Repertory companies, ballet troupes, orchestras where the alien has performed in a leading or starring capacity
- One advertisement placed in a national publication appropriate to the alien's occupation

Filing is with the local Employment Service office.

The local Employment Service office, upon receipt of an application for a college or university teacher or alien represented to have exceptional ability in the performing arts shall:

- Stamp the application and make sure it is complete
- Calculate the prevailing wage for the job opportunity, and
- Advise the employer to increase the amount if the wages offered are below the prevailing wage   *Ref: 20 CFR 656.21*

The local Employment Service office shall transmit a file containing the application, the local officer's prevailing wage findings and any other information it determines is appropriate to the State Workforce Agency (SWA) office or to the Certifying Officer if so directed by the SWA.

The SWA office receiving an application may add appropriate data or comments and transmit the application promptly to the appropriate Certifying Officer for final approval.

Upon receipt of final approval, an I-140 may be filed with the BCIS.

Reduction in Recruitment (RIR)

The Certifying Officer may reduce the employer's recruitment efforts if the employer satisfactorily documents that the employer has adequately tested the labor market with no success at least at the prevailing wage and working conditions. No reduction may be granted for job offers involving occupations listed on Schedule B.

To request a reduction in recruitment efforts, the employer shall file a written request along with the Application for Alien Employment Certification form at the appropriate local Job Service office. The request shall contain:

- Documentary evidence that within the immediately preceding six months the employer has made good faith efforts to recruit U.S. workers for the job opportunity, at least at the prevailing wage and working conditions through sources normal to the occupation, and
- Any other information that the employer believes will support the contention that further recruitment will be unsuccessful

Upon receipt, the local office shall date stamp the request and application form and shall review and process the application without requiring:

- The local office to prepare and process an Employment Service job order
- The employer to place an advertisement for the job opportunity in a newspaper of general circulation or professional, trade or ethnic publication

- The employer to provide the local office with a written report of the results of the post-application recruitment efforts during the normal 30-day period

After reviewing and processing the application, the local office (and the State Employment Service office) shall process the application to the Employment Service agency's state office if not successful or to the regional Certifying Officer, if successful.

The Certifying Officer shall review the documentation submitted by the employer and the comments of the local office and shall notify the employer and the local or state Employment Service office of whether the recruitment efforts may be reduced partially or completely or the application is denied. If it is decided to completely reduce the recruitment efforts, the application shall be returned to the local or state office so that the employer may recruit workers to the extent required in the Certifying Officer's decision.   *Ref: 20 CFR 656.21(i)*

In an effort to expedite processing, a new rule was published on August 3, 2001. The Department of Labor will now permit an employer to file a request with the SWA to have an application which was filed before August 3, 2001 converted to a reduction in recruitment request without losing their filing date.   *Ref: 66 FR 40584*

Schedule B occupations

Schedule B occupations are Third Preference (EB3) for which the Department of Labor (DOL) has determined that there generally are sufficient U.S. workers who are able, willing, qualified and available. Wages and working conditions of U.S. workers similarly employed will generally be adversely affected by the employment in the U.S. of aliens in Schedule B occupations.

Regarding Schedule B occupations, the DOL says:

- Little or no education or experience is required
- Employees can be trained quickly to perform satisfactorily
- Jobs are characterized by relatively low wages, long and irregular hours, poor working conditions and excessive turnover
- Employment of aliens has failed to resolve employment problems
- Aliens often quickly move to other jobs after getting Green Cards

The 49 occupations on the Schedule B list range from Assemblers to Yard Workers. Their job descriptions contain such words as repetitive, routine, service, assist, pack, type, maintain and so on.

An employer or his or her agent or attorney may petition the regional Certifying Officer for the geographic area in which the job opportunity is located for a Schedule B waiver pursuant to 20 CFR 656.23.

- *Additional Schedule B evidence*
  - written request for a Schedule B waiver
  - blind three-day job ad placed in a local newspaper or in technical/academic journals
  - English translation of documents in foreign language

- local job service office had job order on file 30 calendar days and unable to obtain a qualified U.S. worker
- carried out the State Workforce Agency's (SWA) recruitment instructions
- additional documentation submitted to the DOL:
  - newspaper ad and job posting sent to the DOL
  - results of its recruitment with names and résumés
  - justification for the selection of an alien applicant
  - employer has attempted to recruit U.S. workers prior to filing the application for certification
  - reasonable good faith efforts to recruit U.S. workers without success through the Employment Service System or normal labor referral and recruitment sources (listed)
  - job requirements described as normally required for the job in the U.S. and not duly restrictive
  - advertisements and other recruitment efforts have been and continue to be unsuccessful
  - job requirements are the minimum and workers have not been previously hired for similar jobs with less training and experience

The process calls for the petition to be submitted to the local State Workforce Agency (SWA) office serving the geographic area of intended employment. The state office:

- Sends names and résumés of any applications it receives to employer
- Forwards the application to the Certifying Officer at the regional DOL office

After 30 days, the regional Certifying Officer either grants a waiver and issues a Labor Certification or issues a Notice of Findings, a formal request for further documentation. If the additional documentation is not satisfactory, the waiver is denied.

The regional Certifying Officer may refer either Schedule A or B cases to the national Certifying Officer for determination. The employer and the alien will be notified, in writing, when a determination is made on their application.

Upon receipt of a notice of approval, an I-140, Immigrant Petition for Alien Worker may be filed with the BCIS in Step 3.

Option 3 - National Interest Waiver (NIW)

The Secretary of Homeland Security may deem it to be in the national interest to waive the requirement that an alien's services in the sciences, arts, professions, or business be sought by an employer in the United States. Applicants who can prove that their work will be in the national interest of the United States receive a waiver from the Labor Certification.

To qualify, an applicant must demonstrate "exceptional ability in the sciences, arts, or business and will substantially benefit prospectively the national economy, cultural or educational interests, or welfare of the United States."

As the employer does not have to apply, there is no prevailing wage requirement. However, applicants still must prove that they have the necessary personal financial resources to sustain themselves and will not be a financial burden on society.

Third Preference (EB3) NIW waivers are not available.

A greater number of approved cases are in the areas of health and energy-related research, demonstrated extraordinary ability or previous national interest work.

Applicants may file their own concise and well-focused petitions.

To apply for an exemption from the requirement of a job offer, and thus of a Labor Certification, you must file with a BCIS Service Center for a National Interest Waiver. This process combines Steps 2 and 3.

Documentation and supporting evidence includes:

- *BCIS and DOL forms*
  - BCIS I-140, Immigrant Petition for Alien Worker
  - DOL ETA 750B, Statement of Qualifications of Alien (in duplicate)
  - G-28, if represented by an attorney
- *Fees*
  - $135 for I-140
  - $50 for fingerprinting
- *Evidence of financial support*
  - proof of alien's financial solvency (National Interest Waiver cases)
  - an offer of employment as evidence of financial support
  - proof of the employer's financial solvency
- *Additional evidence - alien*
  - evidence to support your claim that such exemption would be in the national interest   *Ref: BCIS Nebraska Service Center*
  - the significance of the program or activity to the economy, defense, environment or labor conditions
  - written substantiation of how your participation would benefit the national interest from:
    - an interested U.S. government agency
    - clients
    - recognized national experts in the field
    - other distinguished scientists/professors/researchers in the field
  - your academic credentials
  - a Ph.D in your field, or a B.S. or M.S if the case is strong
  - what have you already accomplished in the field
  - prizes/achievements in field of expertise
  - articles published in journals

- presentations at conferences
- membership in professional societies
- membership on committees in field of expertise
- the consequences if you are unable to begin or continue to participate

Step 3 - Clearing the BCIS in the United States - Initial Petition

Any U.S. employer may file an I-140, Immigrant Petition for Alien Worker, with the BCIS regional Service Center having jurisdiction over the place where the alien will be employed for classification as Employment-Based Second or Third Preference.
Ref: INA 203(b)(2); TL: VISA-54, 2-28-92

In cases involving Schedule A occupations and sheepherders, the formal request for Labor Certification described in Step 2 is submitted to the BCIS along with the I-140 petition and all necessary supporting documentation required in this step.

In cases involving Schedule B occupations and expeditious handling, Labor Certification must be obtained before an Employment-Based Third Preference petition can be filed with the BCIS.

Whether or not named in the petition, the child or spouse is entitled to a derivative status corresponding to the classification and priority date of the beneficiary of the petition.
Ref: 9 FAM 42.32

Employment-Based Documentation and supporting evidence includes:
- *BCIS forms*
  - I-140, Immigrant Petition for Alien Worker, or
- *DOL forms (Schedule A and sheepherders only)*
  - ETA 750, Part A, Application for Alien Employment Certification
  - ETA 750, Part B, Statement of Qualifications of Alien
- *Fees*
  - $135 for I-140
  - $50 for fingerprinting
  - no DOL filing fee
- *Civil documents*
  - no birth certificate is required
    (as you are not relying on a family connection)
- *Employer's evidence to support request*
  - all necessary supporting employment letters
  - all supporting Step 2 documentation
- *Proof of financial support or solvency*
  - all necessary proof of financial support
  - I-864, Affidavit of Support (if relative's entity filed petition)
- *Professional credentials*
  - all necessary professional evidence, as required

Additional documentation is required for the following categories:

A) Member of the professions holding an advanced degree

Evidence to establish an alien as a member of the professions holding an advanced degree should be in the form of the following:

- An official academic record showing possession of an advanced degree (or foreign equivalent), or
- An official academic record showing possession of a baccalaureate degree (or foreign equivalent) and a letter from current or former employer(s) showing at least five years of progressive post-baccalaureate experience in the specialty
- If the above standards do not readily apply the petitioner may submit comparable evidence to establish the beneficiary's eligibility

Although the BCIS will not evaluate the equivalence of education and experience to a doctorate, if a doctorate (or a foreign equivalent degree) is normally required by the specialty, the alien must possess such a degree.   *Ref: TL: VISA-54; 2-28-92*

B) Aliens of exceptional ability in the sciences, arts, or business who will substantially benefit prospectively the national economy, cultural or educational interests, or welfare of the United States

To establish evidence of exceptional ability, the petition must be accompanied by at least three of the following:

- An official academic record showing a degree, diploma, certificate, or similar award from a college, university, school, or other institution of learning relating to the area of exceptional ability
- Letter(s) from current or former employer(s) showing evidence of at least ten years of full-time experience in the occupation
- A license to practice the profession or certification for a particular profession or occupation
- Evidence that the alien has commanded a salary, or other remuneration for services, which demonstrates exceptional ability
- Evidence of membership in professional associations, or
- Evidence of recognition for achievements and significant contributions to the industry or field by peers, governmental entities, or professional or business organizations

C) National Interest Waiver by the Secretary of Homeland Security

A Form I-140, Immigrant Petition for Alien Worker for an Employment-Based Second Preference National Interest Waiver may be filed by the alien without Labor Certification or job offer with the BCIS regional Service Center having jurisdiction over the place where the alien will be employed for classification as.

Ref: INA 203(b)(2); TL: VISA-54; 2-28-92

Although "national interest" is not defined, some of the factors deemed as being in the U.S. national interest include:

- Improving the U.S. economy
- Creating employment opportunities
- Improving the wages and working conditions of U.S. workers
- Improving the education and training programs for U.S. children and underqualified workers
- Improving health care
- Providing affordable housing for the young, old and poorer U.S. residents
- Improving the environment, making productive use of natural resources
- Research skills would exceed others in the field
- Improving cultural awareness and diversity through artistic endeavors and significant scientific contributions
- A request from an interested U.S. government agency and/or companies benefitting from research or work   *Ref: INS Administrative Appeals Unit*

An I-797 Notice of Action serves as BCIS action on these cases. Mere receipt of Labor Certification does not change an alien's status.

Step 4 - Processing

Aliens living in the U.S. who have not maintained lawful status may pay a $1,000 fine with their Supplement A to Form I-485 for U.S. processing only if they were in the U.S. on December 21, 2000 and had a Green Card application in process by April 30, 2001. Otherwise, they must be processed in their home country and risk a three-year or ten-year bar.

If you are not Out of Status and you are close enough to getting a Green Card to file for adjustment of status, it may be possible to obtain a work permit based on your pending adjustment of status.

Aliens in valid H-1B status when their I-485 and I-765, Application for Employment Authorization (EAD) are filed may remain but not work until their EAD is received.

Option 1 - Adjustment of Status by the BCIS in the United States

If you have maintained lawful status in the United States and you are immediately eligible, you may apply to adjust status from a nonimmigrant classification to permanent resident status by filing with the BCIS office having jurisdiction over your place of residence.

After receipt of an I-797C Notice of Action and approval of the petition, an applicant may file an I-485 for Adjustment of Status.

Documentation and supporting evidence includes:
- *BCIS forms*
  - I-485, Application to Register Permanent Residence or Adjust Status
  - I-765, Application for Employment Authorization, if requested
- *Fees*
  - $255 for I-485 if the applicant is 14 years of age or over
  - $160 for I-485 if the applicant is under 14 years of age
  - $120 for I-765, if requested
  - $50 for fingerprinting
- *Passport and photographs*
  - passport valid for six months beyond intended date of entry
  - two color photographs 40 mm high by 35 mm wide in 3/4 profile showing right ear, no head covering (religious exceptions), light background
- *Prior approval*
  - copy of approved Notice for immigrant petition making visa number immediately available
- *Current and prior immigration status*
  - copy of I-94, if applicable
- *Proof of financial support or solvency*
  - I-864, Affidavit of Support (if relative's entity filed petition)
  - evidence of your own assets
- *Civil documents*
  - birth Certificate of principal alien and dependents - long form
  - marriage certificate, if applicable
- *Police clearance*
- *Employer's evidence to support request*
  - employment letter

Option 2 - By the Department of State (DOS) Abroad

An applicant may be processed at a U.S. Embassy or Consulate abroad after receiving notification that a visa number is immediately available.

The consular officer shall not issue an immigrant visa to any Second or Third Preference Employment-Based immigrant until receiving:
- From the BCIS, a Petition for Immigrant Worker approved in accordance with INA 204, or official notification of such an approval
- From the Department of Labor, an approved petition accompanied by a Labor Certification
- Confirmation of CGFNS or other certification for nurses *Ref: 67 FR 77158*

Documentation and supporting evidence includes:

- *DOS forms*
  - State Department Packet III & IV including:
    - DS-230 Parts I and II
    - G-325A - Biographic information Sheet
- *Fees*
  - $335 for visa processing
  - $65 for Affidavit of Support review (if I-864 required)
- *Passport and photographs*
  - passport valid for at least six months beyond intended date of entry
  - two 50 mm (2") square photographs facing camera directly
- *Prior approval*
  - copy of approved Notice for immigrant petition making visa number immediately available
- *Current and prior immigration status*
  - copy of I-94, if applicable
- *Proof of financial support or solvency*
  - notarized offer of employment
  - evidence of your own assets or support
  - I-864, Affidavit of Support (if relative's entity filed petition)
- *Civil documents*
  - birth certificate of principal alien and dependents - long form
- *Police clearance*
  - proof of police clearance
- *Medical clearance*
  - I-693, proof of medical clearance

If the consular officer is satisfied with the evidence presented, the alien will receive a Second or Third Preference Employment-Based visa, as appropriate.

Step 5 - Clearing the BCBP at a U.S. Port of Entry

The BCBP has the final authority to review the documents presented for compliance and make a decision on whether to admit an alien.

Employment-Based Fourth Preference (EB4)

Special Immigrants
Amerasians, Widow(er)s, Religious Workers, Juveniles Under Court Protection, International Broadcasters

Applicants for Fourth Preference Employment-Based status are a diverse group assembled in this category and exempt from Labor Certification (DOL).

Sub-categories are:

> Fourth Preference (EB4):   Special Immigrants
>
> A Amerasians (AM2)
> B Widow(er)s (IW1)
> C Religious Workers such as Ministers (SD1)
> D Juveniles under Court Protection   (SL1)
> E International Broadcasting Employees (BC1)

Entry Criteria

For Fourth Preference status, you must qualify in one of several sub-categories. See 22 CFR 42.11 for complete list. Several prominent examples follow:

A) Amerasian

An "Amerasian" is an alien who:

- Has not remarried and was born in Korea, Vietnam, Laos, Kampuchea, or Thailand after December 31, 1950 and before October 22, 1982, and
- Was fathered by a U.S. citizen

B) Widow(er)

A "widow(er)" is an alien who:

- Was married for at least two years to a now-deceased U.S. citizen, and
- Had been a U.S. citizen for at least 2 years at the time of death, and:
  - whose citizen spouse's death was less than two years ago
  - not legally separated from the citizen spouse at the time of death
  - who has not remarried

C) Religious Worker

A "religious worker" is an alien who:

- Has been a member of a religious denomination with a bona fide nonprofit, religious organization in the United States, and
- Has been carrying on the vocational, professional work, or other work described below, continuously for the past two years, and
- Seeks to enter the United States to work solely:
  - as a minister of religion, or
  - work for the organization in a professional capacity in a religious vocation (baccalaureate degree required to qualify), or
  - work for the organization or a related, tax-exempt entity in another non-professional capacity in a religious vocation or occupation

This is a temporary program which is renewed in three-year intervals. It is currently extended to September 30, 2003. Five thousand visas are available for this sub-category each year. *Ref: H.R. 4068*

D) Juveniles Under Court Protection

A "juvenile under court protection" is an alien:

- Who is unmarried
- Who has been the subject of administrative or judicial proceedings
- Who is still a dependent juvenile under the law of the state in which the juvenile court is located
- For whom it has been determined that:
  - it would not be in his or her best interests to be returned to:
    - his or her country of nationality, last habitual residence, or
    - his or her parent's country of nationality or last habitual residence
  - he or she is eligible for long-term foster care
- Who may not pass derivative immigration benefits to their natural parents because of their special immigrant status

E) International Broadcasting Employee

An "international broadcasting employee" is an alien who is:

- An employee of the International Broadcasting Bureau of the Broadcasting Board of Governors or grantees of that Board *Ref: INA 203(b)(4)*

One hundred visas are available each year with no numerical limit on spouses and children.

Admission Process

Step 1 - Clearing the Job Offer in the United States

Check whether a written job offer from a prospective U.S. employer is required.

Step 2- Clearing the BCIS in the United States - Initial Petition

The BCIS is responsible for certifying the eligibility of an alien for preference immigrant status.   *Ref: INA 212(a)(5)(A)*

Where to file a petition varies according to the sub-category. Petitions on behalf of battered spouses are filed with the Vermont Service Center. It may take up to eight weeks to receive the BCIS I-797 Notice of Action.

Because of the diverse nature of this Preference category, there are very precise and very different requirements for supporting document and proof.

There are a number of supporting documents required for these aliens which are common to the various sub-categories. The additional requirements which are unique to an individual sub-category follow later.

Whether or not named in the petition, the child or spouse is entitled to a derivative status corresponding to the classification and priority date of the beneficiary of the petition.   *Ref: 9 FAM 42.32*

Documentation and supporting evidence for all sub-categories includes:
- *BCIS form*
  - I-360, Petition for Amerasian, Widow(er) or Special Immigrant
- *Fees*
  - $130
  - no fee for Amerasians
  - $50 for fingerprinting, if applicable
- *Civil documents*
  - no birth certificate is required
    (unless relying on a family connection)
- *Employer's evidence to support request*
  - all necessary supporting employment letters, if employment is involved
- *Proof of financial support or solvency*
  - all necessary proof of financial support
  - I-864, Affidavit of Support (if relative/relative's entity filed petition) with $65 review fee paid
- *Professional credentials*
  - all necessary professional credentials, if applicable

The unique documentation and filing requirements for each category follow.

A) Amerasian

Any person who is 18 or older, an emancipated minor, or a U.S. corporation may file this petition. If you are filing for Amerasian classification and the person you are filing for is outside the United States, you may file this petition at the BCIS local office having jurisdiction over the place of residence.

Documentation and supporting evidence includes:

- Copies of evidence that the beneficiary meets the country and date entry criteria including:
  - the full name, date and place of birth
  - present or permanent address of the mother or guardian
  - the signature of the mother or guardian on the release authenticated by a local registrar, court of minors, or a U.S. immigration or consular officer
- If born in Vietnam, a copy of his or her Vietnamese I.D. card, or an affidavit explaining why it is not available
- Copies of evidence establishing the parentage of the person, and of evidence establishing that the biological father was a U.S. citizen such as:
  - birth or baptismal records or other religious documents
  - local civil records
  - an affidavit
  - correspondence or evidence of financial support from the father
  - photographs of the father with the child
  - affidavits from knowledgeable witnesses which detail the parentage of the child and how they know the facts
- A photograph of the person
- A copy of the marriage certificate if the person is married, and
- Proof of any prior marriages
- If the person is under 18 years old, a written statement from his or her mother or legal guardian which:
  - irrevocably releases him or her for emigration and authorizes the placing agencies to make necessary decisions for immediate care until a sponsor receives custody
  - shows an understanding of the effects of the release
  - states whether money was paid or coercion to obtain the release

The following sponsorship documents are also required and should be filed with the petition to avoid adding to the overall processing time:

- An affidavit of financial support from the sponsor, with the required evidence of financial ability attached (the original sponsor remains financially responsible if the subsequent sponsor fails)
- Copies of evidence that the sponsor is at least 21 years old and is a U.S. citizen or permanent resident
- Police clearance certificates, as required

- If this petition is for a person under 18 years old, the following documents issued by a placement agency must be submitted:
  - a copy of the private, public or state agency's license to place children in the United States
  - proof of the agency's recent experience in the intercountry placement of children and of the agency's financial ability to arrange the placement
  - a favorable home study of the sponsor conducted by a legally authorized agency
  - a pre-placement report from the agency, including information regarding any family separation or dislocation abroad that would result from the placement
  - a written description of the orientation given to the sponsor and to the parent or guardian on the legal and cultural aspects of the placement
  - a statement from the agency showing that the sponsor has been given a report on the pre-placement screening and evaluation of the child
  - a written plan from the agency to provide follow-up services, including mediation and counseling, and describing the contingency placement plans if the initial placement fails

B) Widow(er)

A widow(er) can file this petition on his or her own behalf. The petition must be filed at the BCIS regional Service Center having jurisdiction over your place of residence.

Documentation and supporting evidence includes:

- *Civil documents*
  - copy of your marriage certificate to the U.S. citizen
  - proof of termination of any prior marriages of either of you
  - copies of evidence that your spouse was a U.S. citizen, such as:
    - a birth certificate if born in the United States
    - Certificate of Naturalization or Certificate of Citizenship issued by the BCIS
    - Form FS-240, Report of Birth Abroad of a Citizen of the U.S.
    - a U.S. passport which was valid at the time of the citizen's death
    - copy of the death certificate of your U.S. citizen spouse who is now deceased and who had been a U.S. citizen

C) Religious Worker

Any person, including the alien can file this petition on Form I-360, Petition for Amerasian, Widow(er), or Special Immigrant.

Documentation and supporting evidence includes:

- *Employer's evidence to support request*
  - letter from the authorized official of the religious organization:
    - establishing that the proposed services and alien qualify as above
    - attesting to the alien's membership in the religious denomination and explaining, in detail:
      - the person's religious work
      - all employment during the past two years
      - the proposed employment
- *Additional evidence*
  - religious organization, and any affiliate which will employ the person is:
    - a bona fide nonprofit U.S. religious organization
    - exempt from taxation under section 501(c)(3) of the Internal Revenue Code of 1986

D) Juveniles Under Court Protection

Any person, including the alien can file this petition on Form I-360, Petition for Amerasian, Widow(er), or Special Immigrant, for a juvenile under court protection.

Documentation and supporting evidence includes:

- Copies of the court documents upon which the claim to eligibility is based

E) International Broadcasting Employees

Application for an International Broadcasting Employee may be filed on Form I-360, Petition for Amerasian, Widow(er), or Special Immigrant with proof of qualifying employment status.

Step 3 - Processing for Green Card

Option 1 - Adjustment of Status by the BCIS in the United States

If you have maintained lawful status in the United States and your I-360 petition has been approved making you immediately eligible, you may file with the local BCIS office having jurisdiction over your place of residence to adjust status.

Aliens living in the U.S. who have not maintained lawful status may only pay a $1,000 fine with their Supplement A to Form I-485 for U.S. processing if you were in the U.S. on December 21, 2000 and had a Green Card application in process by April 30, 2001. Otherwise, they must be processed in their home country and risk a three-year or ten-year bar.

Documentation and supporting evidence includes:

- *BCIS forms*
  - I-485, Application to register Permanent Residence or Adjust Status
  - I-765, Application for Employment Authorization, if required
- *Fees*
  - $255 for I-485 for applicants 14 years and over
  - $160 for I-485 for applicants under 14
  - $120 for I-765, if requested
  - $50 for fingerprinting
- *Passport and photographs*
  - passport valid for six months beyond intended date of entry
  - two color photographs 40 mm high by 35 mm wide in 3/4 profile showing right ear, no head covering (religious exceptions), light background
- *Prior approval*
  - copy of approved Notice for immigrant petition making visa number immediately available
- *Current and prior immigration status*
  - copy of I-94, if applicable
- *Proof of financial support or solvency*
  - I-864, Affidavit of Support (if relative/relative's entity filed petition)
  - evidence of your own assets
- *Civil documents*
  - birth Certificate of principal alien and dependents - long form
  - marriage certificate, if applicable
- *Police clearance*
- *Employer's evidence to support request*
  - employment letter, if applicable

Option 2 - By the Department of State (DOS) Abroad

Aliens living outside the U.S. may be processed at a U.S. Embassy or Consulate abroad after receiving notification that a visa number is immediately available.

The consular officer shall not issue an immigrant visa to any Fourth Preference Employment-Based immigrant until receiving from the BCIS:

- A Petition for Immigrant Worker approved in accordance with INA 204, or
- Official notification of such an approval

Documentation and supporting evidence includes:

- *DOS forms*
  - State Department Packet III & IV including:
    - DS-230 Parts I and II
    - G-325A - Biographic information Sheet

- *Fees*
  - $335 for visa processing
  - $65 for Affidavit of Support review, if I-864 required
- *Passport and photographs*
  - passport valid for at least six months beyond intended date of entry
  - two 50 mm (2") square photographsfacing camera directly
- *Prior approval*
  - copy of approved Notice for immigrant petition making visa number immediately available
- *Current and prior immigration status*
  - copy of I-94, if applicable
- *Proof of financial support or solvency*
  - I-864, Affidavit of Support (if relative/relative's entity filed petition), or
- *Civil documents*
  - birth Certificate of principal alien and dependents - long form
  - notarized offer of employment
  - evidence of your own assets
- *Police clearance*
  - proof of police clearance
- *Medical clearance*
  - I-693, proof of medical clearance

If the consular officer is satisfied with the evidence presented, the alien will receive a Fourth Preference Employment-Based visa.

The beneficiary is given a sealed package of documents to carry and give to the BCBP Immigration Inspector at a U.S. port of entry.

Step 5 - *Clearing the BCBP at a U.S. Port Of Entry*

The BCBP has the final authority to review the documents presented for compliance and make a decision on whether to admit the alien.

Employment-Based Fifth Preference (EB5)

Employment Creation (Investors)

T his Preference is for the use of an alien entrepreneur who wishes to establish a new commercial enterprise in the United States and petition for status as a Fifth Preference Employment-Based immigrant.

Applicants are exempt from the requirement to:
- Obtain Labor Certification from the Department of Labor
- Submit a job offer to the BCIS

Fifth Preference permits the entry of aliens to establish their new enterprise in:
- Areas of low unemployment, or
- Areas of high unemployment

Sub-categories are:

> Fifth Preference (EB5):   Employment Creation (Investors)
>
> Employment Creation
> (Investors in targeted rural, or
> high-unemployment centers)

Three thousand visas are available for investors in a targeted rural or high-unemployment area. Three hundred visas are available for regional centers.

Entry Criteria

Both sub-categories require substantial investment with the amount of investment required in a particular area set by regulation. Unless adjusted downward for targeted areas or upward for areas of high employment, the figure shall be $1,000,000. Specific details may be obtained from a BCIS office or U.S. Embassy or Consulate abroad.

The establishment of a new commercial enterprise may include any of:
- Creation of a new business
- Purchase of an existing business with simultaneous or subsequent restructuring or reorganization resulting in a new commercial enterprise

- Expansion of an existing business through investment of the amount required, so that a substantial change (at least 40 percent) in either the net worth, number of employees, or both, results

Proof is required that you have established a new commercial enterprise:

- In which you will engage in a managerial or policy-making capacity
- In which you have invested or are actively in the process of investing the amount required for the area in which the enterprise is located
- Which will benefit the U.S. economy, and
- Which will create full-time employment for at least 10 U.S. citizens, permanent residents, or other immigrants authorized to be employed, other than yourself, your spouse, your sons or daughters, or any nonimmigrant aliens

Full-time employment is defined as being at least 30 hours of service per week.
Ref: INA 203(b)

The following pages deal with the process as it relates to entrepreneurial applicants.

Admission Process

Step 1 - Clearing the BCIS in the United States - Initial Petition

The BCIS is responsible for certifying the eligibility of an alien for preference immigrant status.
Ref: INA 212(a)(5)(A)

While Fifth Preference petitioners do not require Labor Certification or a written job offer since they are the employer, there is a requirement for extensive proof about the new commercial enterprise and their involvement in it.

An entrepreneur may file a petition for status as an immigrant to the United States with either the BCIS regional Service Center in Texas or California depending on where the new commercial enterprise will be principally doing business.

Whether or not named in the petition, the child or spouse is entitled to a derivative status corresponding to the classification and priority date of the beneficiary of the petition.
Ref: 9 FAM 42.32

Documentation and supporting evidence includes:

- *BCIS form*
  - I-526, Immigrant Petition by Alien Entrepreneur
- *Fees*
  - $400 for I-526
  - $50 for fingerprinting

- *Additional evidence*
  - creation of a new business or the expansion of an existing business which includes:
    - evidence that you have created a lawful business entity, or
    - evidence that your investment in an existing business has created at least a 40 percent increase in the net worth of the business:
      - copies of articles of incorporation
      - copies of merger or consolidation
      - partnership agreement or certificate of limited partnership
      - joint venture agreement
      - business trust agreement
      - certificate of authority to do business in a state or municipality
  - evidence of transfer of capital resulting in a substantial increase in net worth or number of employees such as:
    - stock purchase agreements
    - certified financial reports
    - payroll records
    - agreements or documents as evidence of the investment and resulting substantial change
  - if applicable, evidence of the establishment of your enterprise in a targeted employment area such as:
    - an area which has experienced high unemployment of at least 150 percent of the national average rate, or
    - a rural area:
      - not within a metropolitan statistical area, or
      - not within the outer boundary of any city or town having a population of 20,000 or more
  - evidence that you have invested or are actively in the process of investing the amount required for the area in which the business is located:
    - bank statements
    - assets purchased for use in the enterprise
    - money and property transferred from abroad
    - loan, mortgage or security agreements or other evidence of borrowing secured by assets
  - evidence that capital is obtained through lawful means, such as:
    - foreign business registration records
    - tax returns from last five years inside or outside the United States
    - evidence of other sources of capital
    - certified copies of any judgment, pending private or governmental civil or governmental criminal actions against the petitioner from any court within the last 15 years

- evidence that the enterprise will create at least 10 full-time jobs for U.S. citizens, permanent residents, or aliens lawfully authorized to be employed such as:
  - relevant tax records
  - Form I-9 or similar documents, if the employees are already hired, or
  - a business plan of when employees are to be hired within the next two years
- evidence that you will be engaged in the management of the enterprise:
  - through day-to-day managerial control, or
  - through policy formulation:
  - statement of your position title
  - complete description of your duties
  - you are a corporate officer, or hold a seat on the board of directors
- if the new enterprise is a partnership:
  - evidence that you are engaged in either direct management or policy-making activities

Step 2 - Processing

Option 1 - Adjustment of Status by the BCIS in the United States

If you have maintained lawful status in the United States and your I-526 petition has been approved making you immediately eligible, you may apply to adjust status to permanent resident by filing with the local BCIS office having jurisdiction over the place where the employment is located.

Aliens living in the U.S. who have not maintained lawful status may pay a $1,000 fine with Supplement A to Form I-485 for U.S. processing only if they were in the U.S. on December 21, 2000 and had a Green Card application in process by April 30, 2001. Otherwise, they must be processed in their home country and risk a three-year or ten-year bar.

Documentation and supporting evidence includes:

- *BCIS forms*
  - I-485, Application to Register Permanent Residence or Adjust Status
  - I-765, Application for Employment Authorization, if required
- *Fees*
  - $255 for I-485 if the applicant is 14 years of age or over
  - $160 for I-485 if the applicant is under 14 years of age
  - $120 for I-765, if required
  - $50 for fingerprinting

- *Passport and photographs*
  - passport valid for at least six months
  - two color photographs 40 mm high by 35 mm wide in 3/4 profile showing right ear, no head covering (religious exceptions), light background
- *Prior approval*
  - copy of approved Notice for immigrant petition making visa number immediately available
- *Current and prior immigration status*
  - copy of I-94, if applicable
- *Proof of financial support or solvency*
  - I-864, Affidavit of Support (if relative/relative's entity filed petition) with $65 review fee paid
  - evidence of your own assets, as required
- *Civil documents*
  - birth Certificate of principal alien and dependents - long form
  - marriage certificate, if applicable
- *Police clearance*
- *Employer's evidence to support request*
  - employment letter

Option 2 - By the Department of State (DOS) Abroad

An applicant may be processed at a U.S. Embassy or Consulate abroad after receiving notification that a visa number is immediately available.

The consular officer shall not issue an immigrant visa to any Fifth Preference Employment-Based immigrant until receiving from the BCIS, a Petition for Immigrant Worker approved in accordance with INA 204, or official notification of such an approval.

Documentation and supporting evidence includes:

- *DOS forms*
  - State Department Packet III & IV including:
  - DS-230 Parts I and II
  - G-325A - Biographic information Sheet
- *Fees*
  - $335 for visa processing
  - $65 for Affidavit of Support review, if I-864 required
- *Passport and photographs*
  - passport valid for at least six months beyond intended date of entry
  - two 50 mm (2") square photographs facing camera directly
- *Prior approval*
  - copy of approved Notice for immigrant petition making visa number immediately available
- *Current and prior immigration status*
  - copy of I-94, if applicable

- *Proof of financial support or solvency*
  - I-864, Affidavit of Support (if relative/relative's entity filed petition), or
  - evidence of support
  - notarized offer of employment
  - evidence of your own assets
- *Civil documents*
  - birth Certificate of principal alien and dependents - long form
- *Police clearance*
  - proof of police clearance
- *Medical clearance*
  - I-693, proof of medical clearance

If the consular officer is satisfied with the evidence presented, the alien will receive a Fifth Preference Employment-Based visa.

Step 3 - Clearing the BCBP at a U.S. Port Of Entry

The BCBP has the final authority to review the documents presented for compliance and make a decision on whether to admit the alien.

Step 4 - Removal of Conditional Status

The law has created a two-year trial period during which time permanent residence is conditional. Within 90 days of the end of this period, the investor must file Form I-829, Petition by Entrepreneur to Remove Conditions with the $395 fee for removal of the conditional status.

The investor must manage the investment personally.

Chapter 11

Diversity (DV) Lottery

ADiversity (DV) Immigrant Visa or Green Card Lottery Program is run each year by the State Department under INA 203(c) to randomly select and provide 50,000 U.S. Green Card immigration opportunities to natives of countries with low rates of immigration to the United States. No visas are available for countries sending more than 50,000 immigrants to the U.S. in the last five years. Another 5,000 visas are currently reserved for use under the Nicaraguan and Central American Relief Act (NCARA).

Sub-categories:
- DV-1 - Diversity immigrant
- DV-2 - Spouse of DV1
- DV-3 - Child of DV1

In recent years, the month-long mail-in registration period has been held in October. Entries received before or after this period are disqualified regardless of when they were posted. In DV-2004 the mail-in registration period was established from noon on October 7 to noon on November 6, 2002.   *Ref: 67 FR 54251*

The October registration period allows the extra time which the Kentucky Consular Center in Willamsburg, Kentucky and overseas consulates and embassies need to process the qualified entries and notify the successful registrants in a timely manner. By law, Diversity Visas may only be issued during the October 1 to September 30 fiscal year which begins 11 months after the mail-in period ends.

In DV-2003, more than 6.2 million qualified entries were received and another 2.5 million were disqualified for failing to follow the rules. Approximately 87,000 applicants were registered and notified that they could apply for the 50,000 available visas as many winners were not expected to pursue their visas.

In this chapter, the DV-2004 lottery serves as an indication of how future lotteries may be structured.

Eligibility

INA 201(a)(3), 201(e), 203(c) and 204(a)(1)(G), taken together, establish an annual numerical limitation of 50,000 visas for distribution among six geographical regions which approximate the continents.

The law provides a mathematical formula for the BCIS to determine which countries' natives are able to compete for these visas.

In DV-2004, immigrant visas were apportioned so that:

- No single country could receive more than 7 percent of the Diversity Visas available within their region in any one year
- High and low admission regions and high admission foreign states were identified according to a formula based on total immigrant admissions over the most recent five-year period, with:
  - a greater share of the DV numbers for "low admission" countries
  - no Diversity visas for "high admission" countries

In DV-2004, natives of the following countries were not eligible to apply: Canada, China (except Hong Kong, Macau and Taiwan), Colombia, Dominican Republic, El Salvador, Haiti, India, Jamaica, Mexico, Pakistan, Philippines, South Korea, United Kingdom and its dependent territories (except Northern Ireland) and Vietnam. This list has had some minor variations in recent years.

Program information

As the rules are subject to change each year, it is wise to check before applying. For example, some changes were made in 2001. In an effort to clarify the program and combat fraudulent practices, three rule changes were introduced for DV-2003:

- The U.S. Department of Labor's definitions as indicated in the O*Net OnLine database must be used to determine work experience
- Applicants must sign their application with their usual and customary signature in their native alphabet
- Larger photographs must be submitted with name and date of birth printed on the back for the applicant and each dependent

Sources of information on the Visa Lottery include:

- **Written instructions on how to enter the Visa Lottery**
  - call the U.S. State Department's Consular Affairs automated fax service at (202) 647-3000 (Code 1103) from your fax machine
- **Overseas**
  - contact the nearest U.S. Embassy or Consulate for DV instructions
- **DV-2003 Internet instructions**
  - posted at www.travel.state.gov/visa_services.html

Step 1 - Qualification

Educational or work requirements

- At least a high school education or its 12-year U.S. equivalent, or
- Two years of work experience in an occupation requiring at least two years training or experience - See U.S. DOL's O*Net OnLine database at http://online.onetcenter.org and DOS' www.travel.state.gov/ONET.html..

Age requirements

DV-2004 had no minimum age for submission of an application. However, the requirement of a high school education or work experience effectively disqualified most principal applicants under 18.

Nativity

An applicant must be able to claim nativity in an eligible country. Nativity in most cases is determined by the applicant's place of birth. In accordance with INA 202(b)(2), a person born in an ineligible country may be able to claim the spouse's country of birth or that of one of his or her parents if neither parent was born or resided in the ineligible country at the time of the applicant's birth.

Step 2 - Application for Registration

In DV-2004, applications were required to be addressed to a specific address at the Kentucky Consular Center, Lexington, Kentucky related to their country of nativity. All entries had to be received between noon, Eastern U.S. Time on October 7, 2001 and noon on November 6, 2001. All applications arriving outside this period had to be disqualified. However, as "winners" are not selected until after the close of each registration period, there is no advantage to having an application arrive early in the mail-in period. Every properly completed and addressed application received at any time during the one-month period has an equal chance of selection within its region.

The law requires the filing of a separate application for each year's DV Lottery. However, persons already registered for an immigrant visa in another category may also apply for the current DV registration.

Only one application by or for each person is permitted and disqualification results from the detection of more than one entry at either the time of registration or at the visa interview. However, a husband and wife may each submit one application and if either is registered, the other is entitled to derivative status if they enter the U.S. simultaneously. Each applicant must list their spouse and all unmarried natural or adopted children and stepchildren under age 21.

Regardless of whether an application is submitted by the applicant directly, or assistance provided by someone else, it must be signed personally by the applicant, in his or her native alphabet.

There is no application fee other than postage. However, a special DV case processing fee of $100 is payable at the time of visa processing.

Application format

DV-2004 required the request for registration information in the following format:
- Typed or clearly printed on a plain sheet of paper in the English alphabet
- Mailed only by regular or air mail from inside or outside the United States
- Sent in an envelope (no postcards):
  - between 6" and 10" or 15 cm and 25 cm measured from side to side

- between 3½" and 4½" or 9 cm and 11 cm measured from top to bottom
- marked on the front top left hand corner:
  - the applicant's native country
  - the applicant's name
  - the applicant's full return mailing address

1. Applicant's Full Name
- Last Name, First Name and Middle Name
- With last name/surname/family name underlined

2. Applicant's Date and Place of Birth
- Date: Day, Month, Year (Example: 15 November 1961)
- Place: City/Town, District/County/Province, Country
  (Example: Munich, Bavaria, Germany) (Use the country's current name)

3. Applicant's Native Country if Different from Country of Birth
- *Native* ordinarily means someone born within a particular country
- This item must be completed by applicants claiming chargeability to a native country different from their country of birth including:
  - the country of birth of their spouse
  - the country of birth of a parent (minor child only)
  - the country of birth of either parent (if born in a country of which neither parent was a native or resident at the time of the birth)
- This information must match what is put on the upper left corner of the entry envelope

4. Name, Date and Place of Birth of Applicant's Spouse and Natural or Legally-adopted Children and Stepchildren under 21
List the date and place of birth (including the city and country of which the alien claims to be native, if other than the country of birth) of each dependent regardless of whether they reside with you or whether they will immigrate with you or follow. Married children and children 21 or over do not qualify.

5. Applicant's Full Mailing Address
The current mailing address must be clear and complete as any communications will be sent there. A telephone number is optional, but useful.

6. Photographs
Tape a separate recent black and white or color photograph of the applicant, his or her spouse and each natural or legally-adopted child or stepchild under 21 with his or her name and date of birth printed on the back. Each should be taken in front of a light neutral background facing the camera directly with no hat or dark glasses. The face may not be not tilted. Religious head coverings are acceptable. In October 2001, the rules were changed to allow for a range of 37 mm (1½") to 50 mm (2") square photos.

7. Applicant's Signature
The applicant must sign the application using the usual and customary signature in his or her native alphabet. The signature of the spouse and children is not required.

Failure to provide all required information disqualifies an applicant.

Submission of entries

All entries must be sent to the Kentucky Consular Center rather than the National Visa Center in Portsmouth, New Hampshire as in former years.

Sending an application to an incorrect address disqualifies the applicant. Entries must be sent to the exact address including DV Program Year, mailing address and Zip (postal) code according to the applicant's native country or country of chargeability.

Asia:	DV Program Kentucky Consular Center 2002 Visa Crest Migrate, KY 41902-2000 U.S.A.		Africa:	DV Program Kentucky Consular Center 1001 Visa Crest Migrate, KY 41901-1000 U.S.A.
North America:	DV Program Kentucky Consular Center 6006 Visa Crest Migrate, KY 41906-6000 U.S.A.		South & Central America & Caribbean	DV Program Kentucky Consular Center 4004 Visa Crest Migrate, KY 41904-4000 U.S.A.
Europe:	DV Program Kentucky Consular Center 3003 Visa Crest Migrate, KY 41903-3000 U.S.A.		Oceania:	DV Program Kentucky Consular Center 5005 Visa Crest Migrate, KY 41905-5000 U.S.A.

To recap, applications are subject to disqualification if:

- The applicant submits more than one application
- More than one application is in an envelope
- Delivered by hand, fax, registered, certified or express mail
- Any special handling is required
- The application is received on a postcard
- The application is sent to other than the specified address for your country
- The application is received outside the one month reception period

The Federal Trade Commission's Bureau of Consumer Protection has issued a Consumer Alert at www.ftc.gov/bcp/conline/pubs/alerts/lottery.htm to warn against what they called unscrupulous businesses and attorneys who claim that, for a fee, they could increase the chances of winning the Green Card Lottery. They cautioned against statements like:

- They are affiliated with the U.S. government
- They have special expertise or there is a special application form
- They have never had a lottery entry rejected
- They can increase the chances of winning

The State Department advises that if you think you have been cheated by a U.S. company or consultant in connection with the lottery, you may contact the Federal Trade Commission at www.ftc.gov or (877) FTC-HELP or by mail at their Consumer Response Center, 600 Pennsylvania Avenue, Washington, DC 20580.

Step 3 - Selection of "Winners"

In DV-2003, approximately 87,000 applicants were registered and notified that they could make application for the 50,000 annually-allocated diversity visas. As previously noted, an additional 5,000 visas were available for use under the Nicaraguan and Central America Relief Act (NCARA).

Each year, all mail received is separated into the proper geographic region and individually numbered. At the end of each application period, a computer at the Kentucky Consular Center in Williamsburg, Kentucky randomly selects "winners" from among all mail received for each geographic region. Within each region, the first randomly selected applicant is the first case registered, and so on.

According to the DOS, the number registered in each region for DV-2002 was:

- Africa   39,138
- Asia   14,169
- Europe   29,226
- North America   13
- Oceania   1,401
- South America, Central America and the Caribbean   3,407
  Total   87,354

As some 90,000 applicants are expected to be registered for the 50,000 available visas allocated in accordance with INA 203(c)(1) each year, it is important to act quickly, when notified, as "winners" are always processed on a first-come first-served basis. Consequently, each year there is a risk that some could be left out.

Each "selected", or "registered" applicant is sent a notification letter, which provides appropriate visa application instructions and advises of their place on the list. Letters are sent between May and July of the year following the mail-in period.

Spouses and unmarried children under 21 may also apply for visas to accompany or follow to join the principal applicant. Applicants not selected are not notified and only one notification letter is sent for each case registered, to the address provided on the application. Therefore, if a "winner" moves, it is important to promptly advise the program administrators of the move by letter or fax according to the DOS instructions.

Entitlement to immigrant status in the DV category lasts only through the October 1 to September 30 Fiscal (visa) Year for the which the applicant is selected. Successful DV-2004 applicants must be processed and receive their visas during Fiscal Year 2004 (October 1, 2003 through midnight of September 30, 2004). No carry over to the next fiscal year is ever permitted.

Step 4 - Processing

The Kentucky Consular Center will continue to process cases until the point when the "winners" are instructed to make formal application at a U.S. consular office or until those in a legal position to do so may apply for adjustment of status at a BCIS office in the United States.

It must be emphasized that "winners" should complete and file their visa applications quickly as there is no guarantee of the issuance of a visa because the number of entries selected and registered greatly exceeds the number of available immigrant visas.

All registered applicants are informed promptly of their place on the list. Visas are available for issue only to those with DV regional lottery rank numbers below the specified allocation cut-off numbers issued each month. Winners must apply for visa issuance and be processed before the end of the fiscal year on September 30. Once the 50,000 visa numbers are used for the current fiscal year, the program ends.

During the visa interview, principal applicants are required to provide documentary proof of a high school education or its equivalent or show two years of work experience in an occupation that requires at least two years of training or experience within the past five years.

Applicants are subject to all grounds of ineligibility specified in the INA with no special provisions for the waiver of any ground of visa ineligibility other than those ordinarily provided in the act.

Option 1 - Adjustment of Status by the BCIS in the United States

Provided they are otherwise eligible to adjust status, registered applicants who are physically present and in status in the United States may apply to the BCIS for adjustment of status to permanent resident. The BCIS must complete action on their cases before September 30 of the applicable fiscal year, when registrations for the year's DV program terminates.
Ref: INA 245; DOS DV-2004 Diversity Immigrant Visa Program Instructions

Aliens living in the U.S. who have not maintained lawful status may pay a $1,000 fine with Supplement A to Form I-485 for U.S. processing only if they were in the U.S. on December 21, 2000 with a Green Card application in process by April 30, 2001. Otherwise, they must be processed at home and risk a three-year or ten-year bar.

Option 2 - By the Department of State (DOS) Abroad

Aliens living outside the United States will be processed at a U.S. Embassy or Consulate abroad based on instructions received from the Kentucky Consular Center. DV winners, like all other immigrant visa applicants, have to submit required documentation and visa fees in addition to the special Form DSP-122 and DV case processing fee of $100, payable at the time of visa processing.   *Ref: IIRIRA96.636*

Chapter 12

Refugee/Asylee

T he United States was first populated by many religious and political refugees. Consequently, many Americans are sympathetic to requests for asylum.

The United States offers asylum and refugee protection based on an inherent belief in human rights and in ending or preventing the persecution of individuals. Claims of persecution must be based on at least one of five internationally-recognized grounds: **race, religion, nationality, membership in a particular social group, or public opinion**. Some coercive population control programs constitute persecution on account of political opinion and up to 1,000 aliens per fiscal year may be admitted.

The terms "refugee" and "asylee" both relate to a person who is claiming persecution or fear of persecution in his or her home country and wishes to take refuge in the U.S. Simply stated, a refugee is outside the United States and wants to come in while an asylee is already in the U.S. or at its borders and wants to stay.

The asylum procedures were amended on December 6, 2000. *Ref: 65 FR 76121*

An applicant shall be found to be a refugee on the basis of past persecution unless inadmissible, the fear is no longer present or a safe move to another part of the home country could be made. Findings are subject to review and agreement by asylum officers, immigration judges and the Board of Immigration Appeals.

Numerical limitations are established by which the U.S. President with the advice and consent of Congress establishes the number of refugees to be admitted in a given year plus the numerical limit applicable to individual countries or sections of the world.

In 1992, President George Bush approved 144,000 refugee admissions. By comparison, for Fiscal Year 2003, his son President George W. Bush authorized the admission of 70,000 refugees, the same as in the previous year.

The Child Status Protection Act which was signed into law on August 6, 2002, addressed the problem of aging-out. This was an important step in keeping families together.

Previously, a dependent lost child status upon turning 21. Now, an umarried child who was under 21 on the date the parent applied for asylee or refugee status will continue to be classified as a child for purposes of eligibility. *Ref: Pub. L. 107-208*

Establishing Eligibility

To establish eligibility for refugee or asylee status, an alien must be:

- Outside his or her country of nationality or last habitual residence
- Unable or unwilling to accept the protection of that country because of persecution or a well-founded fear of persecution on account of five factors:
  - race
  - religion
  - nationality
  - membership in a particular social group
  - political opinion

The alien's home country must also:

- Target the alien for punishment
- Be aware of applicant's belief or characteristic
- Have the capacity to punish the applicant
- Have the inclination to punish the applicant

A person who ordered, incited, assisted, or participated in the persecution of any person on account of race, religion, nationality, membership in particular social group or political opinion is not eligible. Denial of employment is also not a valid reason.

A. Refugee

A refugee is a person who is physically outside the United States.

In special circumstances, the President after appropriate consultation and in accordance with INA 207(e), may designate any person as a refugee who is in his or her home country or if without nationality, where he or she habitually resides, if he or she meets the criteria for a well-founded fear of persecution. Spouses and minor unmarried children of refugees may also enter as refugees.

Typically, refugee applicants are interviewed in third countries after having fled their country of persecution. Individuals who consider themselves to be at risk should contact the nearest office of the United Nations High Commissioner for Refugees.

Eligibility for a refugee interview is governed by the applicant's nationality and whether they come under one of the processing priorities used to manage the refugee program. The designation of eligible nationalities and processing priorities is decided annually as part of the consultations process.

In addition, the following family members of persons granted refugee status can apply for parole into the United States:

- Family members who reside in the same household and are part of the same economic unit as the refugee
- Unmarried sons and daughters regardless of age or place of residence

Admission Process

Step 1 - Processing

Application may be made abroad at a U.S. Embassy or Consulate. Refugee offices are maintained abroad in embassies and consulates such as:

Athens, Greece	Monterrey, Mexico
Bangkok, Thailand	Moscow, Russia
Ciudad Juarez, Mexico	Nairobi, Kenya
Frankfurt, Germany	New Delhi, India
Hong Kong	Port-au-Prince, Haiti
Islamabad, Pakistan	Singapore
London, England	Seoul, Korea
Rome, Italy	Tegucigalpa, Honduras
Manila, Philippines	Tijuana, Mexico
Mexico City, Mexico	Vienna, Austria

The former INS maintained District Offices at Mexico City, Rome and Bangkok.

Documentation and supporting evidence includes:

- *BCIS form*
  - I-590, Registration for Classification as Refugee

If approved, the applicant is issued a Form I-571, Refugee Travel Document which must be presented at a port of entry. After entry, a refugee can apply for his or her spouse and any unmarried children under 21 to join him or her by filing a Form I-730, Refugee/Asylee Relative Petition. After approval the refugee will receive a Notice of Approval and the information will be forwarded to a U.S. Embassy or Consulate abroad which will contact the dependents for processing.

Step 2 - Clearing the BCBP at a U.S. Port Of Entry

The BCBP has the final authority to review the documents and admit the alien. Aliens who are admitted become eligible for legal permanent resident status in one year. See Asylee Step 5 for details.

B. Asylum

Asylum may be granted if an alien is a refugee within the meaning of INA 208. However, the granting of asylum does not mean that permanent residency has been obtained. That is a later step. To be considered for asylum, you must:

- Be physically present in the U.S. or at a land border or port of entry
- Have been interdicted in international or U.S. waters
- Pay a fee if established   *Ref: IIRIRA96.604*

The two main ways of obtaining asylum in the United States are through:
- The Affirmative Process
- The Defensive Process

Affirmative Process

Regardless of how they entered the United States, individuals are free to file a Form I-589 application for asylum with the BCIS. They are usually seen within 43 days of their application by a BCIS Asylum Officer in one of eight Asylum Offices across the U.S. If the applicant lives far from these offices, interviews may also take place with an Immigration Judge at a District Office. If the BCIS can approve the application at an Asylum Office, the decision is usually issued within 60 days of the initial application.

Affirmative Asylum applicants are almost never detained and are free to live anywhere in the U.S. until their case is resolved. During this time, most applicants are not authorized to work.

If not approved, they are referred to an Immigration Judge at the Executive Office for Immigration Review (EOIR) for further review. They are not detained.

Defensive Process

Applicants are generally placed into Defensive Asylum processing if they were:
- Referred to an EOIR Immigration Judge by a BCIS Asylum Officer who did not grant asylum, or
- Placed in removal proceedings because they were:
  - caught trying to enter the U.S. without proper documentation and were found by an Asylum Pre-Screening Officer (APSO) to have a credible fear of persecution or torture (most are released to relatives, community groups or on their own recognizance)
  - otherwise undocumented or in violation of their immigration status

Application must be filed within one year of the date of arrival in the U.S. However, an asylum officer, immigration judge or Board of Immigration Appeals may allow an extension for extraordinary circumstances not intentionally created by the alien such as serious illness, the effects of persecution since arriving, legal disability or ineffective counsel, or the applicant has maintained Temporary Protected Status, other legal status or the application was denied and refiled.

If you are applying at a U.S. port of entry on the Canadian border, the BCBP Immigration Inspector accepts the I-589 and FD-258 Fingerprint Card which are sent to the Vermont Service Center and the asylee remains in Canada until prior authorization has been received by the port of entry.

Aliens may be detained for being in the U.S. illegally until an immigration judge rules on their asylum claim.

The 1996 law IIRIRA mandated that aliens who arrive at a U.S. port of entry without travel documents or who engage in fraud or material misrepresentation are to be detained and placed in **expedited removal**. However, aliens who express or indicate a fear of persecution during the expedited removal process receive a "credible fear" interview with an asylum officer. Aliens found to have a credible fear are detained and referred for ordinary removal proceedings in which they may apply for asylum before an immigration judge. In 2002, the INS said it had 19,000 detainees.

Withholding of removal is available to refugees in the United States who can show a likelihood that their lives or freedom would be threatened if they were returned to the country in question. Withholding of removal is similar to asylum but governed by a higher standard, requiring applicants to establish that it is more likely than not that they would be persecuted. However, once this standard has been met, they may not be returned to their country. *Ref: INS 10/29/98*

District Directors have discretionary authority to parole, or release an alien from detention if the release would serve an urgent humanitarian need or significant public benefit by considering whether the alien has established his or her identity, poses a threat to the community, demonstrates family ties to the community, presents evidence of a credible asylum claim, or poses a risk of flight.

Asylum is not available if the alien:
- May be removed to a safe third country (other than Canada)
- Has firmly resettled in another country
- Has been in the United States more than one year
- Has previously been denied asylum (unless circumstances have changed)
- Participated in the persecution of any person on account of race, religion, nationality, membership in a particular social group or political opinion
- Has been convicted of a particularly serious crime (such as an aggravated felony) which constitutes a danger to the U.S. community
- Has committed a serious nonpolitical crime outside the United States
- Is a danger to U.S. security (not subject to judicial review)
- Is inadmissible due to terrorist activity
- Is a U.S. citizen
- Is a permanent resident
- Is a conditional resident

An applicant for asylum is not entitled to apply for employment authorization until 150 days after applying for asylum. Employment authorization shall not be granted until 180 days after filing the asylum application. *Ref: IIRIRA96.604*

Other conditions include:
- Fingerprints and photograph by the Homeland Security Secretary
- Asylum cannot be granted until the identity of the applicant has been checked against the BCIS and DOS databases
- A frivolous asylum application shall result in permanent ineligibility for benefits under this act

If you leave the United States pursuant to advance parole granted under 8 CFR 212.5(e), it shall be presumed that you have abandoned your application if you returned to the country from which you are claiming persecution unless you are able to establish compelling reasons for such return.   *Ref: IIRIRA96.604*

Time spent in the United States is not counted against an alien with a legitimate pending asylum application when determining their liability for the three or ten year reentry bars. Refugees and asylees may be eligible for supplementary assistance.

Step 1 - Applying to the BCIS in the United States

Principal alien

If you are not in exclusion or deportation proceedings, you are to mail your application for asylum to the BCIS regional Service Center having jurisdiction over your place of residence unless you have the express consent of the asylum office director or Director of Asylum to file at the asylum office with jurisdiction.

Behind the original package attach two copies of the items in your original package except photographs. Required documentation must be assembled so that it may be easily separated. You must respond to all questions. If any questions do not apply to you, answer "none" or "not applicable".

If you are currently in deportation or exclusion proceedings, you must file your application with the office of the Immigration Judge having jurisdiction over your case.

Documentation and supporting evidence includes:

- *BCIS forms*
  - original signed I-589, Application for Asylum and Withholding of Deportation
  - Form G-28 if represented by an attorney
- *Passport and photographs*
  - copy of every page of the passport and any other U.S. immigration documents for each family member included in your application
  - two ADIT photographs of you and one of every listed family member taken within 30 days of applying:
    - 3/4 frontal profile showing right ear
    - head bare (unless headdress is required by your religious order)
    - white background, on thin glossy paper
    - at least 40 mm high by 35 mm wide
    - approximately 1¼" from top of head to bottom of chin
    - name and A number printed on back
- *Current and prior immigration status*
  - copy of any U.S. immigration documents you possess such as I-94
- *Additional evidence*
  - details of your experiences and/or those of your family which illustrate why you have a well-founded fear of persecution such as:
    - newspaper articles, periodicals, journals, books
    - affidavits of witnesses

- official documents
- other personal statements and evidence such as details of your experiences, events and dates that relate to your claim for asylum
  - original and two copies of any additional sheets and supplementary statements
  - any other supporting documents
- *Civil documents*
  - copy of your birth certificate with adequate translation
  - three copies of any other documentary evidence of relationships to your spouse and unmarried children such as:
    - a birth certificate of the child showing the names of one or both parents if you are applying as the parent(s) plus:
    - certificate of marriage (if applying for your spouse)
  - proof of termination of marriage

If it is not possible to obtain any of the documents, secondary records such as school records, affidavits, photographs and letters may be submitted for consideration.

You must establish why those incidents or other general information are relevant to your specific circumstances and why you have a well-founded fear of persecution.

Accompanying or Following Dependents

A spouse or unmarried child under 21 of an asylee, may, if not otherwise eligible for asylum, be granted the same status as the asylee, if accompanying or following to join the asylee. However, dependents may also choose to file separately.

If a dependent spouse and unmarried child is included in your principal alien application, attach one additional package behind your application and the duplicate packages. In 1998, the INS issued guidelines to evaluate the asylum claims of children.

After being granted asylum in the United States, an asylee may apply for his or her spouse and any unmarried children under 21 to join him or her by filing a Form I-730, Refugee/Asylee Relative Petition.

Take a completed application to the BCIS office having jurisdiction over your place of residence. If filing on behalf of a child under 21, be sure to file in sufficient time for action to be completed and the child receive travel authorization in time to reach the United States before the 21st birthday.

Married dependents must file a separate Form I-589.

Step 2 - Processing by the BCIS in the United States

The applicant is interviewed by an asylum officer.

If the applicant is found to have a credible fear of persecution or torture in the asylum interview, the application will be referred directly to an immigration judge without a separate credible fear interview.

If an applicant is not found to have a credible fear, an asylum officer will conduct a credible fear interview and the applicant will be subject to the credible fear process.

If denied by an asylum officer, a written decision will be given to the applicant in person, unless a mailing is authorized by the asylum office director. Form I-863, Notice of Referral to Immigration Judge is filed in asylum and withholding of removal proceedings and the applicant is sent before an immigration judge who will decide the case. Failure to appear results in denial unless a motion is filed with the judge within 90 days.

An asylum officer may refer or deny if circumstances change and the alien no longer has a well-founded fear of persecution or the applicant could avoid persecution by moving to another part of the home country. In the absence of a well-founded fear of persecution, an alien may be granted asylum by demonstrating compelling reasons for not returning to the home country or there is a reasonable possibility of serious harm upon removal.

Step 3 - Application for Dependents by Asylee in the United States

After approval, the principal alien may file for dependents who will receive a Notice of Approval. The information is forwarded to a U.S. Embassy or Consulate abroad which will contact the dependents.

After processing by the consulate, your family members may proceed to the port of entry where they must apply to the BCBP for entry.

Documentation and supporting evidence includes:
- *BCIS forms*
  - I-730, Refugee/Asylee Relative Petition
  - one copy of Form G-28, if represented by an attorney
- *Photograph*
  - second photograph of each family member stapled to their information
- *Additional evidence*
  - one copy of all continuation sheets and supporting evidence submitted with the original application

Step 4 - Judicial Reconsideration

With a preponderance of supporting evidence, an immigration judge or the Board of Immigration Appeals may reopen an approved case for the purpose of terminating a grant of asylum or withholding of deportation or removal.

An immigration judge may deny if circumstances change and the alien no longer has a well-founded fear of persecution or the applicant could avoid persecution by moving to another part of the home country. An immigration judge has exclusive jurisdiction over an application for withholding of removal filed by an alien subject to a reinstated or administrative removal order.

When an alien's asylum status or withholding of removal is terminated, removal proceedings are initiated unless the alien has other immigrant status.

Step 5 - Application For Employment Authorization

You may file an I-765, Request for Employment Authorization, which is available from your local BCIS office 150 days after filing your asylum application. However, employment authorization shall not be granted until 180 days after filing the asylum application. If you have not received a decision in your case by that time, you will be issued employment authorization. However, any delay that you request or cause in your case will not be counted as part of the 150 or 180 day periods.

There is no fee for filing an initial request for employment authorization.

Step 6 - Processing for Permanent Residence

Option 1 - Adjustment of Status by the BCIS in the United States

In most cases you become eligible after being physically present in the United States for one year after the granting of asylum if you still qualify as a refugee or as the spouse or child of a refugee. Although there is no limit to the number of persons who can be granted asylum in any given year, only 10,000 may adjust status to permanent resident annually. However, an additional 2,000 Jewish Syrian nationals who applied no later than October 26, 2001 could also adjust status.   *Ref: Pub. L. 106-378*

Aliens living in the U.S. who have not maintained lawful status may pay a $1,000 fine with Supplement A to Form I-485 for U.S. processing only if they were in the U.S. on December 21, 2000 and had a Green Card application in process by April 30, 2001. Otherwise, they must be processed in their home country and risk a three-year or ten-year bar.

On an interim basis, asylees and refugees must file their I-485 Application to Adjust Status to permanent resident with the BCIS regional Service Center in Lincoln, Nebraska if:

- You are living in the United States, and
- You have been granted asylum or refugee status, and
- You are eligible for asylum or refugee adjustment

Documentation and supporting evidence includes:

- *BCIS form*
  - I-485, Application to Register Permanent Residence or Adjust Status
- *Fees*
  - $255 if the applicant is 14 years of age or over
  - $160 if the applicant is under 14 years of age

You may expect to:

- File an inquiry sheet

- Have a criminal record check
- Have a check on whether you are still a refugee

Spouse and minor children qualify for a Green Card with the applicant as long as:
- They are on a valid visa in the United States
- They are not subject to the two-year HRR requirement of a J-1 or J-2
- They may be processed with the principal applicant

Option 2 - By the Department of State (DOS) Abroad

Documentation and supporting evidence includes:
- *DOS forms*
  - State Department Packet III & IV, or
  - DS-230 - Parts I and II
  - G-325A - Biographic information Sheet
- *Passport and photographs*
  - passport valid for six months beyond intended date of entry
  - two 50 mm (2") square photographs facing camera directly
- *Prior approval*
  - copy of approved notice for immigrant petition making visa number immediately available
- *Current and prior immigration status*
  - copy of Form I-94
- *Employer's evidence to support request*
  - employment letter
- *Proof of financial support or solvency*
  - evidence of support
- *Civil documents*
  - birth Certificate

Step 7 - Absences From The United States

Being granted asylum does not prevent an alien from going home. However, since the rationale for the granting of asylum is a well-founded fear of persecution, lengthy stays in the home country tend to refute this premise.

As the BCIS codes the Green Card to show that asylum was granted, holders sometimes feel it is prudent to leave their Green Card at home when visiting the home country. However, this conflicts with the alien's obligation to produce his or her Green Card when entering the United States after trips abroad.

Special Programs

Cuban refugees

Along with similar programs in Vietnam and Russia, the U.S. operates an in-country refugee program in Havana, Cuba. In Fiscal Year 1999, a total of 3,406 refugee travel documents were issued to Cuban refugees and their dependent family members.

Potential applicants should contact the U.S. Interests Section of the Swiss Embassy in Havana to request a refugee processing questionnaire to begin the process. Those who appear to meet the criteria are sent an appointment letter for a pre-screening interview. If found to be potentially qualified, a subsequent interview with a BCIS officer will be held to determine whether the refugee definition is met.

Also, the U.S. periodically operates the Special Program for Cuban Migration (SPCM), which is commonly (though incorrectly) called the Cuban Visa Lottery. In addition to the worldwide Diversity Visa Lottery for which Cubans are also eligible, persons in Cuba who do not qualify as refugees or family-sponsored immigrants may enter the SPCM. The 1998 lottery received 541,500 applications.

The SPCM is operated pursuant to the U.S.-Cuban migration agreement of 1994 which mandates that the U.S. authorize no fewer than 20,000 Cuban migrants to enter the U.S. each year. The exact number is based on estimates of the number of approved immigrants needed to complete the target of 20,000 at the end of the fiscal year.

Interested persons may send a letter to the U.S. Interests Section during a specified period. Applications are forwarded to Washington and potential winners are randomly selected and prioritized. Those selected receive forms and instructions by mail and the U.S. Interests Section contacts them for interviews.

Winners must establish that they are not ineligible for admission and meet two of three qualifications - high school education, three or more years' work experience and relatives living in the U.S. Form I-134, Affidavit of Support is used by U.S. sponsors.

The final decision on all cases rests with the BCIS. Winners are not treated as immigrants and issued visas. Instead they receive transportation authorization letters to enter the U.S. under special parole authority.

Cubans entering the U.S. illegally are subject to removal unless they can show that they are the targets of persecution or have valid asylum claims or the Cuban government will mistreat them if they are returned to Cuba.

The Legal Immigration and Family Equity Act of 2000 (LIFE) amended the Nicaraguan Adjustment and Central American Relief Act (NCARA) and Haitian Refugee Immigration Fairness Act of 1998 (HRIFA) to provide that eligible aliens who are nationals of Cuba, Nicaragua or Haiti may apply for Adjustment of Status under NCARA or HRIFA without being subject to certain barriers that existed previously. The INS rule published on May 31, 2001 incorporates the waivers, exceptions, and motion to reopen provisions mandated by the LIFE Act and its amendments. *Ref: 66 FR 29449*

The 1990 ABC settlement provided for different procedures for certain Salvadorans and Guatemalans.

Temporary Protected Status and employment authorization is available to nationals of foreign states designated by the Secretary of Homeland Security due to armed conflict, environmental disasters and other extraordinary and temporary conditions which prevent the return of nationals in safety to their homelands. The status of participating nations changes frequently. Natives of such countries as Angola, Bosnia-Herzegovina, Burundi, El Salvador, Honduras, Liberia, Montserrat, Nicaragua, Sierra Leone, Somalia and Sudan who were living in the U.S. have been eligible, although eligibility procedures vary by country. Applicants file Form I-821, Application for Temporary Protected Status with $50 filing fee and Form I-765, Application for Employment Authorization with $120 filing fee if requesting employment authorization.

Part IV

U.S. Citizenship

Akey element of the immigration process is the realization of the dream of U.S. citizenship. Part IV deals with this very important issue.

According to the U.S. Constitution, all people born in the United States and its territories are U.S. citizens. However, children of foreign diplomats born in the United States are excluded.

All people naturalized in the U.S. are citizens. Also, children born abroad who have at least one U.S. citizen parent may be eligible to claim U.S. citizenship by a form of inheritance or derivation.

Any person in the United States who is not a citizen is an "alien" and falls within the following three broad classifications of aliens:

- **Unlawful** or **unauthorized aliens** who have entered illegally and are not *in status*
- **Nonimmigrants** who have entered legally on temporary visas with limited rights
- **Resident aliens** or **permanent residents** who have received Green Cards and can live and work permanently in the United States

Ref: INS ER 806 3-8-94

Since the final step in the process of *Getting In* to the United States is U.S. citizenship, Part IV offers three chapters of insight into the complex issues surrounding the cherished U.S. citizenship as well as help in preparing for the naturalization test which gets you there.

The U.S. passport is covered in Chapter 35 in Book 2.

Chapter 13-Derivative Status

- An examination of how foreign-born dependents of U.S. citizens qualify for citizenship

Chapter 14-Dual Nationality
- An examination of the issues involved with holding citizenship in two countries simultaneously

Chapter 15-Naturalization and Test Questions
- An examination of the bridge from resident alien to citizen with a detailed list of questions which may be expected in a naturalization interview

Qualifying for U.S. Citizenship

U.S. citizens generally fall into one of five categories:
- Born and living in the United States or its possessions
- Born in the United States and living abroad for any length of time
- Born abroad to U.S. parents and living in the United States
- Born abroad to non-U.S. parents and subsequently naturalized
- Living abroad and unaware of a claim to U.S. citizenship

The United States includes:
- The 50 states
- The District of Columbia
- Puerto Rico
- Guam
- The United States Virgin Islands
- The Commonwealth of the Northern Mariana Islands for purposes of determining U.S. citizenship at birth
- The Pacific islands of American Samoa and Swains Island
  - a person born in either of these islands on or after the date of formal U.S. acquisition is a "national" of the United States

A child may have U.S. citizenship if born abroad to two U.S.-citizen parents or to one U.S.-citizen parent who had lived at least five years in the U.S. before the birth and at least two of those years were after the parent's 14th birthday. Citizenship may also be acquired through a grandparent in some circumstances.

A child born in the United States to foreign diplomats and the foreign parents of a child born in the United States does not qualify for U.S. citizenship.

There has been a dramatic increase in applications for naturalization due to a number of factors such as:
- The three million illegal immigrants who were legalized under the 1986 amnesty law had become eligible to apply for citizenship
- The expiration of pre-1978 Green Cards
- Concern over the loss of benefits following the passing of the welfare reform law in August, 1996 which banned noncitizens from collecting food stamps and Supplemental Security Income

Rights, Benefits and Responsibilities of U.S. Citizenship

Rights
- Voting
- U.S. passport

Benefits
- Work in Federal, State, local government and national security jobs requiring U.S. citizenship
- Work as an FBI agent or federal judge
- Work as a state police officer or teacher, in some states
- Petition for Green Cards for parents, married children, brothers and sisters
- Avoiding deportation or exclusion
- Certain scholarships and other Federally-funded student aid
- Political office

Responsibilities
- Jury duty

Relinquishing U.S. Citizenship

There is no automatic loss of U.S. citizenship. However, the INA identifies ways natural-born or naturalized citizens put their U.S. nationality at risk:

- Obtaining foreign naturalization after age 18
- Taking an oath or formal declaration of allegiance to a foreign state
- Serving in a foreign army in hostilities against the United States or serving as an officer
- Working for the government of another country which requires an oath of affirmation or a declaration of allegiance to that country
- Formally renouncing U.S. citizenship before a U.S. consular officer abroad
- Formally renouncing U.S. citizenship in the United States in war time
- Any act of treason or attempt to overthrow the government *Ref: INA 349*

Leaving the U.S. to avoid military service or desertion makes a person permanently ineligible for citizenship.

A Certificate of Loss of Nationality is issued to former citizens to confirm that they have relinquished their U.S. citizenship. Information on voluntarily renouncing U.S. citizenship may be obtained from U.S. Embassies or Consulates abroad or from:

>Office of Citizens Consular Services (CA/OCS/CCS)
>Room 4811 NS
>Department of State
>Washington, DC 20520-4818   *Ref: INA 349(5); 8 USC 1481(a)(5)*

Persons wishing to regain lost citizenship may contact the same office for guidance on their specific circumstances. This may be a very difficult process.

Chapter 13

Derivative Status

It is not necessary to be born in the United States to obtain U.S. citizenship. This chapter offers insight into the concept of derivative status.

Anyone living abroad who thinks that he or she is entitled to U.S. citizenship should contact the U.S. Embassy or Consulate having jurisdiction over their place of residence or review the options described here.

Persons born abroad may qualify for derivative status if they have one or more U.S. citizen parents. Since the rules for obtaining derivative status are detailed, it is important to follow all steps very carefully.

Reporting a Birth Abroad

Since most children born outside the United States to U.S. citizen(s) are considered U.S. citizens at birth, it is important that their birth be reported to the nearest U.S. Embassy or Consulate as soon after the birth as possible. Form FS-579/SS-5, Application for Consular Report of Birth Abroad of a Citizen of the United States of America, should be filed with a filing fee of $10. Evidence required includes:

- The child's birth certificate
- Evidence of parent(s)' U.S. citizenship
- Evidence of parents' marriage, if applicable
- Affidavit(s) of parent(s)' physical presence in the United States

Upon approval, a Form FS-240 is given the applicant. This serves as the same proof of citizenship as the Certificate of Citizenship issued by the BCIS.

The State Department has eliminated the $100 fee for the adjudication of citizenship cases of persons born abroad with no prior documentation of their U.S. citizenship.   *Ref: 66 FR 17360*

Qualifying for Derivative Status

The Child Citizenship Act of 2000 (CCA)

This Act was signed on October 30, 2000 and became effective February 27, 2001. It addresses U.S. citizenship application procedures for foreign-born children under 18, including adoptive children.

Foreign-born children residing permanently in the United States

Such children acquire U.S. citizenship automatically if they:
- Have at least one U.S. citizen parent by birth or naturalization
- Currently are under 18 years of age
- Have been admitted and are currently residing in the United States as their place of general abode, and are:
  - in the legal and physical custody of the U.S. citizen parent
  - a legal permanent resident in any immigrant classification

If adopted, the child must meet these requirements plus the existence of a final adoption decree.

Such children residing permanently in the U.S. are citizens automatically if they meet these conditions.

Parents may apply for a Certificate of Citizenship at the BCIS district office or sub-office with jurisdiction over the place of residence of the parent and child(ren). They may also apply for a passport from the State Department if they prefer.

Parents of biological children should submit a Form N-600, Application for Certificate of Citizenship with the $185 fee with photographs of the child. Parents of adopted children submit Form N-643, Application for Certificate of Citizenship in Behalf of an Adopted Child with the $145 filing fee and photographs of the child. The BCIS is considering consolidating these forms and Supplement A in a new Form N-600 in the future. Be sure to check before applying.

Foreign-born children residing outside the United States

Such children acquire U.S. citizenship on approval of an application for a Certificate of Citizenship and after taking the Oath of Allegiance unless the Oath is waived under Section 337(a) of the Act if:
- The child has at least one U.S. citizen parent by birth or naturalization
- The U.S. citizen parent has been physically present in the United States or its outlying possessions for at least five years, at least two of which were after the age of 14, or
- The U.S. citizen parent has a citizen parent who has been physically present in the United States or its outlying possessions for at least five years, at least two of which were after the age of 14 (N-600, Supplement A)
- The child is currently under the age of 18
- The child is currently residing outside the United States in the legal and physical custody of the United States citizen parent, and
- The child is temporarily present in the United States pursuant to a lawful admission and is maintaining such lawful status

If adopted, the child must meet these requirements plus the existence of a final adoption decree.

Parents of children residing outside the United States should submit a Form N-600 with the required fee of $185 if applying for a biological child or Form N-643 with the required $145 fee if applying for adopted children. Application may be made at any stateside BCIS district office. The parent should include preferred interview dates at least 90 days in advance. As noted above, it is wise to check whether the future consolidation of these BCIS forms has taken place.

Also required to be submitted for children living abroad are:
- Photographs of the child
- Birth certificate of the child
- Evidence of U.S. parent's U.S. citizenship
- Marriage certificate, if applicable
- Evidence of termination of previous marriages, if applicable
- Evidence of the U.S. citizen parent's or grandparent's physical presence in the United States
- Evidence of the child's lawful admission to the U.S. and maintenance of status
- Evidence of a full and final adoption of adopted children
- Evidence of all legal name changes, if applicable
- Such other evidence as the circumstances may dictate

All applications filed under this section (322) require an interview with both the U.S. citizen parent and the child.

The BCIS intends to remove the Form I-864, Affidavit of Support requirement for children adopted abroad who will receive citizenship at the time of entry as lawful permanent residents. However, children born and residing outside the United States who will not be adopted until after they enter the United States will still require the Affidavit of Support.

Alternatively, parents may apply for a U.S. passport from the State Department and wait until the BCIS has completed re-engineering of the application process.

Orphans

Applications filed for children who immigrated as IR-3s, Orphan Adopted Abroad by a U.S. Citizen may be adjudicated without an interview if the office has the child's A file.

Interviews for IR-4s, Orphans Coming to the United States as Legal Permanent Residents to be Adopted by U.S. Citizen Parent(s) may be waived if the adjudications officer has the child's administrative file and evidence of the final adoption or the recognition by the state of residence of a foreign adoption. They gain citizenship only after the requirements of the adoption or recognition have been completed.

Ref: 66 FR 32138

Chapter 14

Dual Nationality

Dual nationality is the simultaneous possession of two citizenships.

As each country makes its own laws on conferring citizenship, dual nationality is a very complex issue. As what follows is a brief introductory overview to the subject, it may be advisable to discuss specific derivative citizenship issues with legal counsel.

In the United States, dual nationality is not looked upon favorably by some immigration or State Department officers as the act of accepting the rights and responsibilities of U.S. citizenship implies the waiving of other allegiances and the responsibilities which go with them. These officers tend to prefer the term dual national to dual citizen.

Nevertheless, several U.S. Supreme Court rulings reinforce the ability of a person to retain dual status, including:

- Mandoli v. Acheson,   344 U.S. 133 (1952)
- Kawakita v. U.S.,   343 U.S. 717 (1952)
- Afroyim v. Rusk,   387 U.S. 253 (1967)
- Terrazas v. Vance,   444 U.S. 252 (1980)

As a result of these rulings and a 1990 U.S. law, the United States is not challenging the dual nationality of aliens who take advantage of their original citizenship after being naturalized in the United States. However, the U.S. view is that dual nationals:

- Have no extra status in the United States
- Owe allegiance to the United States
- Are obliged to obey U.S. laws
- Who are required to renounce their U.S. citizenship as part of a foreign country's naturalization process may still retain their U.S. citizenship after:
  - taking a routine oath of allegiance to that foreign country, and
  - being employed in a non-policy level foreign governmental position

Many countries do not recognize the act of renouncing their citizenship even though it is part of the U.S. naturalization process. The old country still considers a dual national as one of its citizens.

Canadian law permits Canadian citizens who are naturalized in the U.S. to retain Canadian citizenship. Some observers believe that as many as 5 percent of Canadians have a claim to U.S. citizenship through U.S. ancestors. In certain cases, citizenship could extend automatically to their children, and possibly to their grandchildren.

Other countries, such as India, do not permit dual citizenship and as a result, the citizenship of children of their nationals may be in doubt.

Potential Loss of U.S. Citizenship

Before a U.S. citizen becomes naturalized in another country, the potential dual citizen should check to ensure that the adopted country is not going to require renunciation of U.S. citizenship. From the U.S. perspective, while swearing allegiance to a foreign country may suggest loss of citizenship, it is difficult to prove that a person knowingly and fully intended to abandon U.S. citizenship.

A dual national may jeopardize his or her U.S. citizenship by:

- Accepting a policy-level position with a foreign government
- Being convicted of treason or engaging in conduct so inconsistent with retention of U.S. citizenship that it compels a conclusion that the dual national intended to relinquish his or her U.S. citizenship

U.S. citizenship may also be lost by a person's statements or actions or by signing a document renouncing it. This was formalized in law in 1986.

Citizens who acquired dual status at birth do not risk loss of their U.S. citizenship if they live abroad or of their foreign citizenship when they reach adulthood. These laws and regulations have been repealed by Congress. Citizenship acquired by birth in the United States is practically impossible to lose.

Passports

If a claim to U.S. citizenship can be documented, a passport application may be filed for a grandchild with a U.S. passport office or at an Embassy or Consulate abroad.

The law requires that you show your U.S. passport when entering the United States. There is no need to mention dual status as it may only raise unnecessary questions and delay processing. Similarly, when leaving, show the airline your U.S. passport.   *Ref: 22 CFR 53*

At passport renewal time, consular offices may require that a dual citizen complete a questionnaire to determine whether there is an intention to renounce U.S. citizenship. Further information is available from the State Department's Office of Citizens Consular Services at (202) 647-4000.

It may not be advisable for dual nationals to take their home country's passport or other identifying documents with them on trips to their native country if their departure was under duress, to avoid the draft or was illegal. In these and most other cases your U.S. passport is your best document. See chapter 35 for further details.

Chapter 15

Naturalization
with Test Questions

P ersons 18 years of age or older, who are lawfully admitted permanent resident aliens and meet certain requirements may apply for U.S. citizenship in a process called naturalization.

According to the INS, in Fiscal Year 2002, the number of applicants for naturalization was 700,649 and 589,810 naturalization applicants took the oath of citizenship. This represented a four percent decrease compared to Fiscal Year 2001. During 2002, 139,779 applications were denied and 623,304 others were pending at the end of the 2002 Fiscal Year. The INS attempted to reduce the processing time to six months.

Obtaining Citizenship

Step 1 - Qualifying Period

An immigrant who did not gain permanent resident status through marriage to a U.S. citizen spouse, U.S. military service or through other special circumstances, becomes eligible for naturalization five years from the date of entry as a lawful permanent resident, provided that he or she has been present in the United States for at least two and a half of those five years and without any continuous absences of one year or more. Applicants must be at least 18 years of age.

An immigrant continuously married to and living with a U.S. citizen spouse becomes eligible for naturalization three years from the date of becoming a permanent resident provided that at least one and a half years of the three years have been spent in the U.S. without lengthy absences. The couple must be still be married and living together when citizenship is granted.

An immigrant who has completed three years or more of U.S. military service may also qualify for naturalization after three years as a Green Card holder if applying while still serving or within six months of an honorable discharge. In such cases, the requirement for physical presence and residence is waived.   *Ref: INA 328*

The applicant must have resided for at least the three previous months in the state or service district from which the application was filed.   *Ref: INS N-17*

An immigrant who resided continuously in the U.S. for one year after becoming a legal permanent resident then worked abroad in certain U.S. interests may be eligible to make special application arrangements for naturalization. See Step 2, Form N-470.

Persons working for the CIA may have their one year of continuous physical presence complied with at any time.   *Ref: INA 316*

The Director of Central Intelligence and the Secretary of Homeland Security may allow a person to be naturalized after one year of physical presence if an extraordinary contribution to national security or intelligence activities was made.

A natural or adopted foreign-born child under 18 living permanently in the U.S. automatically becomes a citizen if one parent is a U.S. citizen meeting residency rules.

Time spent in the U.S. on any form of temporary visa does not count toward the waiting period for naturalization. Only the time after gaining permanent residency counts. The waiting period may not be reduced because of the need for specific skills.

The Hmong Veterans' Naturalization Act of 2000 waives the English language requirements and reduces the knowledge of civics for three years for up to 45,000 Green Card holders and their spouses who entered as refugees from Laos and served with Laotian-based guerrillas or irregular forces in support of U.S. forces between 1961 and 1978. Spouses of deceased veterans also qualify.   *Ref: Pub. L. 106-207 as amended*

Step 2 - Absences During Qualifying Period

Continuity of residence is normally broken by absences from the United States for a continuous period of one year or more after becoming a permanent resident. This break could occur either before or after filing for naturalization. In such cases, the qualifying period usually starts over.

With exceptions such as military personnel, applicants must have resided in the state or service district, where the application was filed, for the previous three months.

Before leaving for an extended period it may be possible to help preserve Green Card status and/or naturalization eligibility by:

- Not being absent for a continuous period of six months or more
- Not being out of the United States for a total of more than 30 months during the last five years
- Filing a non-renewable I-131, Reentry Permit to allow an absence of up to two years without protecting residency credits for naturalization

- Filing Form N-470, Application to Preserve Residence for Naturalization Purposes with $95 filing fee if employed abroad by:
  - the U.S. government, including the U.S. Armed Forces
  - an American research institute recognized by the Secretary of Homeland Security
  - a recognized U.S. religious organization
  - a U.S. research institution
  - an American firm engaged in the development of foreign trade and commerce of the United States, or
  - certain public international organizations involving the U.S.

An application is subject to denial if the applicant is on probation following a conviction and must wait until after the probation has been completed.

Step 3 - Application Process

Naturalization application information and N-400 Forms may be obtained on the internet at www.immigration.gov/graphics/services/natz/howapply.htm or by calling (800) 870-3676.

The INS introduced a revised Form N-400 Application for Naturalization (Rev.05/31/01) which was placed in service in 2001. The 10-page form replaces the previous N-400 form and must be used effective January 1, 2002. It includes additional questions about disabilities, illegal voting, terrorism, persecution and removal proceedings. It is intended to be simpler to complete with better topic headings and more specific questions.

According to the INS, the new form was developed to make it easier to capture more required information at the time of initial application rather than later in the process.

Except for military personnel, filing is at the BCIS regional Service Center having jurisdiction over the area of residence. It is later forwarded to the appropriate District Office for further processing. If a couple is temporarily separated for job or other valid reasons, permanent residence is governed by where income tax is filed per 316.5 (a), 316.5 (b) (1) (ii). Military personnel must file the Form N-400 Military Naturalization Packet with the BCIS regional Service Center in Lincoln, Nebraska.

Application for Naturalization Form N-400 may be filed up to 90 days before meeting the "continuous residency" requirement.   *Ref: 8 CFR 334.2*

The countdown to eligibility begins on the date that a person becomes a legal resident as indicated on their Green Card. For a person processed at a U.S. Consulate abroad, the effective date is the date of entry at a U.S. port of entry. However, when a Green Card is obtained through Adjustment of Status in the U.S., permanent residence begins on the date of BCIS approval. The passport stamp may come later.

Processing times are now over a year in some states.

Documentation and supporting evidence includes:

- *BCIS form*
  - Form N-400, Application for Naturalization
- *Fees*
  - $260 for N-400
  - $50 for fingerprinting
- *Photographs*
  - two color photographs 40 mm high by 35 mm wide in 3/4 profile showing right ear, no head covering (religious exceptions), light background
- *Additional evidence*
  - copy of I-551 Permanent Resident Card
  - Form G-325B, evidence of military service, if applicable
  - Form N-426, Request for Certification of Military or Naval Service, if application is based on military service
  - if application is for a child:
    - copy of child's birth certificate
    - copy of parents' marriage certificate
    - evidence of parents' U.S. citizenship

It is suggested that applications be mailed "Certified" and "Return Receipt Requested". To facilitate processing, the BCIS must be notified of changes of address which may now be made by calling (800) 375-5283.

Submit a separate fingerprinting fee of $50 but no fingerprints with your N-400 application. The BCIS will advise you by letter when and where to have your fingerprints taken. Fingerprints taken by a Designated Fingerprinting Service are no longer accepted. By 1999, the INS was operating 76 freestanding Application Support Centers (ASCs), 54 sites in BCIS offices and 38 law enforcement agencies were authorized to do immigration fingerprinting. Questions about fingerprinting may be discussed with a BCIS officer by calling (888) 557-5398.

To expedite the processing of applications for naturalization, applicants must now file with the N-400 Unit in the BCIS regional Service Center serving their area. See www.immigration.gov/graphics/services/natz/statemap.htm.

These changes are designed to:
- Reduce processing times for adjudicating applications
- Enable the Service to provide applicants with more information about their case status in a more efficient and expeditious manner
- Limit the number of in-person visits to local BCIS offices
- Improve the Service's ability to provide service to its customers

Ref: INS 1745-95

There are no restrictions on travel while an N-400 Naturalization application is pending. However, care should be taken to avoid lengthy absences and being out of the U.S. for more than half the period after obtaining the Green Card.

Some states may require the filing of Form N-300, Application to File Declaration of Intention (to obtain naturalization) if you wish to engage in certain occupations or professions or obtain specific licenses.

Documentation and supporting evidence includes:

- *Form*
    - N-300, Application to File Declaration of Intention
- *Fee*
    - $60
- *Photographs*
    - two color photographs 40 mm high by 35 mm wide in 3/4 profile showing right ear, no head covering (religious exceptions), light background
- *Additional evidence*
    - copy of Green Card, or
    - other evidence of permanent resident status

Step 4 - Preparation for the Naturalization Test

By April, 1996, there was a backlog of over 800,000 applicants waiting for naturalization tests. To speed up processing and increase the number of applicants who can be processed by an examiner, the INS authorized private contractors to carry out a pre-test of history and government. However, on August 31, 1998, the INS ended private testing and took over all naturalization testing.

Study textbooks are available from:

Superintendent of Documents
Government Printing Office
Washington, DC 20402

Form M-132, "Information Concerning Citizenship Education to Meet Naturalization Requirements" is available at BCIS offices and contains more information about textbooks and courses available by mail.

You may wish to review the test questions reproduced here before deciding whether you are comfortable enough with the answers to go directly to the interview. Since the INS made a serious effort to reduce its backlog of applicants, examiners have a very limited number of minutes to spend with each candidate and can, therefore, ask relatively few questions.

On March 13, 2003, the BCIS announced the launch of a pilot program to develop a standardized test for all citizenship applicants. The BCIS goal is to have the test in place by late 2004. Until it is implemented, the test questions which follow remain as the core of naturalization test questions.

After reading the test questions in this chapter, you may also wish to test your knowledge at the BCIS internet multiple choice practice self-test site located at www.immigration.gov/graphics/exec/natz/natztest.asp.

Step 5 - Examination

Most applicants are required to pass a naturalization examination. The applicant will be notified when and where to appear. At that time, an interviewer will:

- Test the applicant on his or her:
  - ability to understand, read and write simple English, and
  - knowledge of U.S. history and form of government
    (100 possible questions appear at the end of this chapter)
- Ensure that the applicant has met the requirements for:
  - duration of permanent residency
    - five years in most cases, or
    - three years with a U.S. spouse, or
    - three years in the U.S. military, or
    - other special cases
  - good moral character
  - Selective Service registration (see below)
  - three months residency in the state or BCIS district before filing

Be prepared for questions about the information you have supplied in your original N-400 application. Refresh your memory. Update your list of trips outside the country since filing your N-400 with the reason for and dates of each. Make sure that you can demonstrate that you have been in the United States at least half the time since obtaining permanent resident status.

In an INS study of 7,800 naturalization applications, 48 percent were granted, 43 percent were placed on hold due to missing supporting documents, and eight percent were denied. Of those denied, 44 percent failed the English or civics test, 25 percent did not meet the residency requirements and six percent did not meet the good moral character requirement. Thirteen percent were denied for other reasons.

All males applying for naturalization who have lived in the U.S. as permanent residents between 18 and 26 years of age must show proof that they registered with Selective Service. See Chapter 21, Selective Service. However, the INS instructed its field offices that failure to register bars naturalization only if the applicant knowingly and willfully failed to register during the period for which the applicant must establish good character.   *Ref: INS memorandum, June 18, 1999*

Be sure to study the list of questions about U.S. history and government at the end of this chapter. A minimum of six questions should be answered correctly during the brief interview. However, there is no need to feel intimidated as one interviewer put it, "we try very hard to be compassionate with applicants who try to play by the rules".

The INS says that it tried very hard. As an example, in order to keep up with the major increase in applications, Miami has processed applicants six days a week at 13 minute intervals and each of the many interviewers had approximately 22 applicants per day. The interviews were short and barely left time for the minimum six questions.

Permanent residents who are at least 50 years of age with at least 20 years of legal permanent residence or 55 years of age or more with at least 15 years of permanent residence may be exempted from the English language requirement but not the history and government requirement. Also, applicants 65 or older with at least 20 years legal permanent residence may be given special consideration on the test of government and history and tested on a 20-question list.   *Ref: 316.5(b)(1)(2)*

The application for naturalization can be refused for any of the following reasons:
- Membership in any organization preaching and practicing anarchy
- Membership in communist organizations
- Advocating the overthrow of the U.S. government by force, violence or terrorism
- Publishing any material advocating the methods of overthrow
- Refusal to serve in the armed forces of the U.S. (unless exempt)
- Desertion from military forces and draft evasion

Immigrants who fail the English and civics test still might be eligible for naturalization if they show "satisfactory pursuit" of those subjects. This may be demonstrated by producing any of the following evidence:
- A certificate of satisfactory pursuit from an English-Civics program of at least 40 hours, approved by the BCIS
- U.S. high school diploma
- General equivalency diploma
- Certification from a state-recognized institution for at least one year
- Having passed a proficiency test that demonstrates knowledge equivalent to completing an approved 40 hour course

Ref: Florida Today, January 5, 1996

Step 6 - Naturalization Ceremony

It is possible to have an expedited administration of the oath of allegiance where special circumstances of a compelling or humanitarian nature exist such as illness, disability, advanced age, urgent travel or employment circumstances. In such case, the Certificate of Naturalization, N-550 will be mailed later.   *Ref: 8 CFR 337.3*

Depending on the process being followed in your area, you may be offered the alternative of being sworn in and receiving your Certificate of Naturalization several weeks after your test at either:
- A mass swearing-in ceremony at a regional center, or
- In your county court house

In either case, an oath of allegiance must normally be sworn.

The standard Oath of Allegiance is as follows:

"I hereby declare, an oath, that I absolutely and entirely renounce and abjure all allegiance and fidelity to any foreign prince, potentate, state, or sovereignty, of whom or which I have heretofore been a subject or citizen; that I will support and defend the Constitution and laws of the United States of America against all enemies, foreign and domestic; that I will bear true faith and allegiance to the same; that I will bear arms on behalf of the United States of America when required by law; that I will perform noncombatant service in the armed forces of the United States of America when required by law; that I will perform work of national importance under civilian direction when required by law; and that I take this obligation freely without any mental reservation or purpose of evasion: so help me God."

A special ceremony with a modified oath is offered for those whose religious beliefs prevent them from promising to bear arms and perform military service. However, the applicant cannot be excused from promising to perform a civilian alternative government service deemed important to the nation.

The Secretary of Homeland Security may waive the taking of the oath if the person is unable to understand, or to communicate an understanding of it, because of a physical or developmental disability or mental impairment.   *Ref: INA 337(a)*

If you cannot go to your oath ceremony, you should return the N-445, Notice of Naturalization Oath Ceremony to your local BCIS office. Include a letter explaining why you cannot attend the ceremony. Make a copy of both the notice and your letter for your records. The BCIS will reschedule you and send you a new N-445 to tell you when your ceremony will be held.

Step 7 - Naturalization of Children of Naturalized U.S. Citizens

Children under 18 are not permitted to file an application for naturalization. However, they may derive U.S. citizenship when one or both of their parents are naturalized. To qualify, they must hold a Green Card, be single and under age 18 and reside in the U.S. with their U.S. citizen parent or parents. A U.S. passport may be obtained as proof of U.S. citizenship. If further evidence is needed, a Form N-600, Application for Certificate of Citizenship with $185 fee may be filed.   *Ref: INA 320*

Adopted children file Form N-643, Application for Certificate of Citizenship in Behalf of an Adopted Child with $145 fee.

Step 8 - Residence After Naturalization

The U.S. no longer requires that newly naturalized citizens remain in the U.S. for one year after naturalization. This was repealed by Congress in October, 1994.
Ref: Pub. L. 103-416, 108 Stat. 4305

A U.S. passport may be obtained after naturalization. The Certificate of Naturalization must be attached to the application. See Chapter 35 for details.

Naturalization Test - Questions

The test of history and government is based on your understanding of the answers to the following test questions. If you feel comfortable with the answers to these questions you should be able to take your chances in front of an examiner.

States

How many states are there in the United States?	**Fifty (50)**
What are the 49th and 50th states of the Union?	**Alaska (49th) and Hawaii (50th)**
What is the Capital of your state?	**Your state capital**
What is the head executive of a state government called?	**Governor**
Who is current Governor of your state?	**Your governor**
What is the head executive of a city government called?	**Mayor**
Who is the head of your local government?	**Your mayor**
Can you name the two Senators from your state?	**Your two senators**

History

What is the name of the ship that brought the Pilgrims to America?	**The Mayflower**
Why did the Pilgrims come to America?	**For religious freedom**
Who helped the Pilgrims in America?	**The American Indians (Native Americans)**
What holiday was celebrated for the first time by American colonists?	**Thanksgiving**
What country did we fight during the Revolutionary War?	**England**
What did the Emancipation Proclamation do?	**Freed many slaves**
What is the 4th of July?	**Independence Day**

What is the date of Independence Day?	**July 4th**
Independence from whom?	**England**
What were the 13 original states of the U.S. called?	**Colonies**
Can you name the thirteen original states?	**Connecticut, New Hampshire, New York, New Jersey, Massachusetts, Delaware, Pennsylvania, Virginia, North Carolina, South Carolina, Georgia, Rhode Island and Maryland**
Which countries were our enemies during World War II?	**Germany, Italy and Japan**
Who said "Give me liberty or give me death"?	**Patrick Henry**
Who was Martin Luther King, Jr.?	**A civil rights leader**

Declaration of Independence

Who was the main writer of the Declaration of Independence?	**Thomas Jefferson**
When was the Declaration of Independence adopted?	**July 4, 1776**
What is the basic belief of the Declaration of Independence?	**That all men are created equal**

The Constitution

What is the Constitution?	**The supreme law of the land**
Whose rights are guaranteed by the Constitution and the Bill of Rights?	**Everyone (citizens and non-citizens living in the U.S.)**
In what year was the constitution written?	**1787**
What is the introduction to the Constitution called?	**The Preamble**
Can the Constitution be changed?	**Yes**
What do we call a change to the Constitution?	**Amendments**

How many changes or amendments are there to the Constitution?

27

What are the first 10 amendments to the Constitution called?

The Bill of Rights

Name one right guaranteed by the first amendment.

Freedom of speech, press, religion, peaceable assembly, and requesting peaceable change of government

Where does Freedom of Speech come from?

The Bill of Rights

Name three rights or freedoms guaranteed by the Bill of Rights.

1) The right of freedom of speech, press, religion, peaceable assembly and requesting change of government
2) The right to bear arms (the right to have weapons or own a gun, though subject to certain regulations)
3) The government may not quarter or house soldiers in the people's homes during peacetime without the people's consent
4) The government may not search or take a person's property without a warrant
5) A person may not be tried twice for the same crime and does not have to testify against himself/herself
6) A person charged with a crime still has some rights, such as the right to a trial and to have a lawyer
7) The right to trial by jury in most cases
8) Protects people against excessive or unreasonable fines or cruel and unusual punishment

9) **The people have rights other than those mentioned in the Constitution**

10) **Any power not given to the federal government by the Constitution is a power of either the state or the people**

Form of Government

What kind of government does the United States have?	**Republic**
How many branches are there in our government?	**Three**
What are the three branches of our government?	**Legislative, Executive and Judiciary**

Executive Branch

What is the executive branch of our government?	**The President, cabinet, and departments under the cabinet members**
Who was the first President of the United States?	**George Washington**
Which President is called the "Father of our Country"?	**George Washington**
Which president was the first Commander in Chief of the U.S.	**George Washington**
Who was President during the Civil War?	**Abraham Lincoln**
Which President freed the slaves?	**Abraham Lincoln**
In what month do we vote for the President?	**November**
In what month is the new President inaugurated?	**January**
Who elects the President of the United States?	**The electoral college**

Who is the President of the United States today?	**Current President**
Who is the Commander in Chief of the U.S. military?	**The President**
Who becomes President of the United States if the President dies?	**Vice-President**
Who becomes President of the United States if the President and the Vice-President should die?	**Speaker of the House of Representatives**
For how long do we elect the President?	**Four years**
How many terms can a President serve?	**Two**
According to the Constitution, a person must meet certain requirements in order to be eligible to become President. Name one of those requirements.	**Must be a natural born citizen of the United States; must be at least 35 years old by the time he/she will serve; must have lived in the United States at least 14 years**
Who signs bills into law?	**The President**
Which special group advises the President?	**The Cabinet**
What is the White House?	**The President's official home**
Where is the White House located?	**Washington, DC (1600 Pennsylvania Avenue, N.W.)**
Who is the U.S. Vice-President?	**Current Vice-President**

Legislative Branch

What is the legislative branch of our government?	**Congress**
What is Congress?	**The Senate and the House of Representatives**
Who elects Congress?	**The people**
Who makes the laws in the United States?	**Congress**

What are the duties of Congress?	**To make laws in the United States**
How many senators are there in Congress?	**100**
Why are there 100 Senators in the Senate?	**Two from each state**
For how long do we elect each senator?	**Six years**
How many times may a Senator be re-elected?	**There is no limit**
How many Representatives are there in Congress?	**435**
For how long do we elect the representatives?	**Two years**
How many times may a Congressman be re-elected?	**There is no limit**
Who has the power to declare war?	**The Congress**
Where does Congress meet?	**In the Capitol in Washington, DC**

Judiciary Branch

What is the judiciary branch of our government?	**The Supreme Court**
What is the highest court in the United States?	**The Supreme Court**
What are the duties of the Supreme Court?	**To interpret laws**
Who selects the Supreme Court justices?	**Appointed by the President**
How many Supreme Court justices are there?	**Nine**
Who is Chief Justice of the Supreme Court?	**William Rehnquist**

Citizenship

Name one benefit of being a citizen of the United States.

Obtain Federal government jobs; travel with a U.S. passport; petition for close relatives to live in the U.S.

What is the most important right granted to U.S. citizens?

The right to vote

Flag

What are the colors of our flag?

Red, White and Blue

How many stars are there in our flag?

50

What color are the stars on our flag?

White

What do the stars on the flag mean?

One for each state in the union

How many stripes are there in the flag?

13

What color are the stripes?

Red and White

What do the stripes on the flag mean?

They represent the original 13 states

General

What are the two major political parties in the U.S. today?

Democratic and Republican

What is the national anthem of the United States?

The Star-Spangled Banner

Who wrote the Star-Spangled Banner?

Francis Scott Key

What is the minimum voting age in the United States?

18

What Immigration and Naturalization Service form is used to apply to become a naturalized citizen?

Form N-400, "Application to file Petition for Naturalization"

Name one purpose of the United Nations.

For countries to discuss and try to resolve world problems, to provide economic aid to many countries

Part V

Research Resources

N ow that you are aware of the rationale for, and complexities of, the many immigrant and nonimmigrant classifications available to a person considering a new life in America, you may decide to do more research on your own.

Part V is included as an opportunity for the reader to explore some of the resources which are available to help reach a decision on how to proceed with your own immigration project.

This part contains three chapters which introduce some of the resources you may wish to utilize in your research.

Chapter 16-Legal Assistance

- The pivotal role of attorneys in the immigration process

Chapter 17-New Legislation

- The impact of the Illegal Immigration and Immigrant Responsibility Act of 1996 and the American Competitiveness and Workforce Improvement Act of 1998 on the Immigration and Nationality Act of 1952

Chapter 18-U.S. Government Resources

- An examination of resources available for further home study of the immigration, State Department and Labor Department agencies

Chapter 16

Legal Assistance

Immigration is a complex subject based on a very delicate fabric of intricate legislation, the Immigration and Nationality Act of 1952 and all the subsequent amending legislation.

Many departments of government are involved and a host of immigration classifications have been created to meet the diverse needs of the alien, industry and government alike.

Because of the complexity of the law, and the differing aspirations and skill sets of intending immigrants, many U.S. attorneys are specializing in immigration cases. If you feel that the amount of detail and sensitivity of your case warrants it, you may wish to consider legal assistance.

Selection of an Immigration Attorney

When selecting a particular immigration attorney, consider whether the attorney:
- Is a member of the American Immigration Lawyers Association (AILA)
- Is active in the local or state bar association's immigration committee
- Is licensed in your state
- Is prohibited from practicing in any state
- Receives a favorable opinion from the local attorney referral service
- Has any unfair business practices on record with the local Better Business Bureau in recent years
- Has a good reputation (one source is the internet)
- Is experienced and has a good success rate with cases like yours
- Makes you comfortable with the terms in your first consultation

An immigration attorney may be especially helpful when preparing your case for presentation to a consular or immigration officer if:
- The case or the rules are complicated
- You are unclear about which facts to emphasize
- Your presentation needs organization
- There are prior legal problems and complications

Attorneys should be chosen carefully. Reports suggest that clients who pay their full fee before services are rendered are sometimes ignored by their attorney. Although clients take great comfort in receiving regular status reports, not all attorneys routinely provide that service.

While you should not expect attorneys to make a case move faster than the system allows, they can be very helpful in making sure that it does not bog down. That may mean something as apparently simple as making sure everything is done right the first time. If legal counsel is retained, it is not crucial that he or she have an office in your city. Most of the work is done by telephone, fax, mail and e-mail.

An attorney or other representative must file a Form G-28 signed by the petitioner (8 CFR 103, February 3, 1994) in order to be recognized by the INS. Otherwise, the INS considered the petitioner to be self-represented and the attorney will not be notified of any action taken.   *Ref: BCIS Nebraska Service Center*

American Immigration Lawyers Association

A large number of the immigration lawyers in the United States have joined the American Immigration Lawyers Association (AILA). This association is included as a reference:

> American Immigration Lawyers Association
> 1400 I Street N.W.
> Suite 1200
> Washington, DC 20005
> Phone: (202) 371-9377
> Fax: (202) 371-9449

AILA members may be found in many cities. Each member may have a specialized practice or background. One such attorney is Gene McNary, the former Commissioner of the Immigration and Naturalization Service who wrote the Foreword to this book. He is typical of the very experienced immigration attorneys who are available throughout the United States. He may be contacted at (314) 862-3576 or gmcnary@ix.netcom.com.

An AILA member with a different international perspective is C.C. Abbott. He has been admitted to the bar in both the United States and Canada and is located in the south-eastern U.S. He may be reached at (904) 332-0656 or ecls@fcol.com.

Free Legal Assistance on the Internet

A number of immigration attorneys respond to general immigration questions in internet news groups. Several maintain informative home pages and offer a formal client relationship at prevailing legal rates.

Chapter 17

New Legislation

Congress enacted three pieces of important immigration-related legislation in a four-year period between 1996 and 2000.

First, in 1996, it was the Illegal Immigration Reform And Immigrant Responsibility Act Of 1996 (IIRIRA96). Then in 1998, the American Competitiveness and Workforce Improvement Act of 1998 (ACWIA98) was born. Finally at the end of October, 2000, more flexibility was added to the H-1B classification when President Clinton signed the American Competitiveness in the Twenty-first Century Act of 2000 and a companion bill which increased the supplementary H-1B filing fee to $1,000.

Readers are cautioned that elements of these Acts are constantly being canceled, reconsidered or refined and, consequently, not all may be currently implemented.

The Illegal Immigration Reform And Immigrant Responsibility Act Of 1996 (IIRIRA96)

After much discussion, a number of legal and illegal immigration issues were included together in the Illegal Immigration Reform and Immigrant Responsibility Act of 1996 which was signed into law by President Bill Clinton on September 30, 1996.

IIRIRA96 is divided into six Titles or parts which incorporate several key changes to the Immigration and Nationality Act (INA). As these changes are being phased in gradually, it is always wise to check to see whether any provisions which might affect your case are in force. Original references to the INS are retained for reference.

Title I - Improvements to Border Control, Facilitation of Legal Entry, and Interior Enforcement

Increase in Border Patrol Staff   *Ref: IIRIRA96.101*

- Increase by 300, the number of personnel in support of border patrol agents in each of Fiscal Years 1997, 1998, 1999, 2000 and 2001
- Deployment of additional border patrol agents along the border in proportion to the level of illegal crossing of the border in each sector

Installation of Physical Barriers to Illegal Entry   *Ref: IIRIRA96.102*

- Install additional physical barriers and roads in the vicinity of the U.S. border to deter illegal crossings in the area of high illegal entry
- A maximum of $12,000,000 for the construction of fencing and road improvements in the San Diego, California area

Machine-Readable Border Cross Documents   *Ref: IIRIRA96.104*

INA 101(a)(6) is amended:

- After April 1, 1997, issue border crossing documents with a machine-readable biometric identifier such as the alien's handprint or fingerprints
- After October 1, 1999, an alien presenting a border crossing identification card will not be permitted to enter the U.S. unless the biometric identifier contained on the card matches the alien's biometric characteristics

Increased Penalties for Illegal Entry   *Ref: IIRIRA96.105*

INA 275 is amended by adding:

- Effective April 1, 1997, penalties for illegal entry shall be subject to:
  - between $50 and $250 for each such entry or attempted entry
  - twice the amount if an alien has been previously penalized

Penalties for High Speed Flights from Immigration Checkpoints

INA 241(a)(2)(A) is amended by adding: *Ref: IIRIRA96.108*

- Any alien convicted of fleeing or evading an immigration checkpoint and leading law enforcement agents on a high speed vehicle chase shall be fined and/or imprisoned not more than five years and is deportable

Automated Entry and Exit Control System   *Ref: IIRIRA96.110*

- By October 1, 1998, the Attorney General must develop an automated entry and exit control system that will:
  - record the exit of every alien and match it to the record of the alien's arrival in the United States
  - identify lawfully admitted nonimmigrants who have gone out of status
  - integrate information on out of status aliens into data bases of the INS at ports of entry and State Department consulates abroad
  - be reported annually to the House of Representatives and Senate

Fingerprinting of Illegal or Criminal Aliens   *Ref: IIRIRA96.112*

- Additional funds to ensure the INS "IDENT" program applies to the fingerprinting of illegal or criminal aliens apprehended nationwide

Pre-Inspection Stations at Foreign Airports   *Ref: IIRIRA96.123*

INA is amended by adding new section 235A:

- By October 31, 1998, the INS in consultation with the State Department will establish and maintain pre-inspection stations in at least five of the 10 foreign airports which serve as the last point of departure for the greatest number of inadmissible aliens

Increase in Alien Smuggling and Unlawful Employment Investigators

INA 275 and 275A are amended: *Ref: IIRIRA96.131*

- The INS is authorized to hire an additional 300 staff:
  - in each of Fiscal Years 1997, 1998 and 1999
  - to investigate alien smuggling and unlawful employment violations

Increase in Visa Overstayer Investigators   *Ref: IIRIRA96.132*

- Hire an additional 300 in Fiscal Year 1997 to investigate visa overstayers

Agreements for State Employees to Perform INS Functions   *Ref: IIRIRA96.133*

INA 287 is amended by adding:

- Written agreements with states to enable qualified state employees to perform an INS investigation, apprehension and detention function

Allocation of INS Agents to States   *Ref: IIRIRA96.134*

INA 103 is amended by adding:

- Allocate at least 10 full-time INS agents to each state by January 1, 1997

Title II - Enhanced Enforcement and Penalties Against Alien Smuggling; Document Fraud

Increased Penalties for Alien Smuggling and Hiring   *Ref: IIRIRA96.203*

INA 274A is amended:

- Increased fines and imprisonment for alien smuggling and hiring illegals

Increase in Assistant U.S. Attorneys to Prosecute Persons Harboring or Bringing In Illegal Aliens   *Ref: IIRIRA96.204*

- Increase the number of Assistant United States Attorneys by 25 in Fiscal Year 1997 to prosecute persons harboring or bringing in illegal aliens

Increased Penalties for Document Fraud   *Ref: IIRIRA96.211*

INA 1028(b) is amended:

- Increase penalties for fraud and misuse of government ID documents

Increased Penalties for Improper Document Filing   *Ref: IIRIRA96.212*

INA 274C(a) is amended by adding:

- The penalties are increased for:
  - filing or assisting an alien in the filing of a knowingly false document
  - the improper use of documents before boarding a common carrier, or
  - failure to present documents to an immigration inspector on arrival

False Claims of Citizenship   *Ref: IIRIRA96.215*
- Criminal activity is a false claim of U.S. citizenship with the intent of:
  - obtaining a federal or state benefit or service
  - engaging in unlawful employment
  - registering or voting in any federal, state or local election

Criminal Penalty for Voting   *Ref: IIRIRA96.216*
18 USC 29 is amended by adding:

- Fines and imprisonment of not more than one year for noncitizens voting in a federal election

Title III - Inspection, Apprehension, Detention, Adjudication, and Removal of Inadmissible and Deportable Aliens

Admission Criteria and Unlawful Presence   *Ref: IIRIRA96.301*
INA 101(a) is amended:

- A Green Card holder shall not be considered as seeking an admission into the United States unless he or she:
  - has abandoned or relinquished that status
  - has been absent from the U.S. continuously in excess of 180 days
  - has engaged in illegal activity after having departed the United States
  - has departed from the U.S. while under legal process seeking removal
  - has committed an offence identified in section 212(a)(2) unless waived
  - is attempting to enter at a time or place other than as designated by INS or has not been admitted after inspection and authorization

INA 212(a) is amended:

- An alien is deemed to be unlawfully present in the United States:
  - after the expiration of the authorized period of stay, or
  - without being admitted or paroled
- The alien becomes subject to the following conditions:
  - an alien who is unlawfully present for fewer than 180 days must apply at a consular office responsible for his or her home country
  - an alien who departed voluntarily is:
    - inadmissible within three years of date of departure if unlawfully present between 180 days and one year
    - inadmissible within 10 years of date of departure if unlawfully present for one year or more
  - an alien ordered removed under INA 235 or 240 is:
    - inadmissible within five years of date of removal
    - inadmissible at any time if convicted of aggravated felony
  - an alien who departed while an order of removal was outstanding is:
    - inadmissible within 10 years of departure

- inadmissible within 20 years of departure after a second removal
- inadmissible at any time if convicted of aggravated felony
- exceptions permitted in determining the period of unlawful presence include the periods in which an alien:
  - is under the age of 18
  - has a bona fide application for asylum pending
  - is a beneficiary of family unity protection
  - is a battered woman or child
  - is within 120 days of the filing of a nonfrivolous application for a change or extension of status before the expiration of the authorized period of stay

Stowaways   *Ref: IIRIRA96.302*

INA 235 is amended:

- A stowaway:
  - is not eligible for admission
  - shall be ordered removed upon inspection by an Immigration Officer unless the alien indicates an intention to apply for asylum
  - shall be referred by the officer for an interview by an asylum officer
  - is not be considered an applicant for admission or eligible for a hearing
  - when deemed inadmissible by an immigration officer, the officer shall:
    - order the alien removed without further hearing or review, or
    - refer the alien for an interview by an asylum officer, if requested
- If the asylum officer determines a credible fear of persecution, the alien shall be detained for further consideration, or
- If the asylum officer determines no credible fear of persecution, the officer shall order the alien removed without further hearing or review, or
- If requested, a prompt review by an immigration judge within 24 hours, or not later than seven days, determines a credible fear of persecution

Arrest and Detention Pending Removal Decision   *Ref: IIRIRA96.303*

INA 236 is amended:

- The Attorney General may issue a warrant for the arrest and detention of an alien pending a decision on whether the alien is to be removed
- After arrest and detention, the Attorney General may:
  - continue to detain the alien or release the alien
  - set bond with approved security of at least $1,500
  - approve conditional parole without work authorization unless the alien:
    - has permanent resident status
    - has nonimmigrant status which permits work authorization

Cancellation of Removal of Inadmissible Alien   *Ref: IIRIRA96.304*

INA 239 is redesignated as INA 234 and amended;
INA 240 is redesignated as INA 240C and amended;

INA is amended by adding new section 238:
- The Attorney General may cancel the removal of an inadmissible or deportable alien if the alien has:
  - been lawfully admitted for permanent residence for five years
  - has resided in the United States continuously for seven years after being admitted in any status, and
  - has not been convicted of any aggravated felony
  - has been physically present in the U.S. for a continuous period of not less than 10 years immediately preceding the date of such application
- The number of adjustments are limited to 4,000 in any fiscal year
- The Attorney General may permit an alien to depart voluntarily at his or her own expense in lieu of being subject to removal proceedings if:
  - the alien has been physically present for a period of at least one year
  - the alien has been of good moral character for at least five years
  - the alien is not deportable under INA 237 (aliens excluded from admission or entering in violation of law)
  - the alien has the means to depart and intends to do so
  - the alien was previously permitted to depart after being inadmissible
- Permission to depart voluntarily is valid for a maximum of 60 days

Judicial Review and Fines - Orders of Removal   *Ref: IIRIRA96.306*

INA 242 is amended:
- Section 306 includes such changes as:
  - adding significant restrictions on judicial review of orders of removal
  - establishing fines such as $5,000 for each alien stowaway not removed

Increased Fingerprinting and Registration Authorization   *Ref: IIRIRA96.323*

INA 263(a) is amended:
- Aliens on criminal probation or criminal parole within the U.S. are added to the list of groups authorized for fingerprinting and registration

Criminal Alien Identification System   *Ref: IIRIRA96.326*

Sec. 130002 of the Violent Crime Control and Law Enforcement Act of 1994 is amended:
- The INS Commissioner is directed to operate a criminal alien identification system to assist Federal, State and local law enforcement agencies in:
  - locating aliens subject to removal by conviction of aggravated felonies
  - providing for recording, in automated identification system, fingerprint records of aliens who have been previously arrested and removed

Proof of Vaccination of Permanent Residence Applicants   *Ref: IIRIRA96.341*

INA 212(a) is amended:
- Aliens seeking adjustment of status are excluded for failing to present documentation of having received vaccination against vaccine-preventable diseases including at least mumps, measles, rubella, polio, tetanus and

diphtheria toxoids, pertussis, influenza type B and hepatitis B, and any other vaccinations against vaccine-preventable diseases recommended by the Advisory Committee for Immunization Practices
- Applicable after September 30, 1996

Exclusion of F-1 Violators   *Ref: IIRIRA96.346*
INA 212(a)(6) is amended:
- An alien who obtains the status of a nonimmigrant F-1 and who violates a term or condition of such status is excludable until the alien has been outside the U.S. continuously for five years after the date of the violation

Exclusion of Alien Voters   *Ref: IIRIRA96.347*
INA 212(a)(10) is redesignated as Section 301(b) of this title and amended:
- Any alien who has voted in any Federal, State, or local constitutional provision, statute, ordinance, or regulation is excludable

INA 241(a) is redesignated as section 305(a)(2) of this division and amended:
- Any alien who has voted in violation of any Federal, State, or local constitutional provision, statute, ordinance, or regulation is deportable

Deportation of Aliens Convicted of Crimes Against Spouses and Children
INA 241(a) is amended by adding: *Ref: IIRIRA96.350*
- Any alien who at any time after entry is convicted of domestic violence, stalking, child abuse, child neglect, or child abandonment is deportable

Increased Fee for Processing Out of Status Green Card Applicants
INA 245(i) is amended to: *Ref: IIRIRA96.376*
- Increase the fee for adjusting the status of an out of status alien physically present in the U.S. to $1,000 (subsequently removed and briefly reinstated)

Title IV - Enforcement of Restrictions Against Employment

Three Employment Eligibility Confirmation Pilot Programs
Ref: IIRIRA96.403
- The Attorney General shall conduct the following three pilot programs of employment eligibility confirmation to be used in the hiring, recruitment or referral for employment in the United States:
  - for the basic pilot program in at least five of the seven states with the highest estimated population of illegal aliens in which the alien will provide within three days of hiring:
    - Social Security Account number
    - INS identification or authorization number
    - the original I-9 form in the manner required for inspection

- the citizenship attestation pilot program in at least five states that issue driver's license or similar identification document which contains a photograph of the individual and:
  - has security features
  - is sufficiently resistant to tampering, and fraudulent use that it is a reliable means of identification for this section
- the machine-readable document pilot program in at least five states that issue driver's licenses and similar identification documents issued which include a machine-readable Social Security Account number

Toll-Free or Electronic Identity and Employment Authorization Confirmation
Ref: IIRIRA96.404

Establishment of a pilot program confirmation system to receive inquiries at any time through a toll-free telephone line or toll-free electronic media which provides:
- Within three working days, confirmation or tentative nonconfirmation concerning an individual's identity and authorization to be employed
- Within 10 working days after the date of the tentative nonconfirmation
- Secondary verification to confirm the validity of information provided, and
- A final confirmation or nonconfirmation

Good Faith Employment Verification   *Ref: IIRIRA96.411*

INA 274A(b) is amended:
- A person or entity is considered to have complied with the employment verification system notwithstanding a technical or procedural failure to meet such requirement if:
  - there was a good faith attempt to comply, and
  - not less than 10 business days have been given to correct the failure
  - there is no pattern or practice of violations

Social Security Reporting of Aliens Not Authorized to Work   *Ref: IIRIRA96.414*

INA 290 is amended:
- After January 1, 1997, if a person not authorized to work has earnings reported to Social Security, the Commissioner of Social Security shall provide information in an electronic form to the Attorney General with:
  - the name and address of the alien
  - the name and address of the person reporting the earnings, and
  - the amount of the earnings

Social Security Authorization to Obtain Alien's Social Security Account Number for Attorney General or the INS   *Ref: IIRIRA96.415*

INA 264 is amended:
- Authorization to require any alien to provide a Social Security number for inclusion in any record maintained by the Attorney General or the INS

Limitation on Employment Verification Documentation Proof

INA 274B(a)(6) is amended: *Ref: IIRIRA96.421*

- It is an unfair immigration-related practice to discriminate by:
  - requesting more or different documents than necessary to satisfy the requirements of employment verification
  - refusing to honor tendered documents which appear to be genuine

Title V - Restrictions on Benefits for Aliens

State Illegal Aliens' Driver's License Denial Pilot Programs *Ref: IIRIRA96.502*

- All states may conduct pilot programs on the viability, advisability and cost-effectiveness of denying driver's licenses to aliens not lawfully present

Denial of Social Security Benefits to Illegal Aliens   *Ref: IIRIRA96.503*

Social Security Act.202 is amended:

- No monthly benefit shall be payable to any alien in the United States for any month during which such alien is not lawfully present in the U.S.

Proof of Citizenship for Federal Public Benefits   *Ref: IIRIRA96.504*

- The Attorney General in consultation with the Secretary of Health and Human Services shall establish fair and nondiscriminatory procedures for a person applying for a Federal public benefit to provide proof of citizenship

Eligibility of Illegal Aliens for Postsecondary Education Benefits

Ref: IIRIRA96.505

- Effective July 1, 1998, an alien who is not lawfully present shall not be eligible on the basis of residence within a state or a political subdivision for any postsecondary education benefit unless a U.S. citizen or national is eligible for such a similar benefit regardless of citizenship

Provision of Personal Information to the INS or DOS   *Ref: IIRIRA96.531*

INA 212(a) is amended:

To be considered by the consular officer in a visa application or by the Attorney General in an application for admission or adjustment of status include the alien's:

- Age and health
- Family status
- Assets, resources, and financial status
- Education and skills
- Affidavits of support

Affidavit of Support - Public Charge   *Ref: IRIRA96.551*

INA 212(a)(4) and 213A are amended:

- The terms of the Affidavit of Support contract to establish that the alien is not a public charge:

- must be legally enforceable against the sponsor by the sponsored alien, the Federal Government, any State or political subdivision of the State, or by any other entity that provides a means-tested public benefit
- are not enforceable with respect to benefits provided after the alien:
  - is naturalized, or completes the required period of employment
  - has worked 40 qualifying quarters of Social Security coverage
- The sponsor must:
  - maintain an average income equal to at least 125 percent of the Federal poverty line
  - be the petitioner and may include an individual accepting joint liability
  - agree to submit to the jurisdiction of any Federal or State court
  - be a citizen, national or a lawfully-admitted permanent resident
  - be at least 18 years of age
  - be domiciled in a U.S. state, District, territory or possession
  - be petitioning under INA 204
- The Federal poverty line is defined as the level of income that is applicable to a family of the size involved
- The Attorney General shall ensure that information is provided for alien verification eligibility (SAVE) in Sec. 1137(d)(3) of the Social Security Act
- Any person who fails to notify the Attorney General and the State of current residence or any change of address within 30 days is subject to a civil penalty of:
  - not less than $250 nor more than $2,000, or
  - not less than $2,000 nor more than $5,000 if the sponsored-alien has received any means-tested public benefits if not eligible

Title VI - *Miscellaneous Provisions*

Parole for Humanitarian Reasons or Public Benefit   *Ref: IIRIRA96.602*

INA 212(d)(5)(A) is amended:

- Authority for parole into the United States is only on a case-by-case basis for urgent humanitarian reasons or significant public benefit

Application for Asylum   *Ref: IIRIRA96.604*

INA 208 is amended:

- An alien may apply for asylum if he or she:
  - is physically present or has arrived in the United States
  - has been interdicted in international or U.S. waters
  - pays a fee if established by the Attorney General
- Asylum is not available if the alien:
  - may be removed to a safe third country
  - has been in the United States more than one year
  - has previously been denied asylum (unless circumstances changed)

- has participated in persecution of a person on account of race, religion, nationality, membership in a particular social group or political opinion
- has been convicted of a particularly serious crime (such as an aggravated felony) which constitutes a danger to the U.S. community
- has committed a serious nonpolitical crime outside the United States
- is a danger to U.S. security (not subject to judicial review)
- is inadmissible due to terrorist activity
- has firmly resettled in another country

- Other conditions include:
  - employment authorization shall not be granted until 180 days after filing the asylum application (unless provided by the Attorney General)
  - fingerprints and photograph may be required by the Attorney General
  - asylum cannot be granted until the identity of the applicant has been checked against the INS and State Department databases
  - a frivolous asylum application causes permanent asylum ineligibility
- In the absence of exceptional circumstances:
  - the initial interview or hearing shall commence within 45 days of filing
  - final adjudication shall be completed within 180 days of the filing

Extension and Terms of Waiver of the Two-Year HRR   *Ref: IIRIRA96.622*

Section 220(c) of the Immigration and Nationality Technical Corrections Act of 1994 is amended concerning the Conrad 30 Program:

- The mechanism for a waiver of the two-year foreign country residence requirement for international medical graduates is extended to 2002
- Federally requested waivers are extended to an interested United States Government agency
- The Attorney General shall not grant a requested waiver to an interested State or U.S. government agency unless:
  - the government of the alien's home country furnishes a statement in writing that it has no objection to such waiver
  - the grant of a waiver would not exceed 30 for that state that fiscal year
  - the alien demonstrates a bona fide offer of full-time employment at a health facility or health care organization, and
  - employment is in the public interest
  - the alien agrees to begin such employment within 90 days of the waiver
  - the alien agrees to continue to work for a total of not less than three years (unless extenuating circumstances exist)
  - other than full-time medical research or training, the alien agrees to practice medicine for not less than three years in geographic areas designated by Health and Human Services as having a shortage of health care professionals
- The Attorney General may change the status of an alien who qualifies under this sub-section to that of an H-1B nonimmigrant

- No person who has a waiver and failed to fulfill the terms of the contract with the health care facility is eligible to apply for an immigrant visa until residing and being physically present in the country of his or her nationality or last residence for at least two years after leaving the U.S.:
- The two-year foreign residence requirement shall apply if:
  - the alien ceases to comply with any agreement entered into, or
  - the alien's employment ceases to benefit the public interest

Labor Certification - Professional Athletes   *Ref: IIRIRA96.624*

INA 212(a)(5)(A) is amended for professional athletes:

- An immigrant visa labor certification with respect to a professional athlete shall remain valid after the athlete changes employer, if:
  - the new employer is a team in the same sport as the team which employed the athlete when the athlete first applied for certification
- A professional athlete means an individual who is employed as an athlete by a team that is a member of an association which:
  - has six or more professional teams whose total combined revenues exceed $10,000,000 per year
  - governs the conduct of its members
  - regulates the contests in which its member teams regularly engage
- Any minor league team that is affiliated with such association

F-1 Status - Public Elementary, Secondary and Adult Education

INA 214 is amended: *Ref: IIRIRA96.625*

- An alien may not be accorded status as an F-1 student in order to pursue a course of study at a public elementary school, in a publicly funded adult education program, or at a public secondary school unless:
  - the aggregate period of such status does not exceed 12 months, and
  - the local educational agency has been fully reimbursed
- An alien admitted in F status to study at a private elementary or secondary school or in a language training program that is not publicly funded shall violate status and the F visa shall be voided by terminating or abandoning those studies to undertake a course of study in:
  - a public elementary school
  - a publicly funded adult education or language training program
  - a public secondary school

Increase in Validity Period of Immigrant Visa   *Ref: IIRIRA96.631*

INA 221(c) is amended:

- The period of validity of an immigrant visa is increased from four to six months from the date of issue by a consular officer
- In the case of aliens who are nationals of a foreign country and who are granted refugee or permanent resident status and resettled in another foreign country, the Secretary of State may prescribe the period of validity

of such a visa based upon the treatment granted by that other foreign
country to alien refugees and permanent residents, in the United States

Readmission of Out of Status Aliens   *Ref: IIRIRA96.632*

INA 222 is amended:

- An alien admitted on the basis of a nonimmigrant visa who remained in the
  U.S. beyond the period of stay authorized by the Attorney General shall:
  - have their visa voided after the conclusion of such period of stay
  - be ineligible to be readmitted to the United States as a nonimmigrant
    except on the basis of a visa issued in:
    - a consular office located in the country of the alien's nationality, or:
    - such other consular office as the Secretary of State shall specify if
      there is no office in the alien's country of nationality
      (consulate shopping prohibited)

DOS Nonimmigrant Visa Application Forms   *Ref: IIRIRA96.634*

INA 222(c) is amended:

- At the discretion of the Secretary of State, application forms for the various
  classes of nonimmigrant admissions may vary according to the class of visa

Extension of Visa Waiver Pilot Program   *Ref: IIRIRA96.635*

INA 217 is amended:

- The Visa Waiver Pilot Program was extended to 1997 (made permanent in
  2000) and becomes the responsibility of the Attorney General who:
  - acts in consultation with the Secretary of State
  - places pilot program countries on probation up to two fiscal years if:
    - program country's disqualification rate is between 2 and 3.5 percent
  - shall terminate a program country's designation as a pilot program
    country if:
    - its disqualification rate is 3.5 percent or more
    - after its two-year probationary period:
      - its disqualification rate is greater than 2 percent
      - it has failed to develop a machine-readable passport program

DV Lottery Visa Fee   *Ref: IIRIRA96.636*

- The Secretary of State may establish a fee to be paid by each applicant for
  an immigrant visa under the terms of the Diversity Immigrant Lottery

Electronic Collection of Alien Student Data   *Ref: IIRIRA96.641*

- The Attorney General in consultation with the Secretary of State and the
  Secretary of Education shall develop and conduct a program to collect
  electronically from approved higher education institutions and designated
  exchange visitor programs in the U.S., information concerning the alien's:
  - identity and current U.S. address

- nonimmigrant classification
- date of visa issue, extension or change of status
- current academic and full-time student status
- satisfying the terms and conditions of the program
- disciplinary action and change of program participation as a result of a criminal conviction
- The information shall be provided as a condition of continued approval of the institution's authority to issue documents to demonstrate visa eligibility
- An approved institution shall impose on and collect from each alien when the alien first registers with the institution after entering the United States a fee established by the Attorney General which does not exceed $100

Marriage Fraud   *Ref: IIRIRA96.652*

- The INS estimated the rate of marriage fraud between foreign nationals and U.S. citizens is 8 percent, a portion originating as mail-order marriages
- Each international matchmaking organization is required to:
  - disseminate to recruits, upon recruitment, such information as the INS deemed appropriate in the recruit's native language including:
    - information concerning conditional permanent residence
    - the battered spouse waiver
    - permanent resident status
    - marriage fraud penalties
    - the unregulated nature of the business
  - pay a penalty of not more than $20,000 for each violation

The American Competitiveness and Workforce Improvement Act of 1998

The Act, included in the Omnibus Budget Bill signed by President Clinton on October 27, 1998, established a more strict set of rules for "H-1B-dependent" employers with a proportionately larger share of H-1B nonimmigrants in their full-time workforce. At the same time, it temporarily increased the number of H-1B nonimmigrants to be admitted.

An H-1B-dependent employer is defined as one who has:

- 25 or fewer full-time employees of whom eight or more are H-1Bs, or
- 26 to 50 full-time employees of whom 13 or more are H-1Bs, or
- 51 or more full-time employees of whom 15 percent or more are H-1Bs

The American Competitiveness and Workforce Improvement Act of 1998 is divided into Subtitles A, B and C. While key elements are incorporated into the Immigration and Nationality Act, they are scheduled to terminate on September 30, 2001 because the provisions are meant to act as a temporary measure until permanent solutions can be found for the current shortage of skilled U.S. workers.

Subtitle A - Provisions relating to H-1B Nonimmigrants

Temporary Increase in access to temporary skilled personnel under H-1B program   *Ref: Section 411*

INA 214(g) is amended:

The INS " H-1B "numbers" were increased for the following Fiscal Years:

- 115,000 in fiscal year 1999
- 115,000 in fiscal year 2000
- 107,500 in fiscal year 2001
- 65,000 in each succeeding fiscal year

Protection against displacement of United States workers in case of H-1B-dependent employers   *Ref: Section 412*

INA 212(n)(1) is amended:

On applications submitted between the date the final H-1B regulations are promulgated and October 1, 2001, H-1B-dependent employers must attest that they:

- Will not displace a U.S. worker in the same or essentially equivalent job at the same area of employment within 90 days of filing the H-1B visa petition
- Will not place the H-1B with another employer at the other employer's worksite(s) unless assured that the duties were not previously performed by a displaced U.S. worker within 90 days of the placing of the H-1B
- Will accept a clear liability if the other employer displaces a U.S. worker
- Have taken good faith steps to recruit, in the U.S. using industry-wide standard procedures and have offered compensation that is at least as great as that offered to U.S. workers for the job
- Offered the job to any equally or better qualified U.S. worker who applies
- Used relevant legitimate normal non-discriminatory selection criteria

Changes in enforcement and penalties   *Ref: Section 413*

INA 212 (n) (2) (C) is amended:

H-1B-dependent employers face new rule changes and penalties, after notice and opportunity for a hearing if the Secretary of Labor finds:

- A failure or a substantial failure to meet a condition, or a misrepresentation of material fact in an application, a maximum penalty of $1,000, and no approved H-1B petitions for that employer for at least one year
- A wilful failure to meet a condition or wilful misrepresentation of material fact in an application, a civil monetary penalty of up to $5,000 and no approved H-1B petitions for that employer for at least two years
- A failure to meet a condition or a wilful misrepresentation of material fact which results in the displacement of a U.S. worker within 90 days before or after the filing of any visa petition and if the placing employer knew or had reason to know of the displacement, a monetary penalty not exceeding

$35,000 and no H-1B petitions approved for that employer for at least three years if the employer:
- discriminates in any way against an employee or former employee who cooperates in the investigation of a possible violation
- requires that an H-1B nonimmigrant pay a penalty for ceasing employment prior to a mutually agreed date
- requires that an H-1B nonimmigrant reimburse the employer for any part of the fee for the petition; a maximum $1,000 monetary penalty may be imposed and the amount paid returned to the nonimmigrant
- places an H-1B nonimmigrant designated as a full or part-time employee in nonproductive status or fails to pay the nonimmigrant full wages due to a decision by the employer or due to the nonimmigrant's lack of a permit or license
- fails to offer benefits and eligibility for benefits to an H-1B nonimmigrant on the same basis and criteria as offered to U.S. workers

Collection and use of H-1B nonimmigrant fees for scholarships
Ref: Section 414

INA 214(c) is amended:

The Attorney General shall impose a fee on an H-1B-dependent employer of $500 (increased to $1,000) for each H-1B petition December 1, 1998 to October 1, 2001 for:
- An initial grant of H-1B status
- An extension of stay
- Change of status

Fees are to be deposited into an H-1B nonimmigrant petitioner account and used for scholarships for low-income math, engineering, and computer science students and job training of U.S. workers who are citizens, Green Card holders or refugees as follows:
- Secretary of Labor - 56.3 percent for demonstration programs and projects to provide technical skills training for employed and unemployed workers
- Director of National Science Foundation - 28.2 percent for scholarships of a maximum of $2,500 per year for low-income students to pursue associate, undergraduate or graduate level degrees in mathematics, engineering, or computer science
- National Science Foundation - 4 percent for merit-reviewed grants for academic enrichment courses in mathematics, engineering or science
- National Science Foundation - 4 percent for systemic reform activities
- Attorney General - 1.5 percent for duties related to petitions
- Secretary of Labor - 6 percent for decreasing processing time

Computation of prevailing wage level
Ref: Section 415

INA 212 is amended:

In computing the prevailing wage level for an occupational classification in an institution of higher education, a nonprofit research organization or a Governmental research organization the prevailing wage level shall only take into account employees at such institutions and organizations in the area of employment. When the job opportunity for a professional athlete is covered by professional sports league rules or regulations, the wage set in those rules shall be considered as not adversely affecting the wages of U.S. workers similarly employed and be considered the prevailing wage.

Improving count of H-1B and H-2B nonimmigrants   *Ref: Section 416*

INA 214(g)(1) is amended:

The Attorney General shall take such steps as are necessary to:

- Maintain an accurate count of H-1B and H-2B nonimmigrants
- Revise the forms used for petitions to permit an accurate count of aliens subject to the numerical limitations
- Provide periodic statistical information and background to Congress

Report on older workers in the information technology field *Ref: Section 417*

The President of the National Academy of Sciences shall assess the status of older workers in the information technology field - age discrimination, promotion and advancement, working hours, telecommuting, salary, stock options, bonuses, and other benefits and the relationship between rates of advancement, promotion, compensation related to experience, skill level, education and age.

Report on high technology labor market needs; reports on economic impact of increase in H-1B nonimmigrants   *Ref: Section 418*

The Director of the National Science Foundation shall conduct a study for Congress to assess labor market needs for workers with high technology skills during the next ten years. The study is to include future training and education needs of high tech companies, improvements in teaching and educational level of American students in math, science, computer science and engineering since 1998, projections on U.S. workers employed overseas, relative achievement rates of U.S. and foreign students, cost benefit analysis of foreign high technology workers, needs of high tech sector to adapt products and services to particular local markets abroad.

Subtitle B - Special Immigrant Status for Certain NATO Civilian Employees   *Ref: Section 421*

Subtitle C - Miscellaneous Provision

Academic honoraria   *Ref: Section 431*

An honorarium and associated incidental expenses may be paid to an alien admitted under INA 101(a)(15)(B) for usual academic activities of not more than nine days at a single institution for the benefit of that institution if the alien has not accepted such payment or expenses from more than five institutions during the previous six months.

The American Competitiveness in the Twenty-first Century Act of 2000
Ref: Pub. L. 106-313

When it became apparent that industry needed more skilled foreign workers and there were not enough H-1B "numbers" available, Congress seized the opportunity to develop a new piece of legislation to try to solve, at least temporarily, some of the problems with the supply and demand of temporary skilled workers.

The result was the American Competitiveness in the Twenty-first Century Act of 2000. The following is a brief section-by-section summary of that Act.

Title I -The American Competitiveness in the Twenty-first Century Act of 2000

Short Title
Ref: Section 101

- American Competitiveness in the Twenty-first Century Act of 2000

Temporary Increase in Visa Allotments
Ref: Section 102

INA 214(g)(1)(A) is amended:

The total number of aliens who may be issued visas or provided H-1B nonimmigrant status:

- Fiscal Year 2003 - 195,000
- Fiscal Year 2002 - 195,000
- Fiscal Year 2001 - 195,000
  Petitions from previous years will not be charged against 2001 quota
- Fiscal Year 2000 - cases approved after the limitation was reached, before October 1, 2000, are counted in FY 2000 regardless of when effective
- Fiscal Year 1999 - cases approved after the limitation was reached, before October 1, 1999 are counted in FY 1999 regardless of when effective

Special Rule for Universities and Research Facilities
Ref: Section 103

INA 214(g) is amended:

The numerical limitation shall not apply to any nonimmigrant issued an H-1B visa who is employed or has received an offer of employment from:

- An institution of higher education or related nonprofit entity
- A government or nonprofit research organization
- Unless moving to a non-educational/research organization
- If charged against the cap during the past six years

Limitation on Per-country Ceiling with Respect to Employment-based Immigrants
Ref: Section 104

INA 202(g) is amended:

- If there are more Employment-based visas available in a calendar quarter than are used, then the visas may be made available without regard to

country of origin or per-country ceilings
- H-1B nonimmigrants reaching the six-year limit on their stay who are beneficiaries of pending or approved I-140s and who are from countries subject to per-country limits may receive extensions of H-1B status until decisions are made on their Adjustment of Status applications

Increased Portability of H-1B Status   *Ref: Section 105*
INA 214 is amended:
- An H-1B is authorized to accept new employment on filing of a new petition by a new employer if still in status and not employed without authorization
- Employment will continue until the new petition is adjudicated
- Authorization will cease if the petition is denied

Special Provisions in Cases of Lengthy Adjudications   *Ref: Section 106*
INA 214(g)(4) is amended:
- Nonimmigrant H-1Bs may extend their status beyond six years if an application for Adjustment of Status has been pending 365 days or more since the filing for Labor Certification or the INS petition
- Extensions are in one-year increments until a decision is made
- Nonimmigrant H-1Bs may change to a new job or employer if the new job is in the same or similar occupational classification if their Adjustment of Status has remained unadjudicated for 180 days
- Unused Employment-based immigrant visas are available for future use

Extension of Certain Requirements and Authorities Through Fiscal Year 2002
INA 212(n)(1)(E)(ii) is amended: *Ref: Section 107*
- Extends the authority of the Department of Labor to implement the attestations and investigative authority of the ACWIA to October 1, 2003

Recovery of Visas Used Fraudulently   *Ref: Section 108*
INA 214(g)(3) is amended:
- If a visa is revoked by fraud or willful misrepresentation of a material fact, one number is restored regardless of the fiscal year in which it was issued

NSF Study and Report on the 'Digital Divide'   *Ref: Section 109*
- The National Science Foundation shall conduct a study of the divergence in access to high technology in the United States
- Must report to Congress in 18 months

Modification of Nonimmigrant Petitioner Account Provisions *Ref: Section 110*
INA 286(s) is amended:
- Reallocated the funds collected from the $500 fee enacted in the American Competitiveness and Workforce Improvement Act (ACWIA)

Demonstration Programs and Projects to Provide Technical Skills Training for Workers   *Ref: Section 111*

Section 414(c) of ACWIA is amended:

- Directs the DOL to use funds available to establish demonstration programs or projects to provide technical skills training for workers
- Need for training justified through reliable regional, state, or local data
- 75 percent of grants shall be to workforce investment boards or consortia
- 25 percent of grants will go to partnerships of at least 2 businesses
- 80 percent of grants will be for skills training in high technology, information technology, and biotechnology and no more than 20 percent to training workers for skills in other H-1B-type specialties

Kids 2000 Crime Prevention and Computer Education Initiative

Ref: Section 112

- Provides after-school technology grants to Boys and Girls Clubs of America
- Up to $20 million may be appropriated for FY 2001-2006 to fund grants

Use of Fees for Duties Relating to Petitions   *Ref: Section 113*

INA 286(s)(5) is amended:

Change the percentage allocation of the H-1B Nonimmigrant petitioner fee to:

- 55 percent for DOL training programs
- 22 percent for NSF Scholarships
- 15 percent to NSF for K-12 education programs
- 4 percent to DOL for LCA processing and enforcement
- 4 percent to INS for H-1B case processing, and processing complaints relating to the recruitment attestation of H-1B-dependent employers

Exclusion of Certain "J" Nonimmigrants from Numerical Limitations Applicable to "H-1B" Nonimmigrants   *Ref: Section 114*

- J-1 physicians who are beneficiaries of a Conrad 30 waiver of the two-year home residency requirement who change status to H-1B are not counted toward the cap even if they later change employers or occupations

Study and Report on the "Digital Divide"   *Ref: Section 115*

- The Secretary of Commerce shall conduct a review of existing U.S. public and private high-tech workforce training programs

Severability   *Ref: Section 116*

- If any provision of this title or any amendment, or the application thereof is held invalid, then the remainder shall not be affected

Title II -Immigration Services and Infrastructure Improvements

Short Title   *Ref: Section 201*

- Immigration Services and Infrastructure Improvements Act of 2000

Purposes   *Ref: Section 202*

- Provide the INS with needed mechanisms to eliminate the current backlog in the processing of immigrant benefit applications within one year and maintain the elimination of the backlog in the future
- It is the sense of Congress that the processing of all immigrant benefit applications should be completed by 180 days after the initial filing
- A petition for a nonimmigrant visa should be processed not later than 30 days after filing

Definitions   *Ref: Section 203*

- 'Backlog' means with respect to an immigration benefit application, the period of time in excess of 180 days that such application has been pending before the INS
- 'Immigration benefit application' means any application or petition to convey, confer, certify, change, adjust or extend any INS-granted status

Immigration Services and Infrastructure Improvement Account
                                                                   Ref: Section 204

- The Attorney General to reduce the backlog in the processing of immigration benefit applications by one year after the date of enactment
- Make other improvements to ensure that a backlog does not re-develop
- Authorized to appropriate sums necessary to carry out backlog reduction

Reports to Congress   *Ref: Section 205*

- Within 90 days of the date of enactment, the INS is to submit a report to the House and Senate with their plan for eliminating such backlogs

An Act to Increase the Amount of Fees Charged to Employers who are Petitioners for the Employment of H-1B Nonimmigrant Workers, and for other Purposes   *(Pub. L. 106-311)*

Short Title   *Ref: Section 101*

INA 214(c)(9) is amended:

- Increases employer-paid H-1B alien petition fees from $500 to $1,000
- Excludes any employer that is a primary or secondary education institution, an institution of higher education, a related nonprofit entity, a nonprofit established curriculum-related entity at any such institution or a nonprofit or government research organization filing before October 1, 2003

Homeland Security Act of 2002 (Pub. L. 107-296)

Title I- Department of Homeland Security

Executive Department; Mission   Ref: 6 USC 111; Section 101

There is established a Department of Homeland Security, as an executive department of the United States within the meaning of title 5, United States Code. The primary mission of the Department is to:

- Prevent terrorist attacks within the United States
- Reduce the vulnerability of the United States to terrorism
- Carry out all functions transferred to the Department
- Ensure that the functions of of agencies and sub-divisions within the Department not related to securing the homeland are not diminished or neglected
- Ensure that the overall economic security of the United States is not diminished by homeland security efforts, activities and programs
- Monitor and coordinate efforts to sever connections between illegal drug trafficking and terrorism

Secretary; Functions   Ref: 6 USC 112; Section 102

The Secretary is the head of the department and shall have direction, authority, and control over it.

Other Officers   Ref: 6 USC 113; Section 103

There are the following officers, appointed by the President, by and with the advice and consent of the Senate:

- A Deputy Secretary who shall be the Secretary's first assistant
- An Under Secretary for Information Analysis and Infrastructure Protection
- An Under Secretary for Science and Technology
- An Under Secretary for Emergency Preparedness and Response
- A Director of the Bureau of Citizenship and Immigration Services
- Not more than 12 Assistant Secretaries
- A General Counsel

Title IV- Directorate of Border and Transportation Security

Subtitle A - Under Secretary for Border and Transportation Security

Under Secretary for Border and Transportation Security
Ref: 6 USC 201 Section 401

There shall be in the Department a Directorate of Border and Transportation Security headed by an Under Secretary for Border and Transportation Security.

Responsibilities   Ref: 6 USC 202; Section 402

The Secretary, acting through the Under Secretary for Border and Transportation Security shall be responsible for the following:

- Preventing the entry of terrorists and the instruments of terrorism
- Securing the borders - territorial waters, ports, terminals, waterways and air, land and sea transportation systems, managing and coordinating governmental activities at ports of entry
- Carrying out immigration enforcement functions
- Establishing and administering rules governing the granting of visas and parole
- Establishing national immigration enforcement policies and procedures
- Administering the Customs law of the United States
- Conducting the inspection and administrative functions of the Department of Agriculture
- Ensuring the speedy, orderly and efficient flow of lawful traffic and commerce

Functions Transferred   *Ref: 6 USC 203; Section 403*
The following agencies have been incorporated:

- The United States Customs Service
- The Transportation Security Administration
- The Federal Protective Service
- The Federal Law Enforcement Training Center
- The Office for Domestic Preparedness

Also included are:

- The Immigration & Naturalization Service
- The Animal and Plant Health Inspection Service
- The Coast Guard

Subtitle C- Miscellaneous Provisions

Visa Issuance   *Ref: 6 USC 236; Section 428*
The Secretary shall have exclusive authority through the Secretary of State to issue regulations with respect to, administer, and enforce the provisions of the Act and all other immigration and nationality laws relating to the functions of consular officers of the United States in connection with the granting or refusal of visas in accordance with law. The Secretary is authorized to assign DHS employees to each diplomatic and consular post at which visas are issued unless such assignment would not promote homeland security.

Information on Visa Denials   *Ref: 6 USC 237; Section 429*
Whenever a consular officer denies a visa to an applicant, the consular officer shall enter the facts, basis for denial and name of the applicant in the interoperable electronic data system.

Subtitle D - Immigration Enforcement Functions

Transfer of Functions to Under Secretary for Border and Transportation Security   *Ref: 6 USC 251; Section 441*

The following programs have been transferred:

- The Border Patrol program
- The detention and removal program
- The intelligence program
- The investigations program
- The inspections program

Establishment of Bureau of Border Security   *Ref: 6 USC 252; Section 442*
(Renamed **Bureau of Immigration and Customs Enforcement**)

Functions include:

- Establishing policies
- Overseeing adminstration of such policies
- Advising the Under Secretary of any matters which may affect the Bureau of Citizenship and Immigration
- Administering the program to collect information relating to nonimmigrant foreign students and other exchange (visitor) program participants including the Student and Exchange Visitor InformationSystem (SEVIS) and shall use such information to carry out the enforcement functions of the Bureau

Subtitle E - Citizenship and Immigration Services

Establishment of Bureau of Citizenship and Immigration Services
Ref: 6 USC 271; Section 451

The head of the **Bureau of Immigration and Customs Enforcement (BICE)** shall be the Director of the Bureau of Immigration and Customs Enforcement who shall report directly to the Deputy Secretary. The role of the Director is to:

- Establish policies
- Oversee administration
- Advise Deputy Secretary on policies that affect the Bureau of Border Security
- Establish national immigration services policies and procedures
- Implement pilot initiatives to eliminate any remaining backlog in the processing of immigration benefits applications, and prevent any backlog from recurring

The following functions are transferred from the INS:

- Adjudications of immigrant visa petitions
- Adjudications of naturalization petitions
- Adjudications of asylum and refugee applications
- Adjudications performed at Service Centers
- All other adjudications performed by the INS at the time of transfer

Citizenship and Immigration Services Ombudsman *Ref: 6 USC 272; Section 452*
It shall be the function of the Ombudsman to:
- Assist individuals and employers in resolving problems with the Bureau of Citizenship and Immigration Services
- Identify areas in which individuals and employers have problems in dealing with the Bureau of Citizenship and Immigration Services
- Propose changes in the administrative practices of the Bureau of Citizenship and Immigration Services to mitigate identified problems

Application of Internet-based technologies *Ref: 6 USC 278; Section 461*
Not later than one year after the effective date of the Act, the Technology Advisory Committee shall establish an internet-based system that will permit a person, employer, immigrant or nonimmigrant who has filings with the Secretary for any benefit under the Immigration and Nationality Act access to online information about the processing status of the filing involved.

Subtitle F - General Immigration Provisions

Abolishment of INS *Ref: 6 USC 291; Section 471*
Upon completion of all transfers from the Immigration and Naturalization Service as provided for by this act, the Immigration and Naturalization Service is abolished.

The Bureau of Border Security (renamed Bureau of Immigration and Customs Enforcement) and the Bureau of Citizenship and Immigration Services may not be recombined into a single agency.

Sense of Congress *Ref: 6 USC 294; Section 474*
It is the sense of Congress that the missions of the Bureau of Border Security (renamed Bureau of Immigration and Customs Enforcement) and the Bureau of Citizenship and Immigration Services are equally important.

Immigration Functions *Ref: 6 USC 298; Section 478*
One year after the date of enactment of this Act and each year thereafter, the Secretary shall submit a report to the President and to various Congressional bodies on:
- The number of immigration applications and petitions received and processed
- Region-by-region statistics filed and denied by category
- The quantity of backlog applications and petitions processed, awaiting processing and a detailed plan for backlog elimination
- The average processing period for immigration applications and petitions
- The number and types of grievances filed with the department of Justice and their resolution
- Plans to address grievances and improve immigration services
- Whether immigration fees were used consistent with requirements for their use
- Whether immigration-related questions were answered effectively and efficiently

Chapter 18

United States Government Resources

T he "Big 3" players in the process of U.S. immigration are the U.S. Departments of Homeland Security, the Department of State and the Department of Labor. However, it should be noted that there are also other agencies which play a significant role in the immigration process.

This chapter offers some leads for further research on your own. As you delve into the resources which are made available by each department, you will understand why the immigration process may seem so complex and why such extensive detail had to be incorporated in this book.

Department of Homeland Security

Bureau of Citizenship and Immigration Services (BCIS)

Forms

The BCIS provides most of the forms required for the steps covered in this book. Orders may be placed without charge directly from the BCIS Eastern Forms Center in Williston, Vermont by calling (800) 870-3676. Allow two weeks for delivery. The best time to call is first thing in the morning. If you cannot get the recorded service to take your order, try following the prompts as though you are calling from a rotary telephone.

You may also order or download BCIS forms from the BCIS internet web site at www.immigration.gov/graphics/exec/forms/index.asp.

BCIS National Customer Service Center

The BCIS offers nationwide automated and live telephone information by calling (800) 375-5283. Automated information services are available 24 hours a day, seven days a week.

Live assistance is available with general immigration information from 8 am to 6 pm Eastern Time, Monday to Friday, except holidays. Times vary slightly in Alaska, Hawaii, Puerto Rico and the U.S. Virgin Islands.

The 24-hour menu contains the following recorded information:
- For information on an application that has been filed with the BCIS
  - for inquiries on the status of your application
  - to update your address on a pending application
  - for assistance on rescheduling an appointment
  - for questions regarding a notice received from the BCIS
  - for other questions about a pending application
- For information about fingerprinting, your local BCIS office or for a list of BCIS authorized doctors
  - for ASC fingerprint location information
  - for BCIS local office information
  - for a list of doctors in your area authorized to give a medical exam
- For information about forms or applications
  - to place an order for the BCIS application or forms needed
  - for current application filing fees
  - for information about where to file an application
  - if you have the application but still have questions
- For information on immigration benefits and services
  - for information on how a permanent resident can apply for U.S. citizenship through naturalization
  - for information on how to renew or replace your Green Card
  - for information on bringing a relative, fiancé(e) or orphan to live permanently in the U.S.
  - for immigration services on traveling outside the U.S.
  - for information on immigration benefits available to temporary nonimmigrant visa holders in the U.S.
  - for information on Temporary Protected Status programs
- For information about recent or upcoming changes in immigration programs and procedures
  - for information on changing your address with the BCIS
  - for changes to fees for applications or petitions
  - for information on changes to Temporary Protected Status
- For information regarding other agencies
  - Social Security
  - Passport Office
    - for visa or entry requirements when traveling to another country, contact their Embassy or Consulate

Internet Information Service

The BCIS operates a web site on the internet. It contains a great deal of information on a variety of subjects with heavy emphasis on immigrant and nonimmgrant status. The BCIS may be found at www.immigration.gov.

Bureau of Customs and Border Protection (BCBP)

The border inspection functions of the INS were transferred to the Department of Homeland Security and placed in the Bureau of Customs and Border Protection. The goal of the bureau is to facilitate the flow of legitimate people and goods across the U.S. border. More information is available at their website www.cbp.immigration.gov.

Department of State (DOS)

Visas

The U.S. Department of State is responsible for the issuance of immigration visas to the United States and U.S. passports. For information on visas call the Department of State's visa office at (202) 663-1225.

Green Card Visa Lottery

For specific information on the State Department Visa Lottery program you may call the Visa Lottery hotline at (202) 331-7199. Lottery information is available on the internet at www.travel.state.gov/visa_services.html.

Orphan Adoption

Recorded information about orphan adoption in specific countries may be obtained by calling the State Department at (202) 647-3444 or by autofax at (202) 647-3000.

Passports

Information on U.S. passports is available by calling the U.S. Passport Agency at (900) 225-5674. The cost is 55 cents per minute to listen to automatic recorded messages or $1.50 per minute to speak with an operator. A live operator is available from 8:30 am to 5:30 pm Eastern time, Monday through Friday. A credit card may be used for a flat rate of $5.50 by calling (888) 362-8668.

For the nearest passport agency office or U.S. Post Office authorized to accept passport applications, check the government listings in your local telephone directory under passport services or U.S. Department of State. Further details are available in Chapter 35.

Internet Service

Like the INS, the DOS Bureau of Consular Affairs operates a web site on the internet. It may be found at: www.travel.state.gov.

Department of Labor (DOL)

Forms

Forms may be obtained by calling (202) 219-4369.

Internet Service

The U.S. Department of Labor also operates an internet web site. It contains a great deal of information on a variety of labor-related subjects with emphasis on the Employment and Training Administration. Not all the information offered is still valid. The DOL may be found on the internet at www.doleta.gov.

Federal Information Center

If you need information about these and other U.S. Government departments or agencies, help is available in most major centers by calling the Federal Information Center at (800) 688-9889. Recorded messages are available 24 hours a day, seven days a week and are updated frequently.

Information specialists may be reached between 9 am and 8 pm Eastern time, Monday though Friday. The specially trained staff will answer your question or direct you to a person with the answer in the U.S. Federal government.

Information is available on:
- Federal taxes
- Federal jobs
- Social Security
- Veterans' benefits
- Sales of property or goods offered by the Federal Government
- Copyright, patent, trademark information
- Government publications
- Federal Communications Commission services, rules and regulations
- Government travel information
  - passports
  - visas
  - travel per diem rates.
- Department of State document authentication services
- Selective Service system
- Savings bonds or default student loans

Other U.S. Government Agencies

The functions and responsibilities of the major U.S. government agencies involved in the post-immigration adjustment process are detailed in the chapters which follow in Book 2.

Book 2

USA Orientation: Getting Settled

Adjusting to life in the United States

Book 2

Introduction

Book 2, **USA Orientation: Getting Settled** is devoted to demystifying the process of getting settled in the United States. It will help you navigate through the social and administrative experiences which await you after clearing the immigration processes in Book 1.

As your American friends will tell you, life in the United States is both an adventure and a challenge. To assist you in getting adjusted to your new environment, **USA Orientation: Getting Settled** offers 17 chapters of orientation to a wide range of new social and governmental experiences.

Look for help on these and many other subjects as you settle into your new American home.

Part I - Governmental Procedures

Both the federal and state levels of government have rules to be learned and procedures to be followed.
On the federal side, look for insight into:
- Bureau of Customs and Border Protection
- Social Security
- Selective Service

At the state level, read about:
- Automobile ownership
- Driving privileges and responsibilities
- Employee benefits and obligations

Part II - Finance

Part II includes some tips on the financial side of setting up a new life in the U.S.

The tax system is complex and requires study to take full advantage of your financial position.

Purchasing and financing a home may involve learning a whole new language. Definitions and detailed explanations are provided for the following terms plus many more awaiting the home buyer in the United States:

- Title insurance
- PITI
- Recording fees
- Loan origination fee
- Points

The chapter on banking offers many tips including:

- The legal transfer of funds into the United States
- How to establish your credit rating
- Where to store your valuables

Part III - Insurance

Insurance is a major consideration.

Health insurance can be a big surprise when you find that there is no national government plan to take care of your health needs. To give you a better idea of how the U.S. health care system works, Chapter 29 describes your many options in detail.

Read about a variety of health insurance programs including:

- Medicare
- Medigap
- Managed Health Care
- Fee-for-Service
- Health insurance for expatriates

Home and automobile insurance will also be a necessity. Explanations and definitions are provided for the many new terms you will encounter.

Part IV - Community

A school may be one of the first organizations an alien will encounter in the community. Look for information on:

- Documents needed to register your child in school
- How long a foreign student may attend a public elementary school

Most communities have a mind-boggling choice of organizations which, when joined, can speed the orientation process. Also, marriage is introduced in chapter 33.

Part V - Post-Naturalization Rights

Part V offers some insight into the benefits which become available after naturalization such as:

- Who may vote and who must not
- How and where to obtain a passport

Part I

Governmental Procedures

After clearing the formal immigration steps, as a newly arrived legal alien, you still may be faced with a bewildering list of lessons to learn and agencies to satisfy.

With some exceptions, only "qualified" aliens (in addition to U.S. citizens and nationals) are eligible to receive Federal public benefits. Certain Federal and State departments are required to notify the BCIS of any alien they "know" is not legally present in the United States.
Ref: Sec. 404, Personal Responsibility and Work Opportunity Reconciliation Act of 1996

Part I of Book 2 offers an in-depth study of the rules and roles of several of the agencies you are likely to encounter and what each expects of you. The following five chapters include information on:

Chapter 19 — Importing Belongings
- What you may and may not bring into the country

Chapter 20 — Social Security
- Who participates
- How to obtain a Social Security Card

Chapter 21 — Selective Service
- Who must register and when

Chapter 22 — Buying or Leasing a Car - License & Registration
- Is leasing a car more economical than buying

Chapter 23 — Employment Benefits and Compensation, Welfare
- What an employee can expect

Chapter 19

Importing Belongings

The **Department of Homeland Security** is responsible for securing the borders and transportation systems. To carry out its border security mission, the **Directorate of Border and Transportation Security (BTS)** has been created. Included within this body are two bureaus.

Bureau of Customs and Border Protection (BCBP) - oversees movement of goods and people across borders. The bureau merges:

- Border Patrol
- Inspectors from:
  - INS
  - Customs Service (including canine enforcement)
  - Animal and Plant Health

Bureau of Immigration and Customs Enforcement (BICE) - merges the following enforcement and investigative functions inside the U.S.

- Immigration & Naturalization Service
- Customs Service (including air and marine enforcement)
- Federal Protective Service (provides security for Federal facilities)

Although the new bureaus were officially implemented on March 1, 2003, full integration of the agencies will take months. In the meantime the Customs forms and procedures remain the same.

All persons arriving at a U.S. port of entry are inspected by officials from the Bureau of Customs and Border Protection (BCBP). Each person wishing to enter the U.S. is responsible for sufficient documentation to establish identity, citizenship and if needed, documents which would permit entry into the U.S. The inspectors have the authority to decide whether an alien and his possessions may enter the country.

Advanced Passenger Information System (APIS) requires that all air carriers collect biographical information from passengers and crew prior to travel to and from the U.S. and foreign locations. The names are checked against the combined Federal law enforcement data base, the Interagency Border Inspection System (IBIS), before the plane's arrival at its destination.   *Ref: Pub. L. 107-71*

Officials randomly select individuals for additional inspections to ensure compliance with U.S. laws. Title 19, Section 1582 of the United States Code authorizes officers to search, inspect, and/or examine all persons, luggage, and merchandise entering U.S. from a foreign country. Trained dogs may assist the officers.

Officials recommend that you allow sufficient time for clearance and have all necessary documents ready for inspection before you approach the officer. Before entering the United States as an immigrant you may find it helpful to contact the intended point of entry to determine well in advance whether your documents are satisfactory. For a list of ports see:
www.customs.gov/xp/cgov/toolbox/contacts/ports.

Until the Bureau of Customs and Border Protection is fully operational, Customs information may be found at:

> U.S. Customs Service
> 1300 Pennsylvania Avenue, N.W.
> Room 5.4D
> Washington, DC 20229
> www.customs.gov
> http://cpb.customs.gov
> www.dhs.gov

There is no limit to the amount of money that may be brought into or taken out of the United States. However, if you bring in or take out more than $10,000 in monetary instruments, you must file a Form 4790 with the BCBP. See Chapter 25.

All imported goods are subject to duty unless exempted by law. Certain exemptions are provided to allow persons moving to the United States, either permanently or temporarily, to bring their personal and household effects.

Moving Household and Personal Effects to the United States

You may import household effects such as furniture, kitchenware, appliances, dishes, linens, libraries, home office equipment, artwork and similar household furnishings, for your personal use, free of duty. To be eligible for duty-free exemption, the articles must have either been available for your use or used in a household where you were a resident for one year. The year of use does not need to be continuous nor does it need to be the year immediately before the date of importation.

Household effects from the country where these effects were used, and meeting the above criteria, may be entered into the United States duty-free within 10 years after your initial arrival in the United States as a legal resident. Personal effects are items that belong to and are used by a person, such as wearing apparel, jewelry, photographic and sports equipment (Not Firearms). Personal effects may be shipped or mailed to you at a later date. The package should be marked "Used Personal Effects" and must have been in your possession prior to your entry into the United States. Anything included in the package that is new may be dutiable.

Professional Equipment

A person emigrating to the United States may enter professional books, implements, instruments and tools of trade, occupation or employment free of duty if the articles were owned and used abroad. These items do not need to have been in your possession for one year prior to importation, but they must be imported for your use and not for sale. Included are computers (CPU, monitor, printer, software, etc.), filing cabinets, shredders, fax machines, telephone equipment, calculators, books. etc. Theatrical scenery, properties, or apparel and articles for use in any manufacturing establishment are not eligible for this exemption.

Alcohol and Firearms

The Homeland Security Act divided the Bureau of Alcohol , Tobacco and Firearms into two new agencies.

The **Bureau of Alcohol, Tobacco, Firearms, and Explosives (ATF)** has moved to the Department of Justice. The Bureau oversees firearms, explosives and arson programs and deals with Federal criminal laws concerning alcohol and tobacco smuggling and diversion.

The **Tax and Trade Bureau** (TTB) remains in the Department of the Treasury. The bureau handles the regulatory and taxation aspects of the alcohol and tobacco industries.

Firearms and ammunition are subject to restrictions and import permits. The importation of fully automatic weapons and semi-automatic assault-type weapons is prohibited. Generally, firearms and ammunition acquired abroad may be imported, but only under permit. For more details, see www.atf.gov/firearms/faq/index.htm, www.atf.gov/firearms/rules/foreign.htm www.atf.gov/firarms/022002form6updates.htm.

For complete information, contact:
> Bureau of Alcohol, Tobacco, Firearms and Explosives
> Firearms and Explosives Import Branch
> 650 Massachusetts Avenue, N.W., Room 5300
> Washington, DC 20226
> Phone: (202) 927-8330
> Fax: (202) 927-2697

You will be required to pay duty on liquor that is imported in quantities greater than the exemptions allowed for each category of persons moving to the United States. While there is no Federal limit to the amount of alcohol you may bring in, there will most likely be a state limit. This limit is determined by the state that your goods arrive in, not the state you are moving to. It should be noted that some states prohibit the direct shipment of alcoholic beverages to individuals. Anyone interested in importing alcohol for personal use should contact his or her state liquor control agency.

Householders who are moving to the U.S. with personal wine cellars must remember that all alcohol over the amount eligible for duty-free treatment is dutiable at the applicable duty rate and that all federal, state and local taxes must be paid.

For further information, contact:

The Tax and Trade Bureau
Office of Public and Governmental Affairs
650 Massachusetts Ave, N.W., Room 8290
Washington, DC 20226
Phone: (202) 927-8110
Fax: (202) 927-8605
www.ttb.gov

Goods That Accompany You

Household and personal effects that arrive in the United States on the same vessel, vehicle or aircraft, and on the same day that you do, are considered to accompany you. You must complete Form 6059B, available from the BCBP. List, with their value, all items that you are bringing with you into the United States. BCBP asks that you identify those you believe are entitled to duty-free entry. Generally it is based on the information above, but you should contact them before your move with specific questions. Explain your status to the Inspector and ask any questions that you may have before the inspection of your belongings.

Goods Shipped Separately

Personal and household effects entitled to duty-free entry do not need to accompany you to the United States; you may have them shipped to your U.S. address at a later time. You must fill out Form 3299, Declaration for Free Entry of Unaccompanied Articles, listing the complete inventory. This form is available online through the Customs web site, from a BCBP office or from your mover.

Your shipment of personal and/or household goods must be cleared through BCBP at its first port of arrival unless you have made arrangements with a foreign freight forwarder to have your effects sent in-bond from the port of arrival to a more convenient port of entry for clearance. (Ask your moving company if they offer this service.) BCBP will not notify you that your goods have arrived. It is the responsibility of the shipper to notify you of the arrival of your goods. After receiving this notification you must enter the merchandise promptly. Failure to enter the merchandise within 15 days of its arrival in port may result in the merchandise being moved to a general order warehouse. Failure to obtain that merchandise from the general order warehouse within six months may result in its sale. If you cannot go to the BCBP office yourself, you may designate a friend or relative to represent you. You must give that person a letter addressed to "Officer in Charge of BCBP" authorizing that individual to represent you as your agent, on a one-time basis, to clear your shipment.

If a moving company is handling the transportation from Canada, the driver may take your goods through BCBP. He will need all the necessary papers such as the completed Form 3299 and a Power of Attorney document allowing him to represent you.

Animal and Plant Health Inspection Service (APHIS)

The United States Department of Agriculture could require an inspection of certain articles prior to or following shipment. For instance, persons moving from an area infested with the gypsy moth to a state that is not infested, need to know that their outdoor household articles may require inspection for gypsy moth egg masses.

APHIS also has a rule covering solid wood packing material from China. Wood-boring pests have been found. See www.aphis.usda.gov/ppq.

Importing an Automobile or Other Vehicle - Free Entry

Nonresidents/First-time immigrants may temporarily import a vehicle duty-free for personal use if the vehicle is imported in connection with the owner's arrival. Vehicles do not need to accompany the owner, but should arrive in the United States at approximately the same time, at least within a few weeks. If a delay of more than a few weeks should occur, the importer must prove that the delay was justified. Vehicles are defined as an automobile, trailer, airplane, motorcycle, boat or similar vehicle.

Foreign-made vehicles not in your possession before you leave your foreign residence, and imported into the United States, whether new or used, (i.e., ordered for direct delivery to your U.S. residence, either for personal use or for sale) are generally dutiable. Duty rates are based on the market value of the vehicle and those rates are subject to change on an annual basis.

It is important to know that any imported vehicle, new or used, must conform to U.S. safety, fuel savings, and air pollution control standards. A vehicle must be imported as a nonconforming vehicle unless it bears the manufacturer's label certifying that it meets U.S. standards. Vehicles that don't conform to U.S. safety and emission standards must be exported within one year and may not be sold in the United States. There is no exemption or extension of the export requirement. Conforming vehicles imported under the duty-free exemption are dutiable if sold within one year of importation. Duty must be paid at the most conveniently located BCBP office before the sale is completed.

Safety, Bumper and Theft Prevention Standards

Importers of motor vehicles must file Form HS-7 at the time a vehicle is imported to declare whether the vehicle complies with Department of Transportation requirements. As a general rule, all imported motor vehicles less than 25 years old and items of motor vehicle equipment must comply with all applicable Federal Motor Vehicle Safety Standards in order to be imported permanently into the United States.

Vehicles manufactured after September 1, 1978 must also meet the bumper standard and vehicles beginning with model year 1987 must meet the theft-prevention standard.

Vehicles manufactured to meet these standards will have a certification label affixed by the original manufacturer near the driver's-side door. If you purchase a vehicle abroad that is certified to U.S. standards, you can expedite your importation by making sure the sales contract identifies this fact and by presenting the contract to U.S. Customs at the time of importation.

Emission Standards

Most importers of passenger cars, light trucks, motorcycles and heavy duty engines must complete and submit an Environmental Protection (EPA) entry form (EPA Form 3520-1) to BCBP at the port of entry. These forms may be obtained from Customs at the port of entry or via faxback at (202) 564-9660. The faxback system will work for international calls. Enter your telefax number as if it were dialed from the United States, beginning with 011.

Cars and trucks manufactured in 1971 and later that comply with U.S. emission standards can be identified by a label in a readily visible position in the engine compartment. This label will indicate that the vehicle was originally manufactured to comply with U.S. emission standards. For pre-1971 models, you should verify the original compliance of the vehicle with the vehicle manufacturer.

Beginning with the 1996 model year, Federal emission requirements also apply to some non-road motorized equipment, such as lawn and garden equipment, and farm and construction equipment.

Since EPA and DOT requirements are subject to frequent changes, it is recommended that you contact these agencies for the latest requirements. Individual state requirements may exceed those of the federal government. However, EPA will not accept compliance with a state's emission requirements as satisfying EPA's.

Many automobiles purchased overseas are not manufactured to comply with U.S. standards and require modification. Both the Department of Transportation and the Environmental Protection Agency advise that although a non-conforming car may be conditionally admitted, the modifications required to bring it into compliance may be so extensive and costly that it may be impractical or impossible to achieve such compliance. You should investigate the procedure and necessary modifications before considering importation.

For the latest information about importing vehicles contact:

U.S. Environmental Protection Agency
Investigation/Imports Section
1200 Pennsylvania Avenue, N.W.
Washington, DC 20460
Phone: (202) 564-9240
Fax: (202) 565-2057

Faxback: (202) 564-9660
www.epa.gov/otaq/imports/imptop.htm
www.epa.gov/otaq/imports/quiktext.htm

National Highway Traffic Safety Administration (NSA-32)
400 7th Street S.W.
Washington, DC 20590
Phone: (202) 366-4000
Auto Safety Hot Line: (888) 327-4236
Fax: (202) 366-1024
www.nhtsa.dot.gov/cars/rules/import

For information regarding the entry process, telephone (202) 927-1082 or see www.customs.gov, click on Travel, then Leaving and Returning to the U.S. Under Publications click on Importing or Exporting a Car.

The Department of Agriculture also requires that the undercarriage of imported cars be free from foreign soils before they can be entered into the United States. This may be done by steam spray or by thorough cleaning before shipment.

For your own security and convenience, do not use your car as a container for personal belongings when shipping. Customs will inspect all goods inside which means you cannot lock the doors. Many shippers and carriers will not accept a vehicle with personal belongings.

Registration and Taxes

It is advisable to check with your new state to determine the regulations for registering a car and obtaining a driver's license.

For a list of state driver's license offices:

www.carbuyingtips.com/driver-licenses.htm

For a list of state vehicle registration offices:

www.carbuyingtips.com/dmv.htm

Motorists visiting the U.S. as tourists from countries that have ratified the Convention on International Road Traffic of 1949 may drive in the U.S. for one year with their own national license plates (registration tags) on their cars and with their own personal drivers' licenses.

Motorists from Canada and Mexico are permitted to tour in the U.S. without U.S. license plates or U.S. drivers' permits, under agreements between the U.S. and these countries.

Motorists from a country which is not a party to any of the above agreements must secure a driving permit in the U.S. after taking an examination.

Foreign nationals employed in the U.S. may only use foreign license tags from the port of entry to their destination in the U.S.

Be aware that you may have to pay a tax on the car when you register it in your new home state.

A Federal Gas Guzzler Tax may also be due on certain cars with an EPA gas mileage rating less than 22.5 miles per gallon. The tax increases as the fuel economy of the vehicle decreases from $1,000 to $7,700 and has not changed since 1991. IRS advises that this tax is also due on immigrants' cars when they are imported. IRS Form 6197 must be filed with the Gas Guzzler Tax payment. The tax does not apply to pickup trucks, SUVs, minivans or vans.

Medicines

If you require any medicines containing habit-forming drugs or narcotics (such as cough medicines, diuretics, heart drugs, tranquilizers, sleeping pills, anti-depressants, stimulants), you should:

- Have all medicines and similar products properly identified
- Carry only such quantity as might normally be carried by an individual having a health problem
- Have either a prescription or written statement from your personal physician saying that the medicines are necessary for physical well-being

The Food and Drug Administration prohibits the importation, by mail or in person, of fraudulent or misbranded prescription and non-prescription drugs and medical devices. These may include unorthodox "cures" for medical conditions. However, the FDA might consider allowing a three-month supply of unapproved new drugs into the country for a serious condition for which effective treatment may not be available domestically. The product must not represent an unreasonable risk and the patient must provide the name and address of the U.S. licensed doctor responsible for the treatment or evidence that treatment began in a foreign country.

Congress approved an amendment to the Controlled Substances Act. This amendment allows a U.S. resident to import up to 50 dosage units of a controlled medication without a valid prescription at an international land border. These medications must be declared upon arrival, be for the person's own use and in their original container. Drug products not approved by the USDA may not be acceptable.

Ref: 21 USC 956(a)

A valid U.S. prescription is needed to purchase more than 50 units and should not exceed personal use amounts, generally no more than a 90-day supply.

For additional information, contact the nearest FDA office or:

Food and Drug Administration
Division of Import Operations and Policy
Room 12-8 (HFC-170)
5600 Fishers Lane
Rockville, MD 20857
Phone: (301) 443-3852

(888) 463-6332
Fax: (301) 594-0413
www.fda.gov/ora/import/traveler_alert.htm

Pets

There are controls, restrictions, and prohibitions on entry of animals, birds, turtles, and wildlife.

Endangered species and products made from them are generally prohibited from being imported or exported. This list includes ivory, some animal skins, whale teeth and coral.

For information, contact:

U.S. Fish and Wildlife Service
Office of Management Authority
4401 N. Fairfax Drive
Arlington, VA 22203
Phone: (800) 358-2104
        (703) 358-2093
Fax: (703) 358-2281
www.le.fws.gov

The importation of dogs and cats is regulated by the U.S. Department of Health and Human Services, Center for Disease Control (CDC) in Atlanta, Georgia. In general, cats and dogs must be free of evidence of diseases, and dogs must have a certificate showing that they have been vaccinated for rabies if they come from a country where rabies occurs. This vaccination must have been given at least 30 days, and not more than a year, before the travel date. Airlines may require a health certificate. Puppies may be imported without proof of rabies vaccination but must be confined at a place of the owner's choice until three months of age and then vaccinated. Confinement must continue for 30 days.

For more information and a list of rabies-free areas contact:

Global Migration and Quarantine Division
Center for Disease Control
1600 Clifton Road, Mail Stop E-03
Atlanta, GA 30333
Phone: (404) 498-1670
www.cdc.gov/travel/other/animal-importation.htm

Personally-owned pet birds may be entered, but APHIS (Animal and Plant Health Inspection Service) and Public Health Service requirements must be met, which could include quarantine at an APHIS facility at specified locations, at the owner's expense. Advance reservations are required.

A pet bird coming to the United States from Canada is exempt from quarantine requirements but arrangements must be made for a veterinary inspection at a USDA-designated port of entry. For information call (301) 734-5097. If the birds enter via an airport, an import permit is required. For information, call (301) 734-8364.

Non-human primates such as monkeys, apes and similar animals may not be imported as pets.

Check with state, county and municipal authorities about any restrictions and requirements before importing a pet.

Hours of service and availability of inspectors will vary from port to port. You are encouraged to check with your anticipated port of entry prior to importing a pet, to be sure it will arrive when the necessary staff are on duty to process it.

For information, contact:

> U.S. Department of Agriculture
> Animal & Plant Health Inspection Service
> National Import/Export Center
> 4700 River Road, Unit 40
> Riverdale, MD 20737-1234
> Phone: (301) 734-3277
>   (800) 545-USDA
> Fax: (301) 734-8226
> www.aphis.usda.gov/NCIE
> www.aphis.usda.gov/NCIE/portlist.html

The Homeland Security Act has moved the Animal and Plant Health Inspection Service (APHIS) into the newly formed Bureau of Customs and Border Protection (BCBP).

Plants

All agricultural and food items brought into the U.S. must be inspected to prevent the entry of pests or crop disease.

Plants, cuttings, seeds, unprocessed plant products and certain endangered species either require an import permit or are prohibited from entering the United States. For information contact:

> U.S. Department of Agriculture
> APHIS Plant Protection and Quarantine
> 4700 River Road, Unit 60
> Riverdale, MD 20737
> Phone: (866) SAFGUARD
>   (301) 734-8645
> www.aphis.usda.gov/ppq

Foods

Meats, livestock, poultry and their by-products (such as ham, frankfurters, sausage, paté), are either prohibited or restricted from entering the United States, depending on the animal disease condition in the country of origin. Fresh meat is generally prohibited from most countries. Canned meat is permitted if the inspector can determine that it is commercially canned, cooked in the container, hermetically sealed, and can be kept without refrigeration. Canned, cured, fresh, frozen, cooked or dried meat from most countries is severely restricted.

For information, contact:

> U.S. Department of Agriculture
> USDA-APHIS Veterinary Service
> National Center for Import/Export
> 4700 River Road, Unit 40
> Riverdale, MD 20737
> Phone: (301) 734-7830
> (301) 734-7834 (Meat and poultry)
> (301) 734-4401 (Animal products)
> www.aphis.usda.gov/travel/index.html

> Food Safety and Inspection Service
> Import Inspection Division
> Franklin Court
> 1099 14th Street, N.W.
> Washington, DC 20250
> Phone: (202) 501-7515
> www.fsis.usda.gov

"Duty-Free" Shops

Articles bought in "duty-free" shops in foreign countries are free of duty and taxes only for the country in which that shop is located. The articles are intended for export and are not to be returned to the country of purchase. When brought into the United States, they are subject to U.S. customs duty and restrictions but may be included in a personal exemption.

Articles bought in American duty-free shops are subject to customs duty and IRS tax if reentered into the United States.

Chapter 20
Social Security

In 1935, President Roosevelt signed the original Social Security Act into law. The program now covers more than 141 million workers. It is illegal for your employer not to report your earnings to the Internal Revenue Service and it is also illegal for you and your employer not to pay Social Security taxes on your earnings.

Social Security Administration

Concept

Employees and employers pay taxes into the system during the employees' working years and employees and members of their families receive monthly benefits when the employee retires or becomes disabled. Survivors also collect benefits upon the employee's death. Social Security is meant to supplement pensions, insurance, savings, and other investments.

Historically, people have been eligible for full Social Security benefits at age 65. However, as of the year 2003, the age at which full benefits are payable, increases in gradual steps from 65 to 67.

Reduced benefits are available as early as age 62, while credit is given to people who delay retirement.

No benefits are payable to anyone illegally present in the United States.

Social Security Tax

Social Security taxes are also used to pay part of Medicare coverage.

The 2003 Social Security tax rate, for employees and employers, would be 7.65 percent each on wages up to $87,000. The Social Security portion is 6.2 percent on earnings up to $87,000. The Medicare portion is 1.45 percent on all earnings.

The payroll deduction may be labeled "FICA" on a pay slip. FICA is the Federal Insurance Contributions Act, the law that authorized the Social Security payroll tax.

In 2003, an employee would earn one credit for each $890 in earnings up to a maximum of four credits per year. Most people need 40 credits (ten years of work) to qualify for benefits.

The self-employed pay 15.3 percent of taxable income into Social Security, up to $87,000. Those earning more than $87,000 in 2003 would continue to pay 2.9 percent for the Medicare portion of the Social Security tax on the rest of their earnings.

Social Security Number (SSN)

The Social Security number is used to track earnings during working days and to track benefits once Social Security checks begin. Some medical providers and government agencies use the number for record keeping purposes.

The nine-digit Social Security number is divided into three parts. The first three numbers are determined by the applicant's zip code. The middle two digits have no special significance and the last four represent a straight numerical sequence of assigned numbers.

Social Security Card

Social Security services are free. To obtain a card, an application must be filed at the local Social Security office. Complete an Application for a Social Security Card (Form SS-5) available from your local Social Security office, from the internet at www.ssa.gov/online/ss-5.html or call (800) 772-1213. The card will be mailed to the applicant in about two weeks.

It is wise to phone the 800 number or your local office to confirm that you have the correct documents. You will need to prove your age, identity, U.S. citizenship or lawful resident status.

Three types of Social Security cards are issued.

One has been issued since 1935 and shows the person's name and Social Security number and lets a person work without restriction. It is issued to U.S. citizens and permanent resident aliens.

Green Card holders applying for a Social Security card should make sure that the Social Security agent who accepts the application puts a "Y" in the box marked PRA (Permanent Resident Alien). This should ensure that they issue a Social Security card without restriction. If the agent is not familiar with this box, the authority comes from the *Social Security POMS Manual RM00203.570C.2B*.

Social Security began issuing a second type of card in 1992. It shows the words, "VALID FOR WORK ONLY WITH INS AUTHORIZATION" and is issued to people who are admitted to the U.S. on a temporary basis with INS authorization to work.

The third type of card shows the words, "NOT VALID FOR EMPLOYMENT". Social Security assigns it to people from other countries who are admitted to the United

States without work authorization from the BCIS and who need an SSN because of a Federal law requiring a number to get a benefit or service. Once the BCIS has granted permission to work, you need to apply for a replacement card without that restriction. It will have the same number.

The Social Security Act permits state and local governments to use the SSN to administer laws related to taxes, general public assistance, driver licensing or motor vehicle registration. As of 2002, Social Security is:
- Piloting an online system for employers to verify the names and SSNs of newly-hired employees
- Verifying with the BCIS all immigration documents for non-citizens requesting an SSN
- Verifying with the state bureaus of vital statistics all birth records submitted by U.S. born citizens age one or older applying for an SSN

Social Security continues to issue SSNs to aliens who are otherwise not eligible when a Federal statute or regulation or a state or local law requires an SSN for someone entitled to benefits. In these cases, the SSN application must be accompanied by documentation from the government department explaining the need for the SSN. This letter must be dated and on letterhead stationery. It must identify the non-citizen, the non-work reason for which the SSN is required, the relevant statute or regulation, and the name and telephone number of a person to contact for verification. It should also state that the non-citizen qualifies to receive the benefit or service except for an SSN. If an alien is assigned an SSN for a non-work purpose, he or she cannot use it to work.

Schools are not authorized to use students' Social Security numbers and will assign internal numbers. A student applying for the SAT, ACT, GRE or other tests does not need a Social Security number to take the test.

The Internal Revenue Service assigns individual taxpayer identification numbers (ITIN) for tax purposes to non-citizens who do not qualify for Social Security numbers. Aliens who need individual taxpayer identification numbers may request IRS Form W-7 from the local IRS office, at www.IRS.gov or IRS, Philadelphia Service Center, ITIN Unit, P.O. Box 447, Bensalem, PA 19020 or call (800) 829-3676.

Giving your number to others

If a business or other enterprise asks for your Social Security number, you can refuse to give it to them. However, that may mean doing without the purchase or service for which your number was requested. For example, utility companies and other services ask for your SSN but do not need it; they can do a credit check or identify their customers by alternate means. Medical providers may refuse to see you.

Giving your number is voluntary even when you are asked for the number directly. You may ask:
- Why your number is needed

- How your number will be used
- What happens if you refuse
- What law requires you to give your number

The answers to these questions will help you decide whether you want to give your SSN. The decision is yours.   *Ref: SSA Publication No. 05-10002, May 2001*

Supplemental Security Income (SSI)

SSI is run by Social Security but is financed by U.S. Treasury tax revenues. Generally, monthly benefits are paid to qualified people who have low income and few assets and are:

- Age 65 or older, or blind, or disabled
- Living in the U.S. or on the Northern Mariana Islands
- A U.S. citizen or national
- Certain non-citizens legally in the U.S. or receiving SSI on August 22, 1996, or
- Certain refugee or asylee-type noncitizens during first seven years, or
- Lawful permanent residents with 40 work credits, or
- Certain noncitizens with a military service connection, or
- Certain American Indians, or
- Certain non-citizens granted special entry

For specific information, check www.ssa.gov/pubs/11051.html

Usually people who qualify for SSI can get Medicaid to help pay doctor and hospital bills. They may also get food stamps to help buy food.

Local Social Security offices determine SSI eligibility.

Local social services or public welfare offices have information about all the services available in the community. Some non-profit agencies may provide assistance without regard to citizenship.

Household Workers

In 2002, a household worker would earn Social Security credit only for wages of at least $1,300 from any single employer.

The employer should deduct Social Security and Medicare taxes from the wages, pay the taxes to the Internal Revenue Service, and report the wages to the Social Security Administration. If these wages are not reported, there may not be enough credit for the employee's benefits, or the benefits may be less.

Earnings for household workers (such as baby sitters) under age 18 are exempt from the Social Security tax unless household employment is the worker's primary occupation. You do not pay the tax for contract workers who are paid by the company employer.

Social Security and Visas

Foreign students with F, J or M visas are not subject to Social Security tax if they are working on campus or by special arrangement with the school or performing work connected to their studies. Form 843 may be filed for a refund of FICA (Social Security tax) collected while on a student visa.

Similarly, visitors with Q-1 visas are not subject to Social Security tax. However, Social Security Tax does apply to H-1 visa holders.

Social Security Benefits Outside The United States

It is not necessary to reside in the United States or to have a U.S. visa to receive benefits. A Social Security benefit can be paid at age 65 to any person who has paid the required amount of Social Security tax each year for at least 10 years.

A person who maintains Permanent Residence for 10 years, then leaves the U.S. and abandons Permanent Resident status, may still be eligible for a Social Security retirement benefit. For more information, refer to the Social Security pamphlet, "Your Social Security Checks While You are Outside the United States".

International Agreements

Bilateral Agreements

Since the late 1970s, the U.S. has established a network of bilateral Social Security agreements that coordinate the U.S. Social Security program with the comparable programs of other countries.

Reciprocal programs apply to countries such as Austria, Belgium, Canada, Finland, France, Germany, Greece, Ireland, Italy, Luxembourg, Netherlands, Norway, Portugal, South Korea, Spain, Sweden, Switzerland and the United Kingdom.

These agreements eliminate the need for a worker who is employed in another country to pay Social Security taxes in both countries. Workers who are exempt from U.S. or foreign taxes under an agreement may need to document their exemption by obtaining a certificate of coverage from the country that will continue to cover them.

Workers who have divided their careers between the U.S. and a foreign country sometimes fail to qualify for retirement, survivors or disability insurance benefits from one or both countries. They may not have worked long enough or recently enough to meet minimum eligibility requirements. Under an agreement, such workers may qualify for partial U.S. or foreign benefits based on combined or "totalized" coverage credits from both countries.

The agreements allow Social Security to totalize U.S. and foreign coverage credits only if the worker has at least six quarters of U.S. coverage. Similarly, a person may need a minimum amount of coverage under the foreign system in order to have U.S. coverage counted toward meeting the foreign benefit eligibility requirements.

Further information may be obtained from:

> Social Security Administration
> Office of International Programs
> P.O. Box 17741
> Baltimore, MD 21235-7741
> (410) 966-7808 and Fax: (410) 965-6539
> www.ssa.gov/foreign

Information may also be obtained from U.S. Embassies and Consulates abroad.

Potential Benefit Reductions

If you have earned enough work credits in the U.S. to qualify for a regular U.S. Social Security benefit and you also qualify for a regular government benefit from another country, the amount of your U.S. benefit may be reduced. This is the result of a provision in a U.S. law which can affect the way your benefit is calculated if you also receive a pension based on work which was not covered by U.S. Social Security. This is called the "Windfall Elimination Provision". The formula used to calculate your benefit amount is modified giving you a lower Social Security benefit. It is important to take this into consideration when planning your retirement.

This provision also affects spouses' benefits but does not affect Medicare eligibility.

For more information, call the number below and ask for the fact sheets, "A Pension from Work Not Covered by Social Security" (Publication No. 05-10045) and "Government Pension Offset" (Publication No. 05-10007) or write to the above address or check the web site at www.ssa.gov/foreign.

Information

You may visit your local Social Security office or call (800) 772-1213. You may speak to a representative at that number any business day from 7:00 am to 7:00 pm, Eastern Time. Social Security information is also available to users of the internet at: www.ssa.gov/immigration or http://best.ssa.gov.

Chapter 21

Selective Service

The Selective Service System is a government agency mandated to provide personnel for the Armed Forces in the event of a national emergency.

During times of peace, only citizens and permanent residents may volunteer for military service. However, Selective Service registration is required for all qualifying males between 18 and 26.

Selective Service System

Conscription

Compulsory enrollment into the armed forces is termed conscription.

Congress passed the Selective Service Act in 1948, thus instituting a peacetime form of conscription in order to maintain the strength of the armed forces. Since 1973, with the beginning of the All Volunteer Force, it has been in a "standby" position. The purpose of registration is to allow immediate response in time of war or national emergency.

Legal penalties may apply to those who fail to register. Conviction of this felony may result in imprisonment for up to five years and/or fines of not more than $250,000.

Registration Requirements

All male U.S. citizens, permanent resident aliens, dual national U.S. citizens, refugees, parolees and asylee aliens, special (seasonal) agricultural workers, and undocumented (illegal) aliens are required by law to register with the Selective Service System within 30 days of their 18th birthday or after their arrival in the USA. No one may register after age 26.

The BCIS sends a record of new Green Card holders to Selective Service who may contact males between 18 and 26. All males in this group must be registered with Selective Service.

When a male applies to become a U.S. citizen after five years as a Green Card holder, he must provide proof, during his naturalization interview, that he has registered with Selective Service. Otherwise, he risks citizenship delays or denials. A non-registrant must show substantial evidence that he did not knowingly and purposely fail to register.

Non-registered males may be denied such benefits as Federal student financial aid, Federal job training or Federal employment. Some states also bar non-registered men from state aid and employment as well as driver's licenses.

Males are not required to register with Selective Service while they are:
- Members of the Armed Forces on active duty
- Students at certain military schools
- Lawfully admitted aliens in nonimmigrant status
- Diplomatic and consulate personnel (including their families)
- Foreign students in valid student status
- Tourists with unexpired visas or border crossing documents
- Special agricultural workers with EAD documents
- Incarcerated
- Hospitalized or institutionalized for medical reasons

Upon being released from an institution or the armed forces, a man must register within 30 days or before reaching age 26, whichever is earlier.

For women to be required to register for Selective Service, Congress would have to amend the law which now refers to "male persons". Currently, women are excluded from the draft by the Department of Defense and by policy from front line combat.

Registration Procedure

Eligible males may register by picking up a SSS Form 1M at any U.S. Post Office and mailing the completed form to Selective Service for processing.

Students may register at their schools.

U.S. citizens and Green Card holders living or visiting overseas at the time they are required to register, should do so at the nearest U.S. Embassy or Consulate office.

Registration may also be carried out online at www.sss.gov.

The registrant should receive a Registration Acknowledgment within 90 days and keep it as evidence of his registration. He must report any change in registration information. This includes legal name, mailing address, phone number, and so on. Change should be reported within ten days online or by completing a preaddressed Change of Information Form (SSS Form 2) available at any U.S. Post Office, U.S. Embassy or U.S. Consulate.

Military Inductions

Because there have been no induction draft orders issued since 1973, there are no classifications of eligibility for registrants or local boards who deal with claims for reclassification or postponement. The only requirement is registration.

Should the President and Congress authorize inductions into military service, the Secretary of Defense will request men for the Armed Forces. Selective Service will:

- Conduct a lottery to determine the order of selecting registrants for induction beginning with men whose 20th birthday falls within the calendar year
- Assign each registrant the Random Sequence Number (RSN) drawn by lottery for his date of birth
- Select and order registrants for examination and induction beginning with RSN 1

Postponement or Reclassification

Should a registrant be ordered to report for induction, he must either report or file a claim for postponement or reclassification.

An alien whose other country of nationality has a reciprocal agreement with the U.S. may be exempt from induction or receive credit for military service in that country.

An alien or dual national who has served on active duty in certain countries may qualify for reclassification with the proper documentation. He should first check all regulations with Selective Service to be sure that reclassification is in his best interests.

A word of warning to aliens who are nationals of certain countries. It is important to understand that, if an application for exemption from military training and service in the U.S. Armed Forces is granted, the registrant will be classified as a Treaty Alien and will henceforth be barred from U.S. citizenship.
Ref: SSS, Information For Registrants Oct 1988, Part II, Section B,Classifications, 14

Leaving the U.S. to avoid military service, or desertion from the military, will make a person ineligible for citizenship.

Information

For further information, contact:

Selective Service System
Registration Information Office
P.O. Box 94638
Palatine, IL 60094-4638
Phone: (847) 688-6888
www.sss.gov

Chapter 22

Buying or Leasing a Car - License & Registration

I f you like to negotiate, you'll love buying or leasing a car. A few dealers have set prices with no room to negotiate but most expect a battle of wits.

Buying a Car

Buying a car requires plenty of time to do research. Libraries have magazines like Motor Trend and Consumer Reports. Consumers are increasingly turning to the internet for researching as well as finding and buying cars. Some sites are www.edmunds.com,www.carpoint.com, www.carsdirect.com, www.nhtsa.dot.gov, www.cars.com, www.nada.com, www.consumerreports.org and www.kbb.com. For a car's history, try www.carfax.com (fee required).

Satisfied car buyers recommend that you know as much as possible about the vehicle you are buying beforehand. Try to determine the dealer's costs for the vehicle and options and how much room you have for bargaining.

It is also recommended that you talk to drivers of that model and find out how satisfied they are.

If you have a car to trade in, figure out from buyer's guides, what it should be worth before haggling with the dealer. Much of the dealer's profit is said to come from used car sales rather than new, so obviously it is in their best interest to offer you less than the car may be worth.

The Federal Trade Commission advises that you read an advertised special carefully and call or visit the dealer to find out about all the terms and conditions of the offer. While these advertisements may help you shop, finding the best deal requires careful comparison among several dealers.

Experts say you should first negotiate the price of the car, second, discuss the value of your trade in, third, ask for the dealer's best financing offer. Keep each deal separate. Before signing, be sure that you really want any of the dealer's high profit add-ons such as extended warranties and service contracts.

The demand for used cars has increased greatly as have their prices. The steepest rate of depreciation occurs in the first two years of a car's life (approximately 50 percent). It then levels off considerably. A certified used car has undergone a detailed inspection and is typically backed by an extensive warranty issued by its manufacturer.

Buying a used car from a private individual is usually less expensive than from a dealer. However, the dealer may provide service and support afterward. You will have to decide whether cost or service is more important.

Car Loan

If you are planning to buy a car, chances are you will need a loan. Car dealers will do anything they can to make sure you get financing. However, the loan they find for you might not be the best one available. You should first check on loans from such sources as credit unions (you must become a member), financial institutions and loan companies or research websites listed under buying a car.

Leasing a Car

Some people find that leasing a new or used car is preferable to investing a large amount of money into buying one. You do not own the leased vehicle. Instead, a lease grants you the right to use the vehicle for a fixed period of time. Your lease payments cover the cost of the vehicle's depreciation over the length of the term of the lease instead of the actual purchase price. See the internet sites on previous page.

The short term costs are lower. However, if you want to keep a car for five to ten years, leasing can cost more in the long term. Also, if you drive many miles per year (over 15,000), leasing may not be a good option as you have to pay extra (approximately 10-25 cents per mile) when you exceed the mileage limit.

Leasing may enable you to drive a more expensive car than you can afford to own. If used for business purposes, leasing offers a greater tax write-off than owning.

You can pay for the use of the car for 24 to 60 months, then return it to the dealer and lease a new model. The lease may include an option to purchase the car at the end of that period. However, leasing could be more expensive than financing in that case.

Read the fine print and find out any hidden costs. There are many details you should understand before signing the lease. They include:

- Monthly payment amounts and how they are calculated
- Retail price of the car
- Security deposit
- Down payment
- Lease fee
- Fee if payment is late
- Fee for early termination of the lease

- Mileage limit (may be negotiable)
- Price per mile over limit
- Purchase option at end of lease
- Warranties
- Definition of wear and tear to know how much is considered normal
- Permission for transferring the lease to someone else
- Sales and use tax
- Acquisition Fee - charges for preparation of car and the lease
- Disposition Fee - charges for preparing the car for resale at end of lease
- Residual Value - determine up front projected value of vehicle at lease end

You are responsible for adequate automobile insurance and regular mechanical maintenance whether you lease or buy.

Experts recommend that you negotiate the price of the vehicle before negotiating a lease agreement. Some components of the lease may be negotiable. Shop around and be sure to compare leases on the same model of vehicle with the same options. A good leasing agent will explain all the components of the lease and answer questions.

Used lease cars are available and provide another option for purchasing a vehicle.

Car Registration

A vehicle must be registered and licensed in the state of residence. The cost of the license plate or tag may depend on the age, type, weight or cost of the car, depending on state law. The vehicle must always have a current license plate and the driver must always have the registration in the vehicle. Some states also collect a yearly tax of as much as several hundred dollars. In addition, many states require that all vehicles have an annual inspection. Expect to provide proof of car insurance.

Any car imported to the United States must meet the U.S. highway safety and emission standards. Research should be done in advance if contemplating importing a car. (See Importing Belongings, Chapter 19).

Driver's License

You must have a driver's license in order to legally drive a motor vehicle on public streets or highways. You will need a commercial license in order to drive a commercial vehicle such as a truck or bus.

If you are a temporary resident, you may not be required to get a new license if you have a valid one from another state. Most driver's license offices also issue photo IDs for non-drivers.

It is a good idea to check with the driver's and motor vehicle license offices to find out the rules of your state. If a new license is needed, ask what documents and fees they expect from applicants. Also ask what method of payment they require. Also, if you have an out-of-state driver's license, be prepared to give it up to get your new license.

Most states request a Social Security number. Social Security stopped issuing numbers to non-citizens for driver's licenses but commenced again after losing a court case. Documentation must be provided. See Social Security Card in Chapter 20.

To ensure applicants have legal status, states are tightening procedures. For instance, foreigners may get 30-day temporary permits while police verify their documents and check them against FBI and BCIS records. Their licenses may expire when their immigration status expires. Some states require that non-citizens apply at special processing centers.

Handbooks showing safe driving tips and rules of the roads should be available in state license offices and handbooks and interactive tests are available at most states' driver's license web sites. Some states offer handbooks in other languages.

The driving examination may include any or all of the following: vision and hearing tests, written test on traffic rules, road sign identification, vehicle inspection and a driving test. Some states provide written tests in Spanish. Basic English is required for the driving test.

Before you learn to drive, you must take a test for a restricted license (learner's license). The restrictions may include driving during daylight hours only and having a licensed driver at least 18 years old (21 in some states) sit to the right of the driver.

In an attempt to reduce the rate of teen driving deaths, many states are introducing graduated licensing. Teens must take driver's education courses at school or through a private company. Then, by working their way through the levels of requirements, by age 17, they may be eligible for an unrestricted license. However, they must have passed all the courses and tests, completed the hours of supervised driving and be accident- and violation-free for a specified period.

Some states demand that persons who are 15 to 17 years of age are enrolled in school or have proof of graduation from high school. Those who drop out of school before becoming 18 or graduating, will have their license suspended.

The National Voter Registration Act, or motor voter law enables citizens to register to vote when obtaining their driver's license. Also, driver's license lists are used as a prime resource in the selection of jurors.

Listing of State Vehicle Registration and Driver's License Offices

See /www.sasnet.com/bro/states/1national/dmv.html

Chapter 23

Employment Benefits and Compensation, Welfare

The various levels of government ensure that there are uniform standards of benefits available to employees in the United States. This chapter provides a cursory overview of some of the more important aspects.

Employment Benefits

Legal Public Holidays

The following are legal holidays for federal government employees. Private businesses may vary in which of these holidays they observe.

New Year's Day	January 1
Birthday of Martin Luther King, Jr.	Third Monday in January
Presidents Day	Third Monday in February
Memorial Day	Last Monday in May
Independence Day	July 4
Labor Day	First Monday in September
Columbus Day	Second Monday in October
Veterans Day	November 11
Thanksgiving Day	Fourth Thursday in November
Christmas Day	December 25

Family Leave

California is the first state to offer paid family leave funded by voluntary employee payroll deductions. Eligible employees receive about half of their wages for up to six weeks to care for newborn or adopted children or sick family members.

Vacations

Many businesses allow an employee at least a week's paid vacation after a year of employment. The vacation entitlement generally increases slowly over the years to a set maximum, while the employee remains with the company. Vacation time tends to be shorter in the United States than in many other countries.

Health Insurance

Employers may pay all or part of health insurance premiums for their employees. More information on health insurance options may be found in Chapter 29.

Social Security

Employers and employees share the payments to Social Security. See chapter 20.

Unemployment Insurance

Unemployment insurance is temporary income for eligible workers who become unemployed through no fault of their own and who are ready, willing, able to work and have built up sufficient weeks of credit and wages in previous covered employment.

Each state administers a separate unemploment insurance program within federal guidelines. An employer must provide unemployment insurance coverage for most types of work and several states require minimal employee contributions.

To be eligible for unemployment benefits, you must be available for work and actively seeking employment while you are claiming benefits. In general, these taxable benefits are based on a percentage of an individual's earnings over a recent 52-week period. Each state has a maximum benefit amount that can be paid up to a maximum of about 26 weeks.

The state One-Stop/Employment Service Offices provide free re-employment services such as counseling, testing and referrals to other agencies.

Worker's Compensation

The employer pays into this state fund and the benefits are for workers who have suffered a work-related injury.

Disability Insurance

These policies are designed to replace a portion of your income if you become disabled and cannot work. The level of coverage depends on the plan and premium. Long term disability insurance helps replace income for an extended period of time.

Compensation

Minimum Wage

Congress has set the Federal hourly minimum wage at $5.15. Workers receiving tips may still receive a minimum of $2.13 an hour. Employers must pay more if the employees do not collect enough tips to earn the minimum wage. The "training wage" for the first 90 days on the job remains $4.25 for employees under 20. Overtime pay must be at least one and one half times regular rates of pay after 40 hours of work in a workweek. Some cities have adopted laws mandating minimum wages for their employees well above the Federal minimum.
See www.dol.gov/esa/minwage/america.htm.

Pensions

In recent years, 401(k) savings plans have been replacing traditional pension plans. They provide separate tax-deferred accounts to which workers and sometimes their employers contribute. Employees make the investment choices and can take the proceeds with them if they leave. With the economic downturn, 401(k)s are less attractive and many employers are turning to new less-costly pension plans.

Welfare

The U.S. welfare bill, signed by President Clinton in August of 1996 and effective June, 1997, set a lifetime limit of five years of welfare for a family. Welfare recipients are required to find work within two years. Food stamp funding is reduced and Medicaid will be denied to adults who lose welfare by refusing to work. Training and employment assistance is provided at local One-Stop centers.
 See www.doleta.gov/programs/adtrain.asp.

The Food Stamp Program helps low income households buy food. As of April 2003, the food stamp provision of the farm bill reinstated benefits to some legal immigrants and refugees who have lived in the U.S. at least five years. In October 2003, benefits are also restored for legal immigrant children and disabled people without a residency requirement. Call (800) 221-5689 or www.fns.usda.gov/fsp.

The 1997 Balanced Budget Act restored disability and Medicaid benefits to legal immigrants. Immigrants who were in the United States when the welfare law was signed in August, 1996, will be eligible for SSI if they become disabled in the future. Illegal immigrants are ineligible for a wide range of public benefits. However, local non-profit agencies may provide assistance.

The Legal Immigrant Children's Health Improvement Act of 2001 permits states the option of coverage of legal immigrants, regardless of their date of entry, under the Medicaid program and the state's health insurance program. The Nutrition Assistance for Working Families and Seniors Act of 2001 restored benefits to eligible lawfully present immigrants regardless of date of entry.

Part II

Finance

Part II of Book 2 **USA Orientation: Getting Settled** deals with the inescapable issue of money. As was the case in Part I, several agencies and institutions will be involved in your financial life when you settle in the United States.

USA Orientation: Getting Settled offers an introduction to these financial subjects. Much of the information contained in the following chapters may be new to you. In some cases, it is the terminology, in others it is the process or the obligation which is different from the way things are done back home. So, take a deep breath and read carefully. We hope you will come away with a better understanding of not only how things are done, but why.

The four chapters which follow deal with:

Chapter 24 — Taxation
- Some basic principals, advantages, and responsibilities of the U.S. tax system

Chapter 25 — Banking and Financial Transactions
- A brief introduction to U.S. banking and credit

Chapter 26 — Buying or Renting a Home
- An introduction to the process of buying or renting

Chapter 27 — Mortgages
- Home mortgage programs and terms

Chapter 24

Taxation

T his chapter describes some tax issues for you to think about prior to departure from your home country and provides a brief summary of some aspects of the U.S. income tax and transfer tax system. In the United States, different tax rules often apply to U.S. citizens compared with non-citizens. Except where otherwise indicated, the rules described here apply to individuals who are not U.S. citizens but may also apply to U.S. citizens, depending on the circumstances.

Before departing from your "home" country you should consider obtaining advice on the tax implications of your move in both your home country and the United States so that any helpful pre-move tax planning procedures can be undertaken while they are still available.

Pre-Departure Tax Planning

Becoming a Nonresident of your Home Country

Each country has its own set of rules to determine when you are considered a resident or nonresident of that country for income tax purposes. Since each country's laws are different, it is possible for you to be a resident of two or more countries simultaneously. Therefore it may be helpful to consult a cross border tax advisor to ensure that you understand the circumstances under which your home country will agree that you have become a nonresident.

For example, Canada's domestic law may consider you to be a resident of Canada as long as you have a residence in Canada that is continuously available to you. For a list of additional factors Canada may consider, you can review Form NR 73 issued by the Canada Customs and Revenue Agency at: www.ccra-adrc.gc.ca/E/pbg/tf/nr73/nr73-02e.pdf. However even if Canada considers you to be a resident under its domestic rules, Canada may consider you to be a nonresident under the terms of the tax treaty between the Canada and the United States, since the tax treaty can override Canada's domestic law.

Becoming a Nonresident of Canada

Canadian "Departure Tax"

Individuals becoming nonresidents of Canada will be subject to Canada's so-called departure tax. Under this rule you are considered to have sold (at fair market value) certain of your worldwide property immediately prior to leaving Canada. Thus you may owe Canadian "capital gains" tax on these properties even though you have not actually sold them.

Examples of applicable property include marketable securities, the shares of private Canadian corporations, and U.S. real estate. Excluded are Canadian real estate, Canadian pension-related assets and certain Canadian business property.

Pre-move cross-border tax planning can assist in insuring the combined Canada-U.S. aggregate tax impact resulting from the interplay of Canada's departure tax and the U.S. "historical cost basis" rules (described below) can be minimized, and that double tax can be avoided to the extent possible. Accordingly, consultation with a cross-border tax advisor may be helpful.

Canadian Registered Retirement Savings Plans, etc.

Canada's departure tax generally does not apply to Canadian Registered Retirement Savings Plans, Registered Retirement Income Funds, and similar accounts. However, subject to a special tax treaty election, these accounts are not recognized as tax deferral vehicles under U.S. domestic tax law.   They are simply viewed as regular bank accounts, or brokerage accounts, as the case may be. Therefore it is often beneficial to review these accounts prior to your move to determine if any transactions should be undertaken to increase your "cost basis" in the accounts for U.S. purposes.

U.S "Historical Cost Basis" Rules

The United States income tax law generally provides for a so-called "historical cost basis" for your property when you move to the United States.   In other words, if you move to the United States and later sell property, your profit or loss for U.S. purposes is generally computed with regard to what you originally paid for the property, not what its value was at the date you moved to the United States. Thus it is wise to determine if any of your property should be sold prior to moving to the United States. Similar planning may apply, in some cases, to pension accounts and other assets.

U.S. Rules for Non-U.S. Corporations, Partnerships and Trusts

If you move to the United States and retain an interest in a non-U.S. corporation, partnership or trust (generally excluding publicly traded securities) you will likely have complex U.S. reporting requirements (See "U.S. Filing Requirements" below). You may also be potentially exposed to double tax (i.e. tax in your former home country and tax in the U.S.).   Therefore it can be advisable to determine if reorganization of the entity is justified before you become a U.S. resident.

U.S. Gift & Estate (Death) Tax

Before moving to the United States, you should give consideration to the U.S. gift & estate tax law (described below). Once you move to the United States your flexibility in restructuring ownership of your worldwide property may be significantly reduced.

U.S. Income Tax - Who Pays?

U.S. citizens and U.S. "residents" are subject to U.S. income tax on their worldwide income. Nonresidents of the U.S. who are not U.S. citizens (nonresident aliens) are subject to U.S. tax only on their U.S. source income and certain income effectively connected with a U.S. trade or business.

Who is a U.S. "Resident"

The definition of "resident" is different for U.S. tax law than it is for U.S. immigration law. Under the income tax law you will be classified as a U.S. resident if you meet either the:

- "Green Card test" (i.e. you became a U.S. legal permanent resident), or
- "Substantial presence test" (unless you qualify for the "closer connection exception")

You meet the "substantial presence test" for the year you are testing your residency (i.e. the "current year") if you spend a certain number of days cumulatively in the U.S. over a three-year period ending with the "current year". The following worksheet may be used to determine if you meet the substantial presence test for the "current year":

Number of days in the U.S. in the current year   _____

1/3 the number of days in the U.S. in the previous year   _____

1/6 the number of days in the U.S. in the second preceding year _____

Total   _____

If the total is 183 days or more, and you were present more than 30 days in the current year, you meet the substantial presence test for the current year. In counting days, you may be able to exclude days you were present as an "exempt person", such as due to medical condition arising in the United States, commuting to work in the U.S., or traveling in transit through the United States.

Closer Connection Exception

Even if you meet the substantial presence test, you may avoid being a U.S. resident for tax purposes for the current year by filing IRS Form 8840, (Closer Connection Exception Statement) by the due date for filing, assuming you are qualified to file. You are not qualified for this exception if you have a green card (or have an application pending) or if you spend more than 182 days in the U.S. in the "current year", or you are a U.S. citizen. Additional requirements apply.

Tax Treaty Override

If you meet one of the residency tests described above and you are not eligible for the closer connection exception you may nonetheless be able to compute your U.S. income tax liability as a nonresident of the United States if you are also a resident for income tax in another country that has a tax treaty with the United States.

U.S. Filing Requirements

Tax Return

If you are a U.S. citizen or U.S. resident (for income tax) you must file a U.S. federal income tax return annually (generally on a calendar year basis) if your income is above the filing threshold. Depending upon the individual state in which you reside, a state income tax return may also be required. Some municipalities also levy income tax.

Information Returns

U.S. citizens and U.S. residents must potentially also file numerous reports annually about their contacts and transactions outside the United States. For example, if you have a certain degree of interest in a non-U.S. corporation, partnership, trust, bank account, brokerage account or pension fund, or if you have a transaction with such an entity or account, certain reporting may be required. Penalties of $10,000, or more, may apply annually for noncompliance.

In order to file the income tax return you must have a U.S. taxpayer identification number. For individuals this is usually a U.S. Social Security number obtained from the U.S. Social Security Administration using Form SS-5, or an Individual Taxpayer Identification Number (ITIN) obtained from the Internal Revenue Service (IRS) using IRS Form W-7. Generally, if you have a green card, or have been admitted to work in the U.S. you would obtain a social security number. Otherwise you would obtain an ITIN. U.S. Income Tax - How Much Do You Pay?

Income Tax

United States federal income tax is levied at graduated tax rates, depending upon your level of "taxable" income. Certain exemptions and deductions are available to determine your "taxable" income.

There are actually four different tax rate schedules, depending upon whether you are filing your U.S. income tax return as:

- Married individuals filing a joint return, (in the U.S. it is routine for married individuals to file a "joint" tax return), or a surviving spouse
- So-called "head of household"
- Unmarried individual, other than a surviving spouse or head of household,
- Married individual filing a separate tax return

Tax rates change regularly. At the time of writing, the federal tax rate schedule contains six different tax brackets for each category of filer listed above. The rates vary from a low of 10% to a maximum of 38.6%.

In addition to the federal income tax, there may be state and municipal income tax, depending upon the state in which you reside.

The table below sets out just a few examples of what the 2003 U.S. federal income tax would be for selected levels of taxable income, assuming foreign tax credits, alternative minimum tax, and other special tax issues do not apply.

Federal Income Tax

Taxable Income	Married & Joint	Head of Household	Unmarried	Married Filing Separately
$50,000	$7,206	$8,434	$9,792	$10,353
100,000	20,706	21,987	24,228	25,766
150,000	35,267	36,987	39,553	43,266
200,000	51,531	52,032	54,228	62,351

"Social Security" and "Medicare" tax

In addition to income tax, the U.S. levies federal "social security" tax and "Medicare" tax on "earned" income (for example wages and self employment income). The rate for social security tax is 12.4%, and the rate for Medicare tax is 2.9%. If you are an employee the employer generally pays one-half of the tax.

For year 2003, the social security tax only applies to the first $87,000 of earned income.This latter amount changes annually. The Medicare tax applies to all of your earned income.

U.S. Gift & Estate (Death) Tax - Who Pays?

The United States potentially imposes gift tax or estate tax (referred to as transfer taxes) on the fair market value of property you transfer to another individual or entity. This tax applies regardless of whether the transfer occurs during your life or at the time of your death.

If you are a U.S. citizen or if you are "domiciled" in the U.S. you are subject to this tax on any property you transfer anywhere in the world, subject to certain exemptions. If you are not domiciled in the U.S. and not a U.S. citizen you are only subject to this tax on certain United States property.

The concept of "domicile" is different than the concept of "residency" for income tax. It is generally considered to be a more permanent status than residency for income tax.

Gift Tax

For gift tax purposes there is an annual exemption that is indexed for inflation. For 2003 the exemption is $11,000 per recipient (donee). Thus you can make an unlimited number of tax-free gifts of $11,000 annually, provided they are made to different donees. In some cases your spouse can elect to join with you so that your tax-free gift can be doubled to $22,000 (year 2003).

If the donee is your spouse and is not a U.S. citizen the annual exemption is $100,000 (indexed for inflation). If the donee spouse is a U.S. citizen the tax-free gift is potentially unlimited.

Estate (Death) Tax

For estate tax purposes, for the years 2002 and 2003 there is a tax credit that effectively provides U.S. citizens and U.S. domicilairies an "exemption" from estate taxes for the first $1,000,000 of property owned at the time of death provided there were no prior taxable gifts. If there were prior taxable gifts they are taken into consideration in determining the amount of the "exemption".

The "exemption" rises gradually to $3,500,000 in 2009. Under present law, the estate tax will be repealed in 2010, for at least one year.

If you are not a U.S. citizen and not domiciled in the U.S. you are subject to U.S. estate tax only on your U.S. property owned at the date of death. In this case, there is a general "exemption" from estate taxes equal to the first $60,000 of U.S. property owned at the time of death, or alternatively, an exemption computed under the tax treaty with your country, if one exists.

If the heir to your property is a spouse that is not a U.S. citizen the transfer to your spouse is generally taxable, subject to certain modifications if the surviving spouse contributed to the purchase of the property, or if the property qualifies as community property. However, a deferral of estate tax on a transfer to a non-U.S. citizen spouse is available if the property is transferred to the surviving spouse via a special form of trust referred to as a "Qualified Domestic Trust", or if there is a relevant provision in a tax treaty with the country where you are domiciled.

If the heir is a surviving spouse that is a U.S. citizen there is an unlimited exemption from estate tax, provided the property meets certain requirements.

Generation Skipping Tax

An additional "generation skipping tax" may apply in addition to estate tax if your property is transferred to a "skip person".

Foreign (Non-U.S.) Income Tax - Who Pays?

As a general rule, countries impose a withholding tax at source when payments of interest, dividends, rents, etc, are paid from that country to nonresidents. Therefore once you become a nonresident of your former home country you may still be subject to withholding tax at source in that country on income received from that country.

For example, if you receive interest or dividends from entities located in Canada there may be withholding at source in Canada.

A variety of exemptions may exist under the domestic law of your former home country.   For example, interest received from Canadian federal and provincial government securities is generally exempt from Canadian tax when paid to nonresidents of Canada. A similar exemption potentially applies to interest received on Guaranteed Investment Certificates that are issued by Canadian banks and that have a maturity of five years or more. Other examples exist.

Further, if there is a tax treaty between the U.S. and your former home country the normal withholding tax rate may be reduced or eliminated. For example, while Canada's normal withholding tax rate is 25%, under the present tax treaty this rate is reduced for U.S. residents to 10% for interest, and to 15% or 5% for dividends depending upon the circumstances. The Canadian rate on periodic pensions paid from Canadian plans is reduced to 15%, which also applies in special cases to certain limited payments from Canadian Registered Retirement Income Funds. Payments from Canada Pension Plan and Old Age Security Payments are exempt from tax in Canada under the treaty if you are a U.S. resident.

For more information on Canadian matters you can go to www.ccra-adrc.gc.ca and click on "Forms and Publications".

More information on U.S. matters is available at your local IRS office, or at www.irs.gov by clicking on "Contents" (Individuals) and then "Resources" (Forms and Publications), or you can call (800) 829-1040, or write to the IRS at:

> Internal Revenue Service
> 1111 Constitution Avenue S.W.
> Washington, DC 20024

As the U.S tax system is so complex, cross-border tax planning is vital. Cross-border tax advisor S. L. Richard Brunton agreed to provide comprehensive expert input for this taxation overview. He may be contacted at www.taxintl.com or at (561) 241-9991.

Chapter 25

Banking and Financial Transactions

Banking and financial transactions can, of course, be complicated and bewildering. This chapter explains some of the your more common monetary decisions.

Banking Services

Bank Accounts

There are many types of accounts in which to deposit your money. For instance, some do not have fees but pay no interest. Others give you some interest and allow you to write a certain number of checks. In some accounts, a penalty is assessed if your monthly balance falls below a certain amount. There are also accounts with special privileges for seniors. Bank employees will help you select the most suitable kind.

Credit Unions offer many of the best rates in the country on loans, credit cards and savings products. To find out how to become a member, check Consumer Information at www.cuna.org/data/index.html.

Banks in United States are local, state or regional. Dealing with them may seem very slow or complicated if you are from a country with large national institutions. You may not be able to deposit funds electronically from one bank to an account in another branch of the same major U.S. bank in an adjoining state.

Cash or other deposits, made after 2:00 pm may not be credited to your account until the next business day. Checks from other states or countries may be slow clearing.

If you withdraw or deposit a large amount at your bank, be prepared to explain why you are making the transaction. Banks are required, under federal law, to report all cash transactions over $10,000 to the Internal Revenue Service.

The Federal Deposit Insurance Corporation (FDIC) protects your deposits to a maximum of $100,000 per institution.

Becoming Known to Your Banker

You may be asked for photo identification when you go to a teller. Until getting to know you, they want to be sure they are not letting an imposter make transactions in your account. When you have become established at a bank, they can be very helpful with your financial affairs, such as establishing credit. While an automatic teller machine (ATM) is convenient, you do not become known to bank employees.

Paying for Goods and Services

You may arrange with some businesses such as utilities and credit card companies to automatically withdraw, from your bank account, the amount owing on their bills. They normally send the bill to you for your information before the money is withdrawn. Depending on a company's policy, most monthly bills may also be paid by check, credit card, phone or internet.

In addition to paying for a purchase by cash, credit card, or check, you may also pay by **check card** through a Point-of-Sale (POS) terminal. If you use the check card as a credit card, you sign a slip but if you tell the clerk "debit card" you enter your Personal Identification Number (PIN) instead of signing. The money is taken immediately from your bank account. The standard limit may be $300 a day. You may overcharge the purchase amount and receive cash back. You may also obtain cash directly from ATM machines.

An **ATM card** may only be used at ATM machines and in some stores. A **check card** may be used at any retailer that accepts credit cards as well as at ATM machines.

Various **cash cards** are available such as a disposable type with a magnetic stripe or embedded microchip, loaded with a pre-determined value for small purchases. Some are reloadable when the pre-determined value is depleted. Another type of cash card allows you to you to send or receive money from anyone anytime worldwide. Funds can be immediately accessed from any compatible ATM, converted into local currency.

Transfer of Funds from Outside the U.S.

Instant withdrawals from a foreign bank account may be made by using automated teller machines (ATMs). Depending on the nature of the foreign account and the limits on the U.S. ATM, you can usually bring in between $300 and $1,000 per day in U.S. dollars. You may be charged a transaction fee in either or both countries. You also may open a U.S. dollar account in your home country which you can access in the U.S. by check, debit or credit card.

For larger amounts, your foreign bank can wire funds to a specific account in a U.S. bank or other financial institution. The money should be available within a day. There may be fees of $30-$65 at both ends. Bank customers may pay less.

A foreign bank may also prepare and mail a bank draft to your U.S. bank. There is usually a fee at the foreign end with no guarantee when it will arrive. Money orders and checks from a foreign country drawn on a U.S. bank will clear much faster than those drawn on a foreign bank. Normally, you cannot withdraw that money until your bank has received the cleared funds.

Transfer of Funds for Real Estate Transactions

When buying real estate, you may avoid delays by determining well in advance in what form the closing agent wants the funds. An out-of-country cashier's check or money order could cause a delay in a real estate closing. Ask your bank how long it will take to clear funds from your home country. It simplifies the closing if the money is transferred and deposited into your U.S. bank account in advance so that it is cleared and available when needed.

Automatic Deposit

Many employers and government agencies will automatically deposit checks into your bank account. Also, Federal Government payments may be directly deposited into low-cost Electronic Transfer Accounts (ETAs). You will avoid check cashing fees.

Payroll Cards

A few employers offer the option of transferring wages onto reloadable stored value cards. Each payday, wages show up on employees' cards and they may withdraw money from an ATM or make purchases much like a debit card.

Check Cashing Fees

If you are not a bank customer but want to cash a check, be prepared for a check-cashing fee, possibly with fingerprinting required on the back of the check. Banks are protected because if the check proves fraudulent, the print can be used by police to help identify the person who cashed it. Independent check cashing agencies also charge fees.

PC Banking

With a computer, you can access account information on the internet, pay bills, transfer funds, and so on. There may be a charge for paying bills.

Safe Deposit Boxes

Banks have vaults containing a variety of sizes of boxes - Safe Deposit Boxes. For a yearly fee, you can rent a box where you may keep important documents, jewelry or other valuables. Your key and the bank's must both be used to get into the box.

Non-resident Withholding Tax

While some nonimmigrants are considered to be residents for income tax purposes, many are not. If you are a non-resident and not subject to U.S. income tax, you can submit Form W-8 to the bank. It will let them know that you are a non-resident alien and, therefore, exempt from withholding tax on the interest earned on your account. If tax has already been withheld, you may file for a refund on Form 1040NR (U.S. Nonresident Alien Income Tax Return) by April 15 with:

> Internal Revenue Service
> Philadelphia, PA 19255.

Financial Transactions

Establishing Credit

Establishing credit takes time. Credit reports may possibly be obtained from your home country when you apply for a loan. Bank letter of credit may also help.

If you are planning to remain in the United States, it is important to build a credit reputation. One way of accomplishing this would be to apply for a store credit card with a low credit limit to get you started. Stores may have a higher risk tolerance but charge high interest rates for accounts not paid by the due date each month.

If you pay your bills on time and appear to have stability in your life, such as a home, job, and family, the large credit card companies and lenders may look more favorably upon your application.

You could deposit several hundred dollars to get an initial $500 credit with a bank or credit card company. If you pay your monthly credit card bill on time, eventually your limit may be raised. You may also be able to leave a deposit for a bank to attach as collateral for a loan that will be reported as a normal loan to the credit agencies.

Independent credit bureaus provide credit reports to organizations wanting to know your credit history. However, your credit report may not be available until you have had your Social Security card for a while and made an application for a loan or used the full credit on your credit card. Credit bureau ratings may be adversely affected by such situations as too many queries for several purchases, too many credit cards with the potential for a high aggregate debt, missing a loan payment and continuing to be a month behind in payments. You may check your own credit (fees vary by state):

Equifax	- (800) 685-1111	www.equifax.com
Experian	- (888) 397-3742	www.experian.com
Transunion	- (800) 888-4213	www.transunion.com

Be wary of some "non-profit" credit counseling agencies. Credit monitoring tips are available at www.creditcourt.com.

Do not spend more money than you have in your bank account. If your account is overdrawn, the bank may report you to ChexSystems and your credit can be damaged for five years.

Legal Entry of Funds to the United States

There is no limit to the amount of money that may be brought into or taken out of the United States. However, any person who carries, sends, receives or causes the transport of currency or other monetary instruments totaling more than $10,000 at one time into or out of the country must report it to BCBP. 'Person' includes entities such as an individual, a corporation, any unincorporated organization, a partnership, a syndicate, and all other legal personalities.

Monetary instruments as defined on Form 4790 include:

- Coin or currency of the United States or any other country
- Traveler's Checks in any form
- Negotiable instruments (including checks, promissory notes, and money orders) in bearer form, endorsed without restriction, made out to a fictitious payee, or otherwise in such form that title thereto passes upon delivery
- Incomplete instruments (including checks, promissory notes, and money orders) that are signed but the name of the payee has been omitted
- Securities or stock in bearer form or otherwise in such form that title thereto passes upon delivery

Monetary instruments do not include:

- Checks or money orders made payable to a named person which have not been endorsed or which bear restrictive endorsements
- Warehouse receipts or bills of lading

Each person who receives currency or other monetary instruments (as described above) in the U.S., must file Form 4790, Report of International Transportation of Currency or Monetary Instruments, within 15 days after their receipt, with an Officer in charge at any port of entry or by mail to the address on the form.

Persons who carry currency or other monetary instruments (as described above) may file Form 4790 at the time of entry into or departure from the U.S. with the Officer in charge at the port of entry or departure.

Form 4790 is available at www.customs.gov or from any BCBP office.

Failure to file a report, or the filing of a fraudulent report, could result in civil or criminal penalties such as a fine of not more than $500,000 and imprisonment of not more than ten years. The money may be subject to seizure and forfeiture.

A transfer of funds through normal banking procedures which does not involve the physical transportation of currency or monetary instruments is not required to be reported. Other exceptions include certain banks and businesses involved in the transportation of money.

It is not necessary for non-U.S. citizens or residents to report currency or other monetary instruments mailed or shipped from abroad directly to a bank, broker or dealer in securities through the postal service or by common carrier.

Ref: 31 CFR 103; 31 USC 5316

Financial Education

Money Smart is a program providing financial education for low income people and is available through local One-Stop career centers.

Notary Public

Many U.S. documents must be notarized. U.S. notaries can authenticate papers, such as financial and legal, very economically and quickly. Some banks provide this service without charge. You must have proper identification, usually a photo I.D.

Many businesses have staff who are licensed to notarize documents for employees while others will sign and stamp papers for the public at a fee of several dollars. Look for a "Notary" sign at the front of the store.

The requirement for notarization can become more complicated and expensive if the documents must be signed in a country where there are no notaries. It may be necessary to hire a lawyer to witness your signature.

Accountant

For tax and estate-planning advice, you may contact a certified public accountant (CPA). Talk to several to be sure you are comfortable with one's approach to financial matters. Ask for referrals from people you trust or contact the local CPA organization for names of accountants in your area who specialize in the service you require or contact: American Institute of Certified Public Accountants
1211 Avenue of the Americas
New York, NY 10036
Phone: (201) 938-3000 or (800) 862-4272

Financial Planners

If you require assistance with financial matters, especially in two countries, be sure to find a cross-border planner who is knowledgeable in the services that apply to you. Do not hire a financial planner who is learning at your expense.

Ask for referrals or contact FPA who will refer you to member planners in your area. They may be reached at:
Financial Planning Association
5775 Glenridge Dr. N.E., Suite B-300
Atlanta, GA 30328
Phone: (404) 845-0011 or (800) 322-4237

Chapter 26

Buying or Renting a Home

$\mathbf{B}$uying a home in the United States can be confusing since the rules and practices may be very different from those found in other countries.

This chapter sets out some of the terms a home buyer may encounter. Hopefully, by learning the "language" of U.S. home purchasing, you will avoid some of the misunderstandings.

Overview

Read all contracts, both front and back, to be sure that you understand and agree to all terms before signing. Even if you have the expertise of a real estate agent and attorney, only you know your wishes.

Real estate and relocating literature will have lists of points you should consider when looking for a home. Here are some additional considerations to keep in mind:

- Proximity to shopping, recreation, places of worship, fire station, police, ambulance, medical facilities, post office, schools, day care
- Quality of schools (see www.schoolmatch.com)
- Access to expressways, city center, airport
- Attractiveness of the neighborhood
- Future use of vacant land in the area
- Nuisances (noise, smoke, soot, dust, odors or other hazards)
- Public transportation
- Land in designated flood zone or low elevation that could result in flooding
- Crime rate
- Land in area which qualifies for Homeowner's Insurance
- Erosion protection, if on water (check history of annual rate of erosion and what types of protection are allowed by government agencies)
- Garbage pickup available
- Sewers and other utilities available
- Local restrictions on house design, use of land, and so on
- Tax rate

Useful sources are www.realtor.com, www.homeadvisor.msn.com and www.owners.com.

Buying a New Home

Suggestions

Investigate the builder thoroughly. Talk to the Better Business Bureau and other organizations that keep track of builders' records in your area. See if any complaints have been lodged against the builder and, if so, how the builder addressed them.

A spokesperson for the U.S. National Association of Home Builders, has been widely quoted as suggesting a visit to communities where the company recently built homes similar to the one you're interested in. He suggests that you go on a Saturday morning when everyone is doing yard work. Talk to several homeowners and ask what their experience has been with their builder. Ask if they have had any problems and if they were fixed promptly and properly.

Read the contract carefully. If you don't understand any part, consult a lawyer or real estate expert. The builder may say it's a standard contract but anything in a contract is negotiable and may be changed if both sides agree. A preprinted contract does not mean that you can't cross out and change provisions.

Real estate experts caution you to get everything that is important to you in writing. Oral statements are difficult to prove and enforce. You should put in writing all complaints and problems during and after construction and keep copies.

The most common methods of buying property are:
- The payment of the full amount of money, or
- The combination of a down payment with a **mortgage** for the remaining amount (some may qualify for no down payment)

When paying cash, you avoid the costs connected with a loan but still have **closing costs**. Whether you are buying or selling a home, **closing costs** are a major expense. In spite of local custom, you may negotiate who pays which of the costs.

Condominium - Points to consider when buying
- Solid construction and noise-proof units
- Homeowners association - financial condition - **reserve funds**
- Special assessments - history of, or prediction for such costs as common area repairs, improvements, upkeep
- Maintenance fees - good value, artificially low, or overpriced
- Tolerable rules, restrictions and by-laws
- Amenities - such as pool and tennis courts owned by owners or must they be purchased from the developer in the future
- Management - professionally managed
- Renters - mortgage lenders are concerned with the percentage of renters compared to permanent residents in a complex

Manufactured Homes

Manufacured homes are factory built to meet the Federal Manufactured Home Construction and Safety Standards (HUD Code). These homes come in a variety of styles, sizes and floor plans, and range in price from about $15,000 to more than $100,000 without land. They can be installed on your own land, in a rental community, or in a planned subdivision.

Buying a Used Home

Procedures vary across the country but basically the following main steps occur in buying a home:
- Research areas
- Select a lender, if needed, and get a pre-approval letter
- Research and select real estate agent
- Look at houses for sale
- Select a house
- **Review seller's disclosure**
- Sign offer to purchase; include any contingencies for cancelling the sale
- **Pay earnest money**
- Arrange **home inspection** and **appraisal**
- **Close** deal

Rental Accommodation

Real estate offices usually handle house and condominium rentals. Apartments will normally have a rental office on site.

Some apartment rental leases can be short-term, but condominiums and houses usually have a longer minimum rental period. Most units are unfurnished.

Once you have selected the rental accommodation, you will likely be asked to fill out an application form. There could be an application fee of an amount something like $25. The agent will verify your background and financial history.

By law, you cannot be turned down on the basis of race, religion, color, national origin, sex, handicap or having children.

You will be expected to sign the agreement and to pay the first and perhaps the last month's rent at the beginning of the lease. A deposit is also required but it will be returned to you after you move away at the end of your lease, providing you have caused no damage in excess of the usual wear and tear. If there is damage, the amount of money it takes to make the repair will be deducted before the deposit is returned.

Many apartment complexes offer amenities such as swimming pools, saunas, tennis courts, and fitness equipment.

The apartment unit should have a stove and refrigerator. It may also have a dishwasher and garbage disposal. A heating system is required and air conditioning is a necessity in the southern United States.

There may be large centrally located laundry rooms with coin-operated washers and dryers for the use of all the renters in the complex. Some apartment units have their own washer and dryer connections or appliances.

Pets may be prohibited or restricted as to size. There could be a maximum weight which an animal can be, such as 20 or 50 lbs. There also will probably be a pet deposit (may be non-refundable) and a monthly payment. For instance, one complex demands a $500 deposit plus $30 per month.

Points to consider when renting:
- Inspect the unit carefully and report any pre-existing damage
- Read all rules and regulations applying to the unit
- Check to see how much advance notice must be given before moving out
- Determine the owner's obligation to make the necessary repairs
- Renters of some houses are expected to do the yard maintenance
- Determine clean-up requirements for when you move out. Most clean-up costs can be deducted from security deposit if instructions are not followed
- Check on prohibitions against sub-letting should you wish to leave before the lease has expired
- Determine which utilities are included in the rent, such as garbage pickup, pest control and water
- It is important to always pay the rent on time
- Renter and tenant should have a clear written agreement
- Oral agreements should be indicated on the contract, signed by both parties
- Keep a copy of the lease or agreement

Expenses

Utilities

Before moving into a home, arrangements must be made with the local utility companies in order to have all equipment functioning when you move in. Some utilities have a waiting list so it is wise to contact them in advance.

Utility requirements vary from area to area. Following are samples in one city:

Utility	Deposit	Connect Fee	Advance Notice
Electric	$125-$250*	$16	1 business day
Natural Gas	$75*	$20	2 business days
Telephone	**	$42.75 (1 jack)	3 business days
Cable TV	-	$15-$85 to install	4-7 business days
Water & Sewer	$120	$103	2 business days

* Refunded with interest after 23 months with good payment record
**May be waived with good credit

Once the initial fees are paid, you are then responsible for the monthly charges which will be billed to you.

Property Taxes

Property taxes are collected each year to provide such municipal services as schools, police, fire, sewer, garbage collection, street lighting, street repair, senior citizen and community centers.

Taxes are based on a percentage of the property's assessed value. In at least one state (Florida) a Homestead Tax Exemption of $25,000 may be deducted from the assessed value of the property. To qualify, the owner must:

- Be living on the property
- Hold title to the property
- Be a legal and permanent resident of the state and the U.S.

You may want to check on any similar exemption in your state.

Home Buying Definitions

The following definitions are included as a guide to help prepare a buyer for the complexities of buying a home. Before signing any documents or depositing any money, an attorney should be consulted to ensure that the buyer's rights are properly protected.

Note:

- A bold typed word appearing within a definition indicates that the word appears in the list of definitions in this chapter or in Chapter 27, Mortgages.
- Some terms may have different meanings in another context.
- The definitions are general, non-technical and short.
- State laws, as well as local custom and usage may change the meanings in various regions.

Abstract (Of Title) A summary of the public records of the **title** to a particular piece of land. An attorney or **title insurance** company reviews an abstract of title to determine whether there are any problems which must be cleared up before a buyer can purchase clear, **marketable** and insurable **title**.

Adjustments between Buyer and Seller At **settlement** time, it is necessary to pro-rate all bills such as insurance, taxes and utilities, to determine the adjustments necessary between the buyer and seller. For example, if the taxes have been paid in advance for a year by the seller, credit is given to the seller for the period of the year that he is not occupying the home.

Agreement of Sale Known by various names, such as **contract of purchase**, **purchase agreement,** or **sales agreement,** according to location or jurisdiction, is a contract in which a seller agrees to sell and a buyer agrees to buy. Certain specific terms and conditions are spelled out in writing and signed by both parties. The agreement should include the sale price of the home, method of payment, date for taking possession, what fixtures, appliances, and personal property are to be sold with the home. It should also set out which party pays for specific settlement costs, home inspections, and other items involved in the sale. Attention should be paid to deadlines in the contract for any action that has been agreed upon such as repairs to be made by the seller. Proposed modifications to price and details may be handwritten and initialed on the contract until both parties are satisfied. If real estate brokers are involved they usually carry the **counter offers** between the buyer and the seller. Before signing, both parties may want their own lawyers to review the agreement. If a party does not know a local attorney, he should consult the bar association referral service or a neighborhood legal service office. Be careful. In some areas, once signed, the contract is binding on both the buyer and the seller.

Appraiser Opinion of an appraiser on the value of a home based on the size, features and condition of the residence in relation to the value of comparable homes in the area

Appreciation Increase in value or worth of property.

Assessed Value Value placed on property as a basis for levying **property taxes**.

Attorney's Fees Legal fees paid for examining the title, closing services, etc.

Bathroom - Numerical Descriptions

- Full bath - Toilet, sink and tub or shower
- One-half bath - Toilet and sink, missing tub or shower
- Three-quarter bath - Toilet, sink and shower stall

Binder (Offer to Purchase) A preliminary agreement accompanied by the payment of **earnest money**, between a buyer and seller as an offer to purchase real estate. A binder secures the right to purchase real estate upon agreed terms for a limited period of time. If the buyer changes his mind or is unable to purchase, the earnest money may be forfeited unless the binder expressly provides that it is to be refunded.

Broker State licensed person to represent another for a fee in real estate transactions.

Building Code Local government regulations setting out standards for building.

Building Line or Setback Distances from the ends and/or sides of the lot beyond which construction may not extend. The building line may be established by a filed **plat** of subdivision, by **restrictive convenants** in **deeds** or leases, by **building codes**, or by **zoning ordinances.**

Certificate of Title Certificate issued by a **title** company or a written opinion rendered by an attorney that the seller has good marketable and insurable title to the property which he is offering for sale. A certificate of title offers no protection against any hidden defects in the title which an examination of the records could not reveal. The issuer of a certificate of title is liable only for damages due to negligence.

Chattel Personal property.

Closing or **Settlement** A procedure which occurs at the end of the home buying process when the title to the property is formally transferred from the seller to the buyer. In some areas, the buyer and seller meet with the closing agent and sign the papers. In other cases, they sign the papers in advance and an agent gets everything in order.

Closing Agent (Settlement Agent) Closing practices vary from locality to locality. Typically, they may be conducted by title insurance companies or attorneys. In some parts of the country, lenders or real estate brokers also may hold closings.

Closing Costs (Settlement Costs) (HUD Statements) The numerous expenses which buyers and sellers normally incur to complete a transaction in the transfer of ownership of real estate. One business day before **closing**, the settlement form should be available for inspection. It should itemize all services and fees being charged. These costs are in addition to the price of the property and are paid on the **closing day**. The mortgage provider also will require Lender's Fees to be paid.

The agreement of sale negotiated previously between the buyer and the seller may state in writing who has agreed to pay each of the following applicable costs:

Closing fee to **Settlement Agent**   **Document Preparation**
Notary   **Home Inspection**
Escrow Fees   **Appraisal**
Survey   Attorney or Paralegal Fee
Title Search & Examination   **Commission**
Title Insurance   **Termite Inspection**
Recording & Transfer Charges   **Documentary Stamps**

Closing Day The day on which the formalities of a real estate sale are concluded. The final closing merely confirms the original agreement reached in **agreement of sale**.

Cloud (On Title) Outstanding claim or **encumbrance** which adversely affects the **marketability of title**.

Commission Money paid to a real estate broker by the seller as compensation for finding a buyer and completing the sale. Percentages are negotiable between the agent and seller, based on the agent's cost of doing business.

Conditional Offer Purchase offer in which the buyer proposes to purchase only after certain occurrences such as the sale of another home or securing financing.

Condominium Individual ownership of a dwelling unit within a multi-unit project and access to the common areas and facilities which serve the project.

Contingencies Reasons for cancelling a sale, such as undisclosed liens, financing unavailable, buyer's house not sold, failed home inspection

Contract of Purchase See **Agreement of Sale**

Contractor One who hires and co-ordinates sub-contractors for all phases of construction like heating, electrical, plumbing, air conditioning, roofing and carpentry.

Cooperative Housing An apartment building or a group of dwellings owned by a corporation, the stockholders of which are the residents of the dwellings. It is operated for their benefit by their elected board of directors. Expenses are paid by the shareholders in proportion to the number of shares owned and may include a portion of the mortgage payments, maintenance and taxes.

Counteroffer An amendment or new offer made in response to an offer.

Deed A formal written document by which **title** to real property is transferred from one owner to another. The deed should contain an accurate description of the property being purchased, should be signed and witnessed according to the laws of the state where the property is located and should be delivered to the purchaser on **closing day**. There are two parties to a deed: the **grantor** (seller) and the **grantee** (buyer).

Deed of Trust Like a mortgage, a security instrument whereby real property is given as security for a debt. However, in a deed of trust there are three parties: the borrower, the **trustee**, and the lender, (or beneficiary). In such a transaction, the borrower transfers the legal **title** for the property to the trustee who holds the property in trust as security. If the borrower pays the debt as agreed, the deed of trust becomes void. If, however, he **defaults** in the payment of the debt, the trustee may sell the property at a public sale. In most jurisdictions where the deed of trust is in force, the borrower is subject to having his property sold without benefit of legal proceedings. A few states have begun in recent years to treat the deed of trust like a **mortgage.**

Deed Restriction (Restrictive Covenant) Provision placed in a deed to control use and occupancy of the property by future owners.

Depreciation Decline in value of a house due to wear and tear, adverse changes in the neighborhood, or any other reason.

Document Preparation Fee A fee which covers preparation of final legal papers such as a **mortgage, deed of trust,** note, or **deed**.

Documentary Stamps A state tax, in the form of stamps, required on **deeds** and **mortgages** when real estate **title** passes from one owner to another. The amount varies with each state.

Down payment The amount of money to be paid by the purchaser to the seller upon the signing of the **agreement of sale**. The down payment may not be refundable if the purchaser fails to buy the property without good cause. If the purchaser wants the down payment to be refundable, he should be sure there is a clause in the agreement of sale specifying the conditions under which the deposit will be refunded. If the seller defaults and does not deliver clear **title**, the agreement of sale usually requires the seller to return the down payment and to pay **interest** and expenses incurred by the purchaser. If the seller makes an effort to overcome the problem, the deadline for the sale may be extended.

Duplex A structure with two dwelling units.

Earnest Money The deposit money given to the seller or his agent by the potential buyer upon the signing of the agreement of sale to show that he is serious about buying the property. If the sale goes through, the earnest money is applied against the **down payment**. If the sale does not go through the earnest money may be forfeited or lost unless the **binder** or **offer to purchase** expressly provides that it is refundable.

Easement Rights Right-of-way granted to a person or company authorizing access to or over the owner's land. An electric or telephone company with a right-of-way across private property is a common example.

Encroachment An obstruction, building, or part of a building that intrudes beyond a legal boundary into neighboring private or public land, or a building extending beyond the **building line**.

Encumbrance A legal right or interest in land that affects a good or clear title, and diminishes the land's value. It can take numerous forms, such as **zoning ordinances, easement rights**, claims, **mortgages, liens**, charges, a pending legal action, unpaid taxes, or **restrictive covenants**. An encumbrance does not legally prevent transfer of the property to another. A **title search** is all that is usually done to reveal the existence of such encumbrances, and it is up to the buyer to determine whether he wants to purchase with the encumbrance, or what can be done to remove it. The lender may not allow the sale to be completed with an encumbrance.

Fair Housing Laws Prohibit discrimination in the sale, rental, financing, and other housing-related transactions based on race, color, national origin, religion, gender, familial status or disability.

Fiduciary Person in a position of trust or responsibility with specific duties to act in the best interest of the client.

General Warranty Deed A deed which conveys not only all the seller's interests in and **title** to the property to the buyer, but also warrants that if the title is defective or has a "**cloud** on it (such as mortgage claims, tax **liens**, title claims, judgments, or **mechanic's liens** against it) the buyer may hold the seller liable.

Grantee That party in the **deed** who is the buyer or recipient.

Grantor That party in the **deed** who is the seller or giver.

Hazard Insurance (Homeowner's Insurance) Helps pay for damage caused to property by fire, windstorms, and other common hazards.

Home Inspection Home inspectors determine whether the basic elements of a house are in sound condition. They inspect such features as the heating and cooling system, plumbing, appliances, floors, roof and the electrical system. See www.ashi.com.

Home Warranties

New-Home Warranties
Warranties for new homes generally supplement the builder's warranty and have a deductible, which the homeowner pays when a claim is made.

Typically, new-home warranties cover:
- Workmanship and materials for one year
- Major systems, such as heating, cooling, electrical and plumbing for two years
- The foundation for ten years

New-home warranties do not cover:
- Appliances (covered by manufacturer's warranty)
- "Acts of God" such as hurricanes, floods, earthquakes

Existing-Home Warranties
A limited time warranty may be sold by real estate agents, usually to sellers as a marketing incentive to attract buyers.

Warranties for existing homes cover:
- Appliances such as dishwashers, water heaters, stoves
- Major systems such as heating, air conditioning, electrical and plumbing

Existing-home warranties do not cover:
- "Acts of God"
- Air-conditioning systems and pool equipment (may be optional)

Homeowner's Association (HOA) Fees and Assessments Funds payable to community organizations to maintain common property and perhaps pay for some utilities.

Homeowner's Insurance Several kinds of insurance together in one package - theft, disaster, liability.

HUD Homes (U.S. Department of Housing and Urban Development) Properties that are deeded to HUD/FHA (Federal Housing Administration) by mortgage companies who foreclose on FHA-insured mortgage loans. HUD must sell these homes quickly. The listing price of a HUD property is based on an estimate of its fair market value. Anyone who has the money or can qualify for the mortgage financing can purchase a HUD Home. They are marketed on a competitive basis with sealed bid offers being submitted through any participating licensed real estate broker. The "offer period" is usually a 10-day period. At the end of the period, all bids received on the home will be opened at a public event. When an offer has been accepted, the broker will be notified within 48 hours. Sometimes HUD will accept an offer that is less than the listing price and sometimes buyers make bids higher than the listing price, depending on market conditions. Agents and investors get the good deals quickly.

Joint Tenancy Ownership by two or more persons, each with an undivided ownership; if one dies, the property automatically goes to the survivor.

Lease An agreement that conveys the right to use property for a period of time.

Lease to own Method of renting a home with a substantial amount of rent credited toward the down payment. Eventually the renter has enough rent credit for a down payment to buy the residence.

Lessee Tenant.

Lessor Landlord.

Lien A claim by one person on the property of another as security for money owed. Such claims may include obligations not met or satisfied, judgments, unpaid taxes, materials, or labor (See also **special lien** and **mechanic's lien**).

Listing Agreement Contract between a property owner and a real estate broker, authorizing the broker to find a buyer.

Maintenance Fees Fees a property owner is required to pay in a multiple-owner property which cover such expenses as maintenance and repair of common buildings and property.

Market Value The highest price that a buyer would pay and the lowest price a seller would accept on a property.

Marketable Title A **title** that is free and clear of objectionable **liens, clouds,** or other title defects. A title which enables an owner to sell his property freely to others and which others will accept without objection.

Mechanic's Lien Claim placed against property by unpaid workers or suppliers.

Mobile Home Manufactured home moved by truck and set upon a permanent foundation, usually in a mobile home park where utilities, security, recreation facilities, may all be available.

Multiple-Listing Service (MLS) Many different real estate companies in an area working together to sell properties and share the resulting commissions.

Notary A licensed person who signs and seals documents verifying the signatures.

Plat A map or chart of a lot, subdivision or community drawn by a surveyor, showing boundary lines, buildings, improvements on the land, and **easements**.

Power of Attorney Legal document authorizing a person to act on behalf of another.

Property Taxes Taxes are levied according to the value of the property. The funds are used to support schools, street maintenance, fire, police, and so on.

Purchase Agreement See **agreement of sale**

Quitclaim Deed A deed which transfers whatever interest the seller may have in the particular parcel of land. A quitclaim deed is often given to clear the title when the grantor's interest in a property is questionable. By accepting such a deed the buyer assumes all the risks. Such a deed makes no warranties as to the title, but simply transfers to the buyer whatever interest the grantor has. (See **deed**.) A **title insurance** policy may provide comfort to the buyer.

Real Estate Broker Person licensed to act independently in conducting real estate brokerage business.

Seller's agent
- Is obligated to tell the seller anything known about the buyer that would benefit the seller
- Advises seller on how to make property more saleable
- Researches the market to assist seller in setting the selling price
- May list property with **MLS (Multiple Listing Service)**
- Advertises property for sale
- Shows interested clients through home and makes arrangements for other agents to do the same
- Advises and assists in the contract negotiations
- Usually attends the closing
- Takes a predetermined fee from the sale of the home

Buyer's agent
- Represents the buyer's interests in looking for property
- Shows the buyer available properties
- Assists and advises with contract negotiations
- Shares with seller's agent, the predetermined commission, paid by seller
- May assist the buyer in finding a lender for the mortgage

Real Estate Salesperson Person employed by a **real estate broker** to list and negotiate the sale, lease or rental of real property under guidance of employing broker.

Realtor Registered name for a member of the National Association of Realtors, sworn to abide by the code of ethics.

Realtor Associate Salesperson associated with a broker who is a member of a Board of Realtors.

Recording Fees Money paid for recording a home sale with the local authorities, thereby making it part of the public records.

Reserve Fund Special account for major repair, replacement or renovation of common property.

Restrictive Covenants Clauses placed in **deeds** and **leases** to control how owners and **lessees** may or may not use the property. For example, restrictive covenants may limit the number of buildings per acre, regulate size, style or price range of buildings to be erected, or prevent particular businesses from operating in homes in a given area.

Sales Agreement See **Agreement of Sale**.

Seller's Disclosure List of all home's physical problems and defects of which the seller is aware

Settlement Agent/Costs See **Closing Agent/Costs**.

Special Assessments A special tax imposed on property, individual lots or all property in the immediate area, for such expenses as road or sidewalk construction, sewers, or street lights.

Special Lien A lien that binds a specified piece of property, unlike a general **lien**, which is levied against all one's assets. It creates a right to retain something of value belonging to another person as compensation for labor, material, or money expended in that person's behalf. In some localities it is called "particular" lien or "specific" lien.

Special Warranty Deed A deed in which the seller (**grantor**) conveys title to the buyer (**grantee**) and agrees to protect the buyer against title defects or claims asserted by the seller and those persons whose right to assert a claim against the title arose during the period the seller held title to the property. In a special warranty deed the seller guarantees to the buyer that he has done nothing during the time he held title to the property which has, or which might in the future, impair the buyer's title.

State Stamps See **Documentary Stamps**.

Survey A map or **plat** made by a licensed surveyor showing the results of measuring the land with its elevations, improvements, boundaries, and its relationship to surrounding tracts of land. A survey is often required by the lender to assure him that a building is actually sited on the land according to its legal description. In some areas the buyer may contact the previous surveyor and request an update. Usually the buyer pays the fee.

Termite Guarantee or Bond Bonds are available from pest control services. Some are for re-treatment, but not repair, if termites are found. A more expensive, but many say preferable, bond includes inspection, any necessary treatment and a limited repair guarantee for any termite damage to the wood.

Timesharing A method of dividing up and selling living units for specified lengths of time each year. The buyer may occupy a unit for a certain number of days yearly. The timeshare must be paid in advance and an annual maintenance fee is required.

Title As generally used, the rights of ownership and possession of particular property. In real estate usage, title may refer to the instruments or documents by which a right of ownership is established (title documents), or it may refer to the ownership interest one has in the real estate.

Title Company Searches for hidden problems that might affect the title and provides an insurance policy. May also conduct **closings**.

Title Insurance A form of insurance policy to protect against loss if any problem ever occurs which results in a claim against ownership. Examples of title defects include a forged will or deed, undisclosed heirs, invalid divorces. If a claim is made against the property, the company may either fight the claim in court or pay the loss. If the insurance company decides to fight, the title insurance will, in accordance with the terms of the policy, assure a legal defense and pay all court costs and legal fees. Also, if the claim proves valid, the owner will be reimbursed for the actual loss up to the face value of the policy. Some insurers offer coverage with inflation endorsements. Coverage may be purchased from Title Insurance Companies or attorneys.

The premium is paid only once (usually .5 to 1 percent of the property cost). There are no renewal premiums and there is no expiration date on the policy. Coverage lasts as long as the owner or his heirs retain an interest in the property.

In some areas, there may be no need for a full historical title search if the property has recently changed hands. Some title insurance companies may reissue a policy at a lower premium.

Title Search or Examination A detailed examination of the historical records concerning a property, generally at the local public records, to make sure the buyer is purchasing a house from the legal owner and there are no **liens**, overdue **special assessments,** or other claims or outstanding **restrictive covenants** filed in the record, which would adversely affect the seller's right to transfer ownership.

Townhouse A row of dwelling units with shared walls.

Transfer Charges Recording Fees for documents, including the **deed** or **deed of trust**.

Triplex A structure containing three dwelling units.

Trustee A party who is given legal responsibility to hold property in the best interest of or "for the benefit of" another. The trustee is one placed in a position of responsibility for another, a responsibility enforceable in a court of law (See **deed of trust**).

Walk-through A final inspection of the property just prior to settlement.

Zoning Ordinances The acts of an authorized local government establishing building codes and setting forth regulations that control the specific use of land.

Chapter 27
Mortgages

Areal estate agent should know what financing programs are available in your area and should be a good resource. Agents advise that you start your home financing process well in advance of your offer to purchase by getting a mortgage pre-approval. However, you can't apply for the actual mortgage until you have signed a sales contract. For information: www.fhatoday.com and www.hud.com.

Mortgage Lenders

Financial information a lender may require includes:
- W-2s for prior years
- List of assets and liabilities
- List of all income
- Proof of employment
- Year-to-date pay check stubs
- Bank statements
- Signed sales contract
- Verification of the source of the down payment

Most mortgage lenders will help you determine how much home you can afford.

Experts suggest comparing several lenders and their fees. Online mortgage information is available at http://homeadvisor.msn.com, www.mortgage-net.com and www.bankrate.com. If you plan to stay in the house two or three years, pay attention to your short-term costs such as closing costs (including points), down payment, appraisal and attorney's fees. If you are going to be a long-term owner, then pay attention to the total interest cost on the life of the loan. You may also want to consider **bi-weekly mortgage payments**.

Lenders base their decisions on income, debt, assets, credit history and stability. Federal laws prohibit lenders from discriminating against applicants on the basis of gender or race. See www.ftc.gov/bcp/online/pubs/credit/ecoa.htm.

Some lenders may allow qualifying foreign nationals to borrow up to 75 to 80 percent of the purchase price.

Nonimmigrant aliens may also qualify for a mortgage. To be eligible, they may be required to have a minimum number of years remaining on their visa and proof of a high probability of employment during that time.

In addition to your personal information and credit report (see chapter 25 under Establishing Credit), lenders may also buy a credit score based on your report. Most U.S. credit bureau scores are produced from software by Fair, Isaac and Company (FICO). FICO scores evaluate your payment history, amounts owed, length of credit history, new credit and types of credit use. The higher the score, the lower the risk.

In order for a FICO score to be calculated, your report must contain at least one account which has been open for at least six months and one account that has been updated in the last six months. To obtain a credit report and score, see www.myfico.com.

If you have no FICO score, lenders may accept a letter of reference from your bank. A fee is charged if translation is required. They will also need documents such as a business license to prove that the income source exists.

Additional points to consider when looking for a mortgage loan include:

- A choice of mortgage providers such as banks, savings and loans, mortgage companies, mortgage brokers, credit unions, home sellers, internet
- Types of loans and exact mortgage limits for which you qualify
- Length of loan which is best for you such as 30-year fixed rate, 15-year fixed, one-year ARM
- The down payment required by the lender - the longer the term and the larger the down payment, the smaller the monthly payments
- The interest rate - in some cases the amount of the down payment will influence the interest rate - the larger the down payment, the lower the interest rate
- Interest rates and fees may vary among lenders - differences of as little as a quarter of a percent can mean thousands of dollars in the difference of total payments over the life of the loan
- Penalties may apply for **refinancing** the mortgage or paying off early
- The length of the approval process - in some cases, be prepared for a wait of 30-45 days or longer from the date the lender receives all the information with the application
- Mortgage interest payments are deductible from federal income tax

Some lenders offer mortgage loans insured by a federal agency such as the Federal Housing Administration (FHA loans) or the Department of Veterans Affairs (VA loans). Loans that are not government-insured are called **conventional mortgages**. Insured mortgages may be more attractive than conventional mortgages in some ways such as lower down payment requirements. They may be more restrictive in other ways. For example, they may be available only for certain kinds of homes, or for properties whose value is below a specified price.

Lenders generally charge lower initial interest rates for **adjustable rate mortgages** (ARMs) (indexed to **LIBOR** or **T-Bill** rate plus **margin**) than for **fixed-rate mortgages**. There is a risk that interest rates will increase, leading to higher monthly payments. If you don't plan to keep the property many years, rising interest rates are not of concern.

With most ARMs, the interest rate and monthly payment change every year, every three years, or every five years. The time when one rate period ends and the next begins is called the **adjustment period**.

To choose among **fixed-rate** mortgage loans, you should compare interest rates, monthly payments, fees, **prepayment** penalties, and **due-on-sale** clauses.

If a lender refuses a loan, Federal law requires the lender to tell the applicant, in writing, the specific reasons for the denial. Some companies have stricter credit standards than others. It pays to keep looking.

Items Payable in Connection with Loans may include:

- **. Loan Origination Fee**
- **. Points**
- **. Appraisal**
- **. Mortgage Insurance Application Fee**
- **. Assumption Fee**
- **. Credit Report**

Items that may be required by the lender to be paid by borrower in advance:

- . Accrued Interest
- **. Hazard Insurance**
- . Taxes
- **. Private Mortgage Insurance**

Mortgage Definitions

The following are some terms that you may encounter when arranging a mortgage in order to purchase property. Those words in bold print are defined elsewhere in the following list or in Chapter 26, Buying of Renting a Home. Customs and interpretations of terms may vary from region to region.

Acceleration Clause A condition in a **mortgage** that may require the balance of the loan to become due immediately, if regular mortgage payments are not made or other conditions of the mortgage are not met.

Accrued Interest Interest from the date of settlement to the beginning of the period covered by the first monthly payment.

Adjustable-mortgage Loan See **Adjustable-rate Mortgage**.

Adjustable-rate Mortgage (ARM) Interest rate fluctuates with changes in prevailing rates throughout the life of the loan. Initially the interest rate may be lower than a fixed-rate mortgage. The most common ARMS recalibrate once a year, based on an index of government bond rates.

Adjustment Interval In an **adjustable-rate mortgage**, the time between changes in the interest rate and/or monthly payment, is typically, one, three or five years, depending on the index.

Amortization A gradual process enabling the borrower to reduce his debt gradually through monthly payments that cover both interest and **principal**. As payments are made to the lender each month, the size of the mortgage debt, or principal, declines in most cases.

Annual Percentage Rate (APR) A measure of the cost of credit expressed as a yearly rate. It includes interest as well as other charges. Because all lenders follow the same rules to ensure the accuracy of the annual percentage rate, it provides consumers with a good basis for comparing the cost of loans, including mortgage plans.

Appraisal An expert judgment or estimate of the quality or value of real estate as of a given date.

Assumable Mortgage A mortgage that is transferable from seller to buyer.

Assumption Fee A fee which is charged for processing papers for cases in which the buyer takes over the payments on the prior loan of the seller.

Assumption of Mortgage An obligation undertaken by the purchaser of the property to be personally liable for payment of an existing **mortgage**. In an assumption, the purchaser is substituted for the original **mortgagor** in the mortgage agreement and the original **mortgagor** is released from further liability under the mortgage. Since the **mortgagor** is to be released from further liability in the assumption, the lender's consent is usually required.

The original **mortgagor** should always obtain a written release from further liability if he desires to be fully released under the assumption.

Balloon Mortgage Low fixed-rate payments as though for a 30-year term, but has a short term such as five to seven years at the end of which is a single large payment (the "balloon").

Biweekly Mortgage Payments Payments are made every two weeks rather than monthly (They may even be automatic withdrawals from the homeowner's account.) There are 26 half payments or the equivalent of 13 monthly payments. The extra payment serves to build equity faster and reduce interest costs. Payments are scheduled for a 30-year loan, but the extra payment each year means the loan is paid off in just under 20 years.

Buydown See **Seller Buydown**.

Cap Limit by which an adjustable mortgage rate may be raised at any one time. By law, virtually all ARMs must have an overall cap. Many have a periodic interest-rate cap. Periodic caps limit the interest-rate increase from one adjustment period to the next. Overall caps limit the interest-rate increase over the life of the loan. Payment caps don't limit the amount of interest the lender is earning, so they may cause **negative amortization**.

Ceiling (Lifetime Cap) Limit beyond which an adjustable mortgage rate may never be raised.

Community Reinvestment Act (CRA) Federal law requiring banks to lend to modest-income consumers.

Construction Loan A short-term interim loan for financing the cost of construction. The lender advances funds to the builder at periodic intervals as the work progresses.

Conventional Mortgage A **mortgage** loan not insured by **HUD** or guaranteed by the **VA**. It is subject to conditions established by the lending institution and state statutes. The mortgage rates may vary with different institutions and between states. (States have various interest limits).

Conversion Clause A provision in some **ARMs** that allows you to change the ARM to a fixed-rate loan at some point during the term.

Credit Report A summary which is compiled by a credit reporting agency for the lender. The report shows the buyer's credit history and general reputation. This fee is generally paid by the buyer.

Debt-to-Income Ratio The ratio, expressed as a percentage, which results when a borrower's monthly payment obligation on long-term debts is divided by his or her net income (FHA/VA loans) or gross monthly income (conventional loans). See **Housing expenses-to-income ratio**.

Deed of Trust See **Mortgage**.

Default Failure to make mortgage payments as agreed to in a commitment based on the terms and at the designated time set forth in the **mortgage** or **deed of trust**. In the event of default, the **mortgage** may give the lender the right to accelerate payments, take possession and receive rents, and start **foreclosure**. Defaults may also come about by the failure to observe other conditions in the **mortgage** or **deed of trust**.

Deferred Interest See **Negative Amortization**.

Delinquency Failure to make mortgage payments on time. This can lead to foreclosure.

Department of Veterans Affairs (VA) An independent agency of the Federal government which guarantees long-term, low- or no-down payment mortgages to eligible veterans.

Discount Points See **Points**.

Discounted Rate Some lenders offer initial **ARM** rates that are lower than the sum of the **index** and the **margin**. Discounted rates are often combined with large initial loan fees (**points**) and with higher **interest** rates after the discount expires.

Down payment When a buyer is using a mortgage for the purchase of the property, the down payment is the money paid to make up the difference between the purchase price and the mortgage amount. Down payments usually are 10 percent to 20 percent of the sales price on conventional loans, and no money down up to 5 percent on FHA and VA loans.

Due-on-Sale-Clause A provision in a mortgage or deed of trust that allows the lender to demand immediate payment of the balance of the mortgage if the mortgage holder sells the home.

Equal Credit Opportunity Act (ECOA) Prohibits lenders from discriminating against credit applications on the basis of race, color, religion, national origin, sex, marital status, age, or receipt of income from public assistance programs.

Equity The value of a homeowner's unencumbered interest in a piece of real estate. Equity is computed by subtracting from the property's fair market value the total of the unpaid mortgage balance and any outstanding liens or other debts against the property. A homeowner's equity increases as he pays off his mortgage and/or as the property appreciates in value. When the mortgage and all other debts against the property are paid in full the homeowner has 100 percent equity in his property.

Escrow Funds paid by the buyer to a third party (the escrow agent) to hold until the occurrence of a specified event, after which the funds are released to a designated individual. In FHA mortgage transactions an escrow account usually refers to the funds a mortgagor pays the lender at the time of the periodic mortgage payments. The money is held in a trust fund, provided by the lender for the buyer. Such funds should be adequate to cover anticipated yearly expenditures for **mortgage insurance premiums**, taxes, **hazard insurance premiums,** and **special assessments**.

Fannie Mae See **Federal National Mortgage Association**
Fannie Mae low percent down payment mortgages are available to low income and minority home buyers.

Federal Home Loan Mortgage Corporation (FHLMC) Also called "**Freddie Mac**", a quasi-governmental agency that purchases conventional mortgages from insured depository institutions and HUD-approved mortgage bankers.

Federal Housing Administration (FHA) A division of the Department of Housing and Urban Development. Its main activity is the insuring of residential mortgage loans made by private lenders. FHA also sets standards for underwriting mortgages.

Federal National Mortgage Association (FNMA) Also known as, "**Fannie Mae**", a tax-paying corporation created by Congress that purchases and sells conventional residential mortgages as well as those insured by FHA or guaranteed by VA. This institution, which provides funds for one in seven mortgages, makes more affordable mortgage money available.

FHA Loan Loan insured by the Federal Housing Administration open to all qualified home purchasers. While there are limits to the size of FHA loans, they are generous enough to handle moderate-priced homes almost anywhere in the country.

Fixed-rate mortgage Same interest rate with the same monthly payment for the term of the loan. The longer the loan term, the lower the monthly payment but the higher the ultimate cost.

Foreclosure (Also known as repossession of property) A legal process by which the lender or the seller forces the sale of a mortgaged property because the borrower has not met the terms of the mortgage.

Freddie Mac See **Federal Home Loan Mortgage Corporation (FHLMC)**.

Ginnie Mae See **Government National Mortgage Association (GNMA)**.

Good Faith Estimate When an application for a loan is filed, the lender must provide a Good Faith Estimate of interest and settlement service charges and fees at least three days before the loan is closed.

Government National Mortgage Association (GNMA) Also known as **Ginnie Mae**, provides sources of funds for residential mortgages, insured or guaranteed by **FHA** or **VA**.

Government Recording and Transfer Charges Charges for legally recording the new deed and mortgage. City, county and /or state tax stamps may have to be purchased as well.

Graduated Payment Mortgage (GPM) A type of flexible payment mortgage where the payments increase for a specified period of time and then level off. This type of mortgage has negative amortization built into it.

Gross Monthly Income The total amount the borrower earns per month, before any expenses are deducted.

Guaranty A promise by one party to pay a debt or perform an obligation contracted by another if the original party fails to pay or perform according to a contract.

Housing Expenses-to-Income Ratio The ratio, expressed as a percentage, which results when a borrower's housing expenses are divided by his effective income (FHA/VA loans) or gross monthly income (conventional loans). See **debt-to-income ratio**.

HUD Department of Housing and Urban Development.

Impound See **Reserves**.

Index A published interest rate against which lenders measure the difference between the current interest rate on an adjustable rate mortgage and that earned by other investments (such as one, three, and five-year U.S. Treasury security yields, the monthly average interest rate on loans closed by savings and loan institutions, and the monthly average cost-of-funds incurred by savings and loans), which is then used to adjust the interest rate on an **adjustable mortgage** up or down.

Interest A charge paid for borrowing money (see **Mortgage Note**)

Lending Institutions Lend money to the buyer at either a set or fluctuating interest rate. Lending institutions include commercial banks, mutual savings banks, savings and loan associations and mortgage companies. Settlement charges and fees vary among the lenders. Some local newspapers publish a weekly shopper's guide to mortgage interest rates.

LIBOR (London Interbank Offered Rate) Widely used reference rate for short term interest rates.

Loan Application Application which asks for information such as the borrower's place of employment, assets, and liabilities. False information can lead to severe penalties and loss of the property.

Loan Commitment Lender's promise to make a loan available in a specific amount at a future time.

Loan Discount See **Points**.

Loan Origination Fee A fee to cover the lender's administrative costs in processing the loan. It is often expressed as a percentage of the loan and varies among lenders and localities. It could amount to one percent to two percent of the loan.

Loan-to-Value Ratio The relationship between the amount of the mortgage loan and the appraised value of the property expressed as a percentage.

Lock-in A lender's promise to hold a certain interest rate and certain number of **points** for a specified period of time, while the loan is processed.

Margin The number of percentage points the lender adds to the index rate to calculate the **ARM** interest rate at each adjustment. For example, if the index rate is six percent and the margin is two percent, then the fully-indexed rate is eight percent.

Mortgage (**Deed of Trust** or Security Deed) A loan of money which allows the buyer to purchase property. A **lien** or claim against real property is given by the buyer to the lender as security for money borrowed. Under government-insured or loan-guarantee provisions, the payments may include **escrow** amounts covering taxes, **hazard insurance,** and **special assessments**. There are many types of mortgages usually running from 10 to 30 years, during which time the loan is to be paid off.

Mortgage Bankers Lenders who lend their own funds and later sell off the home loan into the **secondary mortgage market**.

Mortgage Broker Agent who represents many mortgage lenders.

Mortgage Commitment A written notice from the bank or other lending institution saying it will advance mortgage funds in a specified amount to enable a buyer to purchase a house.

Mortgage Insurance Application Fee A fee which covers processing the application for private mortgage insurance which may be required on certain loans. It may cover both the **appraisal** and application fee.

Mortgage Life Insurance Insurance designed to pay off a mortgage in the event of physical disability or death of the borrower.

Mortgage Loan Fee See **Loan Origination Fee**.

Mortgage Note A written agreement to repay a loan. The agreement is secured by a **mortgage**, serves as proof of an indebtedness, and states the manner in which it will be paid. The note states the actual amount of the debt that the mortgage secures and renders the **mortgagor** personally responsible for repayment.

Mortgage (Open-End) Mortgage with a provision that permits borrowing additional money in the future by **refinancing** the loan or paying additional financing charges. Open-end provisions often limit such borrowing to no more than would raise the balance to the original loan figure.

Mortgagee The lender in a mortgage agreement.

Mortgagor The borrower in a mortgage agreement.

Negative Amortization Occurs when the monthly payments are not large enough to pay all the interest due on the loan. This unpaid interest is added to the unpaid balance of the loan. The danger of negative amortization is that the home buyer ends up owing more than the original amount of the loan.

No Cost Mortgage The up-front loan fee is included in a higher interest rate. This loan is often used by buyers who plan to keep their home only a few years.

Nonassumption Clause A statement in a mortgage contract forbidding the assumption of the mortgage without the prior approval of the lender.

Origination Fee The fee charged by the lender to prepare loan documents, make credit checks, inspect and sometimes appraise a property, usually computed as a percentage of the face value of the loan.

PITI Abbreviation for principal, interest, taxes and insurance, elements that commonly make up a borrower's payment on a loan.

Points Sometimes called "**discount points.**" A point is one percent of the amount of the mortgage loan. Lenders frequently charge points in both **fixed-rate** and **adjustable-rate** mortgages in order to increase the yield on the mortgage and to cover loan closing costs. These points usually are paid at closing. Buyers are prohibited from paying points on **HUD** or **VA** guaranteed loans (sellers can pay, however). On a **conventional mortgage**, points may be paid by either buyer or seller or split between them.

Preapproval Letter Lender's letter giving approval for a mortgage up to a certain amount, contingent upon appraisal of the property.

Prepayment Payment of mortgage loan, or part of it, before due date. Mortgage agreements often restrict the right of prepayment either by limiting the amount that can be prepaid in any one year or charging a penalty for prepayment. The Federal Housing Administration does not permit such restrictions in FHA insured mortgages.

Prequalification Letter Potential lender's or broker's estimate whether the buyer qualifies for a loan before shopping for property. This is not necessarily a firm commitment to give a loan.

Primary Mortgage Market Lenders making mortgage loans directly to borrowers, such as savings and loan associations, commercial banks and mortgage companies. These lenders sometimes sell their mortgages into the secondary mortgage markets such as FNMA or GNMA.

Principal The basic amount of money borrowed. In other words, principal is the amount upon which interest is paid.

Private Mortgage Insurance (PMI) Required on all loans greater than 80 percent. Not needed when you have 20 percent equity in home. With this insurance protection, the lender may be willing to make a larger loan, thus reducing down payment requirements.

Refinancing The process of the mortgagor paying off one loan with the proceeds from another loan.

Renegotiable Rate Mortgage See **Adjustable Rate Mortgage**

Reserves Deposited with Lender (Reserves, Escrow, or Impound Accounts) Funds held in an account by the lender to assure future payment for such recurring items as real estate taxes and hazard insurance, mortgage insurance or homeowners fees. At settlement, an initial amount may have to be paid by the buyer to start the reserve. A portion of the regular monthly payments will be added to the reserve account.

Secondary Mortgage Market Agencies to whom primary mortgage lenders sell the mortgages they make to obtain more funds to originate more new loans.

Security Deed See **Mortgage**.

Seller Buydown The seller pays an amount to the lender so the lender can give the buyer a lower rate and lower payments early in the mortgage term. The seller may increase the sales price of the home to cover the cost of the buydown.

T-Bill (Treasury Bill) Indexes Based on the rates on short-term U.S. Treasury securities issued by the U.S. government in order to pay for the national debt and other expenses.

Term Mortgage See **Balloon Mortgage**.

Title Insurance Title insurance may be issued to either the **mortgagor**, as an "owner's title policy," or to the **mortgagee**, as a "lender's title policy." Insurance benefits will be paid only to the "named insured" in the title policy.

If the buyer is satisfied that the title is clear, he may choose not to purchase a policy for himself. However, he will normally be asked to pay for the lender's policy.

Truth in Lending A statement which is prepared by the lender to set out the annual percentage rate, fees and other credit costs.

Underwriting The decision whether to make a loan to a potential home buyer based on credit, employment, assets, and other factors and the matching of this risk to an appropriate rate and term or loan amount.

VA Loan A long-term, low- or no-down payment loan guaranteed by the Department of Veterans Affairs. Restricted to individuals qualified by military service or other entitlements.

Variable Rate Mortgage (VRM) See **Adjustable Rate Mortgage**.

Verification of Deposit (VOD) A document signed by the borrower's financial institution verifying the status and balance of his financial accounts.

Verification of Employment (VOE) A document signed by the borrower's employer verifying his position and salary.

Part III

Insurance

Insurance is a major consideration in the United States. Part III explores the complex subject of insurance for home, health and automobile.

Home insurance covers the structure, its contents and liability protection. Renter's insurance covers the contents. See chapter 28.

Health insurance is an examination of the many kinds of medical coverage in the United States. Millions of U.S. residents are either uninsured or underinsured. Millions more are covered because of their low income level, governmental affiliation or access to insurance through their employer or through their own financial resources. Chapter 29 provides a major insight into this important aspect of getting settled in the United States.

As with residential insurance, there is a need for protection from the liabilities associated with driving a car or truck in the United States. Chapter 30 offers an introduction to this special insurance need.

Insurance company ratings may be found in publications in local libraries or online. Included are A.M. Best (www.ambest.com) and Standard and Poor's (S&P) (www.standardandpoors.com) and   Weiss Research (www.weissratings.com) and Moody's Investors Service (www.moodys.com). State insurance offices are listed at www.pueblo.gsa.gov/crh/insurance.htm.

Chapter 28 — Homeowners' Insurance

- Insurance programs to provide compensation for damage or loss of your home and replacement of contents

Chapter 29 — Health Insurance

- Insurance Programs to provide compensation for sickness or injury requiring hospital and/or medical assistance and treatment

Chapter 30 — Automobile Insurance

- Insurance programs to provide compensation for losses due to automobile accidents

Chapter 28

Homeowner's Insurance

Homeowner's insurance helps pay to repair or rebuild your home and replace personal possessions affected by perils such as theft, fire or other disasters. The policy may also include such coverage as Personal Liability and Medical Payments which offer protection against a claim or lawsuit resulting from bodily injury or damage to property of others. For information, check www.iii.org.

Overview

Homeowner's/Liability insurance is not generally required by law unless your local government demands it. However, it is highly recommended that all homeowners purchase a policy.

The amount of insurance needed should be sufficient to protect the structure and contents (personal possessions), not the land the house is on. An insurance industry standard is to write homeowner's policies for at least 80 percent of replacement cost.

Homeowner's insurance is available from insurance agents in your area. Get quotes from at least three companies. You can decrease your premium by increasing your deductible. Experts advise against making many small claims.

Ask the insurer about discounts for installing smoke detectors, burglar alarms, storm shutters or other security devices.

Some insurance companies check credit scores. They also check Comprehensive Loss Underwriting Exchange (CLUE) reports. This is a database of homeowners' claims histories.

Check out limitations to determine whether additional coverage is needed on potential damage not covered by the homeowner's policy. For example, items such as jewelry and antiques have value limits within the policy. This coverage can be added at extra cost.

The policy may provide either "replacement" or "cash value" coverage. For example, suppose you bought a chair for $200. Ten years later it was destroyed by a fire If you were insured for actual cash value, you would not be paid $200 by the insurance company but rather a lower figure that reflected the depreciated value of the chair - such as $50. If you were insured for replacement cost, and it cost $250 to replace the chair, you should have been reimbursed $250 from the insurance company.

A homeowner's policy may cover wind-driven rain damage and certain other water damage but not the rising water of flooding. If you live in a flood-prone area, talk to your agent about flood insurance.

Be aware of any changes to local ordinances or building codes that affect the home. Check with your agent because the insurance company may not be responsible for paying the cost of upgrading the home to meet these changes.

Most homeowner's policies cover damage caused by windstorm and hail. However, in some areas, mostly coastal, this coverage is excluded. In these cases, coverage may be purchased through a separate agency such as the Florida Windstorm Underwriting Association which insures property in that state. Contact a local insurance agent or your state insurance office for information.

As a result of toxic mold growing on water-damaged wood in homes and the resultant illnesses, mold-related claims have greatly increased. Many insurance companies have restricted mold claims, stopped writing policies in certain states or increased rates. In some states, add-ons are necessary for those homeowners who want mold coverage and those rates can be expensive.

Most mortgage lenders require homeowner's insurance coverage in the loan contract to protect their interest in the property.

Before purchasing property, especially in high-risk areas, make sure that you will be able to find suitable insurance.

After several years of major disasters, many insurance companies in Florida stopped writing or reduced the number of new policies. Premiums rose dramatically, some as much as 100 percent in a year. Florida homeowners have access to the Market Assistance Plan for help in finding available, but not necessarily affordable, insurance. For more information call Market Assistance Plan (MAP) FL at (800) 524-9023.

Florida has a private risk pool of companies that still write insurance. It is a program authorized by the Florida Legislature to provide residential insurance for people who are unable to find coverage for their homes elsewhere. It is sold through regular insurance agents. Coverage costs much more than the average cost of other carriers in Florida. It is a short-term solution to a crisis caused by natural disasters.

Renter's or tenant's insurance is available for contents of a rented property. Insurance options are also available for the owner to cover the structure of the rented building.

If you are a condominium resident, you should find out exactly what portion of the property is covered by the condominium association insurance and what portion is the homeowner's responsibility.

Make a list of belongings. Save receipts showing the year the item was purchased and the amount paid. Dated photographs or video tapes of your possessions are a good idea. Store all records in a safe deposit box or other secure place.

Inform the agent of any additions or major improvements to the home. Each year, check with the agent and make sure the policy provides adequate coverage.

Homeowner's Insurance Definitions

The following is a list of terms which you are likely to encounter when arranging for home insurance:

Additional Living Expense (Loss of Use) Coverage that pays for the extra, above-normal expenses such as food and lodging incurred while the policyholder's home is being repaired.

Adjuster Person who is licensed and professionally trained to assess damage.

All-Risk Policy or "Special Form" A policy that covers the loss of property or damage that results from any peril, except those that are specifically excluded in the contract.

Cancellation Termination of an insurance policy by the insurance company or policyholder before it expires.

Claim A request for reimbursement for a loss covered by the policy.

Condominium Insurance An owner's insurance which covers any items not insured by the condominium association's policy.

Deductible The amount a policyholder must pay per claim or loss before the company will begin paying. (It is a fixed amount set out in the policy. The higher the deductible, the lower the premium.)

Endorsement A change added to an insurance policy that alters the original terms.

Floater Additional coverage added to an insurance policy to cover special items.

Inflation Guard The coverage limit increases annually by a certain percentage that reflects inflation trends.

Insured Loss A loss (theft, damage) that the insurance policy will pay in full or in part.

Liability Legal obligation to compensate for accidental injury or property damage to others.

Licensed Agents and Companies Agents and companies that are approved and monitored by the state insurance department.

Limit The maximum amount an insurance policy will pay in the event of a loss.

Medical Payments Payment for medical expenses of visitors accidentally injured in your home.

Mobile Home Insurance Policy similar to homeowners' policy but specifically for a mobile home.

Mortgage Insurance Pays off the mortgage on your home in the event of your death.

Peril The cause of a loss to a policyholder (theft, fire, windstorm).

Personal Liability Protects against a claim or lawsuit resulting from (non-automobile) bodily injury or property damage to others.

Premium Regular periodic payments made by the policyholder for insurance coverage.

Renters' Insurance Insures renters' household contents against perils.

Risk The chance of loss to insured persons.

Chapter 29

Health Insurance

I n many countries, the government provides a national health insurance program for all residents. In the U.S., over 1,500 insurance companies offer coverage.

Because of the major differences in approach, this chapter has been included to give readers an insight into their health insurance options when they arrive in the U.S. The following individuals will have particular difficulty affording or obtaining health insurance:

- Self-employed
- Early retirees
- Part-time workers
- Unemployed (including those between jobs)
- Those who lose coverage through death or divorce of a spouse
- Those whose employers do not offer coverage
- Immigrants
- Those with pre-existing conditions

In fact, according to the Census Bureau's 2001 survey, 41.2 million Americans were uninsured. If not for Medicaid and the children's program, the story would have been much worse. A Familes U.S. report found that 74.7 million under 65 years of age were uninsured at some point during 2001-2002, most for at least six months. Of the Spanish-speaking population, only 66.8 percent have insurance. A large number are not poor enough to qualify for Medicaid and not rich enough to afford adequate coverage. Access to health insurance should be seriously considered by anyone contemplating a move to the U.S.

With instability in the health insurance field, you may feel that your health care is out of your control. You cannot be sure of continued access to an insurance company or specific doctors. The costs also seem out of control. The insurance policies, even Medicare, seem very complicated.

To better understand how the system works, examine the four sections of this chapter:

- Health care legislation
- Points to consider when choosing health insurance
- Options for health insurance coverage
- Summary of health insurance definitions

Health Care Legislation

The Health Insurance Portability and Accountability Act

In 1996, Congress attempted to address some of the nation's concerns about health care with a new piece of legislation, the Health Insurance Portability and Accountability Act.

The Act mandates that:

- Tax deductions be allowed for long-term care
- Insurers sell to companies with between two and 50 employees (employers are prohibited from excluding employees based on health status)
- Income tax exemptions for the self-employed increase to 80 percent by 2006
- A four-year experiment be established to test tax-deductible medical savings accounts (MSAs)
- Private health insurance coverage for certain employees and individuals be available and renewable
- Employees not be excluded from a new group plan longer than 12 months (18 months for late enrollees) for pre-existing conditions diagnosed within six months of enrollment (states may impose shorter periods)
- Either:
    - states implement laws that allow eligible individuals who leave group coverage plans to purchase individual insurance policies, <u>or</u>
    - all issuers in the individual market must offer individual coverage to all eligible persons moving from group to individual coverage after exhausting their coverage under COBRA or other state programs
- Employees can take their health insurance eligibility with them when they change jobs, providing the new employer offers coverage. It is their eligibility that is portable, not the insurance
- For individuals moving within the group market or from individual to group, the period of pre-existing condition exclusion is reduced by the total of periods of creditable coverage that individual had

The act does not limit the pre-existing condition restrictions in the individual policies, except for eligible people who move from group to individual coverage. It also does not limit waiting periods that plans may impose before an individual is eligible for coverage, although any waiting period must run concurrently with any pre-existing condition restriction period.

The Act does not limit the premiums. People who cannot afford the premiums are not guaranteed coverage.

Other Legislation

In 1996, Congress also passed two other health reform measures. One requires that insurance companies cover at least 48-hour hospital stays, when requested, for mothers and newborns (96 hours, after a Caesarean Section).

The other measure requires businesses with more than 50 workers to make annual and lifetime caps for mental illness equal to the limits for physical illness.

The Balanced Budget Act of 1997 created Medicare+Choice which provides several additional health care options for Medicare beneficiaries. However, not all options are likely to be offered in all parts of the country.

The "Legal Immigrant Children's Health Improvement Act of 2001" permits states the option of coverage of legal immigrants, regardless of their date of entry, under the Medicaid program and the state's health insurance program.

The "Nutrition Assistance for Working Families and Seniors Act of 2001" restored benefits to eligible lawfully present immigrants regardless of date of entry.

Children's Health Insurance

The Federal government created the State Children's Health Insurance Program (SCHIP) in 1997 to help children whose families earn too much to qualify for Medicaid but cannot afford private insurance. Eligibility and coverage vary among states.

For information, (877) 543-7669 or www.insurekidsnow.gov/states.htm.

Points to Consider When Choosing a Health Insurance Provider

Overview

Without insurance, one serious illness or accident could ruin you financially.

Health insurance coverage is available to groups and individuals.

"Group" insurance provides coverage for a group of people under a single policy issued to their employer or organization with which they are affiliated.

"Individual" (Personal) insurance policies are sold to individuals and families.

Health plans can vary substantially in their organizational structure, depending on who sponsors the plan, what state laws govern them and what their individual contracts stipulate. Rules may be interpreted differently, from patient to patient, company to company and state to state.

Group Insurance

Some employers offer employee benefits that include group health insurance. An immigrant working for such a company is very fortunate. The employer may pay all or a portion of the premiums. Because of rising rates, many companies are passing more of the payments on to employees. Deductibles and co-payments also are increasing.

The self-employed, some with as few as one employee, may be able to find a group policy. Although the cost of these premiums is soaring, a tax credit may be available. The insurance companies require proof that it is a legitimate business. They will likely want to see an IRS Schedule C (Form 1040) Profit or Loss from Business.

You may be able to qualify for group insurance through membership in a club or organization. Insurance companies cannot deny coverage or increase rates to specific individuals within a group.

For various reasons, your employer may change insurance companies. There is no guarantee that your doctors and hospitals will be participants in the new plan chosen by the company. You may have to search for new medical providers.

Many company retirees have continued group coverage after retirement. However, in an effort to save money, there is a trend to employers reducing or terminating their pensioners' health benefits. Those individuals who must seek their own insurance will have a difficult experience. Those who are older but do not qualify for Medicare, will have even more difficulty. If coverage is found, it will be very expensive. A Federal law makes it possible for most people to continue their group health coverage for a period of time after leaving a job. Called COBRA (for the Consolidated Reconciliation Act of 1985), the law requires that if you work for a business of 20 or more employees and leave your job or are laid off, you can continue to get health coverage for at least 18 months. You will be charged a higher premium. You will also be able to get insurance under COBRA if your spouse was covered but now you are widowed or divorced. If you were covered under your parent's plan while in school, you may continue in the plan for up to 18 months under COBRA.

Individual Insurance

Before you search for individual health insurance, call your state insurance department to determine which companies in your community offer policies for individuals.

Independent health insurance brokers should be able to offer options suited to your particular situation. You may have to check with more than one as they don't all represent the same companies.

Anyone with a serious health problem who is unable to find coverage from private insurers should check to see if there is a state fund that guarantees membership. However, these policies may be expensive.

Searching for an insurance company can take time. Many insurers require payments with the applications and may take weeks to process them for approval or rejection. When applying for health insurance coverage, list all pre-existing conditions as required. If the company should find that information is incorrect, they might deny a claim and could cancel the policy. You could be an undesirable health insurance applicant if you have pre-existing medical problems such as:

- Heart disease
- Cancer
- Diabetes
- Epilepsy
- Depression
- High blood pressure

Even if an insurance company agrees to insure a person, it may exclude coverage of a pre-existing condition for a period of time. These pre-existing conditions represent some of the greatest concerns for those looking for individual health insurance. One alien said she would never have moved to the United States if she had known how devastating her health insurance problems would be.

Even a condition as non-life threatening as hay fever could result in a refusal for individual coverage or a plan with limited coverage for allergies. Some policies restrict coverage of a condition if the dosage of the prescribed medication for that condition has recently been changed.

As one agent put it, "Insurance companies don't want to buy trouble." They prefer not to insure anyone who is apt to make a claim. The people who need coverage the most are often the ones who are the least likely to qualify. On the other hand, an insurance executive advised not to be discouraged by a negative response from an insurer. Keep trying. Some companies will try to work with you to provide answers to your insurance problems.

Be aware that almost any insurance could be terminated at any time. Your insurer could go bankrupt or just stop writing policies in your state. If you are an employee in a group policy, your employer will find a new insurer. If it is an individual policy, you will have to find a new one.

You should choose a plan that meets your needs and budget. You need to compare plans carefully for cost and coverage. Make sure it provides the kind of coverage that is right for you. Many companies will give you at least ten days to look over the policy. If you decide that it is not the best one for you, you may return it and have the premium refunded.

Setting Your Priorities

When choosing a health insurance provider, set your priorities by considering the importance to you of the following:

- The insurance company:
  - its reputation
  - level of satisfaction of its clients
  - speed with which treatment approval is obtained
  - financial rating of the company
  - state in which the company is licensed (Does that state regulate rates)
  - accreditation by review organizations

- The participating doctors:
  - which of the doctors on insurance lists are accepting new patients
  - percentage of plan's doctors who are board certified (served residency and passed exam in that field)
  - method of payment to doctors (fee for service or per patient basis)
  - physician access (much of the routine care may be handled by nurse practitioners, not doctors)
  - procedure and cost to see a specialist inside and outside the plan
  - length of wait to contact office or get an appointment

- Preventive medical care:
  - physical examination
  - prenatal care
  - immunization

Additional coverage:
  - prescription drugs
  - mental health
  - sports injuries

Choosing a Plan

When researching, make sure:

- Comparison of insurance premiums is based on the same benefits (Beware, the cheapest is not always the best)
- The doctors, hospitals and other facilities are convenient to you
- Coverage can be arranged if you are out of your town, state, country
- You know if your plan permits the use of any hospital in an emergency
- What symptoms create an emergency situation -
  Suppose you have chest pains, suspect a heart attack and go to the emergency room, only to be diagnosed as having indigestion. Find out whether the company's payment will be based on the final diagnosis or on the fact that a prudent person had legitimate symptoms
- You understand the plan's policy on treatments or procedures that are considered experimental, and therefore, not covered
- You know the plan's review procedures for monitoring your care
- You know the plan's procedures for appealing decisions about your care and whether an outside board is available
- You do not over-insure because you cannot collect on the same claim twice
- You determine co-payments, coinsurance and deductibles
- You know whether pre-existing conditions are covered
- You determine any annual or lifetime limits on coverage of services
- The length of waiting period before coverage begins
- You determine a maximum you will have to pay each year.

For helpful information: www.ahcpr.gov, www.ama-assn.org/aps, www.healthinsurance.com, www.healthgrades.com, www.insure.com, http://hprc.ncqa.org and www.abms.org.

Finding a Doctor or Dentist

Contact the local dental or medical association. You may also find some referral agencies which only refer you to professionals who pay for the service. Be sure you understand whether the service provides the names of all suitable practitioners or only those who subscribe to their referral service.

Try to determine the names of those who specialize in the area of importance to you. Ask health professionals such as nurses or pharmacists which doctors or dentists they see. Friends, neighbors or co-workers may also have suggestions. Consider your first visit as a tryout of the office, staff and medical professionals.

Options For Health Insurance Coverage

Other than paying for medical services yourself, you have three basic options for health care insurance in the United States:

- Option 1 - Medicare
- Option 2 - U.S. Private Insurance Companies
- Option 3 - Insurance Companies Offering Coverage to Non-Citizens and Residents

Option 1 - Medicare

Medicare is a two-part Federal health insurance program for:

- People 65 or older
- People of any age with permanent kidney failure
- Certain disabled people under 65

Medicare is administered by the Centers for Medicare and Medicaid Services (CMS), a Federal agency in the Department of Health and Human Services.

The Social Security Administration provides information, collects premiums, and handles enrollment. Various commercial insurance companies are under contract to process and pay Medicare claims.

Aliens must be lawfully admitted permanent residents and must have lived in the United States for five years before they can enroll in Medicare.

Medicare Structure

Medicare - Part A

Part A is hospital insurance which provides coverage of inpatient hospital care, skilled nursing facility care, hospice care, and some home health care.

Medicare provides coverage within the U.S. only, except in a specific emergency where a Canadian or Mexican hospital is substantially closer than a U.S. hospital.

Medicare - Part B

Part B is medical insurance which pays a portion of doctors' services, outpatient hospital services, some home health care, diabetic supplies, flu shots, mammography and Pap smear, prostate and colorectal cancer screening, diagnostic X-Rays, laboratory and other tests, when they are medically necessary.

Medicare - Eligibility and Enrollment

Those eligible to receive Social Security benefits are automatically enrolled in Medicare when they turn 65. Part B may be declined. The initial Part B enrollment window is seven months starting three months before the 65th birthday. Those who are not automatically enrolled, should be aware that penalties and delays may apply if the deadline is missed. Social Security will help sort out the regulations.

As employees work and pay taxes, they earn Social Security credits. Most people need 40 credits to qualify for benefits such as premium-free Part A Hospital Insurance. In 2003, employees earn one credit for each $890 in earnings - up to a maximum of four credits per year.

Those who do not have the 40 work credits may still qualify for hospital insurance by paying a monthly premium. If the employee or spouse has 30-39 credits, the premium for Part A in 2003 is $174 per person per month. For anyone with fewer than 30 Social Security credits, the monthly premium for Part A in 2003 is $316.

The 2003 premium for Part B is $58.70 a month for all applicants.

If you have low income and limited assets, you may qualify for help paying your healthcare costs.

Choice of Medicare Plans

Medicare beneficiaries may choose to receive their hospital, doctor and other health care services covered by the program, either through traditional fee-for-service or some form of managed care. The original Medicare plan is offered by the Federal government while Medicare Managed Care plans and Private Fee-for-Service plans are offered by private companies.

A company may decide that a plan will be available to everyone with Medicare in a state or only in certain counties. Each year the companies can decide whether to join or leave Medicare. Doctors also may join or leave managed care plans at any time.

Medicare via Traditional Fee-for-Service Plan

This traditional plan, available nationwide, allows patients to be treated by any doctor or hospital. However, the patient should ask if a medical provider "accepts assignment" (accepts Medicare). If they do, they will accept the amount Medicare approves for a particular service. If they do not, you may pay more. There is a limit on the amount that a doctor can bill you. However, medical equipment suppliers have no limits.

Medicare does not limit the premiums that private fee-for-service plans may charge. This means that some enrollees may be paying a premium in addition to the standard medicare premium.

With the fee-for-service plan, the patient must deal with the insurance claims, pay deductible and co-insurance and also pay any Medigap premiums.

The following expenses will be encountered:

Part A (Hospital) Deductible and Co-insurance - In 2003 the patient pays:

- One-60 days, a single deductible of $840
- 61-90 days, co-insurance of $210 per day
- Over 90 days, co-insurance of $420 per day (to a lifetime maximum reserve of 60 days)
- After 60 day reserve is spent, all costs

Part B (Medical) Deductible and Co-insurance - The patient pays:

- A single $100 annual deductible
- Remaining amount after Medicare pays 80 percent of a set fee for medical services (co-insurance)

Medigap Insurance

Most people in the fee-for-service Medicare plan also purchase private insurance called "Medigap" to supplement their Medicare coverage. Medigap is designed to fill in some of the gaps in Medicare coverage, created because Medicare generally pays less than 100 percent of the cost of covered services, and does not cover some services at all.

Medicare via Managed Care

In some states, many Medicare beneficiaries join managed care plans, most of which are health maintenance organizations (HMOs). Medicare prepays the HMOs and enrollees may be required to pay the HMO a monthly premium and/or co-payment and must continue to pay Medicare Part B premiums.

In most cases HMO enrollees do not need Medigap supplemental insurance because their plan may offer all or most of the Medigap benefits. Some plans also provide benefits beyond regular Medicare-covered services such as prescription drugs, some eyeglasses and emergency coverage for travel outside the U.S.

Most Medicare HMOs have become established in areas where Medicare pays the highest rates for their enrollees. Consequently, these plans are not found in every state.

Private Fee-for-Service Plan

This is a more flexible form of managed care available in some areas. A monthly premium may be charged and it will likely be higher than an HMO premium.

Medicare pays a set amount every month to the private insurance company. You pay and the insurance company pays a fee for each doctor visit or service you receive. You may go to any doctor or hospital that accepts the plan's payment. Out-of-network doctors or hospitals require higher payments. You may be able to obtain extra benefits such as coverage for additional days in hospital.

Benefits vary from plan to plan and patients should consider out-of-pocket costs and compare options carefully.

For information on Medicare, contact:

> Centers for Medicare and Medicaid Services
> 7500 Security Boulevard
> Baltimore, MD 21244-1850
> Phone: (800) 633-4227
>   (410) 786-3000
> Internet: http://cms.hhs.gov
>   www.medicare.gov

Information is also available from local Social Security offices and (800) 772-1213.

Option 2 - U.S. Private Insurance Plans

Common Insurance Plans

Some common insurance plans which are available to U.S. citizens and some legal aliens are:

- Traditional Fee-for-Service Payment System
- Managed Care -
  - Health Maintenance Organization (HMO)
  - Point of Service Plan (POS)
  - Preferred Provider Organization (PPO)
- Medical Savings Account (MSA)
- Single Employer Plan

Traditional Fee-for-Service Payment System

These insurance companies collect premiums (payments) from clients and put the money into a fund from which they pay patients' eligible medical expenses. They issue an ID card and instructions on how to make a claim.

If an illness or injury is covered by the policy, the company evaluates the claim, checks the usual charge for the service in the patient's home area, then determines how much it will pay. In some cases the company pays the medical provider directly and in others, it partially or entirely reimburses the patient. There may be a great amount of paper work for the patient after making a claim.

The patient may choose from a range of annual deductibles. After paying the annual deductible, the patient usually must pay a co-insurance portion of the eligible charges to a set maximum (stop-loss). After that maximum limit is reached, the insurer pays to the policy limit. The patient is responsible for any extra charges that the insurer does not cover.

With this traditional plan, the patient may go to almost any medical provider. However, these traditional health insurance plans are becoming more and more unpopular as the costs become more prohibitive.

Health Maintenance Organization (HMO)

HMO networks consist of doctors, hospitals and other health care providers who have joined together in a geographical area to provide a unified service.

The patient or employer pays a fixed, prepaid premium. There is usually no deductible. The amount of the co-payment (usually $10 to $25), if any, will likely depend on the plan and premium chosen. There is little or no paper work to file.

The patient must choose a primary care physician (gatekeeper) who is responsible for directing and coordinating the complete medical care for covered services. Some plans may allow you to select a specialist as a primary care physician. When deemed necessary by the physician, the patient will be referred to other participating providers for X-rays, laboratory tests and hospitalization. Often the primary care physician makes all referrals to specialists. Only the medical providers on the list of that particular HMO may be used. Doctors may join or leave an HMO at any time.

Preventive care, such as annual physical exams and prenatal care, is generally included. A suitable plan should provide satisfactory preventive, chronic and acute care.

The company may have an arrangement for emergency medical care for patients who become ill outside the local HMO area. You should check before traveling and make arrangements accordingly.

You may change primary care doctors but if a limited choice of doctors and less control over treatment decisions is a concern, then an HMO may not be your answer.

Some HMOs are easing restrictions with access to care and some PPOs are becoming more restrictive. At least one HMO no longer requires members to go through a 'gatekeeper' doctor for referrals. The difference in PPO and HMO premiums is narrowing.

There may be less oversight for PPOs than with HMOs. The National Committee for Quality Assurance (NCQA) has accredited many HMOs. They have examined the physician's qualifications and HMO's procedures for services and complaints.

Point of Service Plan (POS)

These are essentially HMOs that allow enrollees to use services outside the HMO's network by paying an additional amount (usually a deductible and co-payment). If a doctor makes a referral, the plan may pay most of the bill. These plans' monthly premiums usually cost more than HMOs' but give you more flexibility.

Preferred Provider Organization (PPO)

PPOs are networks of physicians and other health-care providers who negotiate with employers, insurance companies or other organizations and agree to give discounts when servicing the plan's members. If the patients use these providers, a greater portion of their health-care cost will be covered by the plan than if they use other providers outside the network.

There may be deductibles and co-insurance, similar to a traditional medical plan. If you go to a doctor out of the network, and the doctor bills more than the insurance company's allowable charge, you must pay the excess.

PPOs give patients freedom to go without referral to any provider.

Medical Savings Account (MSA)

MSA is a special account in which a worker, or an employer on his or her behalf, sets aside tax-free dollars for ordinary medical costs while covering major expenses with a high-deductible plan.

Single Employer Plan

Under guidelines of the Federal Employee Retirement Income Security Act (ERISA), an employer establishes a health plan and pays the employees' health care and/or other benefits.

The self-insured employer might hire an insurance company to administer the plan, but the employer is responsible for paying the claims. The plan may also be fully insured by the insurance carrier.

Option 3 - Insurance Providers to Non-Citizens and Residents

Canadians who are in the United States fewer than the maximum number of days per year that are allowed by their provincial insurance plan, receive partial coverage for emergency medical services. To help pay the difference, they must obtain supplementary insurance from insurance companies in their home province.

Anyone who qualifies for U.S. Medicare and Canadian health coverage and spends half of the year in each country, may check the feasibility of using both plans.

U.S. law requires universities to verify that international students on J-1 visas (and their J-2 dependents) have health insurance which meets U.S. law. F-1 visa students are not required by law to have health insurance but the school may have its own requirements.

Since health insurance for non-U.S. citizens may be difficult to obtain, we have included brief descriptions of the health insurance programs offered by some of the more prominent companies specializing in the alien community. Be aware that many of these policies will not cover expenses incurred as a result of any act that is part of a declared or undeclared war. Some cover only emergency care.

Some policies are limited to a short term for those intending to return to their home country, while other plans are renewable for a number of years. Some are available to U.S. citizens, only if they are living outside the United States.

For information and assistance on insurance laws, rights and companies, contact your state insurance office or www.ahcpr.gov.

The British United Provident Association Ltd. (BUPA)

BUPA International is based in England and offers a choice of health insurance plans to any expatriates living outside their country of residence.

They may be found at www.bupa.com or at +44 (0) 1273 208 181.

International Health Insurance danmark a/s (IHI)

IHI is a Danish company which:

- Specializes in comprehensive worldwide health insurance
- Covers sports, leisure, study and work

IHI may be contacted at +45 33 15 30 99 and http://travel.ihi.dk

International Medical Group, Inc. (IMG)

Long- and short-term health insurance sold through independent agents to individuals, families and groups who are living or traveling abroad. For more details check www.imglobal.com.

Petersen International Insurance Brokers

Petersen offers International Major Medical Insurance which provides medical coverage with no time limit for foreign nationals visiting or temporarily residing in the U.S.

In addition, they offer The Bridge Plan which is an individual Major Medical Plan for senior age individuals while in the United States. It covers:

- New U.S. permanent residents waiting for Medicare eligibility
- U.S. residents/citizens waiting for Medicare eligibility (who missed the enrollment period and must wait for the next enrollment opportunity)
- U.S. citizens without Medicare Part A or Part B

Petersen may be reached at (800) 345-8816, (661) 254-0006 or www.piu.org.

Specialty Risk International, Inc. (SRI)

SRI's Inbound Immigrant program is designed specifically for immigrants for up to five years in the U.S.

Contact (800) 335-0611, (317) 575-2652 or www.specialtyrisk.com.

Trent Health Insurance

Expatriate insurance is offered to Canadians, under age 80, who are no longer eligible for provincial coverage because they are residing in another country. Contacts are (800) 216-3588, (416) 340-8115 and www.trenthealth.com.

Health Insurance Definitions

Ambulatory Care Medical services provided on an outpatient (non-hospitalized) basis.

Appeal A complaint you make if you disagree with any decision about your healthcare services.

Application A signed statement of facts that an insurance company uses to determine whether to issue coverage. It may ask questions about the patient's age, medical history, and will become part of the health insurance contract.

Assignment A document signed by a policyholder authorizing a company to pay benefits directly to the policyholder's hospital, doctor or other health care provider.

Assignment (Medicare) Arrangement whereby a doctor or other medical provider agrees to accept the amount Medicare approves for a particular service under Part B and will not charge more than the 20 percent coinsurance after the $100 deductible has been paid.

Benefit Period Period an illness or injury is covered before the patient becomes responsible for all of the costs.

Broker A commissioned sales agent who sells the insurance products of more than one company.

Capitation Method of payment for health services in which a hospital or physician is paid a fixed, per capita amount for each person served, regardless of the actual number of services provided to each.

Carrier Insurance company responsible for processing claims.

Catastrophic Policy Pays covered expenses from an extremely costly illness or accident after a patient pays a high deductible.

Claim Reporting of medical expenses to an insurance company by the insured person to request reimbursement.

COBRA (Consolidated Omnibus Budget Reconciliation Act) Under certain circumstances, after leaving a job, COBRA allows an employee to continue coverage for a period of time under the former employer's plan by self-paying all premiums and an administration fee.

Comprehensive Major Medical Insurance Basic plan plus **major medical** insurance.

Conversion Policy An individual policy that replaces a group policy when a policyholder is no longer eligible for group coverage.

Coinsurance Percentage of covered expenses (in addition to the deductible) that a patient must pay. Many policies require the patient to pay 20 percent up to a certain amount.

Co-payment A specified dollar amount the patient pays, as a subscriber to a managed-care plan, for covered health care services. It is paid to the medical provider at the time the service is rendered.

Cost Contract Medicare patient is allowed to go to providers outside the managed care plan but must pay Medicare's coinsurance and deductibles and other charges, similar to fee-for-service.

Cost Shifting Occurs when hospitals charge paying patients extra money for their stay in the hospital. This offsets the cost of caring for non-paying or indigent patients.

Covered Expenses Services listed on the policy that the insurer agrees to pay for.

Custodial Care Care not requiring a nurse that is provided in a nursing home or private home. Includes help with activities such as bathing, dressing, eating or taking medicine. Care must be recommended by a doctor.

Deductible The specified amount the patient must pay per illness or per year before an insurance company begins to pay - the higher the chosen deductible, the lower the monthly premium.

Disability Insurance Replaces a portion of an employee's income if he becomes disabled and cannot work.

Dread Disease Policy Pays benefits for only a specified illness, such as cancer.

Eligible Expenses Procedures that are covered by the insurance policy and costs that are within limits set by the insurance company - not necessarily the full amount of the medical bill.

Elimination Period Length of time a policyholder has to wait before receiving benefits after a covered illness begins.

Emergency A medical condition, manifesting itself by acute signs or symptoms, which could seriously endanger an insured person's health if immediate medical attention is not provided (interpretation may vary among policies).

Emergency Evacuation Transportation is provided to an appropriate hospital if timely treatment for a serious illness or injury is not available locally.

Exclusion Rider Policy excludes coverage for specific ailments, either for a specified period or as long as the policy is in force.

Exclusions Conditions, services or treatments for which the insurance company will not provide benefits.

Exclusive Agent Sells insurance for one company for a commission.

Expatriate A person who has left the home country and is living in another country for either a short or long term.

Fee-for-Service (Traditional) Patient or insurer pays provider for each service.

Gatekeeper See **Primary Care Physician (PCP)**

Home Country (Country of Residence) The country where a person has a permanent home to which he has the intention of returning.

Home Health Care Intermediate or custodial care received at home from a nurse, therapist or home health aide under a doctor's supervision.

Hospital-Indemnity Policy Covers a fixed limit of daily or weekly hospital expenses.

Hospital Insurance Usually pays a portion of room and board and some eligible hospital services such as operating room use and X-Rays.

Independent Agent Represents several insurance companies who pay the agent a sales commission.

Independent Physician Association (IPA) An organization that manages the contracting and claims process for a single group of physicians organized into a medical group or multiple medical groups. The IPA will contract with various insurance plans for the healthcare provided by these groups.

Inflation Protection Benefits are automatically increased each year by a specified percentage to stay in line with the increasing cost of long-term health care.

Inpatient A person who is an overnight patient of a hospital, using and being charged for room and board.

Long-term Care Care an individual needs in the event of a chronic illness or disability - services may be on an inpatient (such as nursing home), outpatient or at-home basis.

Major-Medical Policy Covers inpatient and outpatient hospital stays and physicians' services. Patient pays a deductible and co-insurance. Policy costs more and provides more benefits than basic policy.

Medicaid State assistance plan for Medicare patients with low income and few assets.

Medically Necessary A medical procedure or treatment that is necessary to maintain or resume good health. Many policies will not pay for non-essential procedures such as cosmetic surgery.

Medicare A national health insurance program for people 65 years of age or older and certain younger disabled people.

Medigap Insurance Policies sold by private insurance companies to help pay health care expenses not fully covered by Medicare.

Nurse Practitioner Registered Nurse who has additional training and is able to perform functions such as ordering tests and prescribing medication.

Outpatient A person who receives medically necessary treatment for injury or illness which does not require an overnight stay in hospital.

Physician/Hospital Organization (PHO) A formal organization in which a physician group(s) join with a hospital(s) in a managed-care venture to provide comprehensive healthcare services.

Physician's Assistant Has advanced medical training but is not a Medical Doctor. May order tests, write prescriptions, and do physical exams.

Policy Limits Specific dollar limits on the amount that the company will pay for each service, per policy period, or lifetime.

Portability Allows a covered person to meet the waiting period for a pre-existing condition only once, even if the individual changes employer or insurer.

Precertification Before the patient receives medical treatment, the insurance company is contacted to get clarification and approval on what medical expenses the company is prepared to cover.

Pre-existing Condition A health condition that existed a specific period before the insurance coverage began. Companies may refuse to cover such a condition and its consequences or may demand a waiting period before covering that condition.

Premium A periodic payment a policyholder must make for insurance coverage. Premiums help the insurance company pay policyholders' claims and other expenses, such as commissions to agents, taxes and administrative expenses.

Prepaid Dental Plan A managed care system which requires periodic premium payments. It involves a combination of co-payments and no-charge benefits. Routine examinations, cleanings and X-Rays are provided at no charge. Major services have predetermined co-payments.

Primary Care Physician (PCP) HMO doctor selected by a subscriber to provide or authorize all medical treatment and referrals.

Provider Any physician, hospital or other institution, person or organization that furnishes health care services and is licensed or authorized to practice in the state.

Repatriation Return of body or ashes to a home country.

Rider An attachment to an insurance policy that specifies conditions or benefits the policy covers in addition to the original contract benefits.

Risk Chance of making a claim.

Risk Contract Medicare patient is generally locked into receiving all covered care through a certain managed care plan or through referrals by the plan. The only exceptions are for emergency charges or POS services.

Skilled Nursing Care Twenty-four-hour, daily nursing and rehabilitative care performed by or under the supervision of a registered nurse or a doctor.

State Insurance Pool State-sponsored organization providing health coverage for residents of the state who, by reason of the existence or history of a medical condition, are unable to acquire or afford coverage for the condition.

Stop-loss Limit Provision which limits the amount of coinsurance to a definite amount per individual or per family.

Supplemental Insurance Policy Provides coverage beyond or in addition to what is provided by a basic policy - not a substitute for basic medical insurance.

Underwriter Either a company that receives premiums and fulfills the contract, or the company employee who decides which applicants they will insure.

Usual, Reasonable and Customary Expenses The most common charge for similar services, medicines, or supplies within the area in which the charge is incurred as determined by the Plan Administrator.

Utilization Review Process for deciding whether to approve treatment or referrals recommended by doctors.

Waiting Period Length of time an insured must wait from the date of enrollment to the date the insurance is effective.

Waiver Agreement attached to a policy that exempts certain conditions from coverage.

Chapter 30

Automobile Insurance

Automobile insurance helps pay for medical expenses and car repairs caused by accidents. It provides financial protection from lawsuits as well as loses caused by uninsured and underinsured drivers. It also helps pay for damage due to theft, vandalism and natural disasters. Check information at www.quotesmith.com.

Determine the auto insurance requirements in your state and be sure to purchase at least the minimum limits of coverage as required by state law.

Factors to Consider When Shopping for Automobile Insurance

The chance of injuring or killing another person is the most serious risk that drivers face. Be sure to have enough liability coverage for your situation.

Although not all companies use the same criteria, several common factors may affect your premium. These factors include: the make of car, age of driver, driving record, car's safety equipment, your geographic location and deductible amount.

When you buy a car, keep in mind that premiums are usually higher for cars that are more expensive to repair, such as sport utility vehicles and luxury sports cars, or for cars that have less passenger protection from accidents. Likewise, cars that are favorite targets of thieves are more expensive to insure.

It is wise to shop around and compare coverages and get price quotes. The cheapest is not always the best. Check with trusted friends or your state insurance office to get names of insurance agents. Get quotes on the internet as well as from agents. Rates may vary widely.

Some insurers may have discounts for cars with automatic seat belts, anti-theft devices and anti-lock brakes.

Check into increasing the deductible in order to reduce the premium.

Safe drivers may save as much as 20 percent off premiums. Definitions of 'safe driver' vary by insurance company but include such factors as no major violations, no more than one minor violation or at-fault accident in the last three years, five years driving experience in the U.S. and so on.

Other insurance discounts may be available such as for seniors, new cars or good students. Insuring your home, car, boat or more with one insurance company should reduce rates.

It may not be cost effective to have collision coverage on your car if it is worth less than $2,000.

Ask the agent about the company's policy for renewal and premium rate increases following accidents.

The agent should provide a binder which should show the name of the agent and insurance company, lienholders (if any), policy effective date and time, and the coverage purchased. It should also be signed by the agent. Read the details and ask questions.

Try to pay insurance premiums by check or money order. Always get a detailed receipt. The policy should be issued within 60 days of its effective date.

Keep copies of all insurance records in a safe place. Have proof of insurance in your car at all times.

If coverage is not maintained on a financed car, the financial institution may purchase insurance to protect its own interest. It may be more expensive coverage and inadequate but the owner will have to pay the premiums.

When changing coverage or companies, make sure that your new coverage is in effect before the old policy is canceled.

Keep track of the names of the agent, the insurance company and the insurance agency. They may all be different.

Auto Insurance for Foreign Visitors

If you don't have a U.S. driver's license, most American insurance companies will not sell you auto insurance. However, a few companies that sell policies to risky drivers may issue short-term coverage to someone with a foreign driver's license. Examples are Progressive Insurance Company and Orion Insurance Company. The premiums are much higher than for drivers with a U.S. license and a good driving record.

If you are going to be in the United States for more than six months, it might be worth while to get a U.S. license, if allowed by your state.

If you are staying with American hosts, you may be allowed to be placed on their policies.

If you are renting a car, you can compare the price of the car rental insurance (collision damage waiver) with regular insurance company coverage.

Automobile Insurance Definitions

The following is a brief description of some of the terms that may be found when searching for an automobile insurance policy:

Accidental Death and Dismemberment Coverage up to the policy limit for death or dismemberment (loss of limb) in an auto accident.

Adjuster A person licensed and professionally trained to assess damage.

Agent Local representative who sells and services insurance policies.

At-fault The person who is charged with causing the accident is considered at fault.

Binder The contract a policyholder receives once an insurance application is signed. It provides proof of insurance until the permanent policy is issued.

Bodily Injury Liability Coverage of serious and permanent injury or death to others when the insured's car is involved in an accident in which he is at fault.

Claim A request for financial reimbursement on an insured loss.

Collision Coverage of repairs to a car if it collides with another vehicle, crashes into an object or turns over. It pays regardless of who is at fault.

Comprehensive Coverage of some losses from incidents other than a collision. Examples could be fire, theft, windshield breakage, windstorm, vandalism, flood or hitting an animal. Homeowner's insurance may cover personal items such as cell phone and camera in a stolen car.

Deductible The amount a policyholder must pay per claim or accident, before an insurance company pays its share. The higher the deductible, the lower the premium.

Dismemberment Loss of Limb (arm or leg).

Exclusion A provision in an insurance policy which denies coverage for certain losses.

Identification Card A wallet-sized card issued by an insurance company indicating policy number and coverage.

Insured The persons and items covered under an insurance policy.

Insurer The company that provides the insurance.

Liability Any legally enforceable obligation.

Liability Insurance Insurance covering the policyholder's legal liability for injuries to other persons or damage to their property.

Licensed Agents and Brokers Certification issued by the Department of Insurance which verifies that a company is qualified to sell insurance in the state.

Limit The maximum benefit that the insurance company will pay in the event of a loss.

Loss An occurrence or event resulting in damage or loss of property, or injury or death.

Medical Payments Coverage of medical expenses resulting from accidental injury, up to the limits of the policy.

Personal Injury Protection (PIP) (No-Fault) A system in which the insured is compensated for his loss according to the terms of the policy, regardless of who is responsible for causing the accident.

Personal Liability Umbrella Policy (PLUP) One umbrella policy gives liability protection to home, auto, boat and other areas of risk.

Policy A written contract between the insurance company and the insured person.

Premium The amount paid for coverage. This is based on the type and amount of policy chosen.

Property Damage Liability Coverage of damage to other people's property.

Rental Car Coverage Collision coverage or property damage liability may apply to rental cars, depending on the terms and conditions of the policy.

Rental Reimbursement Coverage Reimbursement for car rental if insured car is in an accident and not driveable.

Towing Towing and road service up to a certain limit.

Uninsured Motor Vehicle Fee This does not provide insurance coverage but allows a driver to operate a vehicle for a certain period of time.

Uninsured/Underinsured Motorist Benefits for injury or death caused by an uninsured or underinsured driver who is at fault.

Emergency Road Service

Emergency road service offers protection for problems not normally covered by regular auto insurance. This coverage is available from various insurance companies such as Allstate and travel clubs such as the American Automobile Association (AAA).

Among the benefits you receive are:
- A certain number of miles of free towing to a repair facility
- Emergency fuel delivery
- Lock service to get you into your locked car if the keys are left inside
- Flat tires changed
- Battery boosts
- Trip routing and maps

Part IV

Community

P art IV explores some of the important social encounters which often tend to be taken for granted or even overlooked.

The following chapters provide a basic explanation of some important social issues you will meet upon entering your new U.S. community.

Chapter 31 — Primary and Secondary Education

- A brief introduction to the U.S. pre-university/college education process

Chapter 32 — Social Activities

- An overview of some of the customs, organizations, and activities awaiting the new resident

Chapter 33 — Marriage Procedures

- A brief introduction to U.S. marriage laws, customs, and procedures

Chapter 31

Primary and Secondary Education

Each state governs its own education system and each local school board is in charge of the schools in its area. Therefore, regulations and traditions vary across the nation.

School Attendance

When you reside in a school district, the property taxes, which you or your landlord pay, give you the right to send your children to a public school without additional charge. If you choose to send your children to private schools, you must pay that tuition but you or your landlord are not exempt from tax for the public school system.

Generally, school is mandatory for all children age five to 16. Home school is permitted if competent instruction and suitable setting are available.

For home school information see: www.hslda.org/laws/default.asp and www.learninfreedom.org/hsguides.html.

Each district has its own age cut-off date to enroll for a school year. For example, in some school boards, a child must be five years of age on or before September 1st in order to qualify for kindergarten for that school term.

A child's English proficiency will be assessed and classes in English for Speakers of Other Languages (ESOL) should be offered free of charge to those in need of instruction.

In order to register at school the following will be required:
- Birth Certificate (for initial entry)
- Proof of Residence - suggested documents:
  - driver's license
  - current utilities statements
  - county voter registration card

- current deed, rental or lease agreement
- Proof of the required immunizations and physical examinations (unless exempt for medical or religious reasons)
- All information documenting previous education (if transferring)

Not required is a child's Social Security number although schools may request it.

Students must be at school each day and on time. They may stay home because of illness or family emergency but must have a note from a parent, guardian or doctor, explaining their absence.

School times are staggered so that the same buses can transport students to all levels of schools.

Sample hours for schools in one district:

- Elementary   - 9:00 am - 3.30 pm
- Junior High   - 7:55 am - 2:45 pm
- High   - 7:15 am - 2:05 pm

Despite practices such as these, research has shown that teenagers do better academically later in the day. It showed that younger children's peek learning times are earlier. As a result, some school districts have changed their hours so that elementary students begin classes at the earliest time.

The following are two methods of dividing the grade levels:

- Elementary   - Kindergarten through fifth grade
- Middle   - sixth through eighth
- High   - ninth through 12th

- Elementary   - Kindergarten through sixth grade
- Junior High   - seventh through ninth
- High   - 10th through 12th

School Term

School terms vary from county to county. For example, one board may have classes from August 12 to May 23 while another may run from September to June. Many schools are also experimenting with year-round classes.

School Policies and Practices

Normally, textbooks are supplied free of charge but the student is responsible for pens, pencils, and notebooks. After-school activities may involve additional expenses.

The United States Department of Agriculture (USDA) regulates a food service program which provides meals at reasonable or reduced prices, or free, depending on the student's family size and income. Students may also take a lunch from home.

Don't be surprised if students are not allowed to go home for lunch, unless arranged for and picked up by a parent or guardian. Schools claim that they are concerned for the health and safety of the students.

The Pledge of Allegiance to the U.S. flag may occur daily. However, students of other nationalities may just stand quietly.

Prayer in public schools has been held unconstitutional but there is some provision for students to have silent reflection inside or to lead prayers off campus. Parochial schools have religious training and prayer within the school.

Dress Code

Schools usually have standards of appearance for students. Certain clothing styles are not permitted. Some schools are introducing uniforms.

Parent-Teacher Association (PTA)

A good way to learn about your child's school is to get involved with the PTA. This organization supports schools by such activities as fund raising, assisting in class, etc.

Foreign Student

An alien in student status such as an F, J or M nonimmigrant may only attend a public elementary or secondary school, or adult education program for a maximum of 12 months. The student must pay the per capita cost of the education.

Attendance at private schools is permitted but transfer from a private to a public school is not. For details, see Chapter 17, New Legislation.   *Ref: IIRIRA96.625*

Choosing a Neighborhood

The following are some issues which should be considered when choosing an area in which to live.

Boundaries

The school boundaries may not be the same for the three levels so you can't assume that because you live in a certain elementary school area you will automatically be within the boundaries of a nearby junior high or high school district.

Some school boards allow students to attend schools other than in their area. There may be a charge.

Busing

School boards have varying rules on busing. One may provide free transportation to all students who live two miles or more from the school. Another may insist that all students ride a bus no matter where they live. They may be concerned about children crossing busy streets near the school or cars stopped on the busy streets to pick up children.

Public schools in some parts of the country have overcrowding or racial inequality and their school boards redistribute the population. To accomplish that end they bus a number of students to schools outside of their home district. Alternatively, parents have the option of sending their children to private schools at considerable cost. It is wise to investigate school policies to be sure that you are comfortable with the potential school placement of your children before settling in an area.

Typical School Choices

Schools having more applicants than space may hold a lottery to select their students. For more information see www.schoolmatch.com and www.nces.ed.gov.

Private Schools

In addition to public education, there are many private schools throughout the country. These cover diverse levels of tuition and specialization. Many are affiliated with religious groups. See www.nais.org.

Charter Schools

These are independent public schools, designed and operated by educators, parents, educational entrepreneurs and others. See www.uscharterschools.org.

Magnet Schools

These are public schools that specialize in enriched academic areas such as technology and science or the preforming arts. See www.magnet.edu.

School Vouchers

In some states, controversial government-run 'voucher' programs distribute monetary vouchers to school-age children, usually in troubled inner-city school districts. Parents can use the vouchers toward the cost of tuition at private schools, including those dedicated to certain religions. See www.schoolchoices.org.

Tuition Tax Credit and Tax Deductions

In some states, legislation allows tuition tax credits and tax deductions for qualifying families. They may also qualify for private school tuition.

School Readiness Programs

Head Start and Early Head Start provide child development programs for low income pregnant women, children up to age five and their families. See www.headstartinfo.org and www.ehsnrc.org.

Chapter 32

Social Activities

The social side of U.S. living holds many surprises and traditions. This chapter offers a little insight into what you can expect.

Social Customs in the United States

Traditions and social behavior

Many traditions and customs may be different from other countries. For example, here are three common situations that could cause concern for newcomers.

Standing in line is usually very orderly and you will be expected to go to the end of the line and wait your turn. You will find great resentment if you cut in front of others who were there before you.

Social interpretations of being on time vary among the regions of the country. However, you will be expected to be prompt for all business appointments.

It is very normal to say sir or ma'am in the southeast. In fact, it is expected. However, some people in the north are uncomfortable when addressed in that manner.

You will find books in the library that will give tips on social customs. Hopefully, your new acquaintances will be able to answer questions you may have.

Even if you speak English, you will find that some of your words or terms are not known in the U.S. Try other words or phrases with similar meanings until you are understood.

There may also be subtle differences in word meanings. For example, 'vacation' is an annual leave from work. 'Holiday' is a day such as Christmas, President's Day or Thanksgiving when banks and government offices may be closed but rarely are all stores closed. In some other countries, 'holiday' means a period of vacation.

Smoking is becoming socially unacceptable and is prohibited or curtailed in schools, airplanes, most office buildings, most public places and homes. Many states have increased tobacco taxes to discourage smoking.

The Pledge of Allegiance

Many activities start off with everyone standing, facing the flag, holding the right hand over the heart, and reciting the Pledge of Allegiance.

Non-citizens may just stand at attention. The pledge states, "I pledge allegiance to the flag of the United States of America and to the Republic for which it stands, one nation under God, indivisible, with liberty and justice for all". Use of the word "God" is being challenged in court.

Community Activities

Sports, social and public service

Most communities have sports facilities and organized sports activities for children as well as adults.

Social organizations also offer you a chance to get involved with the community. Some examples:

- Churches usually have youth and adult groups as well as worship services
- Private clubs such as tennis, golf and health clubs are available for a fee
- Ethnic groups represent nationalities such as Indian, German, Greek and many others
- Social service organizations exist for all kinds of causes. Some examples are Red Cross, Cancer Society and Big Brothers/Big Sisters
- Such public service clubs as Kiwanis and Lions provide fellowship for the members and social benefits for the community
- Community centers offer classes and clubs

Voluntary Service

Work on a volunteer basis is performed by millions of people in their communities. Volunteers come from all social and economic environments and all age groups right across the country.

If your visa doesn't allow you to work, consider volunteering. It's an opportunity to meet people, get work experience, and find great personal satisfaction. You won't be paid, but you will be getting exposure to U.S. society and culture and gaining the satisfaction of helping others.

You may also make contacts that will be of benefit in the workplace if your status changes and you are permitted to work.

However, it is suggested that satisfying volunteering requires patience, flexibility, independence, and perhaps most of all, a sense of humor.

Examples of volunteer jobs:
- Hospital volunteers staffing mobile libraries, providing support to patients, or offering clerical help
- Police office volunteers involved in administrative work or police-trained citizen forces
- Parent-teacher associations supporting schools and school activities

Examples of other areas where volunteers are needed:
- Alcohol and drug addiction
- Assistance for the elderly
- Animal welfare
- Blood and organ/tissue donations
- Youth organizations
- Disease and disability support groups
- Disaster assistance
- Food and housing for the poor
- Veterans affairs
- Museums
- Art galleries
- Zoos
- Theaters
- Libraries
- Political organizations

You may contact a volunteer organization directly or check the phone book listings for an office such as a Volunteer Bureau or Volunteer Information and Referral service. These offices have information on organizations in need of volunteers.

Organizations "Welcoming" Newcomers

Don't be surprised if you find that some community organizations are more welcoming than others. One organization exists for the purpose of giving new residents in the community opportunities to get together but also has a firm rule that each member must have a Voter's Registration card. This means that all members must be citizens of the United States and have proven residency in that particular county. By definition, that eliminates all newcomers from other nations. It saves time and embarrassment if you determine their rules up front.

Chapter 33
Marriage Procedures

Marriage laws are set by the state where you wish to be married. For information see www.usmarriagelaws.com/search/united-states.htm.

Getting Married

Age

Most states require that both the bride and groom be at least 18 to marry without consent of parents or guardian. In Nebraska and Wyoming you must both be over 19, while in Mississippi you must be 21. A few states allow you to marry before the age of 16, with parents' consent.

You will need to provide proof of age. This can be done with your birth certificate, immigration record, adoption record or passport.

License

You must have a marriage license. The fee varies by location. Some states require a waiting period of three to five days between the application for a license and the marriage. In many areas you must also have a medical examination and blood test before getting a license. Some states require pre-marital education.

Ceremony

The wedding may be a religious ceremony, performed in a house of worship or it may be in the form of a civil ceremony, performed anywhere by a civil official such as a judge.

Some states require couples to announce their intention to marry a certain length of time before the ceremony. Many couples follow this practice, started by the Roman Catholic Church, by having their engagements announced in church for several Sundays. These announcements are called "banns".

Other Marriage Laws

Some states prohibit marriage by persons with certain mental or physical limitations.

If you were not born in the United States, be prepared to show proof of your immigration status.

A common requirement is that both parties freely consent to the marriage. If it can be shown that either the bride or groom was threatened or forced, the marriage may be declared void.

State laws do not permit a person who has been married once to marry again while the first marriage is still in effect. Marrying a second time in such a case constitutes the crime of bigamy, and the second marriage is considered void.

You will need a copy of your divorce decree, if applicable.

Some states acknowledge common-law marriages as valid. These are informal marriages in which the parties have not complied with the legal requirements for a license or ceremony. They simply carry out an agreement to live as husband and wife. The community recognizes them as a married couple. In some states where an agreement to live together is all that is necessary, marriages by mail or telephone may be possible.

A marriage by proxy is common in some countries and may be recognized in some states. In this ceremony, one of the parties is not present. Someone else substitutes as the absent person's proxy.

A marriage is usually considered valid according to the laws of the state where the ceremony was performed. Two persons who are not qualified to marry under the laws of one state may go to another state where the laws are different, have the ceremony performed, and then return. However, the couple's home state may, and often does, refuse to recognize the validity of the marriage.

Same-sex Unions

In December, 1999, the Vermont Supreme Court ruled that gay couples are entitled to all the benefits, protections and responsibilities given by the state to heterosexual married couples. A state law went into effect on July 1, 2000 allowing "civil unions" of same-sex couples.

Despite efforts to secure recognition of same-sex unions, many states have taken up efforts to outlaw them and others have passed laws to ban them.

In September, 1996, Congress passed the Defense of Marriage Act which allows states the option of legalizing same-sex marriages. However, states are not obligated to recognize such unions performed in another state. Most states have defined marriage as the exclusive union of a man and woman. Vermont civil unions are gaining acceptance outside the courts and legislatures. Some couples find the certificate helpful in gaining insurance coverage or hospital visitation privileges.

Same-sex unions, even if valid by state law, would not be recognized by Federal laws such as those governing Social Security and immigration.

Many companies are introducing anti-bias policies and offering health benefits to partners of gay and lesbian employees.

California grants legal rights to same-sex partners registered with the state in such areas as medical decision making, use of statutory will form, employee health benefits, adoption of a partner's child, and the right to sue for wrongful death.

Divorce

Divorce laws vary from state to state. There are various grounds for divorce, such as irreconcilable differences, adultery or extreme cruelty.

It is necessary to have proof of a final divorce decree before remarrying.

It is suggested that you find an attorney who is competent in divorce/family law to help you.

See www.abanet.org/family/familylaw/tables.html.

Part V

Post-Naturalization Rights

As was explained in Book 1, USA Immigration: Getting In, the final step in the immigration process is becoming a United States citizen.

With the responsibilities of citizenship come certain benefits.

Clearly the right to vote is the major privilege of U.S. citizenship. After spending several years on the fringe of American society, many Green Card holders look forward to the final step in their transition–citizenship and the right to participate fully in American society.

Chapter 34 – Voting, Jury Duty and Political Office
- Details about the most cherished rights of citizenship

Chapter 35 – Passport
- Foreign travel as a U.S. Citizen

Chapter 34

Voting, Jury Duty and Political Office

In order to participate in any U.S. election, voters in all states except North Dakota, must register in advance.

Voter Registration

The Federal Registration Act which took effect in 1995, regulates all states. Each state has its own laws about registration and deadlines, but must pass legislation to make the provisions of the act applicable to Federal, state and local elections.

The act requires states to register voters in three specified ways in addition to any other procedures the state uses for voter registration:

- Simultaneous application for driver's license and voter registration
- Mail application for voter registration
- Application in person at designated government agencies, including public assistance agencies and agencies that serve people with disabilities

In addition, many states offer registration opportunities at public libraries, post offices, public high schools and universities. You may leave the completed form with the state agency or public office and the application should be submitted for you. Or, you can mail or deliver it in person to your local registration office. In many states the deadline is 30 days before an election.

To register in most states, you must:

- Be a U.S. citizen (Severe penalties apply to aliens who vote illegally)
- Be at least 18 years of age at the time of the next election
- Be a resident of the state where registering
- Not be mentally incapacitated
- Not be convicted of a felony without civil rights having been restored
- Not claim the right to vote in another county or state

See www.fec.gov/pages/faqs.htm or www.fec.gov.

If you are living outside the United States, you will find Federal Postcard Applications for registration at military bases, U.S. Embassies or Consulates.

There is no statutory requirement to show proof of age, citizenship, or residency, but the Supervisor of Elections has the right to ask, if in any doubt. Therefore, it is advisable to take proof if applying in person.

In about half the states, you must register with a party if you want to take part in that party's primary election, caucus, or convention. You can still vote in general elections and nonparty primary elections even if you have no party preference.

If you do not want to register with a party, write "no party" or leave the box blank. Do not write in the word "independent" if you mean "no party" because this might be confused with the name of a political party in your state.

The application must be signed as an oath that all information is true. If it is not true, you can be convicted of a felony of the third degree.

You should receive a voter's registration card in the mail within a couple of weeks of applying.

If you move from one state to another, you must register in the new state.

When you go to your polling place to vote, you may be required to show photo and signature identification such as a driver's license.

In some states you must vote (e.g. every two years) to maintain active registration.

Absentee ballots are available for voters who will be out of town on election day or are physically unable to get to the voting place.

The county Supervisor of Elections office will answer questions about the registration process. Assistance will also be given to anyone who has a problem understanding the ballot or voting procedures on election day.

Some municipalities may allow non-citizens to vote on such local issues as those relating to school boards.

There is no legal prohibition against a U.S. citizen voting in a foreign election. This was struck down by Afroyim v. Rusk, 387 U.S. 253 in 1980 and in 1986 repealed by Congress.

For voting decision-making information, see www.vote-smart.org.

Jury Duty

The right of a trial by jury is a privilege of every person in the United States. This right is guaranteed by the U.S. Constitution. Therefore, jurors are essential to the administration of justice.

Jury selection methods vary from state to state. The most common sources for the jury pool are voter registration and driver's license lists. Local officials use a computerized random-selection process to choose names from the list to be summoned to court. Summonses are mailed to people's homes.

Jurors must be at least 18 years of age and U.S. citizens. Certain people such as those under prosecution for a crime, convicted felons and lawyers may be disqualified.

Generally, at least in one state, the following may be excused from jury duty if they wish:

- Persons who have been summoned for jury duty within one year
- Expectant mothers
- Parents with custody of a young child, meeting specific conditions
- Persons 70 years or older
- Persons who are responsible for the care of someone mentally or physically incompetent
- Persons with physical or medical impairment

Running for Political Office

Once you are qualified to vote, you may be interested in running for office. Without significant financial resources or a political organization to help you through the process, it is difficult to win an election.

In spite of the stress of public office, it can also provide an exciting, challenging and gratifying life. Many political offices require that you be a registered voter over 18 years of age.

To run for the U.S. Senate, the minimum requirement is 30 years of age, nine years as a U.S. citizen and state residency. A candidate for the House of Representatives must be at least 25 years of age, a citizen for at least seven years, and a state resident. You must be a natural-born U.S. citizen in order to run for President.

A declaration of candidacy is the document you sign in order to start the process of becoming a candidate. You "declare" yourself as a candidate for a particular office and if you wish to run as a party candidate, you "declare" yourself to be a member of that party also.

Running for state or national office usually involves working through a political party.

Check for details with the appropriate level of government where you are considering running.

Chapter 35

Passport

Passports are issued to U.S. citizens and nationals by the Passport Office of the Department of State's Bureau of Consular Affairs. They are a symbol of the government and excellent proof of citizenship and identity.

With certain exceptions, it is against U.S. law for U.S. citizens to enter or leave the country without a valid U.S. passport. Those exceptions include short-term travel between the U.S. and Mexico, Canada and some Caribbean countries, where a U.S. birth certificate plus proof of identity or other proof of citizenship may be accepted.

Ref: Department of State Publication 10542, April, 1998

Due to heightened security, the BCIS recommended that U.S. citizens present their passports even when travelling to Canada or Mexico.

Dual Citizens may be required to show the passport of their other country of citizenship when entering and leaving that country. Use of the foreign passport does not endanger U.S. citizenship. However, U.S. documents should be used when entering the United States, as dual citizens could be fined under U.S. law for entering the country on a foreign passport.   *Ref: www.travel.state.gov/tips_canada.html*

If you are certified to Passport Services by the U.S. Department of Health and Human Services (HHS) to be in arrears of child support payments in excess of $5,000, you are not eligible to receive a U.S. passport. Once payment arrangements have been made, it can take two to three weeks until your name is removed from HHS' list.

Ref: 22 FR 51.70(a)(8)

The Department of State will not refund the fee paid for a passport application when, after processing, it is determined that the applicant will not be issued a passport.

Ref: 65 FR 14212

Some countries require that your passport be valid at least six months beyond your trip. Before traveling abroad, make a copy of your identification pages so that it is easier to get a new passport if the original is lost.

Certain acts or conditions may need to be explained as part of your application. For instance, if, since acquiring U.S. citizenship, you have worked for a foreign government or entered into the armed forces of a foreign state, a supplementary explanation under oath may be necessary. Information is on the back of the application.

Children's Applications

Minors under 14 are not required to sign and do not need to appear. However, all persons, including newborn infants, must obtain their passports in their own names. Both parents or guardians must appear with required documents. If only one appears, written consent from the other must be given or primary evidence that person is sole authority.

Minors age 14 to 17 must appear in person and parental consent may be requested.

Parents may request that their children's names be entered in the U.S. passport name-check system. The Children's Passport Issuance Alert Program (CPIAP) provides:

- Notification to parents of passport applications made on behalf of their minor children
- Denies passport issuance if appropriate court orders are on file with CPIAP

Contact (202) 736-7000 for CPIAP information.   *Ref: 22 CFR 51-70*

Application (in person)

You should apply in person if:

- You are applying for your first passport
- Your previous passport was lost, stolen or damaged
- Your previous passport has expired and was issued more than 15 years ago
- Your expired passport was issued when you were under 16
- Your name has been changed since your passport was issued and you do not have a legal name change document
- You are a minor child age 14 or older

Most official Passport Agencies have an automatic telephone appointment system and will accept only those individuals with appointments who are traveling within 14 calendar days or who need extra time because they require visas. In addition to the normal required documents, you must provide proof of travel (airline ticket, confirmed airline-generated itinerary, or a travel letter from an employer for business travel).

First-time applicants may also apply at one of the designated post offices, clerks of court, municipal offices or public libraries authorized to accept passport applications. Go to http://iafdb.travel.state.gov. to find a local center where you can submit an application. Normally, your passport arrives in the mail within about six weeks.

Expedited service is available for an additional $60 fee. You may also arrange for overnight delivery in both directions. Together, these generally ensure receipt of passports in about two weeks.

One- to- two-day service is available from such private companies as www.americanpassport.com,

It is a good idea to phone your local agency to confirm that they still accept passport applications. Also check what form of payment they require.

Documents required for passport applications include:

- *Forms*
  - DS-11, Application for Passport (fill out but **do not** sign until the passport acceptance agent instructs you to do so)
- *Proof of citizenship - any one of:*
  - previous U.S. passport
  - certified birth certificate issued by the state, county, or city of birth (a certified birth certificate has a registrar's raised, embossed, impressed, or multicolored seal, registrar's signature, and the date the certificate was filed with the registrar's office, which must be within one year of birth)
  - Consular Report of Birth Abroad (Form FS-240) or Certification of Birth
  - Certificate of Citizenship
  - Certificate of Naturalization (Note: Attestation of Naturalization is not acceptable)
  - a delayed birth certificate filed more than one year after birth may be acceptable if it:
    - lists the documentation to create it, and
    - is signed by the attending physician or midwife or lists an affidavit signed by the parents or shows early public records
  - if you do not have a previous U.S. passport or a certified birth certificate, you will need:
    - Letter of No Record issued by the state with your name, date of birth, which years were searched for a birth record and that there is no birth record on file for you
    - and as many of the following as possible:*
      - baptismal certificate
      - hospital birth certificate
      - census record
      - certificate of circumcision
      - early school record
      - family bible record
      - doctor's record of post-natal care

* Note: These documents must be early public records showing date and place of birth, preferably created within the first five years of your life. You may also submit an affidavit of birth, Form DSP-10A, from an older blood relative, i.e., a parent, aunt, uncle, sibling who has personal knowledge or your birth. It must be notarized or have the seal and signature of the acceptance agent.

- *Proof of identity*
  - any of the following if you are recognizable:
    - previous U.S. passport
    - Certificate of Naturalization or Certificate of Citizenship
    - current, valid:
      - driver's license, or
      - military ID: military and dependents, or
      - government ID: city, state or Federal
    - if none of these are available :
      - a combination of signed documents such as a social security card, credit card, bank card or library card, and
      - a person who can vouch for you who must:
        - have known you for at least two years
        - be a U.S. citizen or legal permanent resident
        - have valid ID
        - fill out a form DSP-71 in front of the passport agent
- *Photographs*
  - two identical 2" square passport photographs taken within the past six months in color or black and white (showing current appearance)
  - full face front view with a plain white or off-white background between 1 and 13/8 inches from the bottom of the chin to the top of the head
  - taken in normal street attire:
    - uniforms should not be worn in photographs except religious attire that is worn daily
    - do not wear a hat or headgear that obscures the hair or hairline
    - if you normally wear prescription glasses, a hearing device, wig or similar articles, they should be worn for your picture
    - dark glasses or non-prescription glasses with tinted lenses are not acceptable unless needed for medical reasons (a medical certificate may be required)
  - note:
    - passport photographers should have the specifications
    - newspaper, magazine and most vending machine prints are not generally acceptable
    - you should be able to find digitized photo information at: www.travel.state.gov/digitized_photos.html
    - Passport Services encourages photographs of relaxed and happy applicants

- *Fees*
  - $55 for a 10-year passport (plus separate $30 execution fee)
  - $40 for a five-year passport for persons under 16 (plus $30 execution fee)
  - $60 for optional expedited processing
  - the $30 service fee is paid separately at Passport Acceptance Agencies
  - verify the method of payment required by the application agency you choose
- *Social Security Number*
  - you must provide your Social Security Number

According to the Passport Application, 26 USC 6039E of the Internal Revenue Code requires that a passport applicant provide name and Social Security Number. In turn, Passport Services provides this information to the Internal Revenue Service. According to an IRS spokesperson, the IRS wants to be sure that everyone who has proven to be living and working legally in the U.S.A., is also paying taxes. Any applicant who fails to provide the required information is subject to a $500 penalty enforced by the IRS. Any questions on this matter should be referred to the nearest IRS office.

Application at an Official Passport Office (Except at Honolulu)

When you arrive for your pre-arranged appointment:

- Have your Social Security number and all required documents
- Arrive no more than 15 minutes before your appointment
- If you are 15 minutes late, you must reschedule
- You may go through security including metal detectors
- At check-in/information counter in Passport Office, verify appointment
- Take a numbered ticket with approximate waiting time on bottom
- When your number is called and/or appears on TV monitor, go to window indicated

Application (by mail)

You may apply for renewal by mail if you:

- Are a U.S. citizen with an undamaged passport issued within the past 15 years
- Were over 16 years old at the time it was issued
- Have the same name as on the most recent passport or have had your name changed by marriage or court order and can submit proper supporting documentation (you must apply in person if your name is changed by any other means)

Passports may only be mailed to U.S. addresses.

Documentation and supporting evidence includes:
- *Form*
  - DS-82, Application For Passport By Mail
- *Fees*
  - $55 personal check or money order payable to U.S. Department of State
  - $60 for expedited service
- *Photographs*
  - two identical passport photographs, taken within the last six months
- *Attachments*
  - your most recent passport (it will be returned with new passport)

The completed DS-82 application and attachments should be mailed in a padded envelope to:

National Passport Center
P.O. Box 371971
Pittsburgh, PA 15250-7971

U.S. citizens residing abroad cannot submit this form to this address. They should contact the nearest U.S. Embassy or Consulate for information.

If you wish to use an overnight service that will not deliver to a post office box, send it to:

Passport Services - Lockbox
Attn: Passport Supervisor 371971
500 Ross Street, Room 154-0670
Pittsburgh, PA 15262-0001

Include a prepaid overnight return envelope. Overnight service will not speed up processing time unless the $60 payment for expedited service is also included. Mark EXPEDITE on the envelope.

Information

You may write to:

Bureau of Consular Affairs
Passport Services, Room 6811
Washington, DC 20520

Application forms may be found at www.travel.state.gov/get_forms.html, the Information 900 telephone number, a specified post office or courthouse, a Passport Agency or a U.S. Consulate or Embassy abroad.

The Federal Information Center has passport information at (800) 688-9889.

For general information on passports, to check on the status of an application, or for life and death emergencies, phone The National Passport Information Center

(NPIC) at (900) 225-5674. Callers of the 900 number will be charged 55 cents per minute to listen to the automated messages, and $1.50 per minute to speak with an operator. A live operator is available from 8:30 am to 5:30 pm, Eastern Time, Monday through Friday. A credit card call may be made for a flat rate of $5.50 to (888) 362-8668.

Passport Agencies are located at:

Boston Passport Agency**
Thomas P. O'Neill Federal Building
Room 247, 10 Causeway Street
Boston, MA 02222-1094
Appointment: (617) 878-0900*
Region: ME,MA,NH,RI,
Upstate NY,VT

Houston Passport Agency**
Suite 1400
Mickey Leland Federal Building
1919 Smith Street
Houston, TX 77002-8049
Appointment: (713) 751-0294*
Region: KS,OK,NM,TX

Chicago Passport Agency**
18th Floor
Kluczynski Federal Office Bldg
230 South Dearborn Street
Chicago, IL 60604-1564
Appointment: (312) 341-6020*
Region: IL, MI

Los Angeles Passport Agency**
Suite 1000
11000 Wilshire Blvd.
Los Angeles, CA 90024-3615
Appointment: (305) 539-3600*
Region: CA (all counties south of &
including San Luis Obispo, Kern
San Bernardino) & NV
(Clark county only)

Connecticut Passport Agency**
50 Washington Street
Norwalk, CT 06854
Appointment: (203) 299-5443*
Region: CT, Westchester Co.(NY)

Miami Passport Agency**
3rd Floor, Claude Pepper
51 S.W. 1st Avenue
Miami, FL 33130-1680
Appointment: (305) 539-3600*
Region: FL, SC,USVI

Honolulu Passport Agency***
300 Ala Moana Boulevard
Suite 1-330
Honolulu, HI 96850
Information: (808) 522-8283
Region: American Samoa, Guam,
HI, North Mariana Islands,
various U.S. Pacific Islands

New Orleans Passport Agency**
One Canal Place
365 Canal Street, Suite 1300
New Orleans, LA 70130-6508
Appointment: (504) 412-2600*
Region: AL, AR, GA, IA, IN, KY, LA
MS, MO, NC, OH, PR, TN
VA (except DC suburbs), WI

New York Passport Agency **
Federal Office Building
376 Hudson Street
New York, NY 10014
Appointment: (212) 206-3500*
Region: New York City
and Long Island

Philadelphia Passport Agency**
U.S. Custom House
200 Chestnut Street, Room 103
Philadelphia, PA 19106-2970
Appointment : (215) 418-5937*
Region: DE,NJ,PA,WV

Seattle Passport Agency**
Henry Jackson Federal Building
915 2nd Avenue, Room 992
Seattle, WA 98174-1091
Appointment: (206) 808-5700*
Region: AK,CO,ID,MN,MT,NE,ND,
SD,OR,WA,WY

Washington Passport Agency**
Federal Office Building
1111 19th St. N.W.
Washington, DC 20524
Appointment: (202) 647-0518*
Region: Washington, DC, MD, VA,
Counties of Alexandria, Arlington,
Fairfax, Loudon, Stafford,
Prince William
Also accepts applications for diplomatic,
official and No-Fee passports

San Francisco Passport Agency**
95 Hawthorne St., 5th floor
San Francisco, CA 94105-3901
Appointment: (415) 538-2700*
Region: AZ, CA (all counties
north of & including Monterey,
&Kings, Oulare & Inyo, NV (except
Clark County), UT

*   Automated appointments

**   Customers must make an automated appointment and be traveling within 14 calendar days or need foreign visas for travel. Proof of travel is required.

***   This is a 24-hour information line that includes recorded general passport information, passport agency location and hours of operation and information regarding emergency passport services during non-working hours.

Appendix A

Immigration Forms and Fees

Effective February 27, 2003 (2002 Fees Reinstated)

Form No.	Form Name/Description	Fee
I-17	Petition for Approval of School for Attendance by Nonimmigrant Students	$230
I-68	Canadian Border Boat Landing Permit	$16
I-90	Application to Replace Permanent Resident Card	$130
I-94	Arrival/Departure Record	$6
I-94W	Nonimmigrant Visa Waiver Arrival/Departure Record	$6
I-102	Application for Replacement/Initial Nonimmigrant Arrival / Departure Document	$100
I-129	Petition for a Nonimmigrant Worker	$130
I-129F	Petition for Alien Finance(e)	$110
I-130	Petition for Alien Relative	$130
I-131	Application for Travel Document	$110
I-140	Immigrant Petition for Alien Worker	$135
I-175	Application for Nonresident Alien Canadian Border Crossing Card	$30
I-190	Application for Nonresident Alien Mexican Border Crossing Card	$26
I-191	Application for Advance Permission to Return to Unrelinquished Domicile	$195
I-192	Application for Advance Permission to Enter as a Nonimmigrant	$195
I-193	Application for Waiver of Passport and/or Visa	$195
I-212	Application for Permission to Reapply for Admission into the U.S. After Deportation or Removal	$195
I-246	Application for Stay of Deportation or Removal	$155
I-360	Petition for Amerasian, Widow(er), or Special Immigrant (Amerasians fee exempt)	$130
I-485	Application to Register Permanent Residence or Adjust Status	
	• if 14 years of age or older	$255
	• if under 14 years of age	$160
I-485	Supplement A - Application to Register Permanent Residence	$1,000
I-526	Immigrant Petition by Alien Entrepreneur	$400
I-539	Application to Extend/Change Nonimmigrant Status	$140
I-600	Petition to Classify Orphan as an Immediate Relative	$460
I-600A	Application for Advance Processing of Orphan Petition	$460
I-601	Application for Waiver of Grounds of Excludability	$195
I-612	Application for Waiver of the Foreign Residence Requirement	$195

I-690	Application for Waiver of Excludability	$35
I-698	Application to Adjust Status from Temporary to Permanent Resident	$120
I-751	Petition to Remove the Condition on Residence	$145
I-765	Application for Employment Authorization	$120
I-817	Application for Voluntary Departure Under Family Unity Program	$140
I-821	Application for Temporary Protected Status	$50
I-821A	Temporary Protected Status Employment Authorization	$120
I-823	Application - Inspection Facilitation Program - SENTRI	$129
	Application - Inspection Facilitation Program - PACE	$25
I-824	Application for Action on an Approved Application or Petition	$140
I-829	Application by Entrepreneur to Remove Conditions	$395
I-881	NACARA - Suspension of Deportation or Cancellation of Removal	$215
I-907	Request for Premium Processing Service	$1,000
I-914	Application for T Nonimmigrant Status	$200
	T Status - Each Family Member	$50
N-300	Application to File Declaration of Intention	$60
N-400	Application for Naturalization	$260
N-470	Application to Preserve Residence for Naturalization Purposes	$95
N-565	Application for Replacement Naturalization/Citizenship Document	$155
N-600	Application for Certificate of Citizenship	$185
N-643	Application for Certificate of Citizenship - Behalf of Adopted Child	$145

Appendix B

Affidavit of Birth

If it is not possible to obtain a birth certificate to satisfy entry criteria, it will be necessary to submit alternative documentation. In such cases, it may be acceptable to file an affidavit of birth such as the following sample.

An affidavit should be completed and sworn before a Notary Public. The following sample affidavit is provided as a guideline only.

Affidavit of Birth

I, (name of relative), being duly sworn, do depose and say that:

(1) I presently reside at _____.

(2) I am a citizen of _____.

(3) I was born on _____ at_____.

(4) I am the (state relationship to the person whose birth is being verified)

(5) I know that (name of person) was born on _____ at _____.

(6) A request has been made with the proper authorities for (name of person)'s birth certificate.

_____

Signed

Sworn to and subscribed to before me this _____ day of _____ (YEAR), at _____.

_____

Notary Public

My commission expires:_____.

Appendix C

Information Telephone Numbers

American Institute of Certified Public Accountants	(888) 777-7077
American Immigration Lawyers Association	(202) 216-2400
Attorney Referral Service	(800) 954-0254
Bureau of Citizenship and Immigration Services (BCIS)	
National Customer Service Center	(800) 375-5283
TTY	(800) 767-1833
Fingerprinting information	(800) 375-5283
Form Orders	(800) 870-3676
Community Home Buyer's Program - Information	(800) 732-6643
Department of Labor - Labor Certification Processing	
	(212) 337-2193
	(212) 337-2184
Department of State -	(202) 647-4000
American Citizen Consular Information Line	(800) 529-4410
National Visa Center(Immigrant Visa Inquiries)	(603) 334-0700
Nonimmigrant Visa Appointments (fee)	(888) 840-0032
Nonimmigrant Visa Appointment Cancellations	(888) 611-6676
Office of Citizen Consular Services	(202) 647-4000
Public Information	(202) 647-6575
Visa Information	(202) 663-1225
Visa Information - Officer - 2-4 pm Eastern Time	(202) 663-1213
Visa Lottery Hotline	(202) 331-7199
Visa Priority Date Information	(202) 663-1541
Equifax - Credit Report	(800) 685-1111
Experian - Credit Report	(888) 397-3742
Fannie Mae Lenders	(800) 732-6643
FBI - Fingerprint inquiry	(304) 625-5590
Federal Election Commission	(800) 424-9530
Federal Information Center	(800) 688-9889
Freddie Mac Lenders	(800) 373-3343

Green Card Renewal Information	(800) 375-5283
Government Printing Office	
Superintendent of Documents	(202) 512-1800
Fax:	(202) 512-2250
HUD Housing Hotline - Fair Housing Laws	(800) 669-9777
International Association for Financial Planning	(800) 945-4237
Internal Revenue Service (IRS)	
Information	(800) 829-1040
Tax Forms	(800) TAX-FORM
Medicare	(800) 633-4227
O*Net - National Center for O*Net Development	(919) 733-7917
National Flood Insurance Program	(800) 638-6620
Passport Information Center (Fee)	(900) 225-5674
(Fee)	(888)362-8668
Selective Service	(847) 688-6888
Social Security	(800) 772-1213
Visa Lottery Hot Line	(202) 331-7199
Visa Priority Date Information Line	(202) 663-1541

Appendix D

Credential Evaluators

Employment related visas often require analysis of education and work experience to prove that the applicant's background is relevant to the position offered.

The BCIS may ask for an academic credential evaluation from an approved consulting service to determine the equivalent educational level.

Many post-secondary institutions and professional associations prepare their own assessments.

However, if you need assistance, the following is a list of some of the organizations that evaluate credentials. They are members of the National Association of Credential Evaluation Services (NACES) and affiliate members of the American Association of Collegiate Registrars and Admissions Officers (AACRAO). For a complete list of NACES members see www.naces.org. It would be wise to check with BCIS to be sure that they require a professional evaluation and will accept the appraisal of the specific one you choose, before hiring the company.

> Center for Applied Research, Evaluation and Education, Inc
> P.O. Box 20348
> Long Beach CA 90801
> Phone: (562) 430-1105
> Email: evalcaree@earthlink.net

> Education Evaluators International, Inc.
> P.O. Box 5397
> Los Alamitos CA 90720-5397
> Phone: (562) 431-2187
> FAX: (562) 493-5021
> Email: garyeei@ix.netcom.com

> Education International, Inc
> 29 Denton Road
> Wellesley MA 02482
> Phone: (781) 235-7425
> FAX: (781) 235-6831
> Email: edint@gis.net

Educational Credential Evaluators, Inc.
      P.O. Box 514070
      Milwaukee WI 53203
      Phone: (414) 289-3400
      FAX: (414) 289-3411
      Email: eval@ece.org

Foundation for International Services, Inc.
21540 30th Drive S.E., Suite 320
Bothell, WA 98021
      Phone: (425) 487-2245
      Fax: (425) 487-1989
      Email: info@fis-web.com

International Consultants of Delaware, Inc.
109 Barksdale Professional Center
Newark DE 19711
      Phone: (302) 737-8715
      FAX: (302) 737-8756
      Email: icd@icdel.com

International Education Research Foundation, Inc.
P.O. Box 3665
Culver City, CA 90231
      Phone: (310) 258-9451
      FAX: (310) 342-7086
      Email: info@ierf.org

World Education Services, Inc.
P.O. Box 745
New York, NY 10113-0745
      Phone: (800) 937-3895
                                      (212) 966-6311
      Email: info@wes.org

The documents you submit must be in English, or be translated accurately. The translator doesn't have to be a professional, but should be competent in both languages.

The translator must attach the following statement:

"I certify that I am competent to translate this document from (insert foreign language) to English and that this translation is accurate and complete to the best of my knowledge and ability."

Signature

Date

Appendix E

O*Net OnLine Database

In its July 31, 2001 announcement of the regulations for the annual DV Green Card Lottery, the State Department advised that it is amending its regulations as they apply to the use of the Dictionary of Occupational Titles which is no longer current. Its Consular Officers will now make determinations regarding work experience based on the Department of Labor's O*Net OnLine database which is aligned to the new Standard Occupational Classification (SOC) system. This appendix is included as an introduction to O*Net.   *Ref: 66 FR 39435*

The Department of Labor states that O*Net, the Occupational Information Network, is a comprehensive database of worker skills and job characteristics. As the replacement for the Dictionary of Occupational Titles, O*Net will be the nation's primary source of occupational information which will provide a common language for defining and describing occupations.

The database contains information about knowledge, skills, abilities (KSAs), interests, general work activities (GWAs), and work context.

The O*Net may be used by industry and government to:
- Align educational and job training curricula with current workplace needs
- Create occupational clusters based on KSA information
- Develop job descriptions or specifications, job orders, and resumes
- Facilitate employee training and development activities
- Develop and supplement assessment tools to identify worker attributes
- Structure compensation and reward systems
- Evaluate and forecast human resources requirements
- Design and implement organizational development initiatives
- Identify criteria to establish performance appraisal and management systems
- Identify criteria to guide selection and placement decisions
- Explore career options that capitalize on individual KSA profiles
- Target recruitment efforts to maximize person-job-organizational fit
- Improve vocational and career counselling efforts

O*Net OnLine provides individuals with user-friendly access to O*Net occupational information and offers the opportunity to:
- Find occupations to explore
- Search for occupations that use their skills
- Look at related occupations

- View occupational snapshots including the most important characteristics of the worker and requirements of the work
- View details of occupations, such as skills, knowledge, interests, and activities
- Use crosswalks to find corresponding occupations in other classification systems, and
- Connect to other on-line career information resources

In short, O*Net has the goal of straightforward common language designed to improve the quality of dialogue among people who communicate about jobs in the economy, generate employment statistics, and develop education and training programs. Employer hiring requirements will have the same meaning for human resources practitioners, workers, education and training developers, program planners and students.

Given the role of the Department of Labor in the labor certification processes, it is natural that DOL would utilize the O*Net database, their newest and most detailed job vetting tool.

O*Net-SOC Occupations - with Selected Sample Occupations

11-0000   Management Occupations
- *Executive, elected official, marketing, public relations, information systems, human resources, purchasing, agriculture, construction, engineering, food, medical, natural sciences, real estate, community service, gaming, funeral*
- Chief executives, directors, managers, legislators, purchasing, agents, business managers, appraisers, adjusters, specialists

13-0000   Business and Financial Operations Managers Occupations
- *Compliance, insurance, emergency management, management, financial, tax, human resources*
- Agents, business managers, appraisers, adjusters, specialists, analysts, accountants, auditors

15-0000   Computer and Mathematical Science Occupations
- *Computers, information, systems, mathematics, research*
- Scientists, programmers, engineers, support specialists, analysts, administrators, actuaries, mathematicians, analysts, statisticians

17-0000   Architecture and Engineering Occupations
- *Architecture, landscape, engineering, health and safety, marine, mining, petroleum*
- Architects, surveyors, engineers, drafters, technicians, cartographers

19-0000   Life, Physical, and Social Science Occupations
- *Animal, food, agricultural, biology, forestry, astronomy, environment, market research, psychology, nuclear, social science*
- Scientists, foresters, astronomers, physicists, economists, analysts, technicians, planning aides, geographers, historians, sociologists

21-0000   Community and Social Services Occupations
- *Substance abuse, behavioral disorders, family, child, mental health, social, health, religious education*
- Counselors, therapists, social workers, educators, assistants, clergy

23-0000   Legal Occupations
- *Courts, title companies*
- Lawyers, judges, arbitrators, reporters, clerks, title examiners, support workers, paralegal assistants

25-0000   Education, Training, and Library Occupations
- *Postsecondary, secondary, elementary, kindergarten, museums, libraries*
- Teachers, teaching assistants, instructors, archivists, curators, librarians

27-0000   Arts, Design, Entertainment, Sports, and Media Occupations
- *Stage, motion pictures, television, radio, art, fashion, sports, interiors*
- Directors, artists, animators, designers, dancers, actors, photographers, producers, technicians, writers, editors, announcers, musicians

29-0000   Healthcare Practitioner and Technical Occupations
- *Medical, emergency medical, dental, pharmacy, laboratories, optical*
- Medical doctors, dentists, chiropractors, therapists, pathologists, nurses, technicians, hygienists, audiologists, veterinarians, opticians, trainers

31-0000   Healthcare Support Occupations
- *Home health, nursing, therapy, massage, dental, medical, veterinary*
- Occupational and physical therapists, aides, orderlies, pharmacy aides

33-0000   Protective Service Occupations
- *Correctional institutions, fire, police, fish and game, parking, animals*
- Managers, supervisors, officers, detectives, fire fighters, wardens, lifeguards, ski patrols, security guards, gaming investigators

35-0000   Food Preparation and Servicing Related Occupations
- *Food and beverage preparation and serving, related workers*
- Managers, supervisors, cooks, bartenders, hosts, servers, attendants

37-0000   Building and Grounds Cleaning and Maintenance Occupations
- *Housekeeping, janitorial, pest control, landscaping*
- Managers, supervisors, janitors, housekeepers, grounds maintenance

39-0000   Personal Care and Service Occupations
- *Gaming, funeral, amusement, personal care, travel, fitness, child care*
- Managers, supervisors, trainers, barbers, guides, attendants

41-0000   Sales and Related Occupations
- *Retail, non-retail, advertising, insurance, supplies, service, parts, models*
- Managers, supervisors, cashiers, clerks, salespersons, agents, brokers

43-0000   Office and Administrative Support Occupations
- *Office, court, postal, customer service, cargo, legal, medical*
- Managers, supervisors, tellers, interviewers, operators, clerks, assistants

45-0000   Farming, Fishing, and Forestry Occupations
- *Agricultural, horticultural, logging, hunting, fishing*
- Managers, supervisors, inspectors, workers, trappers

47-0000   Construction and Extraction Occupations
- *Building and highway construction, oil and gas*
- Managers, supervisors, installers, painters, laborers, drillers

49-0000   Installation, Maintenance, and Repair Occupations
- *Telecommunications, avionics, automotive, heating, industrial, camera*
- Managers, supervisors, mechanics, technicians, installers, repairers

51-0000   Production Occupations
- *Air, food, electrical, assembly, machine operators, printing, textile, woodworking, water, chemical, gas, medical, painting*
- Managers, supervisors, inspectors, operators, assemblers, laborers

53-0000   Transportation and Material Moving Occupations
- *Air, sea, rail, road, gas*
- Managers, supervisors, pilots, engineers, driver, captains, sailors, crews, laborers, packagers, operators

55-0000   Military Specific Occupations
- *Air, armored, infantry, radar, special forces*
- Officers, crew

More details may be obtained on the internet at the O*Net web site at http://online.onetcenter.org/database.html. Information may also be obtained from the National Center of O*Net Development by calling (919) 733-7917.

Appendix F

Department of Labor - Employment and Training Administration Foreign Labor Certification Contacts - ETA Regional Offices

Region 1   J.F. Kennedy Federal Building
(Boston   Room E-350
Regional   Boston, MA 02203
Office)   Phone: (617) 788-0152
             Telephone Information: (617) 788-0171
Serving: Connecticut, Maine, Massachusetts, Maine, New Hampshire, Rhode Island, and Vermont.

Region 1   201 Varick Street
(New York   Room 755
Regional   New York, NY 10014-4811
Office)   Phone: (212) 337-2184
             Telephone Information: (212) 337-2193
Serving: New York, New Jersey, Puerto Rico, and the Virgin Islands.

Region 2   The Curtis Center
            1705 Independence Mall West
            Suite 825 East
            Philadelphia, PA 19106-3315
            Phone: (215) 861-5200
            Fax: (215) 861-5262
            Telephone Information: (215) 861-5250
Serving: Delaware, Maryland, Pennsylvania, Virginia, West Virginia, and the District of Columbia.

Region 3   Atlanta Federal Center
            61 Forsyth Street, S.W.
            Suite 6M12
            Atlanta, GA 30303
            Phone: (404) 562-2092
            Fax: (404) 562-2149
            Telephone Information: (404) 562-2131
Serving: Alabama, Florida, Georgia, Kentucky, Mississippi, North Carolina, South Carolina, and Tennessee.

Region 4   525 Griffin Street
(Regional   Room 317
Office)   Dallas, TX 75202
              Phone: (214) 767-4989
              Fax: (214) 767-4788
              Telephone Information: (214) 767-4975
Serving: Arkansas, Colorado, Louisiana, Montana, New Mexico, North Dakota, Oklahoma, South Dakota, Texas, Utah and Wyoming.

Region 4   1999 Broadway
(Affiliate   Suite 1780
Office)   P.O. Box 46550
              Denver, CO 80202-5716
              Phone: (303) 318-8831
              Fax: (303) 318-8930
Note: Regional Office functions now served by Dallas, Texas

Region 5   230 South Dearborn Street
(Chicago   Room 605
Office)   Chicago, IL 60604
              Phone: (312) 596-5400
              Fax: (312) 596-5410
              Telephone Information: (312) 353-2595
Serving: Illinois, Indiana, Michigan, Minnesota, Ohio, and Wisconsin.

Region 5   1100 Main Street
(Kansas   Suite 1050
City   Kansas City, MO 64105-2112
Office)   Phone: (816) 502-9000
              Fax: (816) 502-9002
              Telephone Information: (816) 426-3880
Serving: Iowa, Kansas, Missouri, and Nebraska.

Region 6   Mail address - P.O. Box 193767
(Southern   Courier address - 71 Stevenson Street
States)   Room 820
              San Francisco, CA 94119-3767
              Phone: (415) 975-4601
              Fax: (415) 975-4660
              Telephone Information: (415) 975-4617
Serving: Arizona, California, Guam, Hawaii, Nevada, American Samoa, Guam, Marshall Islands, Micronesia, and Saipan.

Region 6   1111 Third Avenue
(Northern   Suite 815
States)   Seattle, WA 98101-3212
                Phone: (415) 975-4601
                Fax: (415) 975-4660
                Telephone Information: (415) 975-4617
Serving: Alaska, Idaho, Oregon, and Washington.

Notes: Regional Office Information Retrieval System is available in ETA Offices.

            A complete list of ETA offices may be found at:
            www.doleta.gov/regions

            LCAs may be filed online at:
            www.lca.doleta.gov/

Glossary

Accompanying Relatives Spouse and unmarried children under age 21 coming with visa holder

Adjudicate To legally judge a document or case

Admission/Admitted Lawful entry of an alien into the United States after inspection and authorization by an immigration officer

Advance Parole Person is granted advance parole if it is necessary to leave the U.S. temporarily before getting a Green Card

Alien Any person in the United States who is not a citizen or a national is an "alien"

The three broad classifications of aliens include:

- **unlawful, unauthorized, undocumented or illegal aliens** who have entered illegally or violated the terms of their visas
- **nonimmigrants** who have entered on temporary visas with limited rights
- **resident-aliens** or **permanent residents** who have received Green Cards and can live and work permanently in the United States

Ref: INS ER 806 3-8-94

Alien Registration Receipt Card Former name of Permanent Resident Card

Appeal To request a new hearing in a higher court

Application A formal request for immigration admission status or for permission or compliance in connection with a government regulation

Asylee An alien who applies for and receives asylum within the United States and must prove a well-founded fear of persecution or physical danger upon return to the home country

Attestation Sworn statement made by employer assuring the U.S. Department of Labor that the job offer meets DOL specifications to protect the U.S. labor force

Attestation of Citizenship Temporary document proving that the alien has been sworn in as a citizen. Does not replace the Certificate of Citizenship

Beneficiary Person who is being sponsored in a petition for a green card or visa

Border Crossing Cards Special, limited approval for Canadians and Mexicans who have legal status to cross the border on a regular basis

Citizens According to the Constitution of the U.S., all people born in the United States and its territories are U.S. citizens except children of foreign diplomats born in the United States who are excluded

All people naturalized in the U.S. are citizens. Also, children born abroad who have at least one U.S. citizen parent may be eligible to claim U.S. citizenship by a form of inheritance or derivation

Consul Department of State representative abroad, responsible for processing nonimmigrant and immigrant applications. A Consul also represents the interests of citizens abroad who are currently within their jurisdiction

Consulate Office of the Consul and government representatives (branch office of U.S. Embassy)

Dual National A person who is a citizen of two countries at the same time

Embassy Office of the Ambassador and representatives of a government in a foreign country, traditionally based in a capital city

ESL English as a Second Language. Students are taught English skills from basic to advanced. At the advanced level they should be able to make oral presentations at university and write essays and reports

Excludability Condition preventing a visa applicant from being allowed into the United States

Foreign National A person who is a citizen of a country other than where residing

Green Card Term used to describe an I-551 Permanent Resident Card issued to permanent resident aliens

High Commission Office of the representative of a commonwealth government in the capital city of another commonwealth country

Immigrant An alien who has a permanent visa allowing him or her to live in the United States permanently (Permanent Resident Alien)

Immigrant Visa Entry permit issued to a permanent resident alien. The Green Card is not issued until after entry into the U.S.

Inadmissable Alien Any alien present in the United States without being admitted or paroled, or who arrives in the United States at any time or place other than as designated by the Secretary of Homeland Security

Labor Certification Official acceptance by the DOL that no U.S. residents are available for the job offered to a foreigner

Legal Alien An alien who has permission to live in or work in the United States

National Could be either a citizen of the United States or a person, who although not a citizen of the United States, still owes permanent allegiance to the country

National Visa Center (NVC) Department of State unit which receives and processes Green Card applications and sends out forms

Naturalization A process which converts permanent resident aliens into citizens

Nonimmigrant Alien An alien who has a visa giving permission to travel, study or work for a fixed period of time

Parolee Someone who does not meet the technical visa requirements but is allowed to come to the United States, without a visa, for humanitarian purposes

Petition Proves eligibility for a green card or visa

Permanent Resident Alien An alien who has received an immigrant visa from the INS or BCIS and has been granted permission to live and work permanently in the United States

Permanent Resident Card Green Card, formerly called Alien Registration Receipt Card

Petitioner A person who sponsors a foreign national for a Green Card or visa

Political Asylum Status is granted to someone who has entered the United States as a nonimmigrant or illegal alien and has a well-founded fear of persecution in the home country

Preconceived Intent Process of applying for a visa but intending to change that status in the future to a more favorable one

Preference Family-sponsored and Employment-Based visas each have several preference categories, with close relatives of U.S. citizens and aliens with extraordinary qualifications having the highest preference

Priority Date Date of first filing of an application for a Green Card

Qualified Alien Category created by 1996 welfare reform consists of lawful permanent residents, refugees (including conditional entrants), asylees, and persons who have had their deportation withheld, parolees admitted for at least one year, and certain battered aliens and alien parents of battered children; all other categories are considered "not qualified aliens"

Quota Number of immigrants who can enter the United States in a year, including a certain number from any particular country

Refugee Person who has a well-founded fear of persecution in the home country, receives permission to come to the United States in refugee status before arriving

Regional Certifying Officer The official (in the Employment and Training Administration) (ETA) in a Department of Labor regional office who is authorized to act on labor certifications and employment attestations on behalf of the Secretary of Labor

Registration Selected entry in a Green Card (diversity) lottery program

Sponsor (in relation to a sponsored alien) means an individual who executes an Affidavit of Support with respect to the sponsored alien, is a citizen or national of the United States or a lawfully admitted permanent resident and meets all criteria of sponsorship

Status Privileges given to aliens who are allowed entry in the United States

Temporary Visa (Nonimmigrant visa) allows an foreigner to enter the United States for a specific purpose and for a certain length of time

TOEFL Test of English as a Foreign Language is a test to measure reading and listening comprehension and writing recognition

TSE Test of Spoken English

TWE Test of Written English

Undocumented Alien An alien whose visa has expired or who has entered the country illegally

Visa An entry document, either on a separate piece of paper or in a passport issued outside the U.S.

Visa Number A number which is immediately available to an intending immigrant for entry in a pre-selected preference category

Visa Waiver Program Tourists from certain countries may come for 90 days without a visa

References

Books

Carroll, Andrew. *Volunteer USA.* New York: Ballantine Books, 1991.

Cutright, Melitta J. *The National PTA Talks to Parents: How to Get the Best Education for Your Child.* New York: Doubleday, 1989.

Daughters of the American Revolution. *DAR Manual for Citizenship.* rev. ed. Washington, DC: National Society, Daughters of the American Revolution, 1993.

Dresser, Norine. *Multicultural Manners.* New York: John Wiley & Sons, 1996.

Harwood, Bruce M. *Real Estate Principles.* 4th ed. Englewood Cliffs, NJ: Prentice-Hall, 1986.

Hogue, Kathleen; Jensen, Cheryl; and McClurg Urban, Kathleen. *The Complete Guide To Health Insurance: How to Beat the High Cost of Being Sick.* New York: Walker Publishing, 1988.

Government Publications

Code of Federal Regulations. Title 8. Aliens and Nationality. Washington, DC, 1997.

_____. Title 20. Employees' Benefits. Washington, DC, 1996.

_____. Title 22. Foreign Relations. Washington, DC, 1996.

Federal Register. Vol. 57, No. 181. 20 CFR Part 655, September 17, 1992.

_____. Vol. 59, No. 243. 20 CFR Part 655. 29 CFR Part 507, December 20, 1994.

_____. Vol. 60, No. 12. 20 CFR Part 655, 29 CFR Part 506, January 19, 1995.

Florida Department of Insurance. Consumer Outreach and Education. *Automobile Insurance Consumers' Guide.* Tallahassee, FL, 1997.

_____. *Health Insurance Consumers' Guide.* Tallahassee, FL, 1997.

_____. *Health Maintenance Organization Consumers' Guide.* Tallahassee, FL, 1997.

_____. *Insuring Your Home Consumers' Guide.* Tallahassee, FL, 1997.

Public Law. *Health Insurance Portability and Accountability Act.* (PL 104-191, August 21, 1996).

_____. *Illegal Immigration Reform and Immigrant Responsibility Act of 1996.*

(PL 104-208, September 30, 1996).

_____. *Immigration and Nationality Act of 1952.* (PL 82-414, 1952).

_____. *Immigration Act of 1990.* (PL 101-649, November 29, 1990).

_____. *International Organizations Immunities Act.* (PL 79-291, 1946).

_____. *North American Free Trade Agreement Implementation Act.* (PL 103-182, December 8, 1993).

Selective Service System. *Information for Registrants.* Fort Worth, TX, 1988.

U.S. Code, Title 8. Aliens and Nationality. Washington, DC, 1994.

_____. Title 22. Foreign Relations and Intercourse. Washington, DC, 1994.

_____. Title 29. Labor. Washington, DC, 1994.

U.S. Department of Health and Human Services. Health Care Financing Administration. *Managed Care Plans.* Washington, DC. Publication No. CDFA-02195.

_____. *Your Medicare Handbook.* Baltimore, MD. Publication No. HCFA-10050, 1996.

U.S. Department of Health and Human Services. Health Care Financing Administration and the National Association of Insurance Commissioners. *Guide to Health Insurance for People with Medicare.* Baltimore, MD. Publication No. HCFA-02110, 1996.

_____. Social Security Administration. Agreement on Social Security Between the U.S. and *Canada.* Washington, DC. Publication No. 05-10198, 1990.

_____. *Medicare.* Baltimore, MD. Publication No. 05-10043, 1996.

_____. *Social Security–Household Workers.* Washington, DC. Publication No. 05-10021, 1997.

_____. *Social Security–How You Earn Credits.* Washington, DC. Publication No. 05-10072, 1997.

_____. *Social Security Numbers for Newborns.* Washington, DC. Publication No. 05-10023, 1995.

_____. *Social Security–Understanding the Benefits.* Washington, DC. Publication No. 05-10024, 1997.

_____. *Social Security: When You'll Get Your Benefit.* Washington, DC. Publication No. 05-10031, 1997.

_____. *Your Social Security Number.* Washington, DC. Publication No. 05-10002, 1993.

_____. *Your Social Security Payments While You Are Outside The United States.* Washington, DC. Publication No. 05-10137, 1995.

U.S. Department of Housing and Urban Development. *The HUD Home Buying Guide.* Washington, DC. Publication No. HUD-1507-SFPD, 1997.

_____. Office of Housing. *Settlement Costs.* Washington, DC. Publication No. HUD-398-H(3), 1997.

U.S. Department of Justice. Immigration and Naturalization. *Service Law Books.*

_____. *Naturalization Requirements and General Information.* Form N-17, 1992.

_____. Eastern Regional Office. *Basic Guide to Naturalization and Citizenship.* Burlington, VT. Publication No. ER 721.

_____. *Guide to the Immigration and Naturalization Service.* Burlington, VT. Publication No. ER 806. March 8, 1994.

U.S. Department of Labor. Employment and Training Administration. *Policy Guidance on Alien Labor Certification Issues.* Field Memorandum 48-94. May, 1994.

_____. *Instructions for Filing Applications for Alien Employment Certification for Permanent Employment in the United States.* Washington, DC.

_____. Pension and Welfare Benefits Administration. *Health Benefits Under the Consolidated Omnibus Budget Reconciliation Act (COBRA).* Washington, DC.

U.S. Department of State. Bureau of Consular Affairs. *Passports: Applying for them the Easy Way.* Washington, DC. Publication No. 10049.

_____. *Foreign Affairs Manual.* 22 CFR, Vol. 9, Sub chapter E - Visas, April 1, 1997.

U.S. Department of the Treasury. U.S. Customs Service. *Importing A Car.* Washington, DC. Publication No. 520, 1995.

_____. *Know Before You Go.* Washington, DC. Publication No. 512, 1994.

_____. *Pets and Wildlife.* Washington, DC. Publication No. 509, 1995.

U.S. Federal Reserve Board. Office of Thrift Supervision. *Consumer Handbook on Adjustable Rate Mortgages.* Washington, DC. Publication No. FRB9-200,000-0892-C.

_____. *A Consumer's Guide to Mortgage Lock-Ins.* Washington, DC. Publication No. FRN 5-30,000-0993-C.

_____. *Home Mortgages: Understanding the Process and Your Right to Fair Lending.* Washington, DC. Publication No. FRB 2-250,000-493C.

U.S. Federal Trade Commission. *Buying A Used Car.* Washington, DC.

_____. *Facts for Consumers–Solving Credit Problems.* Washington, DC. Publication No. F002472, 1994.

Index

Order Form - USA Immigration & Orientation

Phone Orders: (have credit card ready)	(888) US-VISA9, (321) 779-9999
Fax:	(321) 779-3333
Internet orders:	orders@wellesworth.com
Web site:	www.wellesworth.com
Postal Address:	Wellesworth Publishing P.O. Box 372444 Satellite Beach, FL, 32937-2444

Enclose: $US 39.95 per book   _____

Sales Tax (6% for Florida addresses only): $US 2.40 _____

Priority Shipping

             Enter shipping charge (See following
             page for charges to your destination)   _____
                                               _____

                             Total: _____
                                               _____

Cash ____   Check ____

American Express ____   Discover____   Mastercard____   Visa ____

Card Number: _____

Name on Card: _____ Exp. Date: ____/_____

Signature: _____

Name: _____

Address: _____

            _____

City/State/Prov.: _____

ZIP/Postal Code: _____

Country: _____

Telephone: _____

Email: _____

SHIPPING CHARGES
(Subject to Change)

Priority Mail shipping within the United States is $US 3.85.

Global Priority Mail shipping to Canada and Mexico (Guadalajara, Mexico City and Monterrey) is $US 7.00.

Global Priority Mail shipping to the following cities and countries is $US 9.00:

Aruba	Dominican Rep.	Korea, Republic of	Singapore
Australia	Finland	Liechtenstein	South Africa
Austria	France (d)	Luxembourg	Spain (i)
Bahamas	Germany	Malaysia	Sweden
Barbados	Guyana	Monaco	Switzerland
Belgium	Hong Kong	Netherlands	Taiwan
Brazil (a)	Hungary	New Zealand (f)	Thailand
Chile (b)	Iceland	Norway	Trinidad/Tobago
China (c)	India	Philippines	Turks&Cacos Is.
Colombia	Ireland	Poland	United Kingdom
Costa Rica	Israel (e)	Portugal (g)	Vietnam
Czech Republic	Jamaica	St. Lucia	
Denmark	Japan	Saudi Arabia (h)	

(a) Sâo Paolo and Rio de Janeiro only
(b) Santiago, Valparaiso and Viña del Mar only
(c) Check www.usps.gov for current list of cities
(d) Includes Corsica
(e) Haifa, Jerusalem and Tel Aviv only
(f) Includes Cook Islands and Niue
(g) Includes Azores and Madeira Islands
(h) Riyadh, Jeddah and Damman only
(i) Includes Canary Islands

For shipping charges to other destinations, contact Wellesworth Publishing at (321) 779-9999 or info@wellesworth.com.